Essays On Hydraulic And Common Mortars And On Limeburning: Translated From The French Of Gen. Treussart, M. Petot, And M. Courtois. With Brief Observations On Common Mortars, Hydraulic Mortars, And Concretes ......

Clément Louis Treussart, Jean Constant Petot, C. Courtois

ESSAYS

ON

HYDRAULIC AND COMMON MORTARS

AND ON

LIME-BURNING.

TRANSLATED FROM THE FRENCH OF GEN. TREUSSART, M. PETOT, AND M. COURTOIS.

WITH BRIEF OBSERVATIONS

ON

COMMON MORTARS, HYDRAULIC MORTARS,

AND

CONCRETES,

AND AN ACCOUNT OF SOME EXPERIMENTS MADE THEREWITH AT FORT ADAMS, NEWPORT HARBOR, R. I., FROM 1825 TO 1838.

BY J. G. TOTTEN,

LT. COL. OF ENGINEERS, AND BREVET COL. U. S. ARMY.

NEW-YORK:

WILEY AND PUTNAM, 161 BROADWAY.

1842.

TABLE OF CONTENTS.

ON

HYDRAULIC AND COMMON

MORTARS.

Sect. 1.—ON MORTARS PLACED UNDER WATER.

CHAPTER I.

On Lime.—Actual state of our knowledge of this substance.

Lime has been employed from time immemorial. Mixed with sand, or certain other substances, it forms what is called mortar. Although the solidity and durability of masonry depends on the goodness of mortar; still, few experiments have been made with lime; and the manner of making mortar has almost always been given up to workmen. It is only within about fifty years that a few scientific men have attended to this important subject. Comparing the mortars of the ancients, and especially of the Romans, with those of modern times, it was perceived that the old mortars were much better than ours; and the means have, consequently, been sought of imitating them. Several constructors have thought they had discovered the secret of making Roman mortars: others, on the contrary, have thought that the Romans had no particular process, but that, of all their constructions, those only which were made of good lime had survived to our day. We shall see that my experiments tend to confirm this latter opinion.

Lime used in building, is obtained by the calcination of calcareous stones, which occur abundantly on the surface of the globe. Marbles, certain building stones, chalk, calcareous alabaster, and shells, are employed in making lime. The effect of calcination is to drive off the water and the carbonic acid which are combined with the lime. The water and the first portions of carbonic acid pass off easily; but it requires an intense, and long continued heat to dispel the remainder of the acid. Lime, as used in constructions, contains, almost always, a considerable quantity of carbonic acid.

When the stone submitted to calcination is white marble, pure lime is obtained, provided the calcination be carried far enough. According to an analysis which I made of white marble, this substance contained, in 100 parts, as follows: lime 64; carbonic acid 33; water 3. Lime obtained by calcination possesses the following properties. It has a great avidity for water, imbibes it from the air, and has its bulk enlarged thereby. If a certain quantity of water be thrown on lime recently calcined, it heats highly, breaks in pieces with noise, and a part of the water is evaporated by the

1

heat produced. The disengaged vapour carries off some particles of lime. Water dissolves about one four-hundredth of its weight of lime, forming what is called lime-water.* Lime is caustic and turns the syrup of violets, green: its specific gravity, according to Kirwan is 2.3, it attracts carbonic acid from the air, and finally returns to the state of carbonate of lime. To preserve it, it is necessary to keep it in very tight vessels.

Lime was formerly ranked among the alkalis, and it is only lately that the true nature of the substance became known. Davy, the English chemist, succeeded in 1807, in decomposing, by means of Volta's pile, the sulphate, and the carbonate, of lime, or more properly *lime* derived from these compounds; obtaining a brilliant substance, having so strong an attraction for oxygen that it absorbs it rapidly from the air, and from water, which it decomposes. The brilliant substance obtained from lime is regarded as a metal and has received the name of Calcium. Accordingly, lime is only a metallic oxide.

It is rare that lime derived from white marble is used in the arts; that which is commonly employed, and which is derived from ordinary lime stone, almost always contains oxide of iron, and sometimes a certain quantity of sand, alumine, magnesia, oxide of manganese, &c. Some of these substances combine with the lime by calcination: and the lime thus acquires properties which it had not before, and of which I shall speak in the sequel.

If we take lime derived from white marble, or from common lime stone, and reduce it as it comes from the kiln, to a paste with water, and if we place this paste in water, or in humid earth, it will remain soft forever. The same result will be obtained, if lime be mixed with common sand and the resulting mortar be placed in similar situations.

It is a common practice to deluge lime, fresh from the kiln, with a large quantity of water, and run it into large basins, where it is allowed to remain in the condition of soft paste. Alberti says (book II., chap. XI.) he has "seen lime, in an old ditch, that had been abandoned about 500 years, as "was conjectured from several manifest indications; which was still so moist, "well tempered, and ripe, that not honey or the marrow of animals could be "more so."

There is another kind of lime which possesses a singular property: if it be slaked as it comes from the kiln, as above, and be then placed in the state of paste, in water, or in moist earth, it will harden more or less promptly, according to the substances it contains. The same result is obtained if the lime, being mixed with sand, is made into mortar and placed in similar situations. If this lime be slaked and run into vats, as is done with common lime, it will become hard after a little time, and it will then be impossible to make use of it.

On slaking lime, fresh from the kiln, with enough water to reduce it to paste, it is found to augment considerably in bulk; this augmentation is such that one volume of quick lime will sometimes yield more than three volumes, measured in the condition of thick paste. When lime which has the property of hardening in water is slaked in the same manner, it affords a much smaller volume than common lime. Sometimes one volume of this lime, measured before slaking, will give, when slaked to thick paste, scarcely an equal bulk. For a long time, those limes which had the property of hardening in water were called *meagre limes*, and those which had not this property were called *fat limes*. These denominations were affixed because

* One four hundredth, *Davy*—one seven hundred and fifty-eighth, *Thompson*—one seven hundred and seventy-eighth, at 60° Fahr., *Dalton.*—Tr.

the first kind increased but little in bulk when made into paste, while the other give a considerable augmentation of volume; and because fat limes formed, with the same quantity of sand, a mortar much fatter or more unctuous than meagre lime. But the designation "*meagre lime*" is altogether improper to indicate limes which enjoy the property of hardening in water; because there are limes which augment their volume very little, on being made into paste, and at the same time possess no hydraulic property. Belidor gave the name of béton to lime which had the quality of hardening in water; but many engineers continued to call it *meagre lime*. The denomination of *béton* is not suitable; and, in this sense, is not now in use. The following are the terms now employed.

In England, the name of *aquatic lime* has been given to lime which indurates in water; in Germany it is called *lime for the water*; Mr. Vicat, Engineer of roads and bridges, has proposed the name of *hydraulic lime*, and this denomination, which is a very good one, has been generally adopted. I shall therefore call that lime which swells considerably in slaking, *fat lime*, that which swells but little and does not harden in water, *meagre lime*, and that which possesses the property of hardening in water, *hydraulic lime*. *Fat lime* is often called *common lime*, also. The term *quick lime* is applied to all unslaked limes whether *fat lime*, *meagre lime*, or *hydraulic lime*. Although *meagre lime and hydraulic lime* may have been calcined exactly to the proper degree, still they are slower to slake, and give out less heat than *fat lime*. When *fat lime* has been too much burned, it, also, becomes slow to slake; while, if properly burned, it begins to slake the instant water is thrown on. Experiments, to be given in the sequel, will show that iron, in the state of red oxide, causes *fat lime* to slake sluggishly.

Some of the ablest chemists have, at different times, sought to detect the substances which impart to lime the property of indurating under water.

Bergman, a Swedish chemist, was, I think, the first who gave an analysis of a hydraulic lime-stone. That from Léna in Sweden, he found to contain, in 100 parts, the following substances; lime, 90; oxide of manganese, 6; clay, 4. Bergman seems to have attributed the peculiar property of hydraulic lime, to the oxide of manganese; and this opinion prevailed for a long time. On the other hand we find in the *Bibliothèque Britannique* of 1776, vol. III, page 202, that Smeaton, the English Engineer, who built the Edystone Light-house, in 1757, attributed this property to clay: for he says that it is a curious question, which he leaves to chemists and philosophers to decide, why the presence of clay in the tissue of a calcareous stone should give it the property of hardening in water, while clay added to common lime produces no such effects.

Guyton de Morveau, announced in a memoir published in the year 9, that he had detected the presence of oxide of manganese in all the lime stones which afforded hydraulic limes; he announced, further, that in calcining together 90 parts of common lime stone pulverized, 4 parts of clay, and 6 parts of black oxide of manganese, an excellent artificial *meagre lime* would be obtained. It was stated above, that at that time, the name *meagre lime* was given to lime that would set under water; the French chemist was the first therefore to make artificial hydraulic lime; but he, as well as Bergman, was mistaken in supposing that the presence of the oxide of manganese was necessary to the result. He would have obtained his result by burning the pulverized lime stone with clay alone.

Mr. Saussure, in his *Voyage des Alpes*, says that the property possessed by certain limes of hardening in water is due solely to silex and alumine (that is to say, to clay) combined in certain proportions.

Mr. Vitalis, chemist of Rouen, made, in 1807, the analysis of the lime-stones of Senonches and St-Catherines, near Rouen; the analysis is contained in the memoir on the schists of Cherbourg (page 58) published in 1807, by Mr. Gratien, Sen., engineer of roads and bridges. This lime stone contains, according to Mr. Vitalis, in 100 parts, the following substances, water, 12; carbonate of lime, 68; alumine, 12; sand, 6; oxide of iron, 2. In addressing these results to Mr. Gratien, senior, Mr. Vitalis expresses himself thus: "It follows from the analysis that the lime-stones of Senonches and St-Catherines, are two calcareous marles, in which the chalk predominates it is true, but wherein the clay performs an important part. It is this portion of clay which, in my opinion, makes the lime of these two lime-stones, *meagre;* whence it follows that the presence of oxide of manganese is not indispensable to the constitution of such limes, since the analysis proves that the lime-stone in question contains no oxide of manganese, as it would, if present, have coloured the glass violet." I noticed above that these hydraulic limes were then called *meagre limes.* We see that the analysis of these stones confirms the opinion of Mr. Saussure, who had attributed to the clay alone, the property of hardening in water. Thompson, an English chemist, was of the same opinion.

Mr. Descotils, engineer of mines, also made an analysis of the lime-stone of Senonches; which analysis may be found in the *Journal des Mines* of 1813, page 308. According to this trial, the Senonches lime-stone contains a quarter part of silex, disseminated in very fine particles, and only so small a quantity of iron and alumine, that these substances can have no influence on the lime; whence this engineer concludes that the hydraulic property of this lime-stone is owing to the silex. We have, however, seen above, that, according to Mr. Vitalis, it contains twice as much alumine as silex. Mr. Berthier also inserted in the *Journal des Mines* an analysis of the Senonches lime-stone, which will be given further on, and according to which the stone contains very litte alumine. This contradiction has not yet been explained. Perhaps the quarries at that place afford stones of different kinds. If so, it would be important to ascertain what is the composition of the best.

The analysis of the Senonches lime-stone afforded Mr. Descotils occasion to make an important remark on the silex contained in lime-stone: namely, that the silex found in these stones does not dissolve in acids before calcination, but does dissolve after calcination. This fact proves that the properties of silex are changed by calcination with lime, and that it combines in the dry way with this substance.

Mr. Vicat, engineer of roads and bridges, published in 1818 a very important memoir on hydraulic mortars. This engineer set out with the opinion generally admitted at that time, that it was the clay which gave to lime the singular property of hardening in water. He, in consequence, took fat lime, which he mixed with various proportions of clay, according to the following process, extracted from page 7. "The operation we are about to describe (says Mr. Vicat) is a true synthesis, reuniting in an intimate manner, by the action of fire, the essential principles which are separated from hydraulic lime, by analysis. It consists in allowing the lime, which is to be improved, to fall spontaneously to powder in a dry and covered place; afterwards to mix it, by the help of a little water, with a certain quantity of gray or brown clay, or simply with brick earth, and to make balls of this paste, which, after drying, are to be burned to the proper degree.

" Being master of the proportions, we may concieve that the factitious lime may receive any degree of energy desired, equal to, or surpassing at pleasure, the best natural lime.

"Very fat common lime will bear 0.20 of clay to 1.00 of lime; moderately fat lime will have enough clay with 0.15; and 0.10, or even 0.06, of clay will suffice for these limes which are already somewhat hydraulic. When the proportion is forced to 0.33 or 0.40, the lime does not slake, but it pulverizes easily, and gives, when tempered, a paste which hardens under water very promptly."

Such is the process indicated by Mr. Vicat. But this engineer did not content himself with experiments on a small scale: a manufactory was established near Paris by his means, where artificial hydraulic lime is made in large quantities; he moreover exerted himself to extend the use of hydraulic mortar every where, and he succeeded. He has, therefore, rendered an important service to the art of construction, and I have done him the justice to make this acknowledgment, in the notices I have heretofore published.

In 1818, Dr. John, of Berlin, presented to the Society of Sciences in Holland, a memoir, which was published in 1819. This memoir, crowned in 1818, by the Society, answered the following question proposed by the Society: "What is the chemical cause, in virtue whereof stone lime makes generally more solid and durable masonry than shell lime, and what are the means of improving shell lime in this respect?" Dr. John has remarked that shells require to be more highly calcined than common lime-stone: he thinks this owing to the shells being purer carbonate of lime than common lime-stone, which contains earthy substances facilitating the disengagement of the carbonic acid. In making the analysis of sundry lime-stones, he found that those which afforded hydraulic lime contained clay, oxide of iron, &c. He called the foreign matters which gave the property of hardening in water, *cements*; and says that it is possible, by introducing cement in the dry way to ameliorate lime which contains none. On these considerations he made the following experiments. He mixed the powder of oyster shells, 1st, with $\frac{1}{16}$ of silicious sand—2d, with several proportions of clay, varying from $\frac{1}{10}$ to $\frac{1}{3}$— 3d, with $\frac{1}{20}$ of oxide of manganese. He tempered these mixtures with water, formed them into balls, let them dry in the air, and then burned them in a lime-kiln for 96 hours. The following results were obtained: the first mixture was agglutinated but friable, and was not a good result; the second mixture gave good results; and the third possessed no peculiar property. The author concludes that clay is the ingredient which gives to common lime the property of hardening in water; and he says that nothing can be easier than to procure good hydraulic lime, either from shells or from pure lime-stone, following the process indicated: he adds that it is for constructors to determine the best mixture to be made in each case.

The memoir of Dr. John contains the analysis of several ancient mortars; and offers several important observations of which I shall have occasion to speak.

In the third number of the *Annales des Mines* of 1822, there is a very interesting memoir by Mr. Berthier, *Ingénieur en Chef des mines*; it contains the analysis of different lime-stones, and several new views which will contribute to form a more perfect theory of mortars. I shall have more than one occasion to cite his experiments, and his opinion on several important acts.

Mr. Raucourt, engineer of roads and bridges, published at St. Petersburgh in 1822, a work wherein he narrates the experiments he made, following the process used by Mr. Vicat, and adding several of his own. Mr. Bergère, *chef de bataillon du génie*, gave an analysis of this work, in the *Annales des Mines* of 1824, Vol. IX.

In 1825, Mr. Hassenfratz published a memoir on mortars. This work, which is voluminous, contains many practical details on the calcination of lime-stone in different countries, and exhibits the actual state of knowledge, in the art of making mortars at the period of publication.

In terminating this reference to works on hydraulic mortars, which have appeared up to this time, I must introduce a fact, entirely new, announced by Mr. Girard de Caudemberg, engineer of roads and bridges, in a notice published by him in 1827. He states that the proprietors of mills on the river Isle, in the department of Gironde, discovered by accident, a kind of fossil sand to which they gave the name of *aréne*, which has the singular property, without any preparation, of forming, with fat lime, a mortar that hardens under water, and has great durability. I shall have occasion to return to this important fact, and to report what Mr. Girard says, as well as to state the principal experiments which have been made with this substance, in other places where it has been found.

I was employed from 1816 to 1825 at Strasburg, at which place they had made no use of hydraulic lime. I ascertained, however, that such lime was to be found in the neighbourhood. Almost all the hydraulic works connected with the fortifications of the place, having been badly constructed, and dating as far back as Vauban's time, were to be rebuilt. Twenty-five years' experience had taught me the great superiority of hydraulic mortars in the air as well as in the water—where, indeed, they are indispensable. I tried, therefore, the hydraulic limes, afforded by the environs of Strasburg, and found them excellent: they were, consquently, used in all the works both in air and water. All the revetments built from *port de Pierre* to *port Royal*, having a development of about 1650 yards, were rebuilt or repaired with hydraulic mortar. It was the same with the hydraulic works; they were rebuilt or repaired with the hydraulic lime of the neighbourhood.

An engineer who should use fat lime, even for constructions in the air, when there are hydraulic limes at hand, would be very censurable, because the expense is about the same, and, as regards the strength and durability of masonry, there is a vast difference in favour of the hydraulic mortar. But in countries where no hydraulic lime is to be had, or only that of mediocre quality, what should be done? Shall the engineer adopt the process of Mr. Vicat, which consists in making an artificial hydraulic lime? I answer, emphatically, that I think not; in this case, occurring very often, it is, in my opinion, preferable to make hydraulic mortar by a more direct process which I shall point out.

There are two modes of obtaining hydraulic mortar; the first consists in mixing natural, or artificial, hydraulic lime with sand; the second consists in mixing ordinary fat lime with certain substances such as puzzalona, trass, certain coal-ashes, and brick dust, or tile dust. I feel bound to correct here, an assertion touching these mortars, not perfectly accurate, of Mr. Gauthey, Inspector of roads and bridges. In his excellent *Treatise on the construction of bridges*, this Engineer says (Vol. II., page 278) that "fat lime is very proper for constructions out of water; but will not answer in the composition of betons to be placed in water, because the mortars in which it is used, even when mixed with puzzalona, and placed in water as soon as made, do not harden, but remain pulverulent." This is far from exact:

because mortar composed of fat lime and puzzalona hardens very soon in water, and acquires, in a short time, very great strength. This fact was known to the ancients, for Vitruvius speaks of it, as will be seen further on.

I should not refer to the error into which Mr. Gauthey has fallen in this instance, if he did not enjoy a reputation so justly elevated. His highly esteemed work being in the hands of every Engineer, it was to be feared that this remark of his would prevent constructors from making hydraulic mortars by the direct union of common lime and substances analogous to puzzalona. My experiments will show that, in countries where hydraulic lime is not to be had, instead of following the process of Mr. Vicat, it is preferable to make hydraulic mortar by a direct mixture of fat lime with substances of a similar nature to puzzalona. These experiments show also that fat lime is far from being always proper for construction out of water; although Mr. Gauthey, in the beginning of the sentence, states it to be.

CHAPTER II.

On slaking Lime; manner of making Mortar; observations on Hydrate of Lime.

There are three modes of slaking lime. The first consists in throwing on the lime, as it comes from the kiln, enough water to reduce it to thin paste. This process is the one generally employed with fat lime. Too much water is added, almost always—that is to say, as much as is required to make it a thin cream. In this state it is run into vats; after some time it thickens, and it is then covered with a layer of sand or earth to preserve it from contact of the air, which would soon convert the upper portion into a carbonate. It is a common opinion that the longer the lime has been kept in this state, the better it is. My experiments will show that this is not true, at least not always true: since some fat lime that I had experimented with, which had been lying in this condition, gave, in the air, when the mortar was composed of lime and sand only, very bad results.

The thickening of the lime in the vats is due to the escape of water by filtration, by evaporation, and also to a third cause: for this thickening which is quite prompt, occurs equally when the vats are constructed in moist ground, and when the season is rainy. This third cause appears to me to be this: that the lime, having a strong affinity for water, solidifies the first portions very promptly, but requires a considerable time to saturate itself completely. These portions of the lime which have been too much or too little burned are, besides, slow to slake. I made the following experiment to satisfy myself on this point. I took a portion of lime that had been lying wet in a vat for four years, it was quite thick, I added a little water to bring it to the consistence of sirup, and placed it in a stoneware vessel. I took an equal portion of fat lime, slaked fresh from the kiln, reducing this also to the consistence of sirup, and placing it in a similar vessel. After a short time, this last had become very thick, while the former retained its consistence of sirup; I then added water to restore the consistence first given. The thickening again occurred, but more slowly than at first. It was necessary to add water several times before the second lime would maintain the sirupy state. It results from this experiment that fat lime, slaked into a clear paste as it comes from the kiln, retains the power of absorbing water for a considerable time.

The second method of slaking consists in plunging quick-lime into water for a few seconds. It is withdrawn before the commencement of ebullition; slakes with the water it has absorbed, and falls to powder. It is preserved in a dry place. The operation is performed with baskets into which the lime, broken to the size of an egg, is put. Mr. de Lafaye, in 1777, proposed this mode of slaking lime, as a secret recovered from the Romans; it made much noise at the time, but experience has not realized the great results anticipated.

The third process consists in leaving the quick-lime exposed to the air. Its strong affinity for water causes it to attract the greater part of that which is in the surrounding air. Lime, thus exposed, slakes slowly without giving out much heat, and falls at last to powder. This mode of slaking is called air-slaking, or spontaneous slaking. It is employed, more or less, in several countries. It is spoken of in several works on constructions, and is generally condemned. Mr. Vicat, however, appears to give it the preference, for, at page 20 of his memoir, he says: "Such are the three modes of slaking lime: the first is generally used; the second has hardly been tried, except as an experiment at certain works; the third is proscribed, and represented, in all the treatises on construction, as depriving the lime of all energy, to such a degree that those portions which have fallen to powder in the air, are considered as lost. We shall not now speak of the processes of Rondelet, Fleuret, and others, because they do not differ much from those described. We shall see, further on, that, as regards spontaneous slaking, these proscriptions of authors who, believing every thing, repeat without examination the errors of those who preceded them, are founded on false observations and are deserving only of mistrust." Mr. Vicat has announced that a mortar made of sand, and fat lime which was air-slaked, resisted perfectly at the end of ten years, the test indicated by Mr. Berard for frost-proof stones; he says on this subject "a hint, this, to those who have written and spoken so much against air-slaking, and in opposition to the opinion which I have had to maintain singly, unable to invoke to my aid any experiments but my own." The results I have obtained are far from confirming what Vicat says, as will appear by the experiments reported hereafter.

Mr. Vicat gives, at page 20, experiments made by him to ascertain the amount of swelling of fat limes and of hydraulic limes, on slaking by the three modes. He found the first mode to be that which gave the greatest volume of paste, with both kinds of lime. On comparing the bulks obtained by the second and third modes, it was found that with fat lime, air-slaking gave greater bulk than slaking by immersion, and that it was the reverse with hyraulic lime.

At Strasburg, an attempt was made to apply, on a large scale, the mode of slaking by immersion, pointed out by Mr. Lafaye; but the process was found to be attended with inconvenience and embarrassment. It is necessary to procure a stock of baskets—to break up the larger pieces—to secure workmen who will be faithful in holding the lime under water only the given number of seconds, which is not easy; a portion of the lime is lost, falling in powder to the bottom of the vessel of water; when the lime is reduced to powder, it is requisite to measure it before making the mortar, and should there be a wind, much will be lost. These objections caused the process to be renounced in favour of that about to be described, and which amounts to the same thing.

It is founded on the following observation: if quick-lime be plunged into water it absorbs, in a certain number of seconds, a quantity sufficient to reduce it well to powder. We shall have then a like result by throwing the same quantity of water on the lime, and avoid the inconveniences attending the plunging into water. Since 1817, this process has been employed at Strasburg, where considerable masses of lime were operated on. A small building was erected near the works, into which the hydraulic lime, not allowed to arrive too fast from the kiln, was put, to be protected from the weather; the building was boarded on the sides and top, and, in case of rain, covered with a tarpaulin. By the side of this lime-house, a larger shed was constructed, the top only being boarded; a plank floor, on which the mortar was mixed, was laid under this shed. There was a measure, without a bottom, which contained about 10 cubic feet, each dimension of the box being about 2.20 feet, this was placed on the floor and filled with lime; which being done, the same measure was used for the sand, which was placed around the lime, without covering it: with large tin watering pots of known capacity, water, equal in bulk to about one-quarter the bulk of the lime, was thrown on: the workmen knew they were to empty the watering pots but a given number of times; and the lime being all in sight they saw that they should throw the greater quantities on those parts of the heap where lay the largest lumps of lime. As soon as the slaking became energetic, the lime was left to itself until the vapours had ceased; it was then turned a little with a shovel, or a rod was thrust in, and if any lumps were found still entire, either for the want of water, or because they were too much burned, a little water was poured on these lumps. A regular form was then given to the heap, and the surface being slightly pressed with the back of the shovel, the lime was covered with the sand that had been placed around it. This process was completed towards evening—as many heaps being prepared as it was presumed would be required during the whole of the ensuing day. By thus leaving the lime, over night, in heaps, the slaking is complete; portions which have too much water impart it to those which have too little, and the water becomes thus uniformly diffused through the heap. In the morning the sand and lime of each heap were mixed together, and passed twice under the rab (rabot) before adding any water: in this way, if there were any stones, or pieces of lime imperfectly slaked, they were easily found and rejected. Water was then added in sufficient quantity to bring the whole to the state of very soft paste; because in this dilute state the mortar is, with less labour, mixed more perfectly. Experiments which follow will show that it is an error to insist that mortar should be mixed with *"the sweat of the labourers:"* it is enough if the sand be well mixed with the lime; and this mixture is better effected, and in a much more economical manner, when the mortar is in a state rather thin, than when it is thick; another reason for making it rather thin is, that it often becomes stiffer than it ought to be, before it is used, in consequence of the lime preserving, as before stated, for a considerable time, the property of solidifying water. When the lime has been properly burned, the operation just described gives a homogeneous mortar not at all granular, and not exhibiting a multitude of little white specks, which are particles of lime that have been badly slaked. At Strasburg the precaution was always taken of making up only one or two heaps of mortar at a time; so that it should not have too much time to dry before being used, and that the masons might find it in the state of paste, in the heaps in which it was deposited after being well worked. In making the mortar only as it is needed, there is, besides, the advantage of avoiding the labour of remixing, in the frequent case of the works being interrupted by rain: it is best therefore to make the heaps of slaked lime into mortar, no faster than as they are wanted. Lime may be preserved in this way for eight or ten days without losing quality. If at the end of the day, all the heaps of lime have been consumed, new heaps should be formed for the consumption of the morrow: if a portion only have been consumed, this portion should be made good. This manner of slaking lime, and making mortar, gave very good results at Strasburg, and at other places in the vicinity where it was employed. It is seen to be a method analogous to that by immersion, recommended by Mr. Lafaye; but, by throwing upon the lime, just the quantity of water necessary to reduce it well to powder, instead of immersing it, much inconvenience and embarrassment are avoided, especially when operating with large quantities of lime.

An opportunity was presented of convincing ourselves of the goodness of mortar made by this method, it being necessary, in order to make a postern, to pierce through a revetment wall that had been built two years: the mortar had already acquired such hardness that the tools had much difficulty in cutting through the masonry.

In extensive works, it will be very advantageous, as regards economy, to make mortar with a machine. Several have been contrived with this object, but that which has succeeded best is a two-horse machine proposed and executed by Mr. Saint-Léger, formerly Captain of Engineers. The following is a brief description.

A circular trench, having the two sides sloping, is built of masonry; the section of the trench is a trapezoid 2 feet wide at bottom, 3 feet 4 inches wide at top, and 1 foot 4 inches deep; the inner circle of the trench is 9 feet 4 inches in diameter; at the centre there is a mass of masonry, in which is fixed a vertical axis, of wood, 6 feet 8 inches long, and 8 inches square, and which is bedded in the masonry about 5 feet; the top of this axis is formed into a cylinder $5 \frac{2}{10}$ inches in diameter, and 6 inches high; around which is fitted a collar of cast-iron, carrying laterally two horizontal trunions $3 \frac{2}{10}$ inches in diameter, and $4 \frac{8}{10}$ inches long; a piece of wood, 26 feet 8 inches long, is notched at its middle upon the collar of the vertical axis. (Instead of one piece of wood, two might be taken, each 13 feet 4 inches long, by strongly securing, with iron, their junction with the vertical axis.) This piece is placed horizontally, and is about 13 inches square in the middle, lessening towards the ends, so as to serve as an axletree to two vertical wheels with broad felloes—6 feet diameter of wheel, and 6 inches breadth of felloe. These two wheels rest in the circular trench in such a way that the one touches the exterior and the other the interior slope of the trench. A horse is attached to each extremity of the horizontal bar, and their united efforts cause the wheels to revolve in the trench; behind each wheel, attached to the horizontal bar, by means of a hinge, is a scraper of wood armed with iron, these follow the movement of the wheels, scraping the two sides of the trench so as to throw the mortar under the wheels. These scrapers of which the lower end is within two inches of the bottom of the trench, are attached by hinges in order that they may rise over any obstacle.

Mortar is made in this machine in the following manner. A cubic metre (35.34 cubic feet) of lime in the state of paste is thrown into the trench, and the horses are started; a little water is added if necessary, and when the paste has become quite liquid and homogenous, the proper quantity of sand is thrown in by the shovel, without arresting the movement; in about 20 or 25 minutes the mortar is made. With this machine 12 batches of 3 cubic metres each (12 × 3 × 35.34 equals 1272:24 cubic feet) may be made in 10 hours labour; the requisite agents being 4 labourers, 2 horses and their driver, and 1 superintending mason.

The expense of making a cubic metre of mortar, amounts in Paris to about $0.10; this is a considerable saving over the common mode of making mortar.* It is desirable therefore that frequent use be made of this machine, in places where there are important constructions. The description just given is extracted from the *devis-modèle* of the corps of Engineers, and was prepared by Lt. Col. Bergère of the Engineers.

It is stated above that at Strasburg, lime which was to be made into mortar, was slaked to dry powder, and left in that state for twelve hours at least before giving it the quantity of water necessary to convert it into paste. I made the following experiments with limes of the environs of Strasburg, to ascertain the volume obtained in powder and in paste, when the proper quantities of water are used to produce those states.

TABLE I.

Designation of the lime of which the volume is taken as unity.	Volume of water used to bring it first, to a state of dry powder	Volume produced of dry powder.	Volume of water used, in all, to bring to state of paste.	Volume produced in state of paste.
Lime of white marble	$\frac{1}{2}$	$2\frac{1}{2}$	$1\frac{6}{10}$	$1\frac{1}{2}$
Fat lime of Strasburg	1	$3\frac{1}{2}$	2	$1\frac{3}{4}$
Yellow lime of Obernai	$\frac{2}{3}$	2	$\frac{3}{4}$	1
Blue do. do.	$\frac{1}{3}$	$2\frac{1}{3}$	$1\frac{1}{6}$	$1\frac{1}{6}$
Brunstat lime	$\frac{1}{3}$	$2\frac{1}{4}$	$1\frac{1}{2}$	$1\frac{1}{2}$
Villé lime	$\frac{1}{2}$	$3\frac{1}{3}$	$1\frac{1}{2}$	$1\frac{1}{2}$
Altkirch lime	$1\frac{1}{2}$	$1\frac{5}{8}$	$\frac{5}{6}$	1
Verdt lime	$\frac{1}{3}$	$2\frac{1}{4}$	1	1
Metz lime	$\frac{1}{3}$	$2\frac{1}{4}$	$1\frac{1}{2}$	$1\frac{71}{100}$
Boulogne pebbles	$\frac{1}{3}$	$1\frac{1}{6}$	$\frac{1}{2}$	$\frac{3}{4}$

All the limes in the above table, were used fresh from the kiln. I reduced them to powder in a mortar, sifted them, and used, for quantity, about one quart. Thus, for example, I took a measure of quick lime of white marble, and throwing upon it half a measure of water, I obtained $2\frac{1}{2}$ measures of lime slaked to powder, which I measured after it was cold. The quantity of water thrown on is shown in the second column, and the

* One day of superintending mason, . . . $0 66½
  Four days of labourers, at $0 28½, . . . 1 14
  Two days of horses, at $0 42¾, . . . 0 85½
  One day of driver, . . . 0 38
  Wear and tear and repair for one day, . . . 0 09½
  Greasing wheels one day, . . . 0 07
  Wear and tear of shovels and barrows, 1 day for 4 labourers, . 0 07½
  Contingencies, 1-10th of all, . . . 0 32

  Total expense for 36 cubic metres = 1272 cubic feet $3 60

Equal to $0 10 per cub. metre—or $0:0028 per cubic foot.

The quality of the mortar is superior to that made by the common process; and it is well to remark, that the time during which the mortar is made is precisely that in which the labourers repose: it is therefore their interest to let the machine go as long as possible, and consequently to render the mortar more perfect, so that the supervision will be directed chiefly to the proportions of the mixture. This note is extracted from the devis-modèle du corps du Génie, p. 71.—Tr.

quantity of lime obtained in powder is given in the third column. I was obliged to throw upon this lime in powder, one measure and one-tenth of water in addition to reduce it to paste. Adding this last quantity of water to the half measure used in the first instance, the total is $1 \frac{6}{10}$ measures of water, absorbed by the lime, in being reduced to paste: this is shown in the fourth column. The fifth column shows that I obtained $1\frac{1}{4}$ measure of lime in paste. I followed the same process for all the limes of the above table, producing a uniform consistence of paste, by adding the water little by little. Experience had taught me that these limes were reduced to dry powder by throwing on one-fifth of their bulk of water; and that as much as one-half their bulk might be thrown on without the powders ceasing to be dry: beyond this term, a moist powder would be obtained. The only lime on which I threw less than half its bulk, was that at the bottom of the table, of the Boulogne pebbles; on this I poured but $\frac{1}{3}$ its bulk of water; as this lime forms a moist powder with $\frac{1}{4}$ its bulk of water, I was obliged to restrict myself to one-third. This table shows that these different limes afforded very different volumes of powder with the same quantity of water: that the quantities of water absorbed to produce the state of paste were very different, and, also, that the volumes of paste differed much. Experiments which follow will show that, of the limes in the table, those are the most hydraulic which absorbed the least water in passing to the state of paste, and which gave the smallest bulk both of powder and of paste. Those limes, of the table, which are not hydraulic, are those which gave the greatest volumes in powder and in paste. There are in the table two kinds of Obernai lime, one yellow and the other blue; they are of the same limestone, but one more highly calcined than the other. When this lime has been burned just enough, it is of a yellow-fawn colour; when a little more burned, it is of an ashy-gray, and when too much calcined, of a decided blue. It was upon the two extremes of calcination that I made the above experiments, they show that the degree of calcination has a sensible influence on the swelling of this hydraulic lime.

As the swelling of lime, shown in the above table, was obtained with quite small quantities, and with pulverized quicklime, I caused experiments to be made at the mortar beds on a large scale, with fat lime and with Obernai lime; these being the two kinds of lime ordinarily used upon the works. The following results were obtained. Fat lime was taken immediately from the kiln, and measured in the boxes in use at the mortar beds; care being taken to break up a portion of the lumps of quick lime into smaller pieces, in order to occupy the interstices between the larger pieces, and to have the measure well filled: water, in quantity sufficient to bring the lime at once to paste of the consistence of mortar, was thrown on without delay, and the quantity of paste thus obtained was measured. Proceeding thus—one measure of quicklime, just from the kiln, required two measures of water to produce the state of paste, and yielded 1.83 of paste, which differs but little from Table No. 1, wherein the produce is 1.75. The same operation was repeated with Obernai lime, after having rejected vitrified pieces, and those which had not been sufficiently calcined: one measure of this lime absorbed 1.30 of water in being reduced to paste, and in this state gave 1.30 of lime. This differs somewhat from the result in the Table.

The difference may be owing to this, that in the experiments of the Table, the lime was pulverized, and was twice slaked; that is to say had two successive applications of water, while in the larger experiment the lime was not broken up, and had water poured on but once. The degree of calcination might, also, have had some influence.

Many metallic oxides are susceptible of absorbing and solidifying a certain quantity of water forming compounds which possess peculiar properties. It is to these compounds that the term hydrate has been assigned. It has been seen, above, that lime is a metallic oxide, and that this substance absorbs and solidifies a large quantity of water; but the quantity of water absorbed by lime in forming its hydrate is not exactly known. Berzelius asserts that the hydrates are formed of water and oxides in such proportions that the quantity of oxygen contained in the oxide is equal to the quantity of oxygen contained in the water; but Mr. Thenard does not admit this law: he says that the experiments on which it is founded are not numerous enough, nor sufficiently precise, to allow its definitive admission. It is certain nevertheless, says this celebrated chemist, that amongst the hydrates which have as yet been examined, those which contain the most water, are those, also, of which the oxides contain the most oxygen. According to Berzelius, the hydrate of lime is obtained by throwing upon quick lime the water necessary to reduce it to thin paste (*bouille,*) and exposing this paste in a silver or platina crucible to the heat of a spirit-of-wine lamp. After having dried the hydrate of lime in this manner, it is weighed, and the quantity of water it has absorbed is known by the augmentation of weight. Berzelius made two experiments, one with 10 grammes of lime and the other with 30 grammes. He found in the first experiment, that the lime had increased in weight 32.1 per cent., and in the second, 32.5: in this second experiment there was, therefore, an augmentation of four-tenths more than in the first. He attributes this difference to an absorption of carbonic acid, and he admits, as good, only the first experiment, in which 100 parts of pure lime containing 28.16 parts of oxygen, are combined with 32.1 parts of water containing 28.3 parts of oxygen; whence Berzelius concludes that the water absorbed by pure lime contains a quantity of oxygen equal to that contained in the lime.

I have repeated the experiment of Berzelius by operating on 20 grammes of pure lime, using, as he did, a spirit-of-wine lamp, and a platina crucible. I was surprised at obtaining an augmentation of only 22.5 per cent. I repeated the experiment several times, successively diminishing the thickness of the wick, and as I did this, the lime retained more and more water. I inferred, therefore, that the hydrate of lime decomposes with a feeble heat; and that, if Berzelius obtained a greater result in the second experiment than in the first, it was not all due to the absorption of carbonic acid, seeing that the operation lasts only a short time; but to this, that heating with an equal flame, two volumes of hydrate of lime, of which one was triple the other, the smaller volume should lose most water by the heat. But there is a fact which proves with how great facility the hydrate of lime abandons a part of its water. All those who have made mortar of lime newly slaked, have perceived that it becomes very dry in a short time. If, when in this state, it be worked for some time without adding water, it will be brought back nearly to the same moist state it had at first; and drops of water may be seen on the mortar. The same result is obtained with lime alone. It follows from this, that simple friction (working) decomposes the hydrate of lime, and that a feeble heat produces the same effect. To know, therefore, the quantity of water which enters into the hydrate of lime, it appears to me that other means of drying should be resorted to than fire.

The various kinds of lime are used in constructions, only after having been brought to the condition of hydrate: nothing, therefore, that relates to the properties of this compound, is a matter of indifference. As yet, few experiments have been made to determine the quantity of water that should be given to lime in making mortar. I proposed undertaking several experiments on this point, but time failed me. The matter should be attended to, because, opinions are much divided thereon, for want of exact experiments.

The following are the principal properties of hydrate of lime: it is white, pulverulent, and much less caustic than quick lime; it easily abandons to heat the first portion of water, but it requires a high temperature to drive off all the water entering into its composition. This hydrate absorbs carbonic acid; experiments which follow show that it has, also, the property of absorbing oxygen, and that lime sustains important modifications in consequence of this absorption of oxygen. According to the chemists, lime is incapable of absorbing a fresh quantity of oxygen: but according to my observations, there is no doubt that the hydrate of lime absorbs a considerable quantity. I shall give, in the following chapter, experiments which I made on this subject.

CHAPTER III.

Experiments on several hydraulic limes of the environs of Strasburg, on the Metz lime, and on Boulogne pebbles.

When I was sent to Strasburg in 1816, they were in the habit, there, of using fat lime only. One of the two dikes enclosing the navigable canal which passes from the town to the Rhine across the ditch of the place, requiring repairs, I had occasion to remark that while the two facings, which were of cut stone, were much disjointed, the interior of the dike, which was a mass of concrete, was in good condition, and not a drop of water passed through it. The concrete being very hard, and, as it seemed, not made of brick, or tile dust, I conjectured that it had been composed of hydraulic lime, and I made researches accordingly. I learned that the Millers along the Bruche had used, for a long time, in the repairs of their works, a particular species of lime, which they obtained from a village, at the foot of the Vosges, called Obernai.* Mr. Mossère, Engineer of roads and bridges, told me that he had used this lime in the works of the canal of "*Monsieur*," and that he was well satisfied with it; and, on making the essay, I found it to be eminently hydraulic: it appeared to me to be in no respect inferior to the Metz lime, which I had seen employed with success, at that place, in 1800 and 1801. At other stations, I had several times made hydraulic mortars of fat lime and brick, or tile, dust. At the great works of Vésel, where I was employed three years, considerable use was made of trass, which was brought from Andernach by the Rhine; and on the experience I had acquired of hydraulic limes, I introduced the use of the Obernai lime in all the constructions of the works of Strasburg, both in and out of water. I have already observed that all the revetments comprised between *porte de Pierre* and *pont Royal*, giving a development of about 1650 yards, were made with hydraulic lime. Later researches have shown me that hydraulic lime is to be found at the foot of the Vosges, from Belfort to Vissembourg.

* This village is situated between Schelestadt and Strasburg: upon the map of Cassini it is written Ober-Ehnheim, but it is pronounced Obernai, and is so written on some maps.

I shall give experiments which I made with hydraulic lime from Altkirch, Obernai, Rouxviller, Ingviller, Oberbronn, Verdt, &c.

There are no certain means of knowing by inspection whether a lime-stone will give fat lime or hydraulic lime, for there are hydraulic lime-stones of several colours: those of Alsace are generally of a slate blue, like those of Metz, but those of Altkirch, and the hydraulic chalk of Vitry are white; the Boulogne pebbles, and the English lime-stone of which Parker's cement is made, are red. I may say, however, that when a lime-stone is blue, it is a presumption that it will afford hydraulic lime. It is remark-able that in lime-stone giving fat lime, the iron exists as red oxide, while it exists in the lowest state of oxidation in a great proportion of the hydraulic lime-stones, even when left for a long time exposed to the air; the same thing happens with good slate, and it seems to me to be owing to the pre-sence of clay in the hydraulic lime-stones and in the slate, with which the iron is probably in combination. As I have before said, the Boulogne peb-bles, and Parker's cement stone, were exceptions; but this might be due to some peculiar cause: the sea-water might have some influence on the oxida-tion of the iron contained in the Boulogne pebbles.

All the blue hydraulic lime-stones which I have caused to be calcined, gave a yellow ochre colour whenever the heat was not great. If the calcin-ation was raised, the colour passed, successively, to fawn, ash-gray, and, finally, if the heat had been very great, to slate blue. I cannot satisfy my-self as to the cause of the blue colour which the lime-stone takes by a high calcination, because it seems necessary to suppose that this effect is the bringing back of the iron to its first degree of oxidation, which is possible, but does not seem to me easy to explain.

A like effect appears to take place in the calcination of clays that con-tain oxide of iron. Some clays submitted to calcination are blackish, be-cause of the iron being present at the lowest state of oxidation: at a certain degree of heat, the iron passes to the state of red oxide, and the clay takes the decided colour commonly seen in bricks: if the heat be augmented, the red colour weakens, and becomes fawn or straw colour; if the heat be push-ed to a high degree, the clay becomes of an ash colour and afterwards of a very decided slate-blue colour—the iron having then lost a great part of its oxygen. If slate, and the clay just described, be calcined at the same time, the iron will pass with much more difficulty to the state of red oxide in the slate than in the clay. The degree of heat necessary to bring the iron in the slate to the condition of red oxide, will have caused the iron in the clay to pass through all the stages of oxidation before mentioned, and have im-parted the blue colour to the clay. Are these different phenomena due to this, that while, in the slate, the iron is combined with the alumine, there is no such combination in this clay? In clays which are strongly calcined, has the alumine the property of abstracting the oxygen from the iron? It is for chemistry to clear up these points.

M. Berthier has given the following method of detecting hydraulic lime-stones. "The stone must be pulverized and sifted through a silk sieve: 10 grammes of the powder being put in a capsule, muriatic acid, diluted with a little water, must be poured on, little by little. (In want of muriatic acid, nitric acid, or even vinegar, may be used.) The whole should be constant-ly stirred with a glass or wooden rod, as long as there may be any effer-vescence; this having ceased, the solution must be evaporated, in a gentle heat, to the consistence of paste; about one pint of water must be added and the whole filtered; the clay will remain upon the filter; it must be dried in the sun or before the fire, and weighed; or, still better, it must be raised to a red heat in an earthen, or in a metallic crucible before being weighed; limpid lime-water must then be thrown into the solution, as long as it forms a precipitate therein; this precipitate should be separated, as soon as possible, by the filter; it is magnesia (sometimes mixed with iron and manganese;) it should be washed with pure water, and dried at a high heat before taking its weight." The weight of the clay retained by the filter, compared with the weight of the lime-stone, will indicate whether it be hydraulic lime-stone or not. But it might happen that the substance remaining on the filter would be all sand; this may be determined before drying; for if it be sand only, it will be rough to the touch, while if it form a soft and ductile paste, it will be clay, that is to say, a mixture of alumine and silex. Besides, by drying at a high heat, it will be seen if a compact mass be obtained, which will be the case with clay highly heated, or if it be pulverulent matter, which will show that little or no alumine is present. As to the rest, we do not yet know, accurately, in what proportions the silex and alumine ought to be present to constitute the best hydraulic cement. The best manner of ascertaining whether a lime is hydraulic, is the following: take quick lime as it comes, properly calcined, from the kiln; reduce it, with water, to a thick paste, and place enough of it on the bottom of a tumbler to fill it for one-third or one-half of its height; three or four hours after, fill the tumbler with water, and leave all at rest; after two or three days, touch the lime lightly with the finger, to ascertain whether it begins to harden: if it be very hydraulic, it will have taken, after eight or ten days, such a consistence, that no impression can be made on the lime by pressing strongly with the finger. We should assure ourselves whether there has been, in fact, no impression, by throwing off the water and washing the surface of the lime, which will be covered with a thin layer of lime softened by the immediate contact of the water. If the above result be obtained only at the end of twenty, thirty, or forty days, the lime should be regarded as only feebly hydraulic, and if there be no consistence in the lime after the lapse of about forty days, it cannot be regarded as at all hydraulic. This process, which is very simple, is that which I always follow—it was indicated by Mr. Vicat.

Before giving my first experiments, I will explain the processes I followed, both in making mortars, and in breaking them in order to determine their tenacity. In my first experiments, I fixed the proportions of my mortars, by slaking the lime to dry powder with one-fifth of its volume of water, and measuring this lime in powder. Afterwards I measured the lime in paste, in order to approach the mode ordinarily pursued in practice with fat lime. I shall take care to state in every instance, which of these modes of measurement I followed. When I had united the lime to its proper proportion of sand, or other substance, I mixed them well together, adding water, till the consistence was like honey; and I passed the mortar seven or eight times under the trowel. The mortar being made, I put it in wooden boxes which were six inches long by three inches wide, and three inches deep, leaving them in the air for twelve hours, so that the mortars might be somewhat stiffened. They were then placed in a cellar, within a large tub filled with water. I examined the mortars from time to time, and noted the number of days required to harden. I called the mortars hard, when, on pressing them strongly with the thumb, no impression was made on the surface. All the mortars were left in the water one year; at the end of which time they were withdrawn, and I scraped off the four sides or faces with the chisel of a stone cutter until nearly half an inch was removed, when they were rubbed upon a stone until they were reduced to parallelopepids of 6 inches long by 2 inches square. By means of a wooden form which they were made to fit, all were reduced, very exactly, to the same dimensions, and had the four faces well squared. It will be observed that I took off from each side about half an inch, with the view of submitting to rupture only the portion which had not been in contact with water. I ought to notice that in doing this it was often found that the mortars were harder at the surface than in the interior: sometimes the contrary happened. By taking off a portion ($\frac{1}{2}$ inch) from each face, I rejected all, that, from any cause, had received a different degree of hardness from the interior.

To ascertain the tenacity of mortars, the following process was followed. I adapted two pendant, iron, stirrups to a horizontal beam (see plate I. fig. 1.) They were placed parallel to each other and distant four inches in the clear—the lower parts being exactly level. On these stirrups, the parallelopepid of mortar which was to be tested, was placed, passing it through a rectangular collar of iron, a little larger than the prism of mortar, and terminated below by a hook. This collar exercised its pressure upon the mortar by its upper horizontal bar, of which the transverse section had the form of a rounded wedge; and being brought against a bracket, or check, it was midway between the stirrups. To the hook of the collar was suspended a common scale pan, that was loaded by adding successive weights until the prism of mortar broke—which it did with noise. The weights were then summed up, adding, always, 22 lbs. for the weight of the scale pan, cords and collar. In the beginning, as a weight, I poured sand into a box placed on the scale pan, but I renounced this method, because it was too slow. I perceived that it was important to break the mortar promptly; it having several times happened that, when the mortar had supported for some time a weight approaching that which should break it, it would give way, after having taken off a weight of 11 lbs. in order to substitute a greater. On cutting the parallelopepids down to the proper size, I judged nearly of the weight they would sustain; and a weight approaching this was put on at once; after which small weights were added, one after the other, until the mortar broke. When the mortars were capable of sustaining a great weight, I added weights by 10 pounds at a time, because this is a small quantity compared with the total weight, and it is important that the fracture be made promptly. The above are the means I used, and they seem to me to be preferable to any that I have seen described by authors. Some have directed that the mortars should be loaded with weights, until crushed; but the moment when they begin to yield is difficult to judge of, as the angles often break before the middle, and it is not clearly seen when the substance under trial has really yielded to the load. Others have directed that the body of which the strength is to be ascertained, be placed at the end of a strong table to which it is to be fastened; a scale pan is then to be suspended from a portion projecting a certain distance from the table, and weights are to be added till rupture occurs; but it is to be feared that the mortars, or the stones, submitted to this trial, will sometimes project a little more, and sometimes a little less; the weights acting thus at the extremity of unequal arms of levers, will give different results for substances that should exhibit the same tenacity: it is also to be feard that fastening the mortars more or less stifly will influence their resistance.

Mr. Vicat, to judge of the resistance of mortars, employed the following method—reported in pp. 34 and 35 of his memoir: he lets fall upon the surface of the mortar, from a height of 2 inches, a rod of steel slightly conical, and terminated at its end by a plane surface 0.066 inches in diameter; this rod, loaded with the weight of $2\frac{3}{10}$ lbs., penetrates a certain distance into the mortar, giving, thereby, the relative hardness.

As it is the resistance that mortars oppose to steady or unimpulsive forces that it is important to know, he thought he might conclude, from some experiments that he reports, that *"the squares of the numbers which express the penetration of the rod are reciprocally proportional to the resistances to the force which tends to break the mortars."* On this principle he has transformed, by calculation, the penetration of the rod, into numbers proportional to the resistances. I must make, however, on this subject, the following observations.

1st. It is difficult to appreciate exactly the penetration of the rod: 2d. It does not appear to me to be proved, by the few experiments given by Mr. Vicat, that the squares of the numbers expressive of the penetration are always reciprocally proportional to the resistances; 3d. If the rod fall on a grain of gravel, or on a large grain of sand, or even on a grain of lime, we should be liable to infer, from the penetration, conclusions altogether inaccurate as to the resistances of the mortars; 4th. The rod is permitted to fall on the surface of the mortar, and it often happens, as before observed, that the hardness of the surface differs much from that of the interior.

All these causes of error united have conducted Mr. Vicat to conclusions which are sometimes entirely opposite to results obtained in my experiments; I shall take pains to point these out as they present themselves. It will be noticed that to determine the resistance of mortars, I have no calculations to make; by the means employed, these determinations were perfectly independent thereof, and I have only to enter in the table the number of pounds the mortars are loaded with at the moment of rupture.*

I am now about to present the first results of the experiments made with Obernai lime, and with other hydraulic limes of the environs of Strasburg. The Obernai lime being that which was most often used at the works, I sent a specimen to Mr. Berthier, who analysed it, with the following results: Lime, 0.422; Magnesia and iron, 0.050; Silex, 0.105; Alumine, 0.043; Carbonic acid and water, 0.380. This lime-stone differs but little from that of Metz, which contains as follows: Lime, 0.445; Magnesia and Iron, 0.067; Silex, 0.053; Alumine, 0.013; Carbonic acid and Water, 0.412; loss 0.010.

---

* Since the first part of this memoir was written I have seen a new memoir of Mr. Vicat's in which he says, page 117, " We thought ourselves entitled to conclude from a certain number of experiments described in our first work, that the squares of the numbers expressing the penetration of the rod, falling with a given weight, are reciprocally proportional to the relative or absolute resistances of the substance; and, on this principle, the penetrations were transformed by calculation into numbers proportional to these resistances. But, in accordance with the very judicious observations of Mr. Vauthier, Engineer, we have decided to return to the numbers which express the penetration."

I will again observe that it is the tenacity of mortars submitted to unimpulsive or steady forces which it is important to know, and that this will not be obtained by numbers which express the penetration of a rod submitted to an impulsive force.—Au.

Table II.

No. of the mortar.	Composition of mortars.		No. of days required to harden in water.	Weights which they supported before breaking.
	Common bricks of Strasburg			462 lbs.
	Refractory bricks of Sufflenheim			572
1	Yellow Obernai lime alone in paste,*		8	372
2	do. do. do. slaked to powder and measured in powder† 1 / Common sand 1½	} 2½	10	224
3	Lime the same 1 / Sand the same 2	} 3	12	253
4	Lime the same 1 / Sand the same 2½	} 3½	12	176
5	Lime the same 1 / Sand the same 3	} 4	14	92
6	Lime the same 1 / Sand the same 1 / Trass 1	} 3	4	429
7	Lime the same 1 / Trass 2	} 3	4	299
8	Gray Obernai lime alone, in paste		8	354
9	do. do. do. slaked to powder and measured in powder 1 / Common sand 1½	} 2½	10	400
10	Lime the same 1 / Sand the same 2	} 3	10	422
11	Lime the same 1 / Sand the same 2½	} 3½	12	187
12	Lime the same 1 / Sand the same 3	} 4	15	106
13	Lime the same 1 / Sand the same 1 / Trass 1	} 3	4	473
14	Lime the same 1 / Trass 2	} 3	4	328
15	Blue Obernai lime alone, in paste		20	275
16	do. do. do. slaked to powder and measured in powder 1 / Common sand 1½	} 2½	14	136
17	Lime the same 1 / Sand the same 2	} 3	15	154
18	Lime the same 1 / Sand the same 2½	} 3½	16	117
19	Lime the same 1 / Sand the same 3	} 4	18	79
20	Lime the same 1 / Sand the same 1 / Trass 1	} 3	5	378
21	Lime the same 1 / Trass 2	} 3	5	339

* The lime of the hydrates No. 1, 8, and 15 is not of the same burning as the lime of the mortars of the Table.   Av.

† I must premise that by the expression, *slaked to powder*, often used in the Tables, must be understood, lime which was slaked as it came from the kiln, with only a small quantity of water, to reduce it to dry powder.   As to lime reduced to dry powder by being left to spontaneous slaking in the air, it is called *lime slaked in the air*, or *air-slaked lime*.   I sometimes use in the tables the sign + signifying *more*, and the sign — signifying *less*.—*Author*.

Observations on the experiments of Table No. II.

To make the above mortars I took lime as it came fresh from the kiln, and slaked it to dry powder by throwing on one-fifth of its bulk of water; I left it in this state for twelve hours, and then, having measured the powder, I added the quantity of water necessary to reduce it to paste. I afterwards added to the lime the several quantities of sand and of trass indicated in the table, and I, in all cases, mixed the constituents until a homogeneous mortar was obtained, which required that it should pass six or eight times under the trowel. The mortars were made of the consistence of honey; and were put in the small wooden boxes before mentioned; being lightly compressed with the trowel and the hand, they were left in the air during twelve hours: they had then somewhat stiffened, and in this state were placed in a cellar, in a large tub filled with water: I took care to examine them from time to time, and to note the number of days they required to harden to such a degree that on being strongly pressed with the thumb, no impression was made. At the end of a year they were withdrawn from the water and were broken in the manner described, page 17. In order to institute a comparison between the resistance of my mortars and the building materials of the country, I broke, in the same manner, parallelopepids of bricks, having the same dimensions: the average of the common brick of the neighbourhood of Strasburg, gave me 462 lbs., as is expressed in the table; but the refractory bricks of Sufflenheim, are much stronger, and gave 572 lbs.

As I have before remarked, the Obernai lime is yellow when not fully calcined; when a little more burned it is of a dirty yellow; afterwards it passes to ash-gray; and at last, when too much burned, it is of a slate blue, and pieces of vitrified lime are often found. The lime being burned with wood, it is difficult to obtain a uniform calcination: there are always some pieces of lime too much, and others too little burned. Care was taken to reject the pieces of both extremes; but the mortar made at the works always contained, notwithstanding, lime of the three colours mentioned. If the lime-burners would burn their lime for a little longer time, making a less intense fire, they would not consume more wood and would give better results. But it is difficult to change usages.

The object of the experiments of Table No. II. was to know the degree of calcination which is best, and the quantity of sand most proper to mix with the lime. In table No. 1 where I operated with several kinds of lime, I slaked them to dry powder with a bulk of water equal to half the bulk of lime; but the Obernai lime is well reduced to powder with a fifth of its volume of water. With this quantity there is obtained, moreover, nearly the same volume of lime in powder, as when slaked with the half of its volume of water. In fact, 0.005 of yellow Obernai lime reduced to powder and slaked with one-fifth of its volume of water, gave 0.0105 of lime in powder, and, consequently, 1 part would give 2.10, a result differing little from that of table No. 1.

Table No. II. shows that lime-stone which had been calcined so as to yield a lime slightly gray, was that which gave the best result; that which was blue was slow to slake; when reduced to paste it formed with sand and with trass, a mortar susceptible of swelling considerably, because of its preserving, even in this state, the property of absorbing water for a long time. All the boxes containing mortar made of blue lime were totally disjointed by the enlargement of the bulk of mortar. I was not, at first, aware of this effect, and having caused a coat of rough-cast, composed of Obernai lime and sand, to be applied to one of the Government buildings, I was surprised, after five or six months, at seeing, on many points of the surface, swellings of the size, nearly, of a half dollar; these portions finally fell off, and it was then seen that they had been caused by particles of blue lime, about the size of a pea, that were beneath. These particles had not had time to slake thoroughly; and, as imperfectly slaked lime has a strong avidity for water, they absorbed water from the air, and increased in bulk. The force must have been great to break the very hard mortar which covered these particles. This rough-cast has now been on six years; it is very hard, and has perfectly resisted all inclemencies of the seasons. The property which hydraulic lime, too much calcined, has, of swelling considerably after being made into mortar, might be availed of, under certain circumstances. If it were required, for example, to fill cracks in old walls where the hand could not be introduced, or to fill spaces washed from under old foundations, mortar made of highly calcined hydraulic lime might be advantageously used, because the mortar by swelling would more perfectly fill the cavities. But especial care should be taken not to use it in new constructions, as it might cause serious accidents. It is stated that two locks having been made, a short time since, with lime that had not been sufficiently slaked, the mortar swelled to such a degree that all the cut stone was displaced, and it was necessary to rebuild the masonry. This accident happened to the works for the improvement of the navigation of the Vésère.

Table No. II. teaches that the yellow lime and the blue lime gave, alone, greater resistances than when mixed with sand. But I ought to observe that no conclusion should be drawn from this, as the three experiments on hydrates were made with lime different from that used in making the mortars of the table. At the time of making these experiments, I was far from thinking there could be so great a difference between mortars made of pieces of lime which seemed to have sustained the same degree of calcination. The best results with the Obernai lime alone, are 372 lbs. for the yellow, 354 for the gray, and 275 lbs. for the blue. I regret not being prepared for this superiority of the hydrate over mortars, but I was far from expecting it: otherwise, after having made the experiments with the limes alone, I should have made mortars, by adding successively, $\frac{1}{4}$, $\frac{1}{2}$, $\frac{3}{4}$, &c. of sand, so as to judge better of the effect of sand; but it was only on breaking the mortars at the end of a year, that I could know the effect, and I have often, on such occasions, obtained results that surprised me, and been conducted to new experiments, requiring another year to furnish results.

It is seen that after a certain quantity of sand has been added, the mortars lose much of their tenacity: and that for every degree of calcination, trass considerably augments the resistance. It is remarkable that mortars made of lime, sand, and trass, are in general better than those made with lime and trass, without sand: I have, however, found some exceptions. Mr. Vicat thinks that puzzalonas only slightly energetic, suit best with hydraulic limes; but my experiments do not support this opinion; as the trass I used was very energetic, and it will be seen that I always had very good results on mixing it with very hydraulic lime. I obtained, in the above table, better results with Obernai lime, trass, and sand, than with

Obernai lime and trass without sand, and it will be seen, by experiments which follow, that I found the like results with fat lime. In the 7th number of the *Memorial de l'Officier du génie*, I have advanced that, in important constructions, it is not prudent to employ hydraulic lime without a little trass. Mr. Vicat is of a different opinion: for we see a note in the *Annales des Mines*, Vol. X., page 501, wherein he says that the success which has attended the use of hydraulic lime in different works which he cites, ought to suffice to undeceive those who partake my fears as to the insufficiency of hydraulic lime without trass, in important constructions. I have, nevertheless, had an opportunity of seeing the concretes used at the canal *Saint-Martin*, at Paris, and at the basin of the *Palais Royal*, made of the hydraulic lime manufactured by Mr. Saint-Léger, and they are much less hard than those made at Strasburg. I do not doubt, however, that the concrete employed at the *Saint-Martin* canal will well fulfil its object. Being obliged to cover all the bottom of this canal, which has an extent of about 4400 yards, with concrete, in order to keep the water from filtering into the cellars of the inhabitants, it would have much augmented the expense, to have added to this mortar, cements analogous to trass. Concrete composed of Obernai lime and sand, without trass, was often used at Strasburg, for the foundations of revetments, of piers of bridges, &c.; but by "important constructions" I meant Locks and Dams, which have a great pressure of water to sustain, perhaps for a long time. There is no doubt that if such a work were executed with gray lime like that of the preceding table, there would be nothing to fear: but this would require the rejection of a great part of the kiln, and would make the mortar very dear: the extremes, only, can be rejected, so that the lime used is a mixture of the three qualities. If a mean be taken of the three kinds of mortar found under Nos. 3, 10, and 17, we shall have 276 lbs. for the result, while the mean term of the three Nos. 6, 13, and 20, is 427 lbs. I have often, however, had results much weaker than those of the above table, as will be seen in the sequel. I have even had occasion to remark that hydraulic limes coming from the same quarry, and appearing to be calcined nearly to the same degree, have, nevertheless, given very different results: in these cases, the lime, which, mixed with sand had given me a weak resistance, had always afforded a very good mortar, when I used sand and trass with the lime. I am convinced that these last mortars have given, on an average, a resistance more than double the first; I persist, therefore, in thinking that in important constructions, such as Locks and Dikes, which have constantly a strong pressure of water to support, it is prudent to put a little trass, or some analogous substance, into the mortar, even when the hydraulic lime used is as good as the very good hydraulic lime of Strasburg. It is for the Engineer who has the work to execute, to examine the quality of the lime he is to employ, in order to fix the quantity of these matters to be added in the mortar. In my opinion a Government should not regard a light additional expense, when the object is to obtain constructions that will last a long time without needing repairs: unfortunately the contrary system, which I think a very bad one, most commonly prevails.

I ought to premise that in the experiments which I shall report, I shall abstain from conclusions too general. With the limes of Alsace I have often noticed contradictory results, and even, as before mentioned, with limes from the same quarry. We have not, as yet, collected enough facts to establish a general theory: that which may be true as to the limes of one country, may not be true as to those of another. I give the results which I have obtained. It is very desirable that Engineers who have some leisure, should make experiments; as it is only when a great many results shall have been collected that we shall be able to deduce any general principles: those which I shall present must be considered as belonging to only the limes which I shall use.

I now proceed to report other essays upon other limes of the environs of Strasburg.

Table III.

No. of the mortar.	Composition of the mortars.			No. of days which they took to harden in wat'r	Weight which they supported before breaking.
1	Altkirch lime alone, in paste			10	268 lbs.
2	{ do. do. slaked to powder and measured in powder	1	} 3	12	174
	Common sand	2			
3	{ Lime the same	1	} 3	4	539
	Sand the same	1			
	Trass	1			
4	{ Lime the same	1	} 3	4	535
	Trass	2			
5	1st Villé lime alone, in paste			25	119
6	{ Lime the same, slaked to powder and measured in powder	1	} 3	28	68
	Sand	2			
7	{ Lime the same	1	} 3	4	473
	Sand	1			
	Trass	1			
8	{ Lime the same	1	} 3	4	473
	Trass	2			
9	2d Villé lime alone, in paste			25	110
10	{ Lime the same, slaked to powder and measured in powder	1	} 3	28	114
	Sand	2			
11	{ Lime the same	1	} 3	4	396
	Sand	1			
	Trass	1			
12	{ Lime the same	1	} 3	4	475
	Trass	2			
13	Rosheim lime alone, in paste			6	484
14	{ Rosheim lime, slaked to powder and measured in powder	1	} 3	14	209
	Sand	2			
15	{ Lime the same	1	} 3	4	462
	Sand	1			
	Trass	1			
16	Hochfeld lime alone, in paste			12	207
17	{ do. do. slaked to powder and measured in powder	1	} 3	22	136
	Sand	2			
18	{ Lime the same	1	} 3	4	429
	Sand	1			
	Trass	1			

Table III.—(continued.)

No. of the mortars	Composition of the mortars.			No. of days which they took to harden in wat'r	Weight which they supported before breaking.
19	Verdt lime alone, in paste .			8	484
20	do. do. slaked to powder and measured in powder . . Sand	1 2	3	10	279
21	Lime the same . . . Sand . . . . Trass	1 1 1	3	4	510
22	Lime the same . . Trass	1 2	3	4	310
23	Oberbron lime alone, in paste .			10	264
24	Same lime measured in paste . Sand . . .	1 2	3	10	220
25	Same lime do. . . Sand . . .	1 2½	3½	8	352
26	Yellow Bouxviller alone, in paste .			10	299
27	Gray do. do. do. .			30	99
28	Blue do. do. do. .			40	79
29	Yellow do. measured in paste Sand	1 2	3	10	286
30	Lime the same . . . Sand	1 2¼	3¼	10	187
31	Lime the same . . . Sand	1 2½	3½	10	165
32	Lime the same . . . Sand	1 2¾	3¾	12	132
33	Lime the same . . . Sand	1 3	4	12	99
34	Gray Bouxviller lime, measured in paste Sand	1 2	3	25	77
35	Blue do. do. do. . Sand	1 2	3	30	66
36	Yellow do. do. do. . Sand . . . . Trass	1 1 1	3	5	407
37	Metz lime alone, in paste .			15	169
38	Metz lime slaked to powder and measured in powder . . Sand	1 1½	2½	16	312
39	Lime the same . . Sand	1 2	3	16	262
40	Lime the same . . . Sand	1 2½	3½	16	176
41	Lime the same . . . Sand	1 3	4	18	143
42	Lime the same . . . Sand . . . . Trass	1 1 1	3	4	466
43	Lime the same . . . Trass	1 2	3	4	262
44	Lime the same . . . Trass	1 3	4	4	385

Observations on the Experiments of Table No. III.

The Altkirch lime comes from a lime-stone which is grayish: all the others from stones that are blue like those of Obernai and Metz. All were slaked to powder with one-fifth their volume of water, and left in that state for twenty-four hours, before making them into mortars. Several being too remote to be brought into use at the works, I contented myself with some experiments on their hydraulic properties. It is seen that the Altkirch lime is good. The piece of lime brought me had, probably, been out of the kiln a number of days, which should considerably influence the result, as will be soon seen. It is possible, therefore, that this lime is better than the experiments indicate. Two different kinds were brought from Villé. I was told that it was as good as the Obernai lime. The first kind is brown, and the second grayish: we see that the resistances are feeble. The limes of Rosheim, Hochfeld, Verdt, Oberbronn, and Bouxviller gave very good results whether alone or in mortar. It will be seen, also, that with the limes slaked to powder and measured in that state, the mortars consisting of lime and sand, generally supported less weight than the lime alone. It is possible that there was too much sand in them. I began with the principle, admitted by several Engineers, that it is better to err by excess of sand than by excess of lime; but it appears this is not always true, for the experiments of tables Nos. II. and III. show that when the mortars had a little too much sand, their resistance was much diminished. It is possible also that some hydraulic limes may become harder when alone, than when mixed with any proportion of sand whatever.

The Oberbronn lime was measured in paste; it appears that with two and a half parts of sand, it gave a better result than with two parts only, and that this result was superior to that obtained with the lime alone.

As the Bouxviller lime might be used at Strasburg I treated it with more detail. We see that this lime loses much by being too much burned, and that it cannot support as much sand as that of Oberbronn; and, also, that with all these limes, the mortars were much improved by adding trass to the lime and sand. It is an error, therefore, to suppose that energetic puzzalonas are not adapted to good hydraulic limes. Tables Nos. II. and III. show that different limes take very different proportions of sand. Thus, as before observed, various experiments induce me to believe that pieces of lime from the same quarry may give very different results, although calcined to the same degree. It also appears that different degrees of burning require different proportions of sand; it becomes, therefore, difficult to fix accurately the proportion of sand which should enter the mortar.

The above experiments were a first essay only: I proposed making others, with a mixture of lime calcined to different degrees, and to repeat the experiments on several burnings, so as to be able to take a mean. At Strasburg we adopted one part of lime to two and a half parts of sand. The mortar was good, but it, possibly, was not the best that could be made. Supposing the best proportions, as to hardness, were one part of quick lime to two parts of sand, it would still remain to determine whether these proportions should be adopted; because, if in putting a little more sand the result should be but slightly inferior, it might be done unhesitatingly, if the economy were sensible. I was about to make these experiments on the different limes of the environs of Strasburg, when I was obliged to quit the place, in consequence of the new functions to which I was called.

Towards the end of the table, are the experiments made with Metz lime.

It appears that one part of lime in powder, and one and a half of sand, is the mixture which gave the best result, and that it is stronger than the lime alone. Notwithstanding the mortars were made in the month of June, the hardening was slow; and experience teaches that mortars harden sooner in this season, than in winter. The comparisons of No. 42, 43 and 44, show that for the hydraulic limes of Alsace, better results are obtained with sand and trass, than with trass alone. No. 44 which was made with one part of lime in powder, shows that this lime will bear a good deal of trass without losing much of its resistance.

In the above table, the limes used alone, and in the mortars, came from the same piece of limestone, in each case.

I shall conclude my observations on Table No. III, by saying that in the course of my experiments, I have had occasion to observe, more than once, that discordant results were obtained when I used lime that had been slaked for several days. When I made the experiments with the Oberbronn lime, Nos. 23, 24 and 25, I put aside a portion of the lime in powder which I had used. At the end of 15 days, I repeated the experiments recorded at Nos. 23 and 25: for No. 23, which was lime alone, the hardening required 30 days instead of 10 days, which were necessary, when the fresh lime was used. At the end of the year, the piece of hydraulic lime, broke with a weight of 154 lbs, while No. 23, which was made immediately, supported, before breaking, a weight of 264 lbs. As to the mortar made of one part of lime, measured in paste, and two and a half parts of sand, the same as mortar No. 25, the hardening required 25 days instead of 8 days, and the mortar broke with a weight of 154 lbs, while that of No. 25, made immediately, supported 352 lbs, before breaking. I put this lime aside for fifteen days, to see if an old saying of masons, that lime loses its energy in the air, had any foundation. The experiment convinces me that the saying is true, at least as regards the hydraulic limes that I treated; but I wished to see, also, what results I should obtain, with mortars made in the same manner and of the same piece of lime, but at different times. I made, in consequence, the following experiments.

Table No. IV.

No. of the series.	Composition of the mortars.	Made immediately.		After six weeks.		After 2½ months	
		har-den-ing.	w't. sup-port'd	har-den-ing.	w't. sup-port'd	har-den-ing.	w't. sup-portd
		days	lbs	days	lbs	days	lbs
1	Yellow Obernai lime slaked to powder and measured in powder. 1 } 3 Sand . . . . 2 }	9	187	15	44	25	22
2	Lime the same . . 1 } Sand . . . . 1 } 3 Trass . . . . 1 }	6	407	6	407	6	297

Observations on the experiments of Table No. IV.

To make the above experiments, I took the yellow Obernai lime, and slaked it to dry powder by throwing on ¼th of its volume of water. I gave it time to cool, and then made two mortars: one, with one part of lime measured in powder and two parts of sand; the other with one part of lime in powder, one part of sand, and one of trass. The mortars remained in the air during twelve hours, and I then put them in water, where they remained one year, at the end of which time they were broken. The table shows that the mortar of lime and sand, hardened in 9 days and supported 187 lbs, before breaking; it shows also, that the mortar containing lime, sand and trass, hardened in 6 days, and supported 407 lbs. At the end of a month and a half, I repeated the same experiment, using, in powder, the same lime which had served in my first experiment, and which had been lying in an open vessel. I followed, for the second experiment, the same process as for the first: the table shows that in the mortar composed of lime and sand, the hardening was slower, and the resistance much less; and that for the mortar containing trass, the result was the same: again, at the end of two months and a half, I repeated the experiments, using the same lime slaked to powder. The table shows that the hardening was still slower, and that the resistance was still less in the mortar, composed of lime and sand; for by the expression -22, is meant that it could not sustain the weight of the scale-pan, cords, and collar, which was 22 pounds. It also shows that the mortar containing trass experienced a sensible diminution in its resistance, although the time of hardening was the same; but the diminution was not as great as in the mortar made of lime and sand only.

I have thus far gone into particulars, in order that there might be no doubt as to the manner of proceeding : in the following tables, I shall give fewer details. I repeated the above trial, as shown in the following table, using another piece of lime.

Table No. V.

No. of series	Composition of the mortars.	Made immediat'ly		After 15 days.		After 25 days.		After 35 days.		After 45 days.		After 2 months.	
		H	W	H	W	H	W	H	W	H	W	H	W
		d's	lbs	d's	lbs	d's	lbs	d's	lbs	d's	lbs	d's	lbs
	⎧Obernai lime slaked to powder and measured in powder. . 1 ⎫												
	⎨ ⎬ 3	25	264	11	121	15	77	18	88	18	77	20	86
	⎩Sand . . 2 ⎭												
	⎧Lime the same . 1 ⎫												
2	⎨Sand . . 1 ⎬ 3	12	473	5	330	6	297	10	286	12	304	12	299
	⎩Trass . . 1 ⎭												

I made the above experiments, in the same manner as has been explained of Table No. IV; but it will be seen that the periods at which the mortars were made, were brought nearer together. Each experiment in the above table, is divided into two columns: the first contains the number of days, the mortar required to harden, and is marked H; the second column, marked W, expresses the number of pounds that the mortar supported before breaking. I shall adopt, hereafter, this order for all the tables which follow, whenever they contain many columns.

The piece of lime which I used for these experiments, was a petrified cornu ammonis, which was 20 inches in diameter. The table shows that with the first mortar, of lime and sand, the hardening was quite slow, which might be owing to the mortar being made so late as the month of October. It is remarkable that the hardening was not so tardy, for the following, which were made 15 days after slaking. As to the resistance, it was the greatest with the mortar made immediately. That made after fifteen days, lost about half its strength: beyond this period the mortars offered a resistance varying from 77 to 88 lbs, and the hardening was slow.

If the mortars containing lime, sand and trass be reviewed, it will be remarked that the resistance was greatest, with that made immediately, and that it, afterwards, went on diminishing, but keeping well elevated; and that the hardening of the mortar made at the end of fifteen days, was the most prompt.

When making the experiments of the preceding table, I put aside a piece of the same lime, to allow it to slake spontaneously in the air: after two months I made mortar with it, and obtained the following results: it did not harden till the end of twenty-five days, and the mortar broke with 55 pounds, while the table shows that mortar made with the same lime slaked to powder, and which had been left in that state, during the same time, supported a weight of 88 lbs: this result induced me to recommence the experiment with another piece of lime. I proceeded in this way: I divided the lime into two parts; slaking one of these parts into dry powder, by throwing on a fifth of its volume of water, and leaving the other part to slake in the air. I immediately made two mortars with the lime that had been slaked to powder; in one, I mixed sand only with the lime, and in the other I put sand and trass, and at different periods, I repeated the same experiment. It was not till after fifteen days, that the piece of lime which I had left in the air, gave enough lime in powder to begin two similar sets of mortars. The table, following, shows the results I obtained.

Table No. VI.

No. of series	Composition of the mortars.	Made immediat'ly		After 15 days.		After 1 month.		After 2 months.		After 3 months.		After 4 months.	
		H	W	H	W	H	W	H	W	H	W	H	W
		d's	lbs	d's	lbs	d's	lbs	d's	lbs	d's	lbs	d's	lns
1	Obernai lime slaked to powder and measured in powder 1 ⎫ Sand . 2 ⎬ 3	10	121	6	132	4	132	5	117	5	70	6	66
2	Same lime air-slaked and measured in powder . 1 ⎫ Sand . . 2 ⎬ 3			+40	77	+40	44	+40	33	+40	-22	+40	-22
3	Same lime slaked to powder and measured in powder 1 ⎫ Sand . . 1 ⎬ 3 Trass . . 1 ⎭	2	209	2	(1)	2	389	2	352	2	317	3	495
4	Same lime air-slaked and measured in powder . 1 ⎫ Sand . . 1 ⎬ 3 Trass . . 1 ⎭					6	352	5	319	6	275	6	455

(1) This mortar broke on being cut; it was very hard, but I could not determine its resistance. Au.

Observations on the Experiments of Table No. VI.

This table shows, first, that the piece of lime used was not of the best quality. I, however, selected, to make the experiments of Table Nos. IV, V and VI pieces of lime of a yellow fawn colour, which appeared to have been submitted to the same degree of calcination. The trials of tables Nos. IV and V, were commenced in the month of October, while those of No. VI, were begun in June; the febleness of the first result of table No. VI cannot, therefore, be attributed to a cold season of the year; nor can it be attributed to weather too warm, because the experiments of table No. II, which gave very good results, were made in June. We are obliged, therefore, to infer, as I have already noticed, that pieces of quick lime of the same quarry, are far from having, all of them, the same quality.

The first mortar of lime and sand, augmented its resistance a little, after fifteen days slaking, and its hardening was much more prompt after a month. Beyond this term, the time of hardening went on augmenting, and the resistance diminishing, in a sensible manner, as in Table No. V. It will be seen that for the mortar made, in the same manner, with air slaked lime, the hardening was very slow: I pursued the examination for 40 days, and the mortars were not yet hard. The table shows that after 15 days, the mortar gave a resistance much less than that of which the lime had been slaked to powder, and that the resistance went on diminishing. At last it was so weak, that, after three or four months, the mortars were unable to sustain the scale-pan, &c., weighing 22 lbs: the mortars had, in the mean time acquired some consistence, but it was so feeble as to be easily broken between the fingers.

The table shows, also, that mortar composed of lime slaked by water to dry powder, united with sand and trass, hardened promptly. The resistance was less in the mortar made immediately; but it afterwards augmented, and then diminished, and finally, the last gave a great increase. I do not know to what to attribute the anomalies observable in the resistance of these mortars. The last series, made with lime slaked in the air, and in which there is one part of Trass, gave a good result, and the hardening was quite prompt; but the resistance was always less than that of the mortar of which the lime had been slaked by water, to powder. This last mortar also presented, after four months, an anomaly which I cannot explain.

It will be seen by the results of the three tables, Nos. IV, V, and VI, that the presence of trass, corrected the evils resulting from the exposure of the lime to the air, after having been slaked by either process. The air-slaked lime had lost almost all its hydraulic properties; but on mixing it with trass it gave, notwitstanding, very good mortar: this is not surprising, since it appears that exposure to the air, has no other effect, than to cause hydraulic lime to pass to the state of common lime, and this last gives very good mortar when mingled with sand and trass.

The importance of these results, induced me to engage in similar experiments with the Metz lime: they are found as follows.

Table No. VII.

No. of series	Composition of the mortars.	Made immediat'ly.		After 1 month.		After 2 months.		After 4 months.	
		H	W	H	W	H	W	H	W
		d's	lbs	d's	lbs	d's	lbs	d's	lbs
1	Metz lime slaked to powder and measured in powder 1 } 3 / Sand 2	20	116	30	44	30	22		-22
2	Same lime slaked in air and measured in powder 1 } 3 / Sand 2			35	88	15	79	9	88
3	Same lime slaked to powder and measured in powder 1 / Sand 1 } 3 / Trass 1	3	180*	5	312	11	319	11	385
4	Same lime air-slaked and measured in powder 1 / Sand 1 } 3 / Trass 1			13	352	9	209*	7	440

Observations on the experiments of Table No. VII.

I made the above experiments like those in the preceding table. If the first mortar, alone, be compared with No. 39 of Table No. III, it will be seen that the lime used in making the above mortars, was much inferior to that of table No III, although the limes appeared to have been burned to the same degree. The trials, in both these tables, were made in the middle of summer, the quantities of sand and all the other circumstances, were the same; nevertheless, the first mortar of table No. VII, shows a resistance of only 116 lbs, while the similar mortar, No. 39 of table No. III, gives 262 lbs.

It is seen that the first series, composed of lime and sand, shows the greatest resistance when the mortar was made immediately, and that the resistance went on diminishing. At the end of four months, this mortar could not support the scale-pan, and it broke easily in the fingers. We see, therefore, that with Metz lime slaked to powder, the result is the same as with Obernai and Oberbronn lime.

The second series was begun, at the end of a month, with the same lime left to slake in the air: the result varied from 79 to 88 lbs.—a resistance inferior to that obtained by making the mortar immediately: but on comparing these results with those of table No. VI, we see that the Metz lime, when air slaked, gave better mortars, than when slaked to powder with water; while it was the contrary with the Obernai lime, of which the two first series of table No. VI were made. It is also remarkable that the hardening was more and more prompt, with the air-slaked Metz lime, while it required more than 40 days for the Obernai lime to harden, in each case.

As to the two series, of table No VII, made with lime, sand and trass, good results were obtained, whether the lime was slaked with water to powder, or was air-slaked; in both cases, the resistances went on increasing, and the mortars made of air-slaked lime, gave better results than those

* These mortars were split in the middle.

of lime slaked to powder, which was the contrary of the results of table No. VI.

It is to be regretted, that in the first experiment, of the above table, made with lime, sand and trass, the prism of mortar was found split, and separated into two parts. I put the two pieces together, before breaking; but the resistance must have been diminished by the circumstance, and it amounted only to 180 lbs. The last series, also, gives a mortar sustaining 209 lbs. forming an anomaly, when compared with that which precedes, and with that which follows: this mortar was cracked, but the parts were not separated.

It will appear from all the experiments reported, in tables Nos. IV, V, VI and VII, that the saying of masons, that lime loses its energy in the air, is not, as regards hydraulic lime, without foundation. All those which I have treated above have passed to the state of common lime, after some months, when they had been slaked with water; and the Obernai lime gave the same result when air-slaked. I have sought for the cause that might transform hydraulic lime into common lime.

Chemistry teaches us that lime has not the property of absorbing a new quantity of oxygen; but it is not with lime, properly speaking, that we make mortar; it is with the hydrate of lime; that is to say, with lime slaked by water, which enters into combination with it, forming a new body, which may have new properties. It, therefore, occurred to me that hydrate of lime, or, in other words, slaked lime, might absorb oxygen.

In verifying my conjectures in this respect, I could not employ hydraulic lime, because all those I had at command, contained metallic substances capable of oxidation. I proceeded, therefore, in the following manner: I took a piece of white marble which I assured myself contained almost no iron; I had it calcined in a kiln; as soon as it came from the kiln, I pulverized it, and divided the powder into two equal parts, one of these parts was slaked with a little water, and the other was left in the state of quick lime. I put the slaked lime, and the quick lime, each into one of those cylindrical glass vessels used to measure liquids: I placed each of these vessels in a plate containing a little water. I then covered the two vessels containing the lime, with two other vessels, of the same kind, a little larger—the mouths of these covering vessels being immersed in the water. By these means the lime was no longer in connexion with the atmosphere, and it was connected with the water, only through the column of air that was between the two vessels. After five or six days, the water had mounted perceptibly, between the two glass vessels, which contained the slaked lime, and at the end of twenty days, it had mounted four inches. It must be noticed that at this time, the water had risen very little between the two glasses, containing the quick lime. I repeated this experiment several times, and always with the same result. It, therefore, appeared to me that there had been a great absorption of oxygen by the slaked lime, and a slight absorption by the quick lime. I communicated the results I had obtained to Mr. Coze, professor of Pharmacy at the academy of Strasburg, and requested him to ascertain the quantity of oxygen that had been absorbed in the two cases. To that end, a cylindrical glass, graduated, vessel was taken, and one measure of atmospheric air and two measures of deutoxide of azote (nitrous gas) were introduced. As soon as the air in the cylinder had become red, and the water had risen therein, the residue stood at 112 on the scale of the cylinder. The same thing was done with the air that had been in contact with the quick lime: this gave also a red colour, and the residue stood at 117 of the scale. And then the same trial was made with the air that had been in contact with the slaked lime: the red colour was very feeble, and the residue stood at 132 of the scale. In this last case, therefore, there had been a great quantity of gas absorbed by the lime which had been slaked with a little water. To be convinced that it was oxygen, that had been absorbed, hydrogen gas was mixed with the remaining gas, and the mixture submitted to the electrical spark, without any detonation; from which it resulted, that almost all the oxygen had been absorbed by the hydrate of lime.* That the quick lime absorbed but little oxygen, was doubtless owing to this, that this lime could form a hydrate only very slowly, by absorbing water from the dish through the column of air. It appears to me, then, that it is to the absorption of oxygen we should attribute the singular result, that is obtained by leaving exposed to the air, hydraulic limes that have been slaked with a little water. It has been seen that all the above limes, thus treated, have lost, after a little time, almost all their hydraulic properties, and have passed to the condition of common lime.

It appears to me difficult to explain, why the Metz lime which was slaked in the air gave, at the end of four months, a better result than the lime which had been slaked to powder, while the opposite results were obtained with the Obernai lime. Can this difference be owing to the Metz lime containing the oxide of manganese, which the Obernai lime does not? We know that when oxide of manganese is heated, a great part of its oxygen is disengaged, and that it afterwards absorbs it from the air. When the limestone containing it has been calcined, it is possible that this oxide prevents the lime from absorbing oxygen by its own greater affinity for it. It will be interesting to ascertain if the same thing happens with all hydraulic limes, containing oxide of manganese.

It will be seen by the above experiments how important it is not to leave exposed to the air for any time, hydraulic limes which have been slaked to powder, unless well assured that they are not of the same nature as those which become, in this way, common limes. The same observation applies to hydraulic lime slaked spontaneously in the air: we ought to be certain that the same effect will not result as in the Obernai lime of Table No. VI. Without this precaution we shall be liable to make very bad mortars out of very good materials; and to cause very important and expensive constructions to fail. If good results were obtained in tables Nos. VI. and VII. with trass mortars, of which the lime had been slaked for a long time—whether with water to powder or spontaneously in the air, it was because common lime always gives good mortars with trass, whatever may have been the slaking process, as will be seen in the sequel. The above experiments on the absorption of oxygen by hydrate of lime, are contained in a memoir on hydraulic mortars which I addressed to the Committee on Fortifications in October, 1823; an extract from that memoir was printed in 1824, and inserted in the 7th number of the Memorial de l'Officier du génie.

It remains, before closing this article, to speak of the pebbles of Boulogne, of which, having heard, I caused specimens to be brought to Strasburg: but before reporting the experiments therewith, I must refer to a species of lime, much resembling them, well known in England.

In 1796 Messrs. Parker and Wyatts obtained a patent in London for

*It appears from this, that there is reason for forbidding the occupying of newly plastered houses—as they must be unhealthy. Au.

making a particular kind of lime, which was first called *aquatic cement*, and afterwards, improperly, *Roman cement*. At this moment, this cement is an article of considerable commerce, and is sent even to the Indies. This substance has the property of solidifying, like plaster of Paris, almost instantly, when used in the air, and of taking, very soon, a strong consistence in water. It is mixed with 2, 3, 4, and 5 parts of sand, to 3 parts of cement, according to the use to be made of it.

Captain Le Sage, of the Engineers, has brought to notice a substance like the English stone: it was found by an Englishman, by accident, about 20 years ago, upon the shore of Boulogne: a description is given of it in the 2nd vol. of the *mémorial de l'Officier du génie*. This substance is thrown upon the shore by the sea, in the form of pebbles, seldom weighing more than $2\frac{1}{2}$ lbs. Their colour is, in general, a yellowish and dirty gray: several of these pebbles have the surface, to the depth of $\frac{8}{10}$ of an inch, of a rust colour: these stones are of a very fine grain, and they are hard. They are found only in small quantities, and here and there, so that they are used at Boulogne only, where they are advantageously employed in hydraulic works. Mr. Drapier made the analysis of these, and Mr. Berthier of the English stone: from a comparison of these two stones, presented by Mr. Berthier in the same table, after deducting the carbonic acid, and the water which is evaporated by calcination, there remains of the substances employed as lime, viz:

The English stone—lime, 0.554; clay, 0.360; oxide of iron, 0.086.
The Boulogne pebbles— do. 0.540; do. 0.310; do. 0.150.

I ought to add that the analysis gave for the English stone some thousandths of carbonate of magnesia, and of manganese, which are not found in the Boulogne stones: but these quantities being very small, we see that the two are essentially the same. I now give a table of the experiments made with the Boulogne pebbles.

Table VIII.

No. of the mortar.	Composition of the mortars.		No. of days required to harden in water.	Weight supported before breaking.
			days.	pounds.
1	Boulogne pebbles alone, ordinary burning,		$\frac{1}{2}$	108
2	do.		$1\frac{1}{2}$	132
3	do.		1	158
4	do. / Sand	2 / 1 } 3	20	37
5	Pebbles as above / Sand	2 / 1 } 3	22	33
6	Pebbles as above / Sand	1 / 1 } 2		22
7	Pebbles as above / Sand	1 / 2 } 3		— 22
8	Pebbles as above / Sand / Trass	1 / 1 / 1 } 3		22
9	Pebbles as above / Trass	1 / 2 } 3		26
10	Pebbles alone, air-slaked for a month		15	48
11	Pebbles alone, slaked a month with one-fifth the volume of water.	}		— 22
12	Pebbles alone, highly calcined		12	286

Observations on the Experiments of Table No. VIII.

The lime of the first eleven numbers of Table No. VIII. was calcined in a lime kiln, being placed with lime-stone producing fat lime: it was, therefore, calcined with the degree of heat required for burning fat lime. The first three numbers are of the lime alone. We were obliged to pulverize the pebbles as they came from the kiln, because, on throwing on water, instead of being reduced to powder, like fat limes, and ordinary hydraulic limes, they absorb and solidify it. These pebbles afford no vapours on slaking, and give out very little heat. This lime requires less water, than ordinary hydraulic lime, to be reduced to paste. In the above experiments, the pebble lime was reduced to paste a little stiffer than for ordinary hydraulic mortar, because it was perceived that this lime required less water. The first three numbers were made in the same manner; differing only in this, that the first number was put in water after having been formed into paste and exposed three hours in the air; the second number, after two hours exposure, and the third, immediately: it will be seen that this last gave the greatest resistance, but that which gave the least resistance was the quickest to harden, which arose from its having already acquired in the air an evident consistence. We see then, that in constructions in water, when this lime is to be used, it is important to prepare no more mortar than can be used immediately. The numbers from 4 to 9, inclusive, are mixtures of pebble lime with sand in several proportions, and the numbers following contain trass. The hardening was so slow that I was unable to observe them all. We see that the resistance of all these mortars was feeble. It is singular that trass, which gave such good results with all the hydraulic limes I have tried, gave such feeble results with this pebble-lime: it appears that this lime does not bear, with advantage, any mixture. The pebbles of No. 10 were broken up and left to slake in the air for a month; those of No. 11 were exposed during the same time to the air, after having ⅓th of their bulk of water thrown on them. We see that the air-slaked lime gave a very weak result, and that which was slaked with water gave a still feebler, since it was unable to sustain the weight (22 lbs.) of the scale pan, &c.

The weak resistances, shown in the first numbers of the above table, gave me the idea of another experiment, after a higher calcination: to this end, I exposed a piece, in a lime kiln, opposite one of the flues intended to convey the heat through the kiln: the pebble was highly burned; it took a deep rust colour, while those less calcined were of a yellow fawn. No. 12, which is the experiment made with the highly burned pebble, was treated like No. 2, being left, in the state of paste, in the air for one hour before being immersed. We see that the resistance was very good, since this No. 12 supported the weight of 286 lbs. before breaking; but the hardening was quite slow. This trial was made with the remainder of my stock of pebbles; otherwise I should have made several essays to ascertain whether by mixing this strongly calcined lime, with sand and trass, I should obtain better results than those given when less burned.

Taken all together, the experiments of table No. VIII. show, that the lime derived from Boulogne pebbles is a hydraulic lime presenting in several respects, great differences from the other hydraulic limes which I have treated. The ordinary hydraulic limes of which I have spoken, demand only the same degree of heat as is required to calcine fat lime, and it is perhaps proper to calcine them a little less. When these limes are but little burned, they form a good body with sand, and give very good results with trass: if the same degree of heat be given as was received by the pebbles in experiment No. 12, they sustain an incipient vitrification, and give only weak results. A circumstance, quite remarkable, is, that when I treated these limes without mixing them with any other substance, those numbers which hardened the quickest, gave the least resistances, while those which took the longest time to harden, gave results much superior to the others. All these experiments were, notwithstanding, made at the same season— the beginning of the winter. The differences which I have pointed out, between Boulogne pebbles and ordinary hydraulic lime, induce me to suspect there might be, in the pebbles, some substance that escaped detection in the analysis. I have, moreover, attempted to recompose this lime, by a mixture of the substances given by the analysis: on burning it, I had ordinary hydraulic lime, and none of the peculiar results given by the pebbles. To ascertain if the pebbles contained any substance not mentioned in the analysis, I took one of the crude stones, broke it, and examining it with the magnifier, I noticed some very small crystals which did not appear to be calcareous. I pulverized these particles and put them, for some time, in distilled water: I then filtered and concentrated the liquid: it had a decided salt taste, and on leaving it at rest, I obtained quite a quantity of crystals of muriate of soda, which had been previously noticed as being present. It appeared to me that this muriate of soda, contained some crystals of carbonate of soda. This did not surprise me, since we know, from the fine observations of Mr. Bertholet, that Natron, which is brought from Egypt, is formed by the decomposition of muriate of soda, by the carbonate of lime which exists in the bottom of the lakes, situated in the desert of Thaïat to the west of the Delta. In winter, these lakes fill with salt water which enters through the bottom and rises about seven feet; on the return of warm weather, the water of the lakes is completely evaporated, leaving on the bottom, which is calcareous, a stratum of natron, which is a mixture of sea salt, (muriate of soda) sulphate, and carbonate, of soda, constituting the soda of commerce: this natron is broken up from the bottom with iron bars. The muriate of soda which exists in the Boulogne pebbles in notable quantity, and the crystals of carbonate of soda which I thought I discovered, induced me to make several experiments (which I shall soon report,) by adding a little soda and potash to a mixture of lime and clay, which I then burned in order to obtain an artificial hydraulic lime.

Mr. Pitot du Helles, formerly an officer of Engineers, now living at Morlaix, sent me, lately, a singular substance which furnishes hydraulic lime, and seems to me to bear analogy to the Boulogne pebbles. This substance appears to come from the fragments of a species of madrepore of which the geological position does not seem to be well known, but which appears to exist outside the roadstead of Morlaix: these fragments are brought by the currents, and form considerable deposits in the roadstead, whence they are raised with the drag, by the boatmen: the farmers make considerable use of it as a manure for certain soils, and give it the name of *merle*. It is in very small and contorted fragments; its colour is a dirty white; it is light. Mr. Grimm, *pharmacieur en chef de la Marine*, at Brest, made an analysis of this substance, which contains: carbonate of lime, 5.25; sand, 1.35; water and organic matter, 3.30; oxide of iron and phosphate of lime, traces; loss, 0.10. Mr. Pitot made lime of this substance, and I made some trials with the specimen he sent me.

When water was thrown on the calcined *merle*, it was almost a quarter of an hour before any heat was manifested, and that so slight that a little vapour was barely perceptible. This lime does not reduce well to powder by slaking; it would be necessary to reduce it by pestles: in this, it presents similar character to the Boulogne pebbles.

I reduced a portion of this lime to paste with water, and placed it at the bottom of a glass filled with water: the hardening was complete at the end of six days, although the experiment was made towards the close of November. I mixed a portion of this lime with an equal quantity of sand: the hardening took place in eight days; and it seemed to me that this lime would not bear much sand. I was not able to ascertain the tenacity of mortar made of this lime; but the manner in which it hardened, and the degree of induration it had acquired in a short time, led me to think that it is a very good hydraulic lime; and that it will be of great advantage in all hydraulic constructions on the coast of Bretagne. I am astonished that alumine was not found in this lime, so eminently hydraulic.

CHAPTER IV.

Of Artificial Hydraulic Limes.

I stated in the first chapter, that, for a long time, the property possessed by certain limes of hardening in water, was attributed to the presence of oxides of manganese and of iron; several very hydraulic limestones were, however, at last found that contained no oxide of manganese and very little iron. It was observed, at a later period, that almost all hydraulic limestone contained from one to three-tenths of clay. This led to the opinion that when a certain proportion of clay is disseminated in limestone, it combines, by calcination, with the lime, and imparts to it the property of hardening in water. I stated that Mr. Vicat, Engineer of roads and bridges, published, in 1818, an interesting memoir on hydraulic mortars, and that he announced that by reburning fat lime with a certain quality of clay, he obtained very good hydraulic lime. I was bound to state, also, that Dr. John, of Berlin, presented to the Society of Sciences of Holland, a memoir on the subject which was crowned in 1818, and published the following year. He gave the analysis of many common, and hydraulic limes, as well as of many ancient mortars, and he showed that the hydraulic property of lime is due to a portion of clay which combines with it by calcination, and he calls this clay the *cement* of the lime.

The Minister of War sent the memoir of Mr. Vicat to those places where public works were in progress, and directed the experiments announced by this Engineer, to be repeated. I was then occupied at Strasburg, in rebuilding the sluices and other badly constructed hydraulic works; and was using the Obernai hydraulic lime. I had caused trass to be brought from Andernach, having had occasion to employ it at the great works of Vésel in 1806, 1807 and 1808, and knowing its excellence in constructions under water. In the erection of the sluices at Strasburg, we composed the mortar of the Obernai hydraulic lime, sand and trass; but this last substance being dear, I had begun making some essays towards replacing it with cement, when the memoir of Mr. Vicat was sent to me. I caused the experiments given in that work to be repeated, in the first place by an officer of Engineers, who used a clay of which bricks are made in the environs of Strasburg: he obtained no satisfactory result. A second officer was directed to recommence the experiments, and he was not more successful than the first. I repeated them, then, myself, and I took great pains in making the mixture of clay and lime; they were then calcined and I obtained a result, but it was a very feeble one. I then began anew, using other argillaceous earths, richer in clay, (*plus grasses*) and I got much better results. The mortars made with these artificial hydraulic limes, are shown in the following table.

TABLE No. IX.

No. of the mortar.	Composition of the mortar.		No. of days required to harden in water.	Weights supported before breaking.
			days	lbs.
1	Fat lime, reburnt with 2-10 of brick earth, slaked to powder and measured in powder Sand	1⎱ 2⎰3	28	44
2	Same lime, reburnt with 1-10 of Holsheim clay Sand	1⎱ 2⎰3	30	106
3	Same Lime, reburnt with 2-10 of Holsheim clay Sand	1⎱ 2⎰3	20	187
4	Same lime, reburnt with 3-10 of Holsheim clay Sand	1⎱ 2⎰3		—22
5	Lime from white marble, reburnt with 1-10 of Holsheim clay Sand	1⎱ 2⎰3	35	55
6	Same lime reburnt with 2-10 of Holsheim clay Sand	1⎱ 2⎰3	27	174
7	Same lime, reburnt with 3-10 of Holsheim clay Sand	1⎱ 2⎰3	36	130
8	Fat lime reburnt with 2-10 of pipe clay measured in paste Sand	1⎱ 2⎰3	10	132
9	Same lime reburnt with 2-10 of Holsheim clay do. Sand	1⎱ 2⎰3	10	216
10	Same lime reburnt with 2-10 of Yellow Ochre do. Sand	1⎱ 2⎰3	15	90
11	Same lime, reburnt with 2-10 of "Sanguine" do Sand	1⎱ 2⎰3	25	44
12	Same lime reburnt with 2-10 of Sufflenheim clay do. Sand	1⎱ 2⎰3	17	110
13	Same lime reburnt with 2-10 of Frankfort clay do. Sand	1⎱ 2⎰3	17	121
14	Same lime reburnt with 2-10 of pipe clay, but more highly calcined than the lime of No. 8 Sand	1⎱ 2⎰3	16	197
15	Fat lime reburnt with 2-10 pipe clay, measured in paste Trass	1⎱ 2⎰3	5	307
16	Lime from white marble, reburnt with 2-10 of alumine do. Sand	1⎱ 2⎰3		
17	Same lime reburnt with 1-10 of alumine and 1-10 of white sand do. Sand	1⎱ 2⎰3		

No. of the mortar.	Composition of the mortar.		No. of days required to harden in water.	Weights supported before breaking.
			days.	lbs.
18	Same lime reburnt with 2-10 of white sand pulverized do. . . . Sand	1 2 } 3		
19	Fat lime reburnt with 2-10 of white sand pulverized do. . . . . Sand	1 2 } 3	21	51
20	Same lime reburnt with 2-10 of common sand pulverized do. . . Sand	1 2 } 3	28	35
21	Same lime reburnt with 2-10 of magnesia do. . . . . . . Sand	1 2 } 3		
22	Same lime reburnt with several proportions of oxide of manganese do. . Sand	1 2 } 3		
23	Same lime reburnt with several proportions of iron filings, and with oxide of iron in several states of oxidation Sand . . . . . . , .	1 2 } 3		

Observations on the experiments of Table No. IX.

The hydraulic limes of this table were made by the process of Mr. Vicat: care being taken to temper the clays in water, and to make the mixture when they were reduced to the consistence of a homogeneous sirup. If the clays be not diluted, the union with the lime cannot be so well made. The compound of lime and clay was made by taking one part of lime measured in paste, and the several proportions of clay mentioned in the table. All the limes were reburnt by placing them in Hessian crucibles, in the middle of the lime kiln; there was no exception but No. 14, which, as will be stated below, was more strongly calcined than the other limes. All the mortars were made as soon as the artificial limes were withdrawn from the kilns. The proportion of the first seven mortars was got by taking one part of lime in powder to two parts of sand. Some experiments having shown me that in this mixture there was too much sand, the mortars from No. 8 to No. 23 were made by taking one part of lime in paste to two parts of sand.

No. 1 consists of fat lime reburnt with $\frac{2}{10}$ of brick-earth of the environs of Strasburg: this did not give a good result, as may be seen in the last column.

Nos. 2, 3 and 4 were intended as a trial of the clay of the Village of Holsheim, near Strasburg. Lime was mixed, successively, with 1, 2 and 3 tenths of that clay: it will be seen that the best result was with $\frac{2}{10}$; the mixture in which there was $\frac{3}{10}$ of clay gave a mortar which did not bear the scale pan, and broke easily in the fingers. The Holsheim clay is reddish, and greasy to the touch. Further on, I will give its composition.

Nos. 5, 6 and 7 are a repetition of the three preceding experiments, with this difference—that lime made from white marble was employed, in stead of the fat lime of the country. The greatest resistance that I obtained with this lime was in a mixture with $\frac{2}{10}$ of clay. It is remarkable that with $\frac{1}{10}$ of clay, I obtained a passable result, while in No. 4, with the same proportion of clay, and differing from No. 7 only in the kind of lime, the result was very bad. I do not know to what this can be owing.

No. 8 was made with a greasy and very white clay, brought from the neighborhood of Cologne, to Strasburg, to make pipes. This clay gave a tolerable result.

No. 9 is a repetition of No. 8: there is no difference except in the proportions. No. 8 was made by taking one part of lime when reduced to powder after the second burning, and two parts of sand, while for No. 9 one part of lime, when reduced to paste after the second burning, was taken, to two parts of sand: as there is more lime in a given bulk of paste than in an equal bulk of powder, this mortar contained less sand than No. 8, and it gave a better result. It may be seen by Tables No. II and III that the natural hydraulic limes of the environs of Strasburg, will not bear a large proportion of sand; and I think that, in general, hydraulic lime takes less than is commonly supposed.

No. 10 was made with the yellow ochre of commerce, and No. 11, with a substance known under the name of *sanguine:* the results were weak, especially No. 11.

No. 12 was made with the Sufflenheim earth, which is used in making refractory bricks that are highly esteemed in the country, and employed at the cannon foundry at Strasburg. No. 13 contained clay which is brought, because of its containing little or no iron, from the neighborhood of Frankfort, to Strasburg, to make alum. The results of these two trials are not very satisfactory.

No. 14 was made in the same manner, and same proportions as No 8; it differs from it only in the lime being more highly calcined. The result was better. It is possible that each kind of clay requires a particular degree of calcination; this result may be owing also to this—that the lime and the clay contain very little iron, which appears to facilitate vitrification.

The lime of No. 15 was calcined like that of No. 8: but in lieu of making the mortar of sand, it was made of trass: the result was much superior.

No. 16 was made with $\frac{2}{10}$ of alumine mixed with lime from white marble. There was no result: the mortars had no sort of consistence.

No 17 was composed of lime from white marble, mixed with a factitious clay composed of equal parts of silex pounded very fine, and of alumine: this gave a better result. The bad result of No. 16 induced me, at first, to conclude that alumine alone had not the property of rendering lime hydraulic: but a mixture of silecious sand and alumine not having yielded a better result, although forming a factitious clay, I have thought it might be owing to the following circumstance: the alumine which I used was extracted from a quality of alum that I decomposed; this alum had been made of the Frankfort clay, of which I will give the analysis below. In making the alum, the clay is calcined before being dissolved in sulphuric acid. It is possible that the calcination takes away from the alumine the property of combining with lime in the dry way. We ought not, therefore, to conclude, from No. 16, that alumine has not the property of rendering lime hydraulic, but only, that when it has been calcined, it has not that property. What makes me think that calcination deprived the alumine of the property of combining in the dry way with the lime, is, that I have calcined one part of fat lime with $\frac{3}{10}$ of puzzalona, without getting any result. To know if alumine has the property of rendering lime hydraulic, it will be necessary to use this substance before it has been calcined, or acted upon by any acid. Pure alumine exists in some countries: but it is rare: I had none at command.

Nos. 18 and 19 are, respectively, mixtures of marble lime and fat lime, with white sand, and common sand broken very fine. It is remarkable that I obtained a result with fat lime, and no result with the marble lime. I do not know to what to attribute this difference: it may happen perhaps in this way, that the fat lime, of which I shall give the analysis below, contains the red oxide of iron which might facilitate the union of the lime with the white sand, which is entirely silecious.

No. 20, made with fat lime, and with ordinary sand, which is granitic, and coloured by the red oxide of iron, gave a result nearly like No. 9. I regret not having made a fourth experiment with marble lime and ordinary sand, in order to prove, further, that oxide of iron facilitates the combination of silecious and granitic sands with lime, as appears to be inferable from a comparison of Nos. 18 and 19.

No. 21 was designed to ascertain the influence of magnesia: that which I used in this experiment had been calcined to disengage the carbonic acid. We see that no result was obtained. I repeated the experiments, using carbonate of magnesia in order to avoid the use of a substance which had already been calcined: the heat of the lime kiln would drive off the carbonic acid of the magnesia, so that the magnesia would be free to combine with the lime; I, however, got no result.

No. 22 was an attempt to ascertain whether manganese imparted any properties to the lime. I mixed, successively, one part of fat lime with one, two, and three tenths, of oxide of manganese, and calcined the mixtures: I did not observe that the lime had undergone the least change. It is quite astonishing that an opinion should have prevailed for so long a time, that it was to oxide of manganese, hydraulic lime owed its quality of hardening in water: mixing fat lime with this oxide would have shown that lime acquires no new property thereby.

No. 23 indicates that I made various experiments with iron. I took one part of fat lime, which I mixed successively with diverse proportions of filings of iron obtained from a locksmith's shop, and which I reduced to very fine powder. I did the same thing with black oxide of iron, with brown oxide at different degrees of oxidation, and with steel filings: all these mixtures were burned in a lime kiln and I then made mortars by uniting them with sand; the lime had acquired no hydraulic property; but I had occasion to remark that the oxide of iron had, nevertheless, a marked action on the lime. It is known that if we take lime made of white marble, and throw water on it as it comes from the kiln, it slakes at once, giving out much heat and vapour. In making the above experiments with iron, I remarked, that the higher it was oxidized the less heat and vapour were given out by the lime on throwing water upon it, and that it did not slake until after it had been wet for some time: the lime which had been calcined with $\frac{3}{10}$ of brown oxide of iron gave no vapour; I placed in it a thermometer of Réaumur, and at the end of half an hour it had risen but five or six degrees. The Boulogne pebbles contain, as I have observed, a considerable quantity of brown oxide of iron; it is owing to this, no doubt, that if water be thrown on these pebbles as they are taken from the kiln, they give very little heat and no vapour: they do not fall to powder, and must be reduced to that state by pounding. The fat lime of Strasburg, also, contains a certain quantity of brown oxide of iron; the limestone has rusty stains in many places: when water is thrown on it, after calcination, some time is required for it to begin to slake.

A great part of the clays used in the above table were analysed, under the direction of Mr. Berthier, at the school of mines. I give, below, the substances they contain; and also the analysis of the fat limestone of the neighborhood of Strasburg. This stone contains the following substances, viz: carbonate of lime, 0.964; oxide of iron, 0.020; water and loss 0.016. We see that after calcination, which drives off the water and the carbonic acid, there is left lime mixed with about two per cent of oxide of iron.

The following is the analysis made by Mr. Berthier of the different clays used by me.

	CLAYS FROM					
	Hol-sheim.	Vissem-bourg.	Frank-fort.	Cologne.	Sufflen-heim.	Kalb-sheim.
Silex	0.430	0.687	0.500	0.670	0.724	0.442
Sand, Quartzose, mixed	0.365	0.015				0.010
Alumine	0.095	0.182	0.327	0.240	0.118	0.112
Magnesia	0.014	0.006	0.015	0.012	0.020	0.020
Oxide of iron	0.030	0.016	trace	0.012	0.048	0.048
Lime						0.164
Water*	0.056	0.092	0.160	0.066	0.078	0.202
	0.990	0.998	1.002	1.000	0.988	0.998

* The number 0.202 comprises carbonic acid and water. Au.

I used in my experiments two kinds of sand. That which I have designated as white sand is silicious, and is used in making crystals at the manufactory of Saint Louis in the Vosges: it is fine, and very white. The sand which has no particular designation given it in the tables, and which I have sometimes called ordinary sand to distinguish it from the white sand, is that which is commonly used at the works in Strasburg: it is obtained from a plain to the south-east of the town, between the Rhine and the Ill. This sand is rather fine; small gravel is mixed with it, and it is, a very little, earthy; it is coloured quite red by the oxide of iron. This is, for the greater part, granitic, mixed with a little silex.

The above experiments, with iron and oxide of manganese, confirm the opinion now for some time entertained, that these two metals do not confer any hydraulic property on lime. These results were published in 1822, as well as those concerning silex. At the same period, Mr. Berthier published in Vol. VII of the *Annales des Mines*, several interesting experiments, which I shall state. This Engineer, also, having ascertained that iron, and oxide of manganese, imparted no hydraulic quality to lime, says—

"Various mixtures, of chalk and ordinary sand, having been burned in a lime kiln, we obtained only meagre lime not hydraulic, and it was ascertained that only the twentieth part of the sand had been attacked and rendered soluble by the alkalis.

"By substituting, for ordinary sand, the sand of Aumont, prepared for the manufacture of the Sévres porcelain, that is to say, reduced to powder by grinding, the combination is better; but all the silecious matter was not yet attacked, and there remained about one third, which could not be dissolved in alkalis. We afterwards calcined for about one hour, in a platina crucible, at the temperature of about fifty pyrometric degrees, a mixture of ten grammes of chalk and one fifth of gelatinous silex, that is to say, silex separated by acids from its solution in alkalis. The matter slaked with considerable heat, and swelled a little: it formed a consistent paste with water, and, after two months immersion, the paste had acquired strength enough to resist the impression of the finger.

"We calcined, in a platina crucible, ten grammes of chalk with quantities of hydrate of alumine corresponding to 1.942 grammes in one experiment; and 2.36 grammes, in the other: the two mixtures slaked promptly with a strong heat, and swelled considerably. Soft pastes were made of these and put under water: but at the end of two months they had not acquired the least consistence.

"Ten grammes of the magnesian carbonate (of lime) of Paris, and two grammes of gelatinous silex, gave a lime which slaked with feeble heat and little swelling, and after a very short immersion became harder than the best artificial hydraulic lime. This lime may be stated to be composed of lime, 0.560; magnesia, 0.166; silex, 0.274.

"An essay made on a large scale with four parts of chalk, and one part of the kaolin of Limoges, induces the belief that it will be advantageous to have the quantity of alumine equal to the quantity of silex. This lime must be considered as composed of lime, 0.745; alumine, 0.125; and silex, 0.130; it acquired, very soon after its immersion, a consistence stronger than that of the artificial lime prepared with four parts of chalk, and one part of the Passy clay.

"A lime prepared, on a large scale, with four parts of chalk and one part of yellow ochre (in volume,) and which should contain lime, 0.745; alumine, 0.055; oxide of iron, 0.070; silex, 0.130, took but a feeble consistence, even after being immersed a long time. We cannot help attributing the bad quality of this lime to the oxide of iron, because with a quantity of clay equal to the quantity of ochre used, we always obtain a lime eminently hydraulic.

"We calcined, in a platina crucible, ten grammes of chalk, 2.50 of carbonate of magnesia, and 2.50 of gelatinous silex. The matter was purplish; it slaked, giving out heat. A paste was made of it which was placed in water: at the end of two months it had acquired no consistence, while the chalk and silex alone, would have given a lime hardening promptly."

Mr. Berthier thinks that no mixture of which silex does not form a part, will acquire hydraulic properties: that appears probable; but, to be able to affirm it positively, it would be necessary to heat mixtures of lime and alumine or magnesia, which had not already sustained a first calcination. Mr. Berthier does not say whether the alumine which he mixed with his lime was derived from the decomposition of alum, or was natural alumine. In the first case, it is probable it had already sustained a previous calcination, and if so, it is not surprising that no result was obtained.

Mr. Berthier concludes from the experiment which he made with four parts of chalk and one part of ochre, that the oxide of iron was injurious. The oxide of iron enters, however, only in the small quantity of 0.070; and according to the analysis he gives of the English stone, (which furnishes Parker's cement?) it exists therein to the extent of 0.086, and, in the Boulogne pebbles, to the extent of 0.150; this last quantity being more than double, and these two limes being very hydraulic, notwithstanding.

We see that the experiments of Mr. Berthier and mine accord, as to hardening. The learned Professor did not submit his specimens to pressure, to ascertain the tenacity; it is probable he would have had results analogous to mine. I made no experiments by combining, as Mr. Berthier did, carbonate of magnesia with silex, which produced a lime hardening very promptly. It is desirable to repeat this experiment; afterwards submitting the mortars to pressure, to learn their tenacity.

A part of my preceding experiments having been printed in 1824 in a small pamphlet which was sent to the public works, and was inserted in the seventh number of the *Mémorial de l'Officier du Génie*, Mr. Vicat published, in the *Bulletin des Sciences*, in 1825, and in the *Annales des Mines*, Vol. X, 3d livraison, page 501, some observations on the results that I had presented. I propose answering the observations of Mr. Vicat, as the more suitable occasions present themselves. This Engineer commences his remarks in the following manner: "In proscribing hydraulic limes, Mr. Treussart rests upon experiments which do not appear to be conclusive: in the mixtures he made, sometimes he did not employ the clay in suitable proportions, sometimes he used a clay too aluminous, or charged with too great a quantity of oxide of iron, and sometimes he used quartz pounded very fine, as if the degree of fineness obtained by simple trituration could be compared to that of the silex contained in clay."

I do not know what induced Mr. Vicat to say that I proscribed hydraulic lime; the following are the expressions which conclude the pamphlet in question. "We see, by what precedes, that the principal idea of the author (Mr. Treussart) is, that there would be much more advantage in making, *directly*, mortar with fat lime, and trass, or factitious puzzalona, than in seeking first to make hydraulic lime, and afterward to compose mortars of this lime and common sand." This is very different from what Mr. Vicat makes me say. It is now more than twenty-five years since I learned to appreciate the good effects of hydraulic limes, whether for constructions in the air or in water: I have employed them wherever I could procure them: during the nine years that I was at Strasburg, there were built, with hydraulic lime, in the works in water and in air, more than a million of masonry: I have, then, used this lime for a long time, and I think few Engineers have used more; it would be strange, therefore, in me to proscribe it. I was bound to show the precautions that should be taken in using it, so as not to risk making very bad mortar out of very good lime; I was bound to say what my experience had led me to think, namely, that, in places where good natural hydraulic lime could not be found, it is preferable, as regards the quality of the mortar, and as regards economy, to make hydraulic mortar, directly, by using fat lime and factitious trass, in lieu of attempting to make artificial hydraulic lime with which to compose mortars by the addition of common sand: the sequel of my experiments will leave no doubt in this respect. As to the reproach that Mr. Vicat brings, of my having used clays which were not suitable; I have to answer that we were obliged to use those afforded by the locality. I made various essays with argillaceous earths of the environs of Strasburg, and I could do no better. Mr. Vicat says, page 7 of his memoir, that his method consists " in kneading together lime and a certain quantity of gray or brown clay, or simply brick earth, facilitating the operation by the aid of a little water." He gives no other indication as to the nature of the clays that should be used. The experiments that I have given in Table No. IX, prove that it is not indifferent what kinds of clay are used, for the results are not, by a great deal, the same for all. We do not yet know the proportions that a clay should have, to afford the best results. I do not comprehend the reproach connected with having tried silecious sand pounded very fine. I know very well that we cannot compare our mechanical process with the processes of nature; but having seen that Mr. Descotils and Mr. Vitalis gave two different analyses of the Senonches lime, I wished to ascertain whether very fine silecious sand would give a hydraulic result: for if so, I should conclude, however feeble the result might have been, that limestones containing a mixture of silex only, might give good hydraulic limes. The objection that Mr. Vicat makes to me did not prevent his employing, in mixing clay with lime, a mechanical process of which the result cannot certainly be compared to mixtures existing in natural hydraulic limestones; still he was right in trying the mixture, since it succeeds with certain clays.

When I saw that the clays of the environs of Strasburg gave results very inferior to those which I obtained with mortar made of common lime and factitious puzzalona, I requested the *Chef de Battaillon*, Augoyat, of the Engineers, residing in Paris to send me a little of the hydraulic lime made at Paris by Mr. Saint Leger, according to the process of Mr. Vicat. He sent me some, directly as it came from the kiln; a part was in masses, the rest had been broken into small pieces and put into a bottle, which was then well sealed. I made, with the lime as soon as it arrived at Strasburg, experiments like those I had made with natural and artificial hydraulic lime. The following table contains the results of these new experiments.

TABLE No. X.

No. of the mortar.	Composition of mortars.	Made immediately.		At the end of 1 month.		At the end of 2 months.	
		H.	W.	H.	W.	H.	W.
		d's	lbs.	d's	lbs.	d's	lbs.
1	Paris hydraulic lime slaked to powder and measured in powder 1 / Sand 2 } 3	12	187	15	88		
2	Same mortar	14	220				
3	Same mortar	16	246				
4	Same lime slaked in the air and measured in powder 1 / Sand 2 } 3			20	55		
5	Same lime, measured in paste 1 / Sand 2 } 3	1	253	25	99	30	88
6	Same lime 1 / Sand 2¼ } 3¼	18	257				
7	Same lime 1 / Sand 2½ } 3½	20	209				
8	Same lime, measured the same 1 / Sand 2 } 3	15	242				
9	Same lime 1 / Sand 2¼ } 3¼	18	220				
10	Same lime 1 / Sand 2½ } 3½	18	187	24	88		
11	Lime of No. 5 slaked in air and measured in paste 1 / Sand 2 } 3			30	88		
12	Lime of No. 5 slaked to powder and measured in paste 1 / Sand 1 / Trass 1 } 3					6	297

Observations on the experiments of Table No. X.

All the above mortars were made in the same way as the mortars of the preceding tables, that is to say, except for the mortars made of air-slaked lime; the lime was slaked to powder with one-fifth of its volume of water, whether made immediately or preserved for the periods indicated in the table. The mortars being made, they were put into boxes, and left in the air during twelve hours, like the others; after which they were put in water, and at the end of a year submitted to the proof of weights.

The first four numbers were made in the month of April 1823. No. 1 is proportioned with one part of lime slaked to powder, and two parts of sand: of this I made a mortar immediately after the slaking of the lime, and put it in water twelve hours afterwards: this mortar hardened in twelve days, and broke under a weight of 187 lbs. I left the rest of the lime in powder, in the air, and at the end of a month I made a mortar of it in the same way the first mortar was made. We see that the hardening required fifteen days, and that it would support only 88 lbs. No. 2 is a repetition of No. 1, being made of another piece of limestone: this piece appears to have been better than the first, since, of the two mortars made in the same way, the second result is sensibly the best.

The first two numbers were made of lime sent in masses without being defended from the contact of the air. No. 3 was proportioned in the same way, but it was made of broken lime, sent in a well sealed bottle; this number gave a better result than the preceding, which I attribute to the lime being kept from contact of the air. Six or eight days may have elapsed from the time of taking the lime from the kiln, to the time of making the experiment. No. 4 was made of the piece of limestone of which No. 1 had been made; it was left to slake in the air, and at the end of a month I made a mortar with it, taking one part of this lime in powder and two parts of sand. We see that the hardening required 20 days, and that the mortar broke under the light weight of 55 pounds. The lime No. 1 which had been slaked to powder with water, gave a better result, after the same lapse of time.

The first four numbers were proportioned with one part of lime slaked to powder, and two parts of sand; a short time after having made these, however, I became convinced that hydraulic limes would not bear as much sand as had been commonly thought, as I have before stated. I, in consequence, requested Mr. Augoyat to send me some more artificial hydraulic lime from the same manufactory of Mr. Saint-Leger. This lime was sent to me like the first, partly in masses *(en pierre)* in a box, and partly broken up and put in bottles well corked and sealed. This was received in the month of May 1824, and it was with this lime that I made all the experiments of the above table, which follow No. 4, taking, for the proportion, one part of lime measured in paste, against the quantities of sand stated in the table. Mortar No. 5 being made with lime measured in paste, contains much less sand than mortar No. 1, in which the lime was measured in powder. Nos. 5, 6, and 7 were made of the lime contained in the bottles. The object of these three experiments was to ascertain the quantity of sand this lime would bear. We see that the mortar made of one part of lime in paste to two of sand, gave the best result. As I made no experiments with a less proportion of sand, I am not able to say whether this is the best proportion. I anticipated that the best result would be found to lie between two parts and two parts and a half, of sand, because I partook of the common error, that it was better to give too much, than too little sand. In making No. 5,

I had slaked a certain quantity of lime to dry powder, by one-fifth of its volume of water, and I left a portion thereof exposed to the air, as I did with the natural hydraulic lime of the environs of Strasburg; at the end of one and two months, I made new mortars proportioned like those made immediately after slaking. We see that at the end of one month, this mortar had already lost nearly two-thirds of its resistance, and at the end of two months it had lost still more; we see, also, that the hardening was much slower.

Nos. 8, 9, and 10 are repetitions of Nos. 5, 6, and 7, with this difference only, that the former were made of lime sent to me in a box, while Nos. 5, 6 and 7 were made of lime sent in bottles. The best result with these is, again, that in which there is one of lime to two of sand. Of the mortars of these six experiments, if those be compared which have the same proportions, it will be seen that the mortars made of lime secured in bottles were always better than those made of lime which had not been perfectly shut from the air, notwithstanding that only about six days had elapsed from the taking the lime from the kiln to the making it into mortar. I have already remarked that No. 3, made of lime enclosed in a bottle, gave a better result than No. 2, of which the lime had been exposed to the air. We see therefore that this artificial hydraulic lime, loses part of its hydraulic properties, promptly, by exposure to the air, as well as the natural hydraulic limes of *Alsace.*

No. 11 is an experiment made with the same lime as No. 5; but instead of slaking to powder with one-fifth of its volume of water, it was left to slake in the air for one month. At the end of this time it was reduced to powder, and I made it into paste by adding a little water, so that the proportions could be adjusted as in the other trials. The table shows that the hardening required 30 days, and that the mortar broke under a weight of 88 lbs., while mortar No. 5, composed of the same piece of lime, but made immediately, hardened in fifteen days, and sustained a weight of 253 lbs. before breaking. The comparison of No. 5 and No. 10 shows that lime which has been slaked to powder, has lost rather less of its quality at the end of a month, than that left to slake in the air during the same period. I will add, that when they sent me, in 1823, the lime of which the first three experiments were made, they also sent a little lime which had fallen spontaneously to powder. I left it in this state for two months; and I presume it had then been about three months exposed to the air: I made a mortar of this lime, taking one part of lime in powder to two parts of sand: the mortar which resulted was not able, after a years' immersion in water, to support the weight of the scale pan, which was 22 lbs.

No. 12, containing trass, was made with the same lime as No. 5, slaked to dry powder for two months. We see that No. 5, which was made of one part of this lime measured in paste, and two parts of sand, required thirty days to harden, and broke under the light weight of 88 lbs., while No. 12 hardened in the space of six days and supported 297 pounds before breaking. We see, therefore, that trass has the same influence on artificial hydraulic limes, as on natural hydraulic limes, and that it restores to them properties which they had lost by too long exposure to the air. I will here state that I was, last year, at the country seat of a Paris banker, who, having a spring of water, had caused a pond to be made in his garden. The spring being small, they had been obliged to cover the bottom of the pond with concrete, and to form the sides with a wall, all made of the artificial hydraulic lime of Mr. Saint-Leger. The basin had been finished about a year, but a great deal of the water filtered through it: I examined the mortar and found it had a very feeble consistence: I questioned the architect as to the manner he had treated the lime, and he told me that he had caused a considerable quantity to be brought at once, and deposited in a spot sheltered from the rain; that sometimes he used it immediately, as it arrived, and sometimes, after it had fallen to powder. This explanation showed me that the evil proceeded from having used the lime that had been too long from the kiln, and which had already lost a great part of its hydraulic property.

Mr. Vicat appears not to have observed the bad results obtained with hydraulic limes which have been exposed some time in the air, whether slaked to powder with water, or slaked spontaneously: he even appears to incline to the process of air-slaking, for, after having given the three modes of slaking, he says, page 20: "such are the modes of slaking: the first is generally used; the second has hardly been employed except by way of experiment at certain works; the third is proscribed, and represented in all treatises on construction, as depriving the lime of all energy, to such a degree that all lime fallen to powder by air-slaking is considered as lost. We do not now allude to the processes of Rondelet, Fleuret, and others, because they do not differ enough from those described to be separated from them. We shall see, further on, relative to spontaneous slaking, how necessary it is to be mistrustful of condemnatory assertions, springing out of false observations, and accredited by authors who know how to doubt of nothing, and who repeat, without examination, the errors of others."

At page 25, Mr. Vicat says, again, "the three modes of slaking arranged in the order of superiority, relative to the resistance, and the hardness they communicate to the hydrates of common fat lime, are: 1st. Ordinary slaking; 2nd. spontaneous slaking; 3d. slaking by immersion. The mean relative resistances, in the three cases, are the numbers 2490, 1707, 450, and the hardness as $0.^d1696$, $0.^d0850$, $0.^d0713$.

"The order changes for hydraulic lime, and becomes: 1st, ordinary slaking; 2d, slaking by immersion; 3d, spontaneous slakings. The mean relative resistances are as the numbers 864, 392, 245, and the hardness as $0.^d0488$, $0.^d0446$ $0.^d0358$."

The above experiments of Mr. Vicat were made with hydrate of lime, that it to say, with limes reduced to paste with water. We see that ordinary slaking gave better results than spontaneous slaking; with both fat lime and hydraulic lime. In his table No. XVIII., which contains eight mortars made with diverse hydraulic limes, and sand; the first five gave greater resistances when the lime was slaked in the ordinary way than when slaked spontaneously. The mortars made of fat lime and sand, as exhibited in tables Nos. XIX., XX.. and XXI., gave, it is true, better results when these limes were slaked spontaneously: but with hydraulic limes he, himself, obtained results very different, since the mortar No. 5 of table No. XVIII. gave a resistance represented by 4102 when the lime had been slaked by the ordinary process, while it was only 3082, when the lime had slaked spontaneously. The experiments of Mr. Vicat are, therefore, far from causing us to reject the old saying of masons as to the bad results obtained from air-slaked lime; and we do not perceive how he could regard this saying as a condemnatory assertion growing out of false observations. This old saying appears to me to be well founded as to the greater number of hydraulic limes. Mr. Vicat, in giving his experiments, had not said for how long a time he left the limes which he slaked by the second and third processes, in the air. If he had made comparative experiments, he would have had very variable results, according as the hydraulic limes used had been, for a greater or less time, exposed to the influence of the air.

All that precedes proves that hydraulic limes, whether natural or artificial, lose much of their hydraulic property if not used soon after they are calcined. As an exception, a single piece of lime, of which the experiments in table No. VI. were made, gave to the mortar, after fifteen days slaking, a better result than to the mortar made immediately; but we see that the resistances of the mortars made at periods more remote from the slaking, diminished rapidly: we may therefore say, in relation to all the hydraulic limes that I have treated, that it is necessary to make the mortars soon after they come from the kiln; for I assured myself that the same deterioration took place with the limes of Bouxviller, Oberbronn, Verdt, &c., although I did not make as detailed experiments with them as with the Obernai lime. All, in fine, induces me to believe that the greater part of hydraulic limes are thus affected. It is consequently very important, before using them, to see if they do not soon lose, by exposure to the air, a great part of their hydraulic quality.*

The artificial hydraulic lime, made by Mr. Saint-Leger at Meudon, to supply the wants of the Capital, is made of chalk which is mixed with $\frac{3}{10}$ of clay brought from Vanvres, near Paris. This clay contains the following substances: silex, 0.630; alumine, 0.282; oxide of iron, 0.068. A cubic metre of this lime (35.34 cubic feet) costs at Paris about $13,50. If it be examined minutely, there will be seen small portions of clay that have not been well mixed. This is an inevitable result, because we cannot, by a mechanical operation, obtain a mixture as intimate as that existing in natural hydraulic limes. The results which I obtained with this lime are a little superior to those that I got from the Holsheim clay, of which the resistances varied from 187 to 215, while with the hydraulic lime of Paris, I obtained from 187 to 253. This might be owing to their having sent me choice pieces of lime. I made, besides, too few experiments with the Holsheim clay to be able to affirm that it is really inferior to that of the environs of Paris for making artificial hydraulic lime.

Captain Petitot of the Engineers sent me from *Vitry-le-Francais* a little hydraulic lime of the environs of that place of which he had made trial, obtaining, as he informed me, good results. This lime comes from chalk; it is very white; water being sprinkled on it, as it comes from the kiln, about five minutes elapses before slaking begins. One part of quick lime gave 1.30 of paste. I do not know the degree of resistance that mortars made of this lime would give; but I made the following experiment with it: I took a portion which was sent to me in a well stopped vessel, as soon as it was withdrawn from the kiln; I made a paste of this with water; I left it in the air for one hour, and then plunged it in water: it took a good consistence in a very short time, and at the end of four days it was very hard. This lime, therefore, hardens more promptly than any of the hydraulic limes of Alsace and Metz, and than any of the artificial hydraulic limes that I have examined. The only exception is the Obernai lime, shown in table No. VI. The Boulogne pebble lime hardened sooner; but it is remarkable that the mortars of this lime which hardened soonest, presented a weak resistance;

---

* We see, by the above, how many precautions should be taken with hydraulic lime. Parker's cement which has been burned and pulverized, is brought from England: this lime may be good in England, and have lost a great part of its properties on arriving in France. It is necessary, therefore, to try, before using it.—*Author.*

while those which were slower to indurate, gave a greater. The Vitry lime appeared to me to harden in the manner of good hydraulic lime, and to promise to furnish very good mortars. This lime costs in the neighborhood, only $5.50 per cubic metre (35.34 cub. feet,) while we see, above, that the Meudon lime costs about $13.50. It would therefore, be a good speculation to bring the hydraulic lime necessary for the Capital, from Vitry. The river Maine, which is navigable as far as Vitry, would give great facility to the transportation. As wood is scarce in the neighborhood of Vitry, as coal is not easy to be obtained, and as it is advantageous to use hydraulic limes soon after calcination, it would perhaps be best to bring the chalk, of which the lime is made, to Paris; and to burn it with coal, as it might be wanted—profiting of favourable seasons for collecting a stock of the chalk.

The experiments which I made with the Boulogne pebbles, induced me to think that the soda it contained, might have some agency. I made, therefore, various experiments, by reburning fat lime with a little clay, and adding some water containing soda or potash. I proceed to give the results.

Table No. XI.

No. of the mortar.	Composition of the mortars.		LIME			
			Burned as commonly.		Burned more highly	
			H	W	H	W
			days	lbs	days	lbs
1	Fat lime, reburnt with 2-10 of pipe clay, and measured in paste . . . Sand	$\left.{1\atop2}\right\}3$	8	132	15	187
2	Same lime, reburnt with 3-10 of pipe clay, 1-10 of solution of soda at 5°, and measured in paste . . . Sand	$\left.{1\atop2}\right\}3$	8	176	20	209
3	Same lime reburnt with 2-10 of pipe clay, and 1-5 of solution of soda at 5°, and measured in paste . . . Sand	$\left.{1\atop2}\right\}3$	8	220	15	242
4	Same lime, reburnt with 2-10 of pipe clay, and 1-4 of solution of soda at 5°, and measured in paste . . . Sand .	$\left.{1\atop2}\right\}3$	8	176	18	231
5	Same lime, reburnt with 2-10 of pipe clay, and 1-3 of solution of soda at 5°, and measured in paste . . Sand . . .	$\left.{1\atop2}\right\}3$	9	154	18	220
6	Same lime reburnt with 2-10 of pipe clay, and 1-2 of solution of soda at 5°, and measured in paste . . . Sand . . .	$\left.{1\atop2}\right\}3$	10	121	18	198

Observations on the Experiments of Table No. XI.

To make the above experiments I took fat lime which I reduced to paste, with water: I then mixed it well, with $\frac{1}{10}$ of the Cologne pipe clay, of which the analysis has been given: this is lime No. 1. For No. 2, I added $\frac{1}{10}$ of the solution of soda of the strength of 5° of the *pèse acid.* The volume of solution of soda was taken in relation to that of the lime in paste and with it I diluted the pipe clay before mixing it with the lime. In the succeeding numbers, I successively tempered the pipe clay with $\frac{1}{2}$, $\frac{1}{3}$, $\frac{1}{4}$ and $\frac{1}{5}$ of the solution of soda of the same strength. Each of these experiments was made in duplicate; one half of each mixture was placed in such a situation in the lime kiln, that it would receive only the mean degree of heat: the other half was exposed to a higher temperature. I satisfied myself of the degree of heat sustained, by placing unburnt bricks by the side of the crucible containing the mixtures. From the colour of these bricks I knew that the second set had been more highly calcined than the first. Immediately after the calcination, I made mortars with one part of lime in paste and two of sand. The mortars are given in the table in two series according to the two degrees of calcination. It will be noticed, at once, that the more highly calcined lime, gave the greater resistance, but the slower rate of hardening. No 1, containing pipe clay only, gave a resistance of but 132 lbs. for the lime the least burned, and 187 lbs. for that most burned, No. 2, which contained $\frac{1}{10}$ of solution of soda, gave a slight augmentation of resistance, and No. 3, which contained one-fifth of solution of soda, gave a greater resistance for both degrees of calcination. Beyond the proportion of one-fifth solution of soda, the weight supported went on decreasing; but up to the proportion of one-fifth the resistance was increased, by the addition of a little soda, about in ratio of 6 to 7. These experiments were made in the month of January.

Having made the above experiments with clay and soda, I made similar ones with potash: the results obtained are in the following table.

Table No. XII.

No. of the mortar.	Composition of the mortar.	No. of days required to harden. in water.	Weight supported before breaking.
		days	lb.
1	Fat lime, reburnt with 2-10 of pipe clay and 1-10 of solution of Potash at 5°, measured in paste . . . 1 ⎱ 3 Common sand . . . 2 ⎰	6	242
2	Same lime, reburnt with 2-10 of pipe clay and 1-5 of solution of Potash at 5°, measured in paste . . . 1 ⎱ 3 Sand . . . 2 ⎰	8	297
3	Same lime reburnt with 2-10 of pipe clay and 1-4 of solution of Potash at 5°, measured in paste . . . 1 ⎱ 3 Sand . . . 2 ⎰	12	242*
4	Same lime reburnt with 2-10 of pipe clay and 1-3 of solution of Potash at 5°, measured in paste . . . 1 ⎱ 3 Sand . . . 2 ⎰	15	407
5	Same lime, reburnt with 2-10 of pipe clay and 1-2 of solution of Potash at 5°, measured in paste . . . 1 ⎱ 3 Sand . . . 2 ⎰	18	275

Observations on the experiments of Table No. XII.

The experiments in the above table were made in the same way, and at the same time, as the experiments of table No. XI. These limes were burned by the side of those of table No. XI, which gave the best results. No. 1 of table No. XI, containing pipe clay alone, serving equally as a term of comparison for the above table. We see, in table No. XI, that the greatest resistance obtained by the mixture of lime and pipe clay only, was 187 lbs. The experiments of tables Nos. XI and XII differ only in substituting in the latter, potash for soda. We see that the results obtained with potash are superior to those obtained with soda., No. 3 of the above table being cracked, I am uncertain whether the greatest resistance belonged to No. 3 or No. 4. No. 5 shows that the proportion of one-half potash, diminished the resistance. I made a sixth experiment by putting one-half of potash at 10°: the mortar resulting broke under a load of 242 lbs. It is remarkable that the mortars which gave the greatest resistance were those which hardened the most slowly. Several of the preceding tables gave the same result; it was quite striking with the Boulogne pebbles of table No. VIII. It will there be seen that No. 1 which hardened in twelve hours, supported a weight of only 108 lbs., while No. 12. which supported 286 lbs., required 12 days to harden. An inspection of the preceding tables will show that, in general, the mortars which gave good results, took from 8 to 15 days to indurate, whether made of natural or artificial hydraulic lime. The experiments of table No. XII were made in the month of January. I also made essays with the soda and potash of commerce, which, as is known, are composed of sub-carbonates, sulphates and muriates of these substances: the results obtained were not so good.

I made several experiments with lime and solutions of potash and soda without other admixture. I operated in this way: I took several pieces of fat lime as they came from the kiln, and slaked them to dry powders thus,—on the first piece I sprinkled the fourth of its volume of solution of soda standing at 5° of the *pèse-acid*; on the second, the same quantity of solution of the sub-carbonate of soda of commerce, of the same strength; on the third, the same quantity of an equally strong solution of potash: on the fourth a like quantity of solution of the same strength of the sub-carbonate of potash of commerce; and on the fifth an equal quantity of solution of muriate of soda, also standing at 5°. I left these several powders in the air for one month; I then added the quantity of water requisite to produce a paste, and had them reburnt in a lime kiln. As they were drawn from the kiln I slaked them with a little water, and left them in the air, for some days: I afterwards made mortars of them, by mixing them with sand, and having allowed them to harden in the air for twelve hours, I placed them in water: the two first mortars hardened in two days; the third, the fourth and the fifth hardened in a day and a half. At the end of a year, I wished to break these mortars: and I was much surprised to find that, notwithstanding they had hardened so promptly, they had become entirely soft. As the boxes containing these mortars were covered with others, I had not been able to observe them at the period to their beginning to lose hardness.

It follows from experiments made up to this time, that it is clay,—that is to say, a mixture of alumine and silex, united with the lime, that gives good hydraulic lime by calcination. (An exception exists in the lime of Senonches, which is said to be very hydraulic, and which appears to owe this property to silex alone.) We do not as yet know the proportions in which silex and alumine ought to exist, to give the best results. Hydraulic limes are improved by adding to the mixture of clay and lime, a little soda: the result is still better if potash be used instead of soda. We have seen that the Boulogne pebbles gave a lime which hardened very quickly, but which would not bear mixture with any other substance, in making

---

* This mortar was cracked on being cut, which diminished its strength. Au.

mortar—this being the only lime which gave this result. I before observed that it appeared to me these pebbles contained a little soda: but we have just seen that limes which I caused to be reburned with a little soda or potash gave good mortars when mixed with a considerable quantity of sand: it seems, therefore, as I have remarked, that these pebbles contain some substance which escaped analysis, or else that some of the substances known to be present are modified by the sea-water.

In comparing artificial hydraulic limes, I have been led to remark that better results were obtained when, in lieu of making the mixture of clay, with lime just from the kiln, I first slaked the lime with one fifth of its bulk of water, and left it, in this state, in the air for a month or two. I do not attribute the better effect solely to a more minute division of the lime: but I think that the slaked lime exposed to the air, absorbing much oxygen, as I have shown in page 31, is capable, in this state of oxidation, of combining better with the clay which is mixed with it. I proposed making experiments to ascertain what might be the advantages of this process, and also during what time it would be proper to have exposed to the air, lime that had been slaked to powder, or lime designed to be left to spontaneous slaking; but I was obliged to quit Strasburg, before having it in my power to make these experiments.

CHAPTER V.

On Hydraulic Mortars made of fat lime and trass, or fat lime and puzzalona.

Trass is a substance obtained from the village of Brohl, near Andernach, on the Rhine; this village is situated at the foot of an extinct volcano. Trass is of a grayish colour, much resembling gray clay which has been calcined. I have seen several pieces of trass which were covered with lava. This last substance differs much from trass: the separation is distinct: the lava which covers the trass is of a blackish colour, and its surface is full of asperities and cavities, showing that it has sustained a very high heat, and very rapid cooling: trass seems to have been exposed to a much lower heat.

Puzzalona is likewise a burned clay—deriving its name from the village of Puzzoles, at the foot of Vesuvius; it is found at or near the surface. According to Mr. Sganzin, there are a great many varieties of puzzalona: it is found white, black, yellow, gray, brown, red, and violet.

It is not known whether trass and puzzalona result from banks of clay which have been highly heated by incumbent lava, or whether they have been thrown out of volcanos during irruptions; it is possible that both suppositions may be true; an examination on the spot can alone remove uncertainty in this respect.

Puzzalona is, according to Mr. Sganzin, also obtained near Rome: this is of a red-brown, and contains brilliant particles having a metallic lustre.

The Dutch have a great trade in Trass. They get out this substance in masses, and reduce it to a very fine powder, by means of wind mills. Much has been sent to France, to the North, and to England; but it seems that the commerce has diminished a little. Some authors call this substance the Terras of Holland.

Arches, in several of the gothic churches, in Belgium were built of pieces of the Andernach Trass: as was the case in several edifices on the Rhine. The great lock of Slikens in Belgium, was rebuilt with pieces of the arch of a demolished church; and by pulverizing the same material, a very good trass was obtained.

On the shores of the Mediterranean, much puzzalona, furnished from the environs of Rome and Naples, is used. The good effects of this substance were known to the Romans, for Vitruvius, Book II., Chapter VI., has the following passage. "There is a kind of powder to which nature has given an admirable quality: it is found near Baie, and in the grounds around Mount Vesuvius. This powder mixed with lime and stones, not only renders common masonry very firm, but it even unites and hardens in a remarkable manner, masonry at the bottom of the sea."

I had occasion to appreciate the good effects of trass in the great works of Vesel. It was brought in powder, and as it was transported in batteaux descending the Rhine, it was not dear. Before becoming acquainted with the excellent qualities of the Obernai hydraulic lime, I caused some of it to be brought to Strasburg, and the first hydraulic works that I constructed at Strasburg were made of mortar composed of fat lime, sand, and trass. But the trass cost much more at Strasburg than at Vesel, on account of the export duties that the Prussians levied on it, and because of the difficulty of ascending the Rhine. A cubic metre (35.34 cub. feet) cost 120 francs (about $23.00) at Strasburg, which raised the cost of the hydraulic mortar enormously. I had begun some researches with a view to make artificial trass, when I became aware of the hydraulic properties of the Obernai lime. This lime was afterwards used without trass in the foundations of revetments, in the construction of bridges, and in all masonry exposed to the air; but in the foundation of locks and dams and in the construction of caps for under-ground casemates, a little trass was always mixed in the mortar, with the lime and sand. I continued my experiments on the forming of artificial trass, less for our particular advantage at Strasburg, therefore, than for those places which do not afford good natural hydraulic limes. I succeeded, in the end, as will be seen in the following Chapter, in making artificial trass equal in quality to natural trass or puzzalona. The cost of a cubic metre (35.34 cub. feet) was about 30 francs (about $6.00.) I caused the puzzalona to be brought from Naples, it was red, and much resembled brick or tile dust.

An analysis of trass and puzzalona, made many years ago, may be found in the *Précis du cours de construction* of Mr. Sganzin of the Polytechnic school. Mr. Berthier asked me for samples of the trass and puzzalona which I used at Strasburg, and made an analysis of them. Both analyses are given below.

	Old analysis.		Mr. Berthier's analysis.	
	Trass.	Puzzalona	Trass.	Puzzalona
Silex -	0.570	0.350	0.570	0.445
Alumine -	0.230	0.400	0.160	0.150
Lime -	0.065	0.050	0.026	0.088
Magnesia -			0.010	0.047
Oxide of iron*	0.085	0.200	0.050	0.120
Potash -			0.070	0.014
Soda - -			0.010	0.040
Water -			0.096	0.092
	0.950	1.000	0.992	0.996

* In Mr. Berthier's analysis, there was in the Puzzalona, oxide of iron and titanium 0.120.—Author.

We see that the new analysis of trass and puzzalona by Mr. Berthier differs in several points from the preceding analysis. According to that of Mr. Berthier, trass and puzzalona contain potash and soda which were not before noticed in those substances. According to the old analysis, puzzalona contains much more alumine than trass, but according to Mr. Berthier, about the same. The proportion of alumine to silex is greater, for both substances, in the old, than in the new analysis. I will add that Mr. Berthier discovered that the trass and puzzalona which I sent him attracted the magnetic needle.

We ought not to be surprised that these analyses differ sensibly, because it has been known for a long time that different puzzalonas give very different results, and it is the same with trass. We can conceive that these substances may vary considerably, because the several strata of clay in the same bank often vary sensibly. I proceed to give different experiments made with fat lime, puzzalona, and trass.

Table No. XIII.

No. of the mortars	Composition of the mortars.		No. of days which they took to harden in wat'r	Weight which they supported before breaking.
			days.	pounds.
1	Fat lime of Strasburg slaked to powder and measured in powder Sand Trass	1 1 } 3 1	5	411
2	Lime the same, do. Trass	1 } 3 2	4	330
3	Lime the same, do. Sand Puzzalona	1 1 } 3 1	4	499
4	Lime the same Puzzalona	1 } 3 2	3	444
5	Fat lime from Vasselone, do. Sand Trass	1 1 } 3 1	5	449
6	Lime the same, do Trass	1 } 3 2	4	385
7	Fat lime from Brunstat, do. Sand Trass	1 1 } 3 1	5	510
8	Lime the same, do. Trass	1 } 3 2	4	535
9	Lime from white marble, do. Sand Trass	1 1 } 3 1	5	308
10	Lime the same, do. Trass	1 } 3 2	4	407
11	Same lime, do. Sand Puzzalona	1 1 } 3 1	4	396
12	Lime the same, do. Puzzalona	1 } 3 2	3	367
13	Strasburg fat lime measured in paste Puzzalona	1 } 3 2	4	495
14	Lime the same Puzzalona	1 } 3½ 2½	5	550
15	Same lime slaked to powder and measured in powder Trass	1 } 3 2	3 to 16	231 to 580

Observations on the experiments of Table No. XIII.

The lime of the first twelve numbers was measured in powder and mixed with the substances indicated in the table. It will be seen that I used various fat limes of the environs of Strasburg. I satisfied myself that these limes had no hydraulic property. The first four numbers were designed to ascertain whether puzzalona is preferable to trass. The puzzalona gave me rather the best results—the lime being the same in all. The experiments 9, 10, 11, and 12 confirm the first four. We see that I had a greater resistance by mixing sand with the lime and puzzalona, or lime and trass, than when there was no sand. The limes of Nos. 13 and 14 were measured in paste, and we see that I obtained a better result by augmenting the proportion of puzzalona.

No. 15 contains the results of many trials made with 1 part of fat lime measured in powder and 2 parts of trass. The time of hardening varied from 3 to 16 days, and the resistance from 231 to 580 lbs. But I had few mortars giving a result so feeble as 231 lbs., or so strong as 580 lbs. We might say that the mean resistance with mortars composed of fat lime, sand and trass, was between 352 and 374 pounds. The mortar which gave 580 pounds contained lime and trass only. If, with the same substances, I had composed a mortar of lime, sand, and trass, I should have had, probably, a still better result. I found fewer variations with puzzalona than with trass, probably because, having but a small quantity of the former, my experiments were few. We shall, however, see in table No. XX., that a mortar like No. 13 of the above table, broke under a weight of 286 lbs. I am uncertain whether this weak result was due to particular circumstances or to the quality of the puzzalona. It appears to me, in general, that there was no great difference between the trass and the puzzalona, that I used.

In comparing the results of table XIII., with those of the preceding tables in which mortars were made of natural or artificial hydraulic lime and sand only, we see that these last hardened much more slowly, and gave much less resistance, than mortars made of fat lime, sand, and trass or puzzalona. Mr. Gauthey was therefore in error, as I noticed page 6, when he stated that mortars made of fat lime and puzzalona did not take consistence in water and remained pulverent.

In the observations made by Mr. Vicat on the pamphlet which I published in 1824, and of which I have already spoken, this Engineer remarks as follows: "The greatest resistance that Mr. Treussart found for trass mortars immersed for one year, is $17 \frac{6}{10}$ lbs. for four-tenths of an inch square, and I have made mortars with lime and sand, which, after a year's exposure on a roof to all the inclemencies of the seasons gave a resistance of 31 lbs. and even of 40 lbs." The results that Mr. Vicat and I obtained are very different. These differences can only be attributed to our having used means of measuring the resistance, or rather the tenacity, of mortars, which do not admit of comparison. I will observe, however, that the greatest resistance I found was 579 lbs., for mortar made of artificial trass, and that the section being four square inches, there results 23.1 lbs. for four-tenths of an inch square instead of $17 \frac{6}{10}$ lbs., as Mr. Vicat supposes. He does not say what were the dimensions of the mortars he submitted to proof in order to compare his results with mine; and as a year had not elapsed from the publication of my pamphlet to the appearance of his observations, I conclude that he did not use the same method in breaking the mortars of which he speaks and which he says had been made a year, that I did. Of twenty-five tables that Mr. Vicat's memoir contains, the weights supported by mortars, are given only in three instances—to be found in table No. III. All the other results of the tables are resistances obtained by calculation from the penetration of a rod subjected to an impulsive force, and deduced from the few experiments of table No. III. This table indicates that the mortars had 1 inch 6-10 of base, by 1 inch in height, and that the weights were applied at the extremity of a lever of only $1.\frac{2}{10}$ long. But the mortars which I submitted to fracture, were two inches square, they rested on two points of support, distant four inches from each other; the weights were applied to the middle of the mortar: thus the dimensions of the mortars and the arms of the levers to which the weights were applied, were entirely different, in the two methods. We, cannot therefore, compare the weights supported by four-tenth of an inch square, when the methods were so different. I will add to what I said page 18, that if Nos. 26 and 33 of my table No. III. be submitted to the proof of the rod of Mr. Vicat, it is possible that the rod would penetrate less into No. 33, which contains three parts of sand, than into No. 26 which contains none. Whence we might assign to No. 33 a higher resistance than to No. 26, whereas its actual resistance is three times less. If sand (alone) be compressed in a metallic tube, and then submitted to the rod of Mr. Vicat, which is terminated by a flat portion, it will penetrate but little into the sand; and the false consequence would appear that the sand possessed tenacity. It is to be noticed that when the lime takes consistence, it fulfils, as regards the resistance of the sand to the shock of the rod, the function of an enclosing vessel. The means used by Mr. Vicat to determine the tenacity of mortars, appears therefore to be bad, and his results not of a nature to be brought into comparison with mine.

The experiments stated in the above table, and especially those comprised under No. 15, suggested anew to me an idea that I had already entertained regarding hydraulic limes: namely, that the differences in the results might not be attributable solely to diversity in the trass, but might result from using the lime sometimes immediately from the kiln, and sometimes after having been left for a period exposed to the air after having been slaked to powder. I consequently made experiments to know the influence exercised by the air on fat lime—these are stated in the following table.

Table No. XIV.

No. of series	Composition of the mortars.	Made immediately.	After 5 days.	After 10 days	After 20 days	After 1 month.	After 2 months.	After 3 months.	After 4 months.	After 5 months.	After 6 months.	After 7 months.
		lbs	lbs	lbs	lbs	ls	lbs	lbs	lbs	lbs	lbs	lbs
1	Fat lime slaked to powder and measured in powder 1, Sand 1, Trass 1 }3	242 days (20)	261 d (18)	253 d (16)	275 d (12)	319 d (5)	96 3d (4)	363 d (5)	374 d (6)	86 d (8)	407 d (10)	396 d (12)
2	Lime the same 1, Trass 2 }3	374 (16)	341 (11)	341 (8)	407 (6)	440 (4)	440 (3)	462 (3)	418 (4)	429 (6)	506 (8)	462 (10)
3	Fat lime air-slaked and measured in powder 1, Sand 1, Trass 1 }3					253 (9)	308 (6)	286 (6)	308 (7)	319 (9)	352 (12)	330 (12)
4	Lime the same 1, Tass 2 }3					319 (7)	363 (4)	385 (4)	352 (5)	341 (5	385 (7)	352 (8)

Observations on the Experiments of Table No. XIV.

For making the above experiments I took fat lime as it came from the kiln, and slaked a part to dry powder with a quarter of its volume of water. I then made two mortars, taking for the first, one part of this lime in powder, one of sand, and one part of trass, and for the second mortar the same quantity of lime and two parts of trass. These two mortars are in the first column, and will serve as terms of comparison for the rest. I then put in a vessel the remainder of the lime slaked to powder, and made mortars of it, of the series No. 1 and 2, at the periods indicated in the table. When I slaked this lime to powder I left another portion to slake in the air, and at the end of a month I commenced the series of experiments therewith, marked Nos. 3 and 4. I took care to use the same trass in all the mortars. I must remark that the figures in brackets express the number of days the mortars required to harden, and the figures over those in brackets, express the weights supported before breaking.

The series comprised under No. 1 was made of one part of lime in powder, to one part sand and one part trass. We see that the hardening of the mortars which were made soon after the slaking, was slow; at the end of a month it was much more prompt, and after three months, it again became slower. The numbers representing resistances present prominent anomalies; but we must look at the whole rather than at the particulars. The *whole* of this series shows that mortars made of lime slaked to powder, and exposed to the air for a month and more, gave better results than those made immediately, or soon after the slaking of the lime.

These experiments were commenced in the middle of April, 1823; the numbers, therefore, which express the most prompt hardening, correspond to the hottest months, and according to the observation of Mr. Vicat, mortars harden in the water more promptly in summer than in winter. The two last columns correspond to the months of October and November, and although the hardening had then, again, become slower, the resistance had not lessened. The experiments of table No. XIII. were made with lime which had remained slaked in powder about one month. The first twelve numbers were made in September and October and No. 13 and 14, in the month of January: I, however, got a prompt hardening. It appears that by exposing fat lime which has been slaked to powder, to the air for some time, the induration is favoured: but there is no doubt that heat contributes much thereto.

The series of experiments comprised under No. 2, were made of one part of lime in powder to two parts of trass. We see, here also, that the resistances that I obtained a short time after the slaking are inferior to those got one month after the slaking. The experiments of table No. XIII. often gave me with sand and trass, better results than with trass alone, while it is the contrary in the above table. I attribute this anomaly to the difference in the trass used.

The series comprised under No. 3 and 4, were made in the same manner as the two first series, with this difference that air-slaked lime was used. It was not before the expiration of a month that I had enough of this lime to commence the experiments. If we compare the third series with the first, and the fourth with the second, we shall see that the results are in general inferior with the air-slaked lime. I will add that all the mortars made of lime slaked to powder were very homogeneous, while those of air-slaked lime exhibited, in the interior, a multitude of white points which appeared to me to be particles of lime that had absorbed carbonic acid; they were very apparent when the mortars were broken. I think, therefore, that it is better to slake fat lime to a powder, than to air-slake it.

I ought to observe that before making the experiments of table No. XIV, I had made several of the same kind but less complete; and that I had often got contradictory results, that is to say, sometimes, I obtained a greater resistance when I had made mortar of lime just as it came from the kiln, than when I slaked it to powder and left it for some time in the air. Sometimes, also, I got better results with air-slaked lime than with that slaked to powder; the differences were not great but they existed. On examining my notes, I saw that in making my first experiments, I changed the trass several times; this induced me to keep back these previous results, and the anomalies that I found therein determined me to make the experiments of the above table, in all of which the same trass was used.

These experiments should, no doubt, be repeated with several kinds of lime, to ascertain whether it will always be better to use fat lime as soon as it is burned, or some time after having slaked it to dry powder. It is necessary to repeat the experiments both in summer and in winter. As to air-slaked lime, it appears to me that this process ought not to be adopted, because of the great quantity of white particles which I found in all the mortars of this kind that I made.

This manner of slaking fat lime is that which Mr. Vicat prefers: he, in *Annales de chimie*, Vol. XIX. page 22, publishing as follows: "The assertion of Mr. John relative to lime exposed to the air is in contradiction to recent facts, so presented, and so multiplied, that I am constrained to combat it. It was I who first announced that fat lime slaked spontaneously, and abandoned for one year to the action of the air, under cover and protected from winds, gives better results, than when employed immediately, according to the common method. This conclusion is founded on a hundred and fifty experiments, varied in several ways: it results, for example, that the force of ordinary mortar being, in the most favourable case of a series of experiments represented by 1506, that of mortar made of air-slaked lime gave, under the same circumstances 2293." Mr. Vicat acknowledges that the ideas, commonly received, on this point of the doctrine of mortars, are all in favour of Mr. John, and he says, because of this sentiment, almost general, he presumes Mr. John did not examine the matter. I will remark, touching this point, that Lieut. Col. Bergere of the Engineers, notices, in the last *devis instructive*, and in the account he has given of the work of Mr. Raucour, that several Engineers have thought, in times long gone by, that air-slaking gave better results than the other two processes, and that this mode has been in use, from time immemorial, in Spain, and in a part of Italy. Mr. Bergere says that he used it at Flushing; and that this method is recommended in a letter written in 1764 by Mr. Sienne, an Engineer officer, resident at Graveline. I do not however counsel the process of air-slaking in making hydraulic mortar with fat lime and trass, or other analogous substance; because the mortars made in this way contain a great many white specks which appear to be lime passed to the state of carbonate. We may conceive, in fact, that when lime is left to slake spontaneously, every successive small portion of lime remains for some time exposed to the contact of the air, as the lime falls off in successive layers: there ought, therefore, to be a considerable absorption of carbonic acid: whereas lime slaked to powder with water and formed into heaps, has the surface only exposed to the air.

Besides the experiments of the above table, I have made others of the same kind, by slaking fat lime into thick paste, and into thin paste—comparing these results with each other, and with those I got from the same lime slaked to powder.

These experiments are in the following table.

Table No. XV.

No. of series	Composition of the mortars.	Made immediately.	After 5 days.	After 15 days.	After 1 month.	After 2 months.	After 3 months.	After 4 months	After 5 months.	After 6 months.	After 7 months.	After 8 months.	After 9 months.	After 10 months.	After 11 months.	After 12 months.
1	Fat lime slaked to thick paste 1 } Sand 1¼ } Trass 3¼	lbs 319 (12)	lbs 341 (12)	lbs 352 (14)	lbs 374 (16)	lbs 341 (18)	lbs 363 (20)	lbs 341 (18)	lbs 385 (16)	lbs 352 (10)	lbs 341 (5)	lbs 319 (5)	lbs 341 (6)	lbs 330 (8)	lbs 341 (10)	lbs 363 (13)
2	Fat lime slaked to thin paste 1 } Sand 1¼ } Trass 3¼									308 (10)	297 (5)	308 (6)	275 (6)	286 (8)	253 (10)	275 (13)
3	Fat lime slaked to powder and measured in paste 1 } Sand 1¼ } Trass 3¼									396 (8)	352 (5)	341 (5)	352 (6)	363 (8)	341 (10)	352 (13)

Observations on the experiments of Table No. XV.

To make the experiments of the above table, I took fat lime as it came from the kiln, and divided it into three portions: one of these portions we slaked to a thick paste and left in a vessel; another portion was slaked to a thin paste, and, as it thickened, I added a little water so as to keep it in the consistence of sirup; the third portion was slaked to a dry powder with one-fourth of its bulk of water, and put, like the others, in an open vessel. I, immediately, made the mortar in the first column, which may serve as a term of comparison. The others were made, at the periods expressed in the table, of lime slaked in the several modes mentioned. In proportioning the parts, I added, when I made the mortar, a little water to the lime which had been slaked to a thick paste and also to that which had been slaked to powder, so as to bring all to the condition of that slaked to thin paste. These experiments were begun in the month of November, 1823, that is to say seven months after the experiments of table No. XIV. In table No. XV, I have followed the same mode of expressing the time required to harden, as in table No. XIV. The mortars of three series were made of the same quantities of lime, sand and trass; and I took care, as in the preceding table, to use the same trass, and the same sand, for all.

In the first series of the table, the mortar made immediately gave a result rather weaker than those made afterwards: the hardening was more prompt in summer than in winter.

I left the lime of the second series for six months in a state of clear paste before using it. We see that the results were not so good as those obtained from the thick paste. There are, certainly, several anomalies in the results, but, as before remarked, we must look at the *whole*.

The third series was likewise commenced at the end of six months. In table No. XIV, the mortars of the first series, made of lime slaked to powder, were formed at appropriate periods, which were not extended beyond seven months. The resistances obtained in table No. XIV are not the same as those obtained in Table No. XV, because the proportions were different: but if we compare the experiments of the first series of table No. XIV with those of the first and third series of table No. XV, we shall see that instead of making hydraulic mortar of fat lime, sand and trass, immediately after slaking the lime, it will be more advantageous, after slaking the lime, with a little water, as it comes from the kiln, to leave it exposed to the air for some time. We see, here again, that the hardening was more slow in winter than in summer. If we compare the results obtained in the preceding tables, we shall see that there is a great difference in the effects of mortars made of natural or artificial hydraulic lime and sand, and of these made of fat lime, sand and trass. When the first are made of lime which has for some time slaked to powder, or which has been air-slaked, they generally lose much of their force. There is not the same disadvantage with fat lime: whether the mortars are made as soon as the lime comes from the kiln, or after it has been slaked with a little water and left exposed for some time in the air, or after the lime has been air-slaked, good results are always obtained: but we have seen that the best are got by slaking the lime with a little water as soon as it is burned and leaving it exposed for some time to the air in a covered place. Experiments, to be given by and by, will show that I obtained good results, also, by making hydraulic mortars of sand, trass, and fat lime which had been lying wet in basins for four or five years.

We have also seen by comparison of the preceding table, that mortars made of hydraulic lime, natural or artificial, without trass or puzzalona, did not harden, with sand, until from eight to fifteen days, although giving resistances; while those made of fat lime, sand and trass, hardened at the same season of the year, in the space of from four to six days, and, on the average, gave much greater resistances.

These results induced me to make researches in order to the fabrication of factitious trass or puzzalona. In the following chapter I shall give the results I obtained—commencing with several essays that have previously been made by others, with this view.

CHAPTER VI.

Of Artificial Trass and Puzzalona.

Mr. Baggé, a Swedish Engineer, was, I think, the first who attempted to make artificial puzzalona. This Engineer used, in his experiments, a species of black, and quite hard, schistus; he heated it highly several times; afterwards reduced it to powder, and having mixed it with lime, announced having obtained an excellent mortar, having all the properties of mortar made of puzzalona.

I do not at all doubt the success of Mr. Baggé: but his experiments having been repeated elsewhere, a less satisfactory result was secured. This was owing to using schists of a different composition, and which, in lieu of being heated highly, like those of the Swedish Engineer, required to be heated moderately.

Mr. Faujas de Saint-Fond made several researches in 1778 with the puzzalonas of Vivarais, which he found to be equal to the puzzalonas of Italy. He showed, also, that the trass of Andernach was a true puzzalona.

In 1786 Mr. Chaptal repeated the experiments of Mr. Faujas de Saint-Fond, on the puzzalonas of Vivarais, and found that they were inferior to those of Italy. This contradiction between the results obtained by Mr. Faujas de Saint-Fond and Mr. Chaptal is easily explained, for one used hydraulic lime in his experiments, and the other used fat lime.

Mr. Chaptal published in 1787 a memoir on the use of the ochreous earths of the south of France. These earths were calcined in a kiln like those used in some countries for burning lime. The kilns are reversed cones from about eight feet eight inches to about ten feet ten inches in height, and are from six to eight feet in diameter at the base: an opening is left near the apex of the cone, through which to withdraw the products of calcination: these kilns are filled by placing alternately, a layer of seacoal or turf, and a layer of the ochreous earth; the fire is kindled, after a few layers have been placed, and, when it is in full action, other alternate layers are added until the kiln is full. When the lower portion, which was the first heated, is sufficiently calcined, it is withdrawn as fast as necessary, and other new layers of clay and fuel are successively added above. Thus the burning is continual; the clays heat gently near the top of the kiln, and are subject to a much greater heat in the middle: they gradually cool towards the bottom, by the action of the current of air, after the fuel is consumed. This manner of burning earths, possesses great advantages as I shall have occasion to show. It would be equally advantageous to calcine hydraulic limes in these kilns, because, as we have seen above, it is very important to use these limes soon after they are burned. By constructing several kilns of this kind, there might be as great a supply of fresh lime as could be needed.

Mr. Chaptal attributed to iron, a great effect in improving puzzalonas;

and he appears to have attributed a very feeble one to alumine. Mr. Vicat says, on this subject, in his memoir: "If, as Mr. Chaptal assures us, clays deprived of iron, and calcined, cannot be employed as puzzalonas, it must be the oxide of iron that acts principally on the silex and modifies it, by the aid of fire in the ochreous earths, as the lime does in the hydraulic limestones: the alumine, therefore, appears to take the least part in these reactions; it does, nevertheless, make part of good puzzalonas."

Experiments which follow will show that iron plays no part in the preparation of puzzalonas, while alumine is very active. We shall see, also, that there is another substance which is very active and which has occasioned the divergencies of opinion on the preparation of puzzalona; but I will not anticipate; and will go on with the statement of the various attempts made to produce factitious puzzalona.

From experiments made at Cherbourg in 1787 by Mr. de Cessart, it appeared that basalts, obtained in the Department of the *Haute-Loire*, and pulverized after having been calcined, produced a mortar possessing all the qualities of those made with Italian puzzalona. Analysis shows this basalt to contain in one hundred parts, the following; Alumine, 16.75; Silex, 44.50; Oxide of iron, 20.00; Lime, 9.50; oxide of Manganese, 2.37; Soda, 2.60; Water, 2.00; loss, 2.28.

· The works in the port of Cherbourg required a great quantity of puzzalona; but the war which broke out with England on the rupture of the treaty of Amiens, raised the substance to an exorbitant price: it was calculated that the price of a cubic metre (35.34 cubic feet) cost, in 1803, more than 400 francs (about $76.00.)

They might easily have procured on the spot, clays which would have given results absolutely the same as those afforded by Italian puzzalona, at the cost of about 30 francs (about $6.00.) And had they understood the manner of making puzzalona, there would have been a great saving. Considerations of this sort induced Mr. Gratien, Senior, Engineer of roads and bridges, to occupy himself with the subject. He made a few essays with the porcelain clay of Valognes, and made many with the schists of Haineville, which he calcined, in repetition of the experiments of the Swedish engineer. The Valognes clay calcined, gave but feeble results; the Haineville schists gave better; analysis showed this schist to consist, in 100 parts, of the following: alumine, 26.00; silex, 46.00; magnesia, 8.00; lime, 4.00; oxide of iron, 14.00; loss and water, 2.00. The results of the experiments of Mr. Gratien, Senior, are given in two memoirs which he published, one in 1805, the other 1807. A commission of the Institute was charged with examining experiments, comparative of mortars made of puzzalona, of trass, and of the Cherbourg schist; the judgment of this commission is inserted by Mr. Gratien in his memoir of 1807, page 9; it declares "that after taking from the water the twelve boxes of beton of different compositions:

"1st. All had acquired a certain consistence, but very different amongst themselves.

"2nd. The difference was striking between the betons composed of puzzalona and trass, and those into which these substances did not enter.

"3rd. The two compositions of burnt and pulverized schistus offered a resistance quite satisfactory, but not so great as it probably would be after a longer immersion.

The above report shows that Mr. Gratien obtained with the schists, results inferior to those given by puzzalona.

In 1806 Mr. Le Masson, Engineer of roads and bridges, at Rouen, attempted, in concert with Mr. Vitalis, to make factitious puzzalona by calcining yellow ochreous earths, according to the process of Mr. Chaptal. The betons made with the calcined earth, having acquired a remarkable consistence, Mr. Le Masson, in 1807, repeated the experiments on a larger scale: he immersed, in the Seine, casks filled with beton made of the calcined ochreous earth. After six months, the casks were taken out, and it was found that the betons had acquired such hardness that it was necessary to strike it two hundred times with a mass of iron weighing 26$\frac{4}{10}$ lbs. to break in a depth of ten to twelve inches; the tenacity was so great, that the entire mass weighing 2800 lbs. was suspended by means of a *tire fond* (lewis?) Mr. Gratien and Mr. Vitalis judged that the masonry had acquired a hardness greater than could ever be absolutely necessary, even in constructions that require the greatest solidity in their foundations. These experiments are reported in the memoir of Mr. Gratien 1807—page 46 and following.

Mr. Vicat in his memoir of 1818 confined himself to reporting the different attempts that had been made, up to that time, to form artificial puzzalona: but in 1819 he sent to the Institute a memoir on that subject. I do not know whether this memoir was printed, but an extract is contained in the *annales de chimie et de physique* of 1820, Vol. XV, page 365 and following. After several observations on limestone, on the action of fire on calcareous stones, and the combination of water with lime, the author gives a succinct history of puzzalona. We find afterward the following passage.

"Since the quality of natural hydraulic lime, depends solely on the presence of a certain quantity of clay, combined by fire with the calcareous matter, it was natural to think that by mixing clay in suitable proportions with fat lime, slaked, no matter how, and then submitting the mixture to calcination, a similar result would be obtained: experiments made on a large scale, and in many places, have confirmed this idea in a manner so complete, that it is now possible to fabricate any where, and at a very moderate price, artificial lime superior to the natural analagous lime."

"In like manner, since chemical analysis gave, for the constituents of natural puzzalona, silex, alumine, oxide of iron, and a little lime; it was easy to suppose that our clays, of which the composition is altogether similar, might be transformed, by burning, into artificial puzzalonas. This idea was already old at the period of the experiments of the author of these researches; but by a remarkable fatality it was as if stricken with sterility: the circumstances on which the quantities of good puzzalona depend, had not been determined with sufficient precision. There was a persuasion, for example, that iron was very active therein; that, therefore, only ochreous clays should be used; that in order to a more perfect imitation of nature, there should be a high degree of heat, 'because,' said they, 'the fire of volcanos is much more intense than the fire of our kilns.' (Several geologists are of a contrary opinion.) Certain puzzalonas, came, beyond doubt, in the form of lava, from volcanos: they were in fact subject to a high degree of heat; but since the very distant epoch of their formation, they have sustained diverse decompositions, either from intestine modifications or from the action of acid vapours, or from other causes, and these decompositions have totally changed the mode of combination of their principles. As to the red puzzalonas of the neighbourhood of Rome, every thing shows that they were only vast beds of ochreous clay variously burned, either by subterranean fires, or by currents of lava which covered them and broke them up in every direction. Thus their quality is very variable according to the disposition and depth of the beds. But whatever may be the process of the formation of these substances, it is demonstrated that all the mystery of their properties, resides, not in the presence of iron or lime, but in a particular state of combination of silex and alumine—a state to which all clays, soft and greasy to the touch, may be brought, with the greatest facility, by a light calcination. The means which hitherto appear to have succeeded best, consists in reducing the dry clay to a very fine powder, and calcining it, for some minutes, on metallic plates heated to an obscure (*brun*) red. The truth is, that practice has not yet fully matured the process, and it is probable that full success requires the contrivance of a mode of calcination more expeditious and convenient than the above: but the problem is not the less resolved."

Such is the mode proposed by Mr. Vicat for making factitious puzzalona; and he teaches us nothing new, for he does not tell us what is the particular condition in which the silex and alumine should be found to afford good results. Opinions were for a long time divided on the question whether the clays, which it was desired to convert into good cements, should be heated much or little—these cements being, really, artificial puzzalonas.* Mr. Vicat has adopted the opinion of those who thought they should be burned but little; but experiments which are to follow will show that this (as a general principle) is erroneous—it being necessary to burn more or less, according to the composition of the clay. The problem, therefore, was not resolved by Mr. Vicat, though he says it was; and the experiments which follow will show in what it really consists.

I made several essays, substituting brick and tile dust for trass. To this end I composed a number of mortars of fat lime and the dust of bricks or tiles taken from all the kilns of the neighbourhood. A part of the mortars were made of brick dust, and a part of tile dust. I obtained many results: —sometimes very good, sometimes indifferent, and sometimes very bad. What struck me much, at first, was, that mortars made of different dusts coming from the same burning gave very different results: notwithstanding that the dusts were of the same burning, were all made of the same clay, were used with the same lime, and that all other circumstances were the same. I saw from this, that great risk was run of making bad mortar, by taking brick or tile dusts without discrimination. I know that the great majority of constructors preferred highly burned dusts, and that, although made of the same clay, they much preferred dust of tiles to that of bricks. To settle my opinion on these two points, and to explain up contradictory results that I had obtained, I made the experiments reported in the following table.

* By the term *ciment*—translated, in the above sentence, *cement*, the French often mean, simply brick dust or tile dust; and it will be so rendered wherever it is supposed to bear that meaning.—Trans.

Table No. XVI.

No. of the mortar.	Composition of the mortar.		No. of days required to harden in water.	Weight supported before breaking.
			days.	lbs.
1	Fat Lime slaked to powder and measured in powder . Dust of bricks but little burned .	1 2 } 3	11	330
2	Lime the same . . Dust of bricks well burned .	1 2 } 3	+40	180
3	Lime the same . . Dust of tiles but little burned . .	1 2 } 3	5	275
4	Lime the same . . . Dust of tiles well burned .	1 2 } 3	+30	125 *
5	Lime the same . Dust of tiles same as No. 3 but which had been reburned in a reverberatory furnace for six hours.	1 ... 2 } 3		

Observations on the experiments of Table No. XVI.

In order to make the above five experiments, I went to the nearest brickyard, at Strasburg; and there got bricks and tiles, both lightly burned, and well burned. It was easy to dintinguish them, for the first were very red, and but feebly sonorous, while those which were *well burned*, as it is called, were of a fawn colour (*fauve*) (pale red) and quite sonorous. The burners are never mistaken in this particular.

The first four experiments show that I obtained much better results with bricks and tiles but little burned, than with those well burned. We see, also, that the hardening was much more prompt, with the slightly burned dusts: for No. 2 required more than forty days to harden, while No. 1 required but 11 days; No. 4 took more than 30 days to indurate, while No. 3 took but 5 days. We see, also, contrary to the general opinion, that brick dust gave better results than tile dust. No. 5 was made with the same dust as No. 3, after it had been reburnt for six hours in a reverberatory furnace, keeping it constantly at a low red heat. The mortar made of this last dust took no consistence, and when I withdrew it from the water after a year, it was as soft as if it had been made of lime and sand only. This shows how important it is not to use these dusts at hazard; for they are always costly and are sometimes no better than so much sand. More than one fault of this kind has been committed in great works, as I shall have occasion to remark. The experiments of the above table agree with the opinion of Mr. Vicat, who says, that clay should be submitted to a feeble heat only. But on resorting to another tile kiln, where they used another clay in making bricks and tiles; and making therewith four new experiments exactly like the first four in the above table, I was surprised to find results directly opposite to those before obtained; that is to say, the dusts furnished by bricks and tiles but little burned, gave results much inferior to those afforded by the dusts from well burned bricks and tiles. The experiments in the following table, were made with this cement.

* In my pamphlet of 1824, and in the 7th number of the *mémorial*, copied therefrom the resistance, by a typographical error, is set down as 87 kil. (194 lbs.) Au.

Table XVII.

No. of the mortar.	Composition of the mortar.		No. of days required to harden in water.	Weight supported before breaking.
			days.	lbs.
1	{ Fat lime slaked to powder and measured in powder	1 } 3	12	139
	{ Dust of tiles but little burned	2 }		
2	{ Lime the same	1 } 3	12	176
	{ Dust of No. 1 reburnt for half an hour	2 }		
3	{ Lime the same	1 } 3	15	282
	{ Dust of No. 1 reburnt for one hour	2 }		
4	{ Lime the same	1 } 3	20	319
	{ Dust of No. 1 reburnt for two hours	2 }		

Observations on the experiments of Table No. XVII.

To make the experiments of table No. XVII, I took dust from the tile kiln which had given results opposite to those in table No. XVI, dust but lightly burned, and made mortars therewith, in its then state, and also after it had been reburnt.

Mortar No. 1 contains the slightly burned dust, and Nos. 2, 3 and 4 the same dust after it had been reburnt for the periods of time expressed in the table. According as the dust was burned more and more, the resistance increased; and it is probable it would have been further augmented by further burning. It should be noticed that the induration became slower as the resistance became greater. We shall see, below, that the slowness of the hardening is due to the dusts having been heated in crucibles, where they were out of contact of the air.

We see that the dusts of table No. XVI gave me good results only when they had been but little burned, while it was the contrary with those of table No. XVII. These opposite results led me to examine the composition of the clays of these two brick yards; and I ascertained that the clay which gave the dust of table No. XVII contained very little carbonate of lime, while that which produced the dust of table No. XVI, contained almost a fifth of its weight of that substance. I repeated the experiment with the clays of several other tile kilns, and I always obtained this remarkable result, namely, when the clays contained little or no carbonate of lime, gentle burning imparted only mediocre qualities, while strong burning gave them excellent qualities. When, on the contrary, the clays contained from one to two tenths of carbonate of lime I procured good results only by heating lightly, and, if I augmented the degree of calcination the quality was impaired; and if the heat had been very great, all hydraulic property was lost. We see, consequently, that Mr. Vicat was in error in saying, as I have already quoted him at page 65, "that all the mystery of puzzalona resides, not in the presence of iron or lime, but in a particular state of combination of silex and alumine." It is certain, on the contrary, that the presence of lime in clays has a great influence on the quality of the puzzalona. At the same time we may conceive why those who had been engaged in producing this substance, were induced to announce, some, that it was necessary to heat clays but little, and others that it was necessary to heat them highly. It follows from what I have said that what was true of one kind of clay might not be true of another, although having the same aspect. We in no degree contest the point, for example, of Mr. Le Masson having obtained, at Rouen, very good results with a calcined ochreous earth; but had he submitted to the same degree of calcination an ochreous earth of the same appearance, but containing more or less lime, he would have had very different results. If two clays, equally greasy to the touch, be taken, of which one shall contain one fifth of lime, while the other contains none, and if they be equally heated, it may happen that neither of the results will possess hydraulic properties of any moment: that which contained the lime will have been too much burned, while that which was without lime will not have been burned enough. On the other hand if that containing lime be less burned and that having no lime be more burned, then very good results may be had from both.

The above experiments were made in the autumn of 1821. As they are the foundation of the fabrication of artificial puzzalonas, and as the important part that lime acts in this fabrication had not been noticed, I addressed, in 1822, to the Minister of War, a memoir containing the result of my experiments. An extract from this memoir may be found in the *Moniteur* of January 22nd, 1823.

Mr. Sganzin reports, page 31 of his *cours de construction*, that "they prepare at Amsterdam an artificial trass: it is clay taken from the bottom of the sea, which they burn highly as they do bricks. These brick-like pieces are broken by pestles worked by horses: the substance is then put under millstones, where it acquires the fineness necessary to be converted into mortar by mixture with lime.

"Bergman analysed this artificial trass, which bears the name of *privileged cement of Holland:* he found that it contained in about 100 parts Silex, from 55 to 60; Alumine, 19 to 20; Lime, 5 to 6; Iron, 15 to 20.

There is no doubt, considering the composition of this clay, and the degree of heat to which it is subjected, that it must give very good artificial trass.

I give below, in a table, some experiments on clay which I calcined after mixing with it a little lime.

Table No. XVIII.

No. of the mortar.	Composition of the mortar.		No. of days required to harden in water.	Weight supported before breaking.
			days	lbs.
1	Fat lime slaked to powder and measured in powder . . Dust from Holsheim clay .	1 2 } 3	12	319
2	Lime the same . . Same clay calcined with 0.10 of lime	1 2 } 3	23	169
3	Obernai lime slaked to powder and measured in powder . Dust of Holsheim clay .	1 2 } 3	10	440
4	Obernai lime do. . Same clay calcined with 0.10 of lime	1 2 } 3	23	216

Observations on the experiments of Table No. XVIII.

To make the above experiments, I slaked fat lime to dry powder, and fixed the quantity by measuring in powder: and I took Holsheim clay of which the composition is given at page 41; it contains no lime. I calcined a portion of this clay in a crucible placed in a reverberatory furnace, keeping it at a red heat during twelve hours. I took the same clay, mixed it with one-tenth its volume of fat lime reduced to paste, and heated the mixture in the same way and for the same time, as the clay alone. I then made mortars 1 and 3 of the above table, mixing fat lime and the Obernai hydraulic lime, with the clay dust that contained no lime: the numbers 2 and 4 were made with the clay dust mixed with one-tenth of lime.

The results of the table show that the mortar made with fat lime, and clay dust containing lime, gave a resistance only one half of that obtained with same lime, and clay dust containing no lime. The table shows that I got like results with mortars made of Obernai lime. It will also be seen that the hardening was slower, by one half, with the dust containing lime, than with that without lime. Besides, these mortars took much more time to harden than they should have taken; this is owing to the clay dusts having been calcined in a crucible, and to the experiment having been made in winter.

Mr. Sganzin states, page 27 of his *cours de construction* that the officers of Engineers who constructed the sluice-bridge at Alexandria reburnt their brick dust to a high degree; and he says it was because, before this operation, the mortars melted (*se délayait*) in the water. Mr. Vicat also, mentions this process which he approves, but for another reason; his opinion is that energetic puzzalonas suit better with fat lime than with hydraulic lime; he has remarked that on highly heating puzzalona, it loses all its energy, and I have obtained the same effect. But the lime used in building the Alexandria bridge was Casal lime, which is eminently hydraulic. Mr. Vicat thinks, therefore, that the brick dust was calcined to diminish its energy, so that it might make better mortar with the Casal lime. This is a great error. The officers of Engineers in calcining this brick dust to a high degree, committed a serious fault as I shall prove. But it is first necessary to show in what the error of Mr. Vicat consists. This Engineer relies on the principle, that mortar made of hydraulic lime, sand, and good cement, is superior to that made of lime and cement without sand. The first experiments of my tables, Nos. II and III, also show, that with good hydraulic lime, sand and trass or puzzalona, I obtained better results than with lime and trass or puzzalona without sand. But if we refer to table No. XIII, we shall see that, with a few exceptions, I obtained similar results with fat lime. If we compare the results of Nos. 9, 10, 11 and 12, all made of the same lime from marble, same trass and puzzalona, we see that if No. 9, containing sand, is inferior to No. 10, containing only lime and trass, on the other hand No. 11 which contains sand, is superior to No. 12 containing puzzalona without sand. To complete the conviction, it will suffice to cast the eyes over table No. XVIII; wherein we see that by the addition of one-tenth of lime to the Holsheim clay, and the degree of burning to which I submitted it, I considerably diminished the energy of this factitious trass: but it appears that this slightly energetic clay dust, gave, both with common lime, and with the Obernai hydraulic lime, a result only one half as good as that obtained with the same lime, and the clay dust in all its energy. The experiments cited, prove then, that energetic puzzalonas suit equally with very hydraulic lime and with fat lime. They prove that with these two kinds of lime it is in general more advantageous and economical to make mortars of lime, sand and puzzalona whether natural or artificial, than with lime and puzzalona only. If in certain cases, there is found to be a superiority in mortar without sand, we see that it is not great, and, on account of the considerable economy that results, we ought not to hesitate to use sand.

The observation cited by Mr. Sganzin, as to the sluice-bridge at Alexandria, would be entirely in opposition to the results Mr. Vicat and I have obtained by calcining clay dusts and puzzalonas to a high degree. We found that these substances thus calcined, lost all their energy, while, according to Mr. Sganzin, they require to be submitted to an elevated temperature. I did not doubt that Mr. Sganzin had been incorrectly informed as to what occurred at Alexandria; but, to be certain, I examined at the Depot of fortifications the documents relative to the works of that place, and I found, in a memoir of the *Chef de bataillon* Maynial, of the Engineers, dated 28 *brumaire an* 13, relating to this sluice-bridge what follows: The first season the floor (*radier*) was constructed of brick masonry in puzzalona mortar: the difficulty of procuring puzzalona, and its high price, led to the construction of a reverberatory furnace in which brick dust was reburnt to incandescence, so that when stirred it would flow like lava (*jusqu'a incandescence, de maniére que, lorsqu'on le remuait, on le voyait couler comme de la lave.*) The mixture of mortar, was one third of this reburnt brick-dust, one third sand, and one third Casal (lime,) and it produced the same effect as a like mixture of puzzalona."

We see that it was the difficulty of procuring puzzalona, that gave the idea of reburning the clay dust to the point of fusion, and that they were led to this degree of calcination by the false notion that puzzalona was lava—these two substances, being in fact, very different. It is not said in the memoir that the mortar made of this dust, before reburning it, melted in water, as Mr. Sganzin states: and it could not have been so, since they used the Casal lime, which is very hydraulic. We see, moreover, that it was not with a view to diminish the energy of the cement, and because it was to be used with very hydraulic lime, that it was reburnt; on the contrary they wished to impart to it the force of puzzalona, which they imagined had been melted like lava. The memoir says that this recalcined dust, produced the same effect as a like mixture of puzzalona. If they had mixed it with fat lime, there would have been a great difference between the results with this dust and those obtained in the same way with puzzalona. It is evident that their result ought to have been good, as it is stated to have been, at the end of the memoir, but it was owing entirely to the Casal lime being so eminently hydraulic. We have seen in the first tables that very hydraulic limes gave very good resistances without any admixture: if they had been mixed with broken nut shells, or with chopped straw, we should still have had a good result, but it would have been very wrong to attribute the result to those substances. By reburning the brick dust at so high a heat, they destroyed all its hydraulic properties; and they would have had as good a mortar by mixing this very hydraulic lime with sand, instead of the dust they used; and at a much cheaper rate. I repeat then that they committed a great fault at Alexandria in reburning the clay dust thus highly, since they necessarily caused it to part with all its hydraulic properties, and, in order to do this, encountered great expense. Before calcining the dust, if they thought proper to use it, they should have tried it with a little fat lime, to ascertain whether, or not, it would be advantageous to burn it more. I have enlarged on this example of the works of Alexandria, to show how important it is not to have false ideas as to puzzalonas, or the substances which are substituted for them. I proceed now to repeat other experiments that I made with diverse clays mixed with lime and calcined to different degrees.

Table No. XIX.

No. of the mortar.	Composition of the mortars.	The clay having been burnt with lime.		The clay having been burnt with bricks.	
		H	W*	H	W
		days	lbs.	days	lbs.
1	Fat lime slaked to powder & measured in powder 1 Trass 2 } 3				
2	Lime the same 1 Puzzalona 2 } 3				
3	Lime the same 1 Dust of Holsheim clay 2 } 3	25	187	15	275
4	Lime the same 1 Dust of Holsheim clay with lime water 2 } 3	25	143	15	286
5	Lime the same 1 Dust of Holsheim clay with 0.01 of lime 2 } 3	25	165	15	297
6	Lime the same 1 Dust of Holsheim clay with 0.02 of lime 2 } 3	30	110	10	319
7	Lime the same 1 Dust of Sufflenheim clay 2 } 3	25	165	15	297
8	Lime the same 1 Dust of Sufflenheim clay with lime water 2 } 3	25	220	15	286
9	Lime the same 1 Dust of Sufflenheim clay with 0.01 of lime 2 } 3	25	143	15	286
10	Lime the same 1 Dust of Sufflenheim clay with 0.02 of lime 2 } 3	25	121	12	275
11	Lime the same 1 Dust of pipe clay 2 } 3	25	264	15	308
12	Lime the same 1 Dust of pipe clay with lime water 2 } 3	25	264	15	330
13	Lime the same 1 Dust of pipe clay with 0.01 of lime 2 } 3	25	275	15	341
14	Lime the same 1 Dust of pipe clay with 0.02 of lime 2 } 3	25	275	12	363

Observations on the experiments of Table No. XIX.

To make the above experiments I took three kinds of clay, that of Holsheim, of Sufflenheim, and the pipe clay of the environs of Cologne: the composition of these clays may be seen at page 41. I made four bricks of each of these clays: the first contained no foreign substance: the second was made by adding a quantity of lime water equal to the bulk of clay; the third by adding one per cent. of fat lime in paste, and the fourth by adding two per cent of the same lime; they were placed in a lime kiln in the midst of the

*In this table and several others which follow, the columns marked H, express the number of days the mortar required to harden in water, and those marked W, indicate the weights supported before breaking. Au.

lime.* With each of the same clays I made, also, four other similar bricks which I placed in the same kiln with the common bricks. Lastly, having calcined these cements, I made the mortars which are given in the table, taking one part of fat lime, measured in powder, to two parts of each of these cements. No. 1 and 2, were made of the same lime and trass or puzzalona, to serve as comparisons with the other experiments. The mortar of trass hardened in six days, and broke under a weight of 264 lbs: that of puzzalona hardened in four days and supported 352 lbs. before breaking. The hardening has in general been a little slower; although these experiments were made at the end of summer. That may possibly be owing to the degree of burning of the lime.

On examining the above table we shall remark that all the clays that were burned with the lime, including the natural clays, gave results, less good, than when burned with the bricks; this difference is much greater with the clays which contain lime; we see that when burned with the bricks the Holsheim clay, and the pipe clay, gained a little by the addition of a small quantity of lime, while the Sufflenheim clay, on the contrary, lost a little. When they were burned with the lime, the Holsheim clay lost strength; that of Sufflenheim presented anomalies which I cannot explain, and the pipe clay was but little changed.

The Holsheim clay being most at command. I made with it several mixtures of lime up to one tenth, and I burned them in the same way as the above clays: the following table contains the results.

*Throughout all Alsace, they burn lime in large square, and elevated kilns, lime is put at bottom, bricks are placed above the lime, and tiles above the bricks: they burn with wood, which is placed at the bottom: so that the lime is most highly heated, and the tiles the least. Au.

Table No. XX.

No. of the series.	Composition of the mortars.		Clay burned with lime.		Clay burned with bricks.	
			H	W	H	W
			days	lbs	days	lbs
1	Fat lime measured in paste — 1 / Trass — 2	} 2				
2	Lime the same — 1 / Puzzalona — 2	} 3				
3	Lime the same — 1 / Dust of Holsheim clay — 2	} 3	25	253	15	396
4	Lime the same — 1 / Dust of Holsheim clay with 0.01 of lime — 2	} 3	25	209	15	319
5	Lime the same — 1 / Dust of Holsheim clay with 0.02 of lime — 2	} 3	25	242	15	297
6	Lime the same — 1 / Dust of Holsheim clay with 0.03 of lime — 2	} 3	25	231	15	286
7	Lime the same — 1 / Dust of Holsheim clay with 0.04 of lime — 2	} 3	25	253	15	341
8	Lime the same — 1 / Dust of Holsheim clay with 0.05 of lime — 2	} 3	25	275	15	352
9	Lime the same — 1 / Dust of Holsheim clay with 0.06 of lime — 2	} 3	25	231	15	297
10	Lime the same — 1 / Dust of Holsheim clay with 0.07 of lime — 2	} 3	25	198	15	275
11	Lime the same — 1 / Dust of Holsheim clay with 0.08 of lime — 2	} 3	25	198	15	286
12	Lime the same — 1 / Dust of Holsheim clay with 0.09 of lime — 2	} 3	25	231	15	297
13	Lime the same — 1 / Dust of Holsheim clay with 0.10 of lime — 2	} 3	25	242	15	286
14	Lime the same — 1 / Dust of Holsheim clay with 0.04 of lime — 2	} 3			4	187
15	Same mortar				4	209
16	Same mortar				3	297
17	Same mortar				3	385

Observations on the experiments of Table No. XX.

The above experiments were made in the same manner as those of table No. XIX, as to the burning of the clays; but in proportioning the mortars I took one part of lime in paste to two parts of cement. I made two comparative experiments, No. I and No. 2 with trass and puzzalona. The mortar with trass hardened in four days and supported 319 lbs; that with puzzalona hardened in three days and broke under a weight of 286 lbs. We have seen in table No. XIII, an exactly similar mortar support 495 lbs. Whence it appears that with puzzalona as with trass, results are various.

The present table concurs with No. XIX in showing that the cements calcined with the lime gave inferior results to those calcined with the bricks. This table shows also that the proportions of lime mixed with the clay, which gave the best results for the degrees of calcination tried, were four or five per cent; but here, the best result obtained from clay mixed with lime, is inferior to that of No. 3 where there was no lime. It appears that the mortars of the two tables whereof the clay had been calcined with 0.02 of lime do not greatly differ. A greater difference observable between the mortars No. 3 of the two tables, neither of which contain lime, may be owing to two circumstances: the first is, that in table No. XIX the proportions were adjusted with lime in powder, while in No. XX, they were fixed with lime in paste; the second is, that the cement of mortar No. 3 in the present table may have received a more suitable degree of calcination than that of table No. XIX.

All the four mortars No. 14, 15, 16 and 17 were made with clay that had been mixed with 0.04 of lime, but they were heated to different degrees in another kiln, and gave different results. Cement No. 14 was burned with the tiles and placed in the upper part; No. 15 was placed in the middle of the kiln; No. 16 between the tiles and the bricks, and No. 17 in the middle of the bricks. Whence it appears that No. 14 was least and No. 17 most heated. This last mortar gave about the same resistance as No. 3 which contained no lime.

There are several anomalies in the last column of table No. XX which appear to me to be due to the degree of calcination. We notice, in fact, that in a brick kiln, not only the different layers sustain different degrees of heat, but even the bricks in the same layer are not all burned to the same degree. All the mortars of the last column of the last two tables, required about fifteen days to harden, with the exception of the last four which hardened in the short space of three to four days. I attribute this effect to the circumstance that these four cements were placed by the side of one of the flues left in the mass of bricks in order to distribute the heat; and thus they were exposed, during the burning, to a current of air which contributed to the promptitude of the induration, as I shall have occasion to show.

The experiments given in tables Nos. XVI, XVII, XVIII, XIX and XX, show that the presence of lime has great influence, when it exists in the state of carbonate in the clays, as to the effect of calcination upon them; because the heat disengages a great part of the carbonic acid, and the lime mixed in the clay, causes the beginning of vitrification, which is distructive of all hydraulic properties in these cements. These experiments show, besides, 1st. that clay containing no lime requires a rather high calcination to form good artificial puzzalonas, and that the heat required to burn bricks suitably, is about the proper degree for such cements: 2nd. that when the clays contain as high as one tenth of carbonate of lime, the temperature used to burn tiles is sufficient: 3rd. that this degree of heat is too great for them, provided they contain from a tenth to a fifth of carbonate of lime, as sometimes happens, but that good results may still be got by burning them with a lower heat than that required for tiles: 4th. it does not appear that the presence of lime in clays tends to make the cements more energetic. If it gives energy to some clays, it is but slight: and there may result from the mixture, if the burning be carried too high, a loss of all hydraulic property. At the close of the chapter I shall explain all the means necessary to the fabrication of good artificial puzzalona.

Among the substances which, after lime, occur most frequently in clays, is magnesia. I, in consequence, made the following experiments with Holsheim clay and various proportions of carbonate of magnesia.

Table No. XXI.

No. of the mortars	Composition of the mortars.		No. of days required to harden in water.	Weight supported before breaking.
			days.	pounds.
1	Fat lime measured in paste . . Dust of Holsheim clay . .	1 } 3 2	20	330
2	Lime the same . . . Dust of the same clay with 0.01 of carbonate of magnesia . .	1 } 3 2	20	341
3	Lime the same Dust of the same clay with 0.03 of do.	1 } 3 2	20	330
4	Lime the same Dust of the same clay with 0.05 of do.	1 } 3 2	20	341
	Lime the same . . Dust of the same clay with 0.07 of do.	1 } 3 2	20	330
6	Lime the same . . Dust of the same clay with 0.10 of do.	1 } 3 2	20	¿330
7	Lime the same . . Dust of the same clay, highly heated, with 0.05 of carbonate of magnesia	1 } 3 2	20	231

Observations on the Experiments of Table No. XXI.

I made the above mixtures of Holsheim clay with carbonate of magnesia in the same manner as, in the preceding tables, the mixtures of clay and lime. We see that the hardening was slower than usual; but this is owing to the experiments having been made during very cold weather in the month of January.

These clays were placed in the lime kiln between the bricks and the tiles, and we see by the result of No. 1 that the degree of heat was not quite sufficient to impart to this clay all the energy of which it is susceptible. We see also, that at this degree of heat, the carbonate of magnesia has had no great effect in transforming this clay into puzzalona. The cement No. 7 was more highly heated, being placed between the bricks and the lime: the clay of this number contained the same quantity of carbonate of magnesia as No. 4 and we see that it supported 110 lbs. less. We should not conclude that this effect is due to the magnesia; because the Holsheim clay loses, when alone, much of its force when too highly heated, as we see by No. 1 of table XXIII. It appears, therefore, that magnesia is nearly passive in the perfecting of artificial puzzalonas.

Clay, we know, is a mixture of silex and alumine: I, in consequence, made the following experiments, adding sand to the clay which I heated.

Table No. XXII.

No. of the mortars.	Composition of the mortars.	No. of days required to harden. in water.	Weight supported before breaking
		days	lbs.
1	Fat lime slaked to powder and measured in powder . 1 }3 Dust of pipe clay heated for six hours in a reverberatory furnace . 2	12	418
2	Lime the same . . 1 Same clay deprived of part of its sand, and to which was added 0.10 of white sand pounded fine . . 2 }3	14	374
3	Lime the same . . 1 Dust of clay No. 2 with 0.20 of sand do. 2 }3	15	378
4	Lime the same . . 1 Dust of clay No. 2 with 0.30 of sand do. 2 }3	15	383
5	Lime the same . . . 1 Dust of clay No. 2 with 0.40 of sand do. 2 }3	15	473
6	Lime the same . . . 1 Dust of clay No. 2 with 0.50 of sand do. 2 }3	15	462
7	Lime the same . . . 1 Dust of yellow ochreous clay . 2 }3	16	187
8	Lime the same . . 1 Dust of yellow ochreous clay, deprived of part of its sand . . 2 }3	20	143
9	Lime the same . . . 1 Dust of clay No. 8 with 0.10 of white sand pounded fine . . 2 }3	20	165
10	Lime the same . . . 1 Dust of clay No. 8 with 0.20 of sand do. 2 }3	18	176
11	Lime the same . . . 1 Dust of clay No. 8 with 0.30 of sand do. 2 }3	16	189
12	Lime the same . . . 1 Dust of clay No. 9 with 0.40 of sand do. 2 }3	18	154
13	Lime the same . . . 1 Dust of clay No. 8 with 0.50 of sand do. 2 }3	20	132
14	Lime the same . . . 1 Dust of clay called Rintzel . 2 }3	12	352
15	Lime the same . . . 1 Dust of Rintzel clay deprived of part of its sand . . . 2 }3	10	418

Observations on the experiments of Table No. XXII.

To make the first six experiments, I took the white clay which is sent from the environs of Cologne to Strasburg, to make pipes. The analysis of this clay, given at page. 41, shows that it contains very little iron, and that the alumine in it, is about one third of the silex. I took a portion of this clay, diffused it through a large quantity of water, and decanting it several times, deprived it of a part of its silex. I then made the mortar No. 1 with the natural clay: the other mortars up to No. 6 inclusive were composed with the clay deprived of part of its silex, to which I added, successively, the portions of sand stated in the table. The sand which I used was white and silecious: it was pounded very fine and mixed with the clay.

I omitted composing a mortar of lime, and this white clay deprived of part of its sand, like that, No. 8, made of another kind of clay. The clay of the first six numbers was calcined during six hours in a reverberatory furnace. No. 2, which had less sand than No. 1, gave a result less strong. The quality of the succeeding mortars improves up to No. 5, to which I had added 0.40 of sand; No. 6, which contained 0.50 of sand, was inferior to No. 5.

The experiments from No. 7 to No. 13 were made with a very greasy clay: a yellow ochreous earth ot which I had not the analysis. I treated this clay like the other, that is to say; I took a portion which I washed in a great quantity of water, decanting several times to separate a portion of the sand it contained. No. 7 was made with the natural ochreous earth: No. 8 with the clay deprived of a portion of its sand. To make the following mortars up to No. 13, I added to the washed clay the several portions of sand indicated in the table; these clays, like the pipe clay, were heated for six hours in a reverberatory furnace, keeping them at a low red heat (*rouge tendre.*) We see that, with this clay as with the pipe clay, we obtained an inferior result when it was deprived of much of its sand, and that its energy was augmented by adding a little sand, up to a certain quantity, beyond which it went on diminishing. The comparison of the above experiments with ochreous clay and pipe clay, shows that ochreous earths are not, as was for a long time believed, to be preferred in forming artificial puzzalonas: several other results confirm this remark.

The experiments No. 14 and 15 were made with a clay which is found in the environs of Haguenace, and is used for various purposes; this clay is gray, and contains no lime: it is refractory. It is used in the construction of furnaces for heating madder. On working it in the hands, it is perceived to contain a considerable quantity of sand. No. 14 is composed of the natural clay: in No. 15, the clay is deprived of part of its sand, and in this state it is much more greasy to the touch. A comparison of No. 14 and 15 shows that this clay gave the best result when deprived of part of its sand.

The experiments made with the above three kinds of clay prove that clays containing a great quantity of sand are not so suitable for making artificial puzzalonas as those which, having more alumine, are greasy to the touch. When clays contain one part of alumine to three of silex, they are very greasy: they are also quite greasy when the proportion is one to five, but beyond this they become meagre: it is therefore amongst the clays a little greasy, that we should seek for those whereof to make artificial puzzalona.

We have seen, according to the analysis, by Mr. Berthier, of trass and puzzalona, that these substances contain potash and soda. I therefore mixed these with the clays to be heated, and the following are the results.

Table No. XXIII.

No. of the mortar.	Composition of the mortars.		Clay having been burned with bricks.		Clay having been burned with lime.	
			H	W	H	W
			days.	lbs.	days.	lbs.
1	Fat lime measured in paste . Dust of Holsheim clay .	$\begin{smallmatrix}1\\2\end{smallmatrix}$ 3	15	330	25	99
2	Lime the same . . Dust of same clay with 1-10 of solution of soda at 5° .	$\begin{smallmatrix}1\\2\end{smallmatrix}$ 3	15	319		
3	Lime the same . . Dust of same clay with 1·5 do.	$\begin{smallmatrix}1\\2\end{smallmatrix}$ 3	15	308		
4	Lime the same . Dust of same clay with 1-4 do.	$\begin{smallmatrix}1\\2\end{smallmatrix}$ 3	15	297		
5	Lime the same . . Dust of same clay with 1-3	$\begin{smallmatrix}1\\2\end{smallmatrix}$ 3	15	297		
6	Lime the same . . Dust of same clay with 1-2 .	$\begin{smallmatrix}1\\2\end{smallmatrix}$ 3	15	286	15	297
7	Lime the same . Dust of same clay with 1-10 of solution of potash at 5° .	$\begin{smallmatrix}1\\2\end{smallmatrix}$ 3	15	341		
8	Lime the same . . Dust of same clay with 1-5 do.	$\begin{smallmatrix}1\\2\end{smallmatrix}$ 3	15	363		
9	Lime the same . . Dust of same clay with 1-6 do.	$\begin{smallmatrix}1\\2\end{smallmatrix}$ 3	15	374		
10	Lime the same . . Dust of same clay with 1-3 do.	$\begin{smallmatrix}1\\2\end{smallmatrix}$ 3	15	363		
11	Lime the same . . Dust of same clay with 1-2 do.	$\begin{smallmatrix}1\\2\end{smallmatrix}$ 3	15	341	25	264
12	Lime the same . . Dust of same clay with 1-2 of solution of saltpetre at 5° .	$\begin{smallmatrix}1\\2\end{smallmatrix}$ 3		(*)	25	264
13	Lime the same . . Dust of same clay with 1-2 of solution of saltpetre at 10° .	$\begin{smallmatrix}1\\2\end{smallmatrix}$ 3			25	242
14	Lime the same . . Dust of same clay with 1-2 of solution of com. salt at 5° .	$\begin{smallmatrix}1\\2\end{smallmatrix}$ 3	15	330	25	264

Observations on the experiments of Table No. XXIII.

To make the above experiments I took Holsheim clay and mixed it with various quantities of solutions of soda standing at 5° of the *pèse acid.* The quantities of solutions of soda that the clays contain are taken with reference to the volume of clay. I did the same with potash, as is shown in the numbers from 7 to 11. Nos. 12 and 13 have the clay mixed with water containing saltpetre; and No. 14 has the clay wet with salt water.

The clays of the first eleven numbers of the first column of the table were heated in a lime kiln, between the tiles and the bricks, so as to give them only a moderate heat. Those of No. 1, 6 and 11 of the second column were burned with the lime, and subjected to a very high heat.

If the result of the first eleven numbers, wherein the clay was heated with bricks, be observed, it will be seen that the first of those which con-

*This mortar broke, on being cut, but was very hard. Au.

tain soda, differ but little from No 1 which contains none, but that the resistances, in the succeding numbers, go on diminishing a little, as the proportion of soda was increased. With potash, I obtained a different result; the resistance of the mortars augmented up to No. 9, and afterward diminished. The clays placed between the tiles and the bricks received a degree of heat rather too slight—for No. 1 supported a weight of only 330 lbs, while we have seen that this clay could sustain a weight of 396 lbs, when the clay had been properly calcined.

The clays No. 1, 6 and 11, which had been placed in the middle of the lime, received a much higher degree of heat than ordinary: for the cement No. 1 had become of a slate blue, while it is commonly of a liver colour (*d'un rouge foncé*) a good deal like the puzzalona that I used.

We see that mortar No. 1 lost much of its strength when its cement had been calcined with the lime, since, instead of 330 lbs, it supported only 99 lbs: but it is singular that Nos. 6 and 11 which had received the same degree of heat, and of which the cements were equally blue, offered a resistance much greater than the corresponding one of No. 1. The effect of soda and potash, then, has been to prevent this clay from losing a great part of its hydraulic property in consequence of a too high calcination. I thought I should obtain an opposite result, because these substances, heated with silex, form glass, and all vitrified substances make very bad puzzalonas. But these gave no trace of vitrification. I obtained a slight advantage by moistening the clay with the lye of ashes standing at 5°.

No. 12 and 13 are composed of the same clay tempered with water containing saltpetre (nitrate of potash.) This trial was made in duplicate; the cement in one being but little, and in the other, much burnt. Unfortunately the first mortar broke on being cut to the proper size; the second experiment gave a good result, like that obtained from potash. This trial was designed to ascertain whether the *aqua-fortis cement*, which has been a long time in use, merits its high reputation. This cement is an argillaceous residue, derived from distillation of nitrate of potash and clay, to extract nitric acid. This operation is performed in matrasses of stoneware or glass: the residue being a combination of ferruginous clay, potash and some alkaline salts. Being pulverized, this is what is called *aqua-fortis cement (le ciment a l'eau-forte.)* Very good results are got from it. But I presume, after what has been shown above, that the quality of the cement must be very variable, according to the composition of the clays used, and especially, as they may sometimes contain lime. It is unfortunate that the mortar No. 12, of which the clay had been moderately calcined, was broken. We see that the trial, in the case where the clay had been highly calcined, gave an average result. No. 13 only differed from No. 12, in being mixed with water more highly charged with nitrate of potash. The experiment of No. 13 having given a result sensibly superior to the No. 1 corresponding, I am induced to think that the *aqua-fortis cement* may be very good; but these experiments should be repeated.

I have stated above that the Dutch make a very good factitious trass, by calcining a clay which they extract from the bottom of the sea; I, consesequently, made No. 14, of the Holshiem clay, and salt water. If we compare No. 14 of the first column and the corresponding No. 1, we see that the result is the same. If we make the same comparison in the second column, which comprises the clays calcined with the lime, we shall remark that the clay mixed with salt water has a great superiority. We have a right to conclude then that the marine salt acted like the potash and soda—

that is to say, it prevented a high degree of calcination from depriving the clay of a great portion of its hydraulic property. It results from this, that when fabricating artificial puzzalouas near the sea, it will be proper to try whether, on mixing the clays with salt water, the bad effects of too high a heat will be prevented. This would be advantageous, because it is difficult to give an equal degree of heat to a kiln, when the temperature is high. These experiments should be made at different degrees of temperature, so as to compare results. Even in the interior of the country, it would not be expensive to add salt to the clays which are to be calcined—using a solution of common salt.

Although, according to table No. XXIII, soda, mixed with Holsheim clay, gave results a little inferior to those given by the natural clay, it was not so with potash. When the proportions were not too great, potash gave results sensibly better. This resort cannot always be had, because of the cost of the materials, and of the operation of mixing. I shall show in the sequel that it is easy to arrive at the same end in a less expensive mode, by choosing proper clays; but the observation of the effects of potash will serve to throw some light on the theory of puzzalona and trass.

The hardening of the mortars in the above table was rather slow; one of the causes was, that the experiments were made in the beginning of winter. The mortars of the first series all took about fifteen days to harden, and those of the second, twenty-five days.

I now proceed to give the results obtained with the dust of clays found near Strasburg, or carried thither for various uses.

Table No. XXIV.

No. of the mortar.	Composition of the mortars.	No. of days required to harden in water.	Weight supported before breaking.
		Days.	lbs. lbs.
1	Fat lime, sand and trass	4 to 20	231 to 510
2	Do. and Trass	3 to 16	264 to 583
3	Fat lime, sand and puzzalona	4 to 5	352 to 499
4	Do. and puzzalona	3 to 5	286 to 550
5	Do. sand, and dust of Frankfort clay	4 to 6	418 to 561
6	Do. and dust of Frankfort clay	3 to 5	422 to 578
7	Do. sand, and dust of Cologne clay	14 to 18	286 to 473
8	Do. and dust of Cologne clay	12 to 15	308 to 495
9	Do. sand, and Dust of Wissemburg clay	14 to 16	242 to 429
10	Do. and dust of Wissemburg clay	12 to 15	220 to 462
11	Do. sand, and dust of Holsheim clay	12 to 18	253 to 418
12	Do. and dust of Holsheim clay	10 to 15	275 to 440
13	Do. sand, and brick dust of Sufflenheim	16 to 20	231 to 407
14	Do. and brick dust of Sufflenheim	15 to 18	253 to 462
15	Do. sand, and dust of Kilbsheim clay	10 to 12	231 to 308
16	Do. and dust of Kilbsheim clay	8 to 10	253 to 319
17	Do. and dust of whitish bricks of Ackenheim	12 to 15	242 to 286
18	Do. and dust of red bricks of Ackenheim	25 to 35	77 to 121
19	Do. and dust of yellow bricks of Kehl	25 to 40	55 to 77
20	Do. and several kinds of dust from Depot	10 to 30	121 to 330
21	Do. and slate dust	12 to 15	319 to 451
22	Do. and " ciment de sanguine"	15	352
23	Do. and dust of yellow ochre	18	297
24	Do. and two parts of Paris cement	4	187*
25	Do. sand, and Paris cement	5	99*

*These two mortars were cracked.

Observations on the experiments of Table No. XXIV.

I have united in the above table several trials to produce hydraulic mortar with fat lime and different kinds of clay calcined, without adding anything to them. At the top of the table, I put the results obtained with trass and puzzalona. I have united all the experiments of the same kind in a single statement, because I sometimes made the mortars by taking the lime in a powder, and sometimes in paste. The proportions of sand, trass and cement, also varied. We see that it would have required a very extended table to separate all these experiments. By uniting them, as I have done, the general result may be seen.

No. 1 comprises mortars composed of various fat limes, sand and trass; several causes contributed to vary the hardening and the resistance: these are, principally, the quality of the trass; the time it was left in the air after being slaked with a little water; the proportion, and, lastly, the season of the year. This observation applies to all the following mortars. The weakest resistance of the mortars No. 1, is 231 lbs., and the strongest 510 lbs.

No. 2 comprises a series of experiments made with fat lime and trass, without sand, the resistance varied from 264 to 583 lbs.; this last result is the greatest that I obtained in all my experiments. This mortar was made in summer, with lime that had been slaked to powder for two months; it is probable that the piece of trass was of an unusually good quality.

The two series of experiments under Nos. 3 and 4, were made with fat lime, sand and puzzalona; and with lime and this last substance without sand. The puzzalona behaved like the trass. From the column showing the hardness, it might be supposed that the puzzalona mortars hardened quicker than those made of trass, but it is not so. In the instances of the trass, the mortars were made in winter as well as in summer; but with the puzzalona, the experiments were made only in summer, and during that season, the hardening was about the same for the two substances. There is, however, a light advantage in favor of puzzalona, but which cannot be estimated at more than half a day. I therefore, as stated above, regard these two substances as having given me like results.

Nos. 5 and 6, comprise experiments made with clay brought from a village called Kinglesburg, twelve leagues from Frankfort; this clay is used at Strasburg to make alum; it is preferred to the clays of the vicinity because it contains almost no iron; they calcine it for thirty-six hours before dissolving it in sulphuric acid. When this clay is in its crude state, it is blackish, owing to vegetable remains. By calcining it a little, it becomes blue; in which state it gives bad results; when strongly calcined, it becomes very white, and forms an excellent artificial puzzalona, as appears from those two numbers, 5 and 6. The analysis of this clay shows that it contains no lime, and the iron found in it in small quantity may be considered as without action. It has been an error, therefore, to attribute great influence to iron in the improvement of artificial puzzalonas: these experiments, 5 and 6, showing that a very good artificial puzzalona may be obtained from a clay containing neither iron nor lime. The analysis of this clay exhibits the alumine as existing in the proportion to the silex, of about three to five, (see page 41:) it is very greasy to the touch. Mortars made of this cement and sand, sometimes gave superior results to those in which there was no sand, and sometimes inferior, as happened with trass. The hardening was always as quick as with puzzalona; which I shall explain in the sequel.

The series Nos. 7 and 8, were made of the white clay which is brought from Cologne to Strasburg to make pipes. We see, at page 41, that it contains no lime and very little iron. The table shows that the mortar made of this cement gave very good results also, although the clay does not contain as much alumine as that from Frankfort; the hardening was slower.

The mortars Nos. 9 and 10, were composed of clay from the environs of Wissemburg; it is used at Strasburg to make common pipes. This clay contains no lime; it is, as it were, marbled with veins of red oxide of iron; the analysis indicates but little more iron than the Cologne clay, but it is because the specimen analysed was taken from between the veins. The table shows the results to have been very good.

The series Nos. 11 and 12, were made of Holsheim clay; which contains no lime, but a quantity of iron; it is of a reddish color, and quite greasy to the touch, although the proportion of alumine to the silex is hardly one to four. The dust of this clay gave very good results, but the hardening was slow.

The series Nos. 13 and 14, were made of bricks of Sufflenheim, of which the clay contains no lime, but a considerable quantity of iron; it is not very greasy, and, indeed, the alumine is only about one seventh of the silex. The cement of which I made the several mortars, were made from bricks which I reduced to powder; we see that these results are also very good.

The series Nos. 15 and 16, were made of Kolbsheim bricks; the clay of this kiln is quite greasy—containing one of alumine to four of silex. It contains a considerable quantity of iron, and more than one tenth of lime; the results were not so good as with Holsheim and Sufflenheim cements. The trials were made with brick dust; I did not make many, and it is possible that I used bricks that had been too much burned.

Nos. 17 and 18 were made of the dust of Achenheim bricks. No. 17, of the dust of a whitish brick, containing but little iron and little lime. The results were pretty good. No. 18 was made of the dust of bricks which are very red—containing much iron, and a great quantity of lime. The mortars of this cement were very bad. I am not certain whether the bricks of No. 17 were made of clay from Achenheim itself, or its environs.

The experiments under No. 19, were made with yellow bricks from Khel. I do not know the analysis of this earth, but it is a yellow ochreous earth, containing a considerable quantity of lime; we see that I got bad results, only.

The series No. 20, was made with various cements taken from the place of deposit of a contractor—being derived from a mixture of various tiles and bricks. We see that I had sometimes good results, and sometimes quite bad; as might be expected from the manner in which the cements were composed.

The experiments under No. 21, were made of slates from the neighborhood of Mayence. I do not know the analysis, but being assured that they contain little or no lime, I calcined them highly, and they gave me a very good cement. I had occasion to notice that, to obtain a good result, it was necessary to calcine these slates until they began to take a light red color on cooling, which requires quite a high heat. I am surprised that in the experiments of Mr. Gratien, senior, at Cherbough, better results were not obtained; this appears to me to have been owing to the degree of burning, which they did not sufficiently vary, to ascertain the best. I presume that good cements could be made of the tender strata found near the surface of the slate quarries, and which are too tender to be formed into slates. They will be easier to reduce to powder after calcination.

No. 22 was made of a cement obtained from a substance known under the name of "*sanguine;*" the resistance of this mortar was quite good.

Mortar No. 23 was made of cement resulting from the calcination of a clay known by the name of yellow ochre; the result was less than that of the preceding mortar. It appears to me that the yellow ochreous clays are not so good as others for the production of artificial puzzalonas; it is possible it may be owing to the oxide of iron being found therein in combination with the silex, as shown by Berzelius.

In the *Annales de Chimie* of 1824, it is stated that in 1823, Mr. Saint Leger made factitious puzzalona at Paris from the clay of Passy and Meudon, in the proportion of three parts of these clays to one of lime slaked and measured in paste. In 1825, I made two mortars of some cement given me by Mr. Saint Leger. Mortar No. 24 is an experiment therewith; it was made of one part of fat lime measured in paste, mixed with two parts of this cement: this mortar hardened promptly. At the end of a year, I submitted it to rupture, with the others; but it was cracked, and supported only 187 lbs.

No. 25, was made of the same lime, of sand, and of cement, in equal parts; this mortar hardens promptly; but it, also, was cracked, and bore only the light weight of 99 lbs. We shall see, in the second section, that I made of this cement a mortar which was exposed in the air for one year, and that it had so little consistence, that it crumbled easily in the fingers.

The bad results that I obtained from the cements of Mr. Saint Leger seem to be due to the quantity of lime which they mix with the clay in making the cement. I said in my memoir of 1822, of which an extract is contained in the Moniteur of January 22, 1823. "The substance of which it is most important to observe the proportions, is lime. If the argillaceous earth used contains a tenth, or more, of lime, and it be heated to the degree necessary to burn bricks properly, the trass obtained will be very bad; if this earth be heated to the degree employed to burn those bricks which are called *light burned bricks*, the trass will be of a mediocre quality only, but may be used in works not requiring prompt induration. It appears that a very small quantity of lime, as four or five per cent, in the clayey earths, far from injuring the quality of the puzzalona or trass, brings, on the contrary, the clay to that condition that the cement produced will cause the mortar to harden very promptly, and at the same time impart to it a high degree of force. When there is no lime in clay, a higher burning is required and the hardening is rather slower."

In 1822, therefore, I regarded lime as a substance to which the greatest attention should be paid, when it was found to be a natural constituent of the clays to be turned into puzzalonas; but that I considered it rather to be avoided than sought after; observing, nevertheless, that a small percentage of this substance was rather useful than injurious, with proper care in managing the heat. The expense of mixing lime with clays that are to be converted into puzzalonas, should, therefore, be avoided.

On mixing fat lime slaked to paste, with clay, I have observed a singular phenomenon, for which I have not been able to account: it is this, if clay be diffused through water, till we bring it to the consistence of clear sirup, and, after having brought the lime to the same state, the two mortars be mixed together, as soon as the mixture is made, it becomes so thick that it will be difficult to continue the operation without adding a considerable quantity of water. I do not know to what this is owing.

The results of experiments 18, 19 and 20, show how dangerous it would be to use, without examination, the first cements encountered. I will cite an example in point. When Marshal Vauban built the citadel of Strasburg, three great casemates were constructed in each of the two bastions which lie on the town side. The casemates of the right bastion are very dry, and they are often used as powder magazines. The casemates on the left were, on the contrary, very wet; the water filtered, every where, through the arches; all the casemates had caps of cement, but those of the right had been made of good, and those of the left, of bad cement. In 1808, they were obliged to make the caps of the casemates on the left anew. On breaking up the old caps, it appeared that they had been made of cement, (brick dust?) but that moisture had penetrated for a long time, and that several parts had scaled off. In the report on the reconstruction, it is said, "We followed vigorously, in the execution of this work, the method indicated by Mr. Fleuret. The cement was made under the supervision of a workman employed by him, and it was put on by masons practised in this kind of work. The thickness of the cap was two and four-tenth inches, and was composed of three layers of cement, applied successively with the trowel, and compacted by ramming. The last course was rammed, and afterwards polished off with a stone, until the cement had acquired such hardness as to receive no further impression." (Report of Captain Gleizes of the Engineers, January 30, 1808.)

We see that it was no want of precautions that caused the work to fail. Notwithstanding these precautions, the water, after ten years, filtered through every part of these arches, and they were again, necessarily, remade. On demolishing them a second time, it was observed that several portions of the three layers of mortar that had been successively placed to form the caps, had no connexion with each other. I think it is a great fault to make the caps of arches in successive layers; they should, in my opinion, be made of a single one, let the thickness be what it may. Mr. Fleuret attaches great importance to beating mortars well, and we shall see further on, that this is also an error. The caps at Strasburg failed the second time because they used fat lime, and brick dust? taken at hazard; it was found to have no hydraulic property, and the mortar had no consistence. Mr. Fleuret succeeded very well in making factitious stones, and water pipes, when he used the Metz lime; but a contractor at Phalsbourg who attempted to apply this process to the construction of the military fountain—using the materials of the country, failed in his work, and was ruined. At Landau, also, the caps of arches made according to the process of Mr. Fleuret, failed. The caps of the above casemates of Strasburg were constructed in 1819, with good materials: they succeeded well, and the casemates have become very dry. I thought it my duty to give these details to show how important it is not to use cements without a previous trial, because it is always an expensive substance, and if badly chosen, it may happen that the result is no better than if so much sand had been used instead thereof.

I am now about to state how I detected an important action exercised by the air in perfecting artificial puzzalonas. We may remark that all the experiments made with Frankfort clay, hardened very quickly, and gave great resistance. I took these clays from a certain furnace where they had been calcined for the purpose of making alum. Having, one day, burnt in a lime kiln, some bricks made of this clay, I was surprised to see that the hardening was much slower, although the degree of heat had been about the proper degree, as was easy to perceive by the colour. Examining the construction of the two furnaces, I remarked that the bricks were burnt by being placed above the lime; that above the bricks tiles were placed, and, lastly, above all, pieces of burnt clay covered with fragments in such a way as to leave openings only in certain places, thereby directing currents of air into certain parts only of the kiln. It resulted from this arrangement, made with a view to save as much heat as possible, that only certain bricks and tiles were exposed, during calcination, to a current of air. I will remark, that the dust of these bricks always caused the mortars to harden more promptly than the others. On the other hand, I noticed that the hearth of the alum furnace was pierced with many holes, which caused a strong current of air throughout all the mass of clay submitted to calcination. Pl. I, Fig. 2, gives a plan and section of this furnace. The calcination is effected by wood placed in the lower arches. It then occurred to me that the reason why I obtained good results with this clay, and especially a rapid induration, might be, that at a high temperature the hydrate of alumine might absorb oxygen. I was led to this supposition because I had ascertained, as stated page 81, that the hydrate of lime absorbed oxygen. I calcined a little clay in a current of air, and also a little in a close vessel, and I ascertained that the alumine that had been calcined in a current of air dissolved in sulphuric acid more easily than the other. This was a presumption for my hypothesis, but no proof. I had, likewise, heated in these two ways, a little alumine extracted from alum, and had made mortars by mixing it with lime from white marble. The mortar made of alumine burned in a current of air appeared to me to take consistence sooner than the other; but, after some time, both were equally soft, and at the end of a year had no consistence. This experiment seems to prove that alumine alone will not form puzzalona, and that it requires to be mixed with a certain quantity of silex; this result is besides in accordance with table No. XXII, in which we see that by taking away from clay too much sand, the energy of the cement was diminished, and that it was augmented on adding very fine siliceous sand. The alumine which I used having already been calcined and dissolved in sulphuric acid, to form alum, it is possible that this had taken from it the property of forming puzzalona, and the experiment should have been made with natural alumine; but this substance is very rare, and I had none at command. After these first essays, I made the last four experiments of table No. XX. We have seen that the hardening was very prompt; which was owing, as I said in speaking of those experiments, to the bricks being exposed to a current of air during the calcination. The bad mortar—the cement having been properly burned, gave a good resistance, and at the same time a very prompt induration. I then made the following experiments: I took Holsheim clay, of which I made two bricks; one of these bricks was of the natural clay, the other was of the natural clay mixed with 0.02 of lime in paste. I calcined these two bricks in a lime kiln, placing them where, as it seemed to me, they would be but little exposed to the current of air. I, at the same time, made balls of the size of a nut, of the same Holsheim clay, both in its natural state, and also mixed with 0.02 of lime, and afterward calcined these two kinds of balls in a reverberatory furnace, keeping them red during six hours, in a hessian crucible having a hole in the bottom. These last clays were, therefore, calcined in a current of air, and the former, not. The following results were obtained. The mortar of the natural clay heated in the lime kiln did not harden till the end of thirty days, and supported a weight of 385 lbs. before breaking; that which was made of the same clay mixed with 0.02 of lime, hardened in seventeen days, and broke under a weight of 352 lbs. The mortar made of the natural clay that had been heated for six hours in a current of air, hardened in five days; but it broke under a weight of 330 lbs. Lastly, the mortar made of the clay which contained 0.02 of lime, and which was, also, heated for the same time in a current of air, hardened in three days; but this mortar was cracked, and broke under a weight of 198 lbs. These experiments were made in the beginning of 1825.

Having communicated these results to Mr. Bergère, *chef de bataillon*, of the engineers, he informed me that Mr. Raucourt, engineer of roads and bridges, had published at Petersburg, in 1822, a memoir in which he mentioned the influence of air on the calcination of clays that are to be transformed into puzzalonas. I procured this work, and quote the following remarks from page 130. "I had thought for a long time that the degree of calcination could not be the only cause of the superior qualities that argillaceous earths acquire by a few minutes' torrefaction: if it were otherwise, slightly burned bricks would furnish excellent puzzalonas, which is far from being the case, and several essays made with pounded bricks, burnt with various degrees of intensity, gave me no result comparable to that given by clay exposed on a red hot plate.

"It was thence inferred that the contact of air is necessary to modify, in the most favorable manner, the oxides which the earths contain, so that they may form good hydraulic combinations with lime. To assure myself more completely, I made direct experiments which fully confirmed this induction, and which led me to more particular researches than had before been made on factitious hydraulic lime."

The experiments of table No. XVI show, in opposition to the opinion of Mr. Raucourt, that lightly burned bricks may furnish very good puzzalonas, when they contain lime, and the burning has been properly managed. This engineer asserts positively, in this quotation, the necessity of contact of air to modify the clays advantageously; but he reports none of the experiments that he announces as having made.

At page 135 of his memoir he says:

"If it be true, as is said, that the earths are metallic oxides, one might be led to think that they have need of a certain degree of burning in contact with the air, to form with lime, and the concurrence of water, insoluble compounds; and as several chemists have already shown that the presence of silex in the state of gelly will contribute to render a fat lime hydraulic, that it is the same with the oxides of iron and magnesia; that Mr. Vicat, by his transformations with clay, proves that alumine, also, might enjoy this property; that if the very hydraulic lime I H (Art. 163) be observed, it will be allowed that magnesia must necessarily fulfil analogous functions; one would be almost convinced that all the metallic oxides, properly prepared with fire, would form, with lime, combinations susceptible of hardening in water."

There are many errors in this passage; for it is demonstrated that iron and manganese act no part in hydraulic limes; and what Mr. Raucourt says in this particular, proves that he has not consulted experience. Nothing has proved, as yet, that alumine, or magnesia, possesses the property of forming hydraulic lime. (The lime cited art. 163, contains clay.) Lastly, nothing is more doubtful than such properties as Mr. Raucourt has attributed to almost all metallic oxides. In a matter so delicate as this, the imagination must not get in advance of facts.

As Mr. Raucourt has not given the experiments which led him to the opinion that the air acts an important part in perfecting artificial puzzalonas, I am obliged to draw my conclusions from the facts presented in my preceding table, and principally from the last four experiments reported in page 85. There are two things to consider in artificial puzzalona; the first, is the promptitude of induration of the mortars whereof they form part; the second, is the resistance of these mortars. The experiments at the end of table No. XX, the observations I made on Nos. 5 and 6, of table No. XXIV, and the few experiments cited in page 85, prove that when these clays are calcined in a current of air, they harden much the more promptly. But is the resistance of the mortars greater, also? I cannot affirm positively that it is.

We see, for example, in the four experiments cited, that the case of the most prompt hardening, coincides with the weakest resistance; but we ought not to conclude from thence, in a positive manner, that the calcination in a current of air diminishes the resistance at the same time that it increases the promptitude to harden; because the result obtained may have depended on some other cause—as, for instance, the degree of calcination. What induces me to think that calcination of clays in a current of air, far from diminishing the resistance of mortars, will, on the contrary, augment it, is, that all the clays Nos. 5 and 6, of table No. XXIV, having been heated in this manner, the hardening was very prompt, at the same time that the resistances were very great. I cannot positively affirm that this last effect will follow, but I think it probable. I have not had time to make the direct experiments that I intended, in order to clear up this point.

In a note printed by me in 1825, I stated that I was induced to think that at an elevated temperature, the alumine contained in clays absorbed oxygen, and that this absorption rendered cements more proper to combine with fat lime in the moist way. Mr. Vicat is of a different opinion. He inserted a note in the *Annales de Chimie*, of 1827, Vol. XXXIV, wherein he says that he calcined, for half an hour, pulverised clay in close vessels, and that he heated the same quantity, during five minutes, on a metallic plate kept at a common red heat. After cooling, the substances were weighed, and were found to weigh nearly the same. Mr. Vicat concludes from the small differences found between the weights of clays calcined in close vessels, and those calcined in the air, that there is, incontestably, no absorption.

I will remark, that nothing can be concluded from this experiment. A part of the clay was calcined during half an hour, and the other part during five minutes only; the quantities of water lost by these two portions could not, therefore, have been the same, since they were not equally heated. It is, besides, possible that a small quantity of oxygen, difficult to appreciate with a balance, might suffice to give new properties to the clay. To know whether alumine absorbs oxygen, it would be necessary to heat it highly in a tube not susceptible of oxidation, and to pass, during the calcination, at different times, a given volume of oxygen gas, over the incandescent alumine, and, afterward, to measure the volume of gas, in order to ascertain whether it had been diminished. I had not under my control the means necessary for making this experiment; the observation that I made, that alumine calcined in a current of air, dissolved more easily in sulphuric acid than when calcined in a close vessel, led me to think there was an absorption of oxygen, but it is no proof; I offer it as a presumption only.

Several Engineers have proclaimed the good results obtained with ashes derived from the combustion of coal in furnaces, or lime kilns; others on the contrary, have denied the effect of this substance. With this question, it is the same, I am satisfied, as with the question whether dust of tiles or bricks, much, or little burned, should be taken. The good results of the Tournay ashes* have been known for a long time, and are contested by no one. Having been employed at Lille, in 1815 and 1816, I had an opportunity of knowing the good effects. But when I wished to use, in the same way, the coal ashes at Strasburg, I could not obtain a good result. I made mortars composed of one part of fat lime measured in paste, and two parts of coal ashes: after an immersion of a year, these mortars were as soft as if made of sand. These opposite effects surprised me, and on examining different coals and their analyses, I saw that several of them contained quite a quantity of clay, while others contained little or none. But coals are generally burned on a grate: the clay they contain is thus calcined in a current of air; and it is the mixture of this clay with a little iron, constituting the residue, that is used, when we take these ashes: we see, therefore, that it is a real puzzalona that they have been making, for a long time, without knowing it. Should the coal contain no clay, or should the clay be mixed with too much lime; in the first case no result will be got; and in the second, if the calcination has been too high, the ashes will possess but an indifferent quality.

I think Mr. Sganzin is wrong when he says in his *cours de construction*, page 32, "Experience teaches that the ashes of all coals which have served for the calcination of lime, will form a mortar hardening promptly in water." We know that when lime is calcined with coal, the ashes of the combustible is mixed with a considerable quantity of particles of lime. Although the coal should contain no clay, if the lime calcined be very hydraulic, I conceive that a mortar of fat lime and these ashes would harden in water; but the result would be due to the presence of the hydraulic lime; I think that no result would be obtained if, with such coal, the calcination were of fat lime.

In 1826, I was charged with the inspection of several places along the Straits of Calais. Much coal is used in these departments. At Boulogne where the forts of the sea coast were to be repaired, I requested Capt. Le Marchand of the Engineers, to make some experiments with cements and the coal ashes of the neighbourhood, because the use of the Boulogne pebbles, before mentioned, was very expensive, and it was difficult to obtain them in quantity. This Engineer took great pains in his researches, and informed me that he had obtained good results with some cements, and especially with the ashes got from the coal burned in several manufactures in Boulogne. He procured the analysis of this coal, which is composed of the following substances; combustible matter, 96.62; alumine, 2.00; silex and iron, 1.38. Therefore the ashes he used were nothing else than a very aluminous clay, which contained no lime, and which had been calcined in a current of air during the combustion of the coal, and it is not astonishing that it gave very good mortar. The cinders of forges, another residue of the combustion of coal, may be assimilated to ashes: there are some that give very good, and others that yield no results: neither should, in any case,

*Rondelet, in his *art de batie* thus describes this substance. "This powder is made of half burned fragments of a very hard blue lime-stone. These fragments fall, during the burning, through the grate of the lime kilns, and are mixed with the ashes of the coal. The Tournay ashes are considered equal to the Dutch trass, and are used for the same purposes." Tr.

be employed without our being assured of their quality. To know if they may be used with advantage, the practical process for distinguishing good cements from those that have no hydraulic property, that I will soon point out, should be followed.

I commenced my experiments on artificial puzzalonas in 1821; and the first operation I performed was to see whether I could make puzzalona and trass anew out of their constituents. I accordingly took the substances contained in trass and puzzalona, according to the old analysis which is given in p. 53; with these I made a paste with water; afterward, I calcined the mixture at a low red heat for six hours; and, lastly, reduced it to very fine powder. As I had no natural alumine at my command, and as I doubted the efficacy of that to be obtained from the decomposition of alum, I took the Cologne pipe clay, washed it several times with a great deal of water, and decanted, to separate the greater part of the sand from the alumine. I assured myself, by calcining a small portion of this earth, and dissolving it in sulphuric acid, that it contained hardly any silex. This is the substance to which I added the other matters in the proportions given in the old analysis. We see then that, by this operation, my artificial trass and puzzalona had a little more silex than the natural productions, by the quantity retained in the aluminous earth; but this augmentation of silex was the same for both mixtures. I made two mortars by taking one part of Obernai lime, and two parts of each of these compounds: the mortar of the factitious trass hardened in four days, and broke under the weight of 385 lbs: that made of the artificial puzzalona hardened in three days and supported 477 lbs. before breaking. The lime was the same in both experiments: all other circumstances were alike: wherefore we must attribute the superiority of the artificial puzzalona over the artificial trass, to the clay of the first mixture containing much more alumine than the second. I was wrong in using hydraulic lime: I should have used fat lime, which I, afterward, always used when I wished to determine the quality of puzzalonas or other analagous substances. This experiment, and those which were made of the very aluminous clays of Frankfort and Cologne, prove that results, exactly like those furnished by natural puzzalona, are obtained, by suitably calcining greasy clays.

I was not able to determine the proportion in which the silex and alumine should exist to give the best results; but I am led to think that the alumine should equal, at least, a third of the silex. We have seen, however, that the Sufflenheim clay, which contains seven parts of silex to one of alumine, sometimes produced very good cements; but it is probable the best were obtained with portions of clays more aluminous than the others. The results contained in table No. XXII support this opinion. It is true we might be inclined to infer the contrary from the new analysis of trass and puzzalona made by Mr. Berthier, and given in p. 53. The proportion of alumine is about the same in Trass and Puzzalona, according to Mr. Berthier, and is much smaller than according to the older analysis: but the analysis of a single specimen must not fix the proportions of a substance which gives, as we have seen, very various results; and every thing leads to the belief that the several pieces of trass and puzzalona vary much in their composition. It is possible that the specimens of trass and puzzalona that I sent to Mr. Berthier, were possessed of a high degree of energy, although containing but little alumine, by reason of the potash they contained; for this substance augments, in a sensible manner, the energy of puzzalonas, as we have seen in the experiments of table No. XXIII. But the good results obtained from the calcination of greasy clays, prove that cements without potash, may be made to be quite equal to trass and puzzalona.

The experiments above show that, with artificial puzzalona and fat lime I have obtained mortars much superior to those made with artificial, or even natural, hydraulic lime, and sand. Although I happened, with some pieces of Obernai lime, to obtain results approaching those afforded by artificial puzzalona, such instances are rare; and, in cases like these, it is the general bearing of the facts that we are to regard. I announced these results in a little pamphlet published in 1824, and I stated, moreover, that there would accrue a sensible economy. Mr. Vicat, in a criticism on this pamphlet has endeavoured to prove the contrary; but it will not be difficult to show that he was deceived in his calculations. This Engineer says "The objection of Mr. Treussart to the high price of artificial limes is without foundation. In fact the trass mortars are as follows:

For two cubic metres of trass (70.68 cub. feet) a $5.22½   . $10.45
For one cub. metre (35.34 cub. ft.) of fat lime in paste   .   .   2.28
<hr>
$12..73

"The three cubic metres of materials are reduced by the mixture to 2.30m; it follows that the cubic metre costs $5.53 (35.34 cub. ft. cost $5.53 equal $0.16 per cub. foot.)

On the other hand to make a cubic metre of hydraulic lime
    mortar, requires 0.90m of common sand a $0.28⅓ $0.26
0.43m of hydraulic lime in stiff paste, which at the mean price
    will cost (one foot cost $0.34)   .   .   5.27
<hr>
$5.53

The prices then will be exactly the same, since in each case it is found to be $5.53: but let us see if the basis of this calculation is exact. I will first remark, what I did not neglect to state in my pamphlet of 1824, namely that the mortars of fat lime, sand and trass, gave me results which were often superior to those in which there was trass without sand; and that it was the same with mortars made of puzzalona. We may satisfy ourselves by table No. XIII that when the mortars of trass and puzzalona, alone, were superior to those containing sand, the advantage was not sufficient to lead to a preference of the former. I obtained a like result with artificial puzzalona of table No. XXIV. It is, therefore, an error of Mr. Vicat's to compare the price of mortars made of artificial hydraulic lime, with that made of fat lime and trass without sand: it is necessary to compare it with mortar made of lime, sand and trass. If the first calculation, above, be thus rectified, the price of $10.45, given by two cubic metres of trass at $5.22½, will be reduced to $5.51, resulting from one cub. metre of sand at $0.28⅓, and one cub. metre of trass at $5.22½: consequently the cubic metre of mortar composed of fat lime, sand and trass, will amount to $3.39 = $0.10 per cub. foot, only, instead of $5.53. The objection that I made, therefore, is not, as Mr. Vicat thought, without foundation. I feel bound to state that the prices I have given, using the data established by Mr. Vicat, appear to me to be too low for the principal places in France; but I was obliged to use the elements he had employed.

It is possible that in countries where chalk is abundant it will not cost more to make hydraulic mortar with artificial hydraulic lime and sand, than with fat lime, sand and factitious trass: but in many countries chalk is not to be procured; and then it will be necessary to mix fat lime with clay, and to give a second burning for the mixtures; which will cause embarrassment, and an augmentation of expense. I am convinced that, in such cases, there will generally be economy in making hydraulic mortar at once of fat lime, sand and artificial trass: and besides the relation of the resistance of these two kinds of mortar, is no important consideration. If we compare the results obtained in all the preceding tables, we shall see that the mortars made of sand and hydraulic lime, whether natural or artificial, afford an average resistance hardly amounting to 220 lbs., while it is 352 lbs. for the mortars made of fat lime, sand and natural or artificial trass. To compare the expense justly, therefore, it would be necessary to lessen the preparation of trass, substituting sand, until we arrived at an equal resistance.

I must, besides, observe that we are much more certain to obtain uniform results with hydraulic mortars, composed of fat lime, sand and factitious trass, than with those that can be made of artificial, or natural hydraulic lime, and sand only. We have seen, in fact, that hydraulic limes deteriorate when a little too highly calcined; it is necessary to keep them carefully from the rain; and they, in general, lose a great part of their hydraulic property, unless used soon after leaving the kiln; which often occasions embarrassment. With fat lime and factitious trass, all these difficulties are avoided; because the lime loses nothing by being a little more calcined than necessary. It is not necessary to use it immediately, nor to take any troublesome precautions. As to factitious trass, once prepared, it needs no particular care: for neither the influence of the air, nor humidity, will deprive it of any of its properties.

It results from what I have said that, in a country where there are good natural hydraulic limes, they should be used in preference to fat lime, which requires, always, to be mixed with natural or artificial trass, for constructions in water or in damp places. There will be economy, and no bad results to fear, in taking the precautions I have pointed out. When, however, works demanding great care, are to be made, such as floors of Locks, caps of Arches, &c., I think it will be proper to add to the mortar a little natural or artificial trass. The proportion to be added depends on the quality of the hydraulic lime and of the trass. If both are of good quality, and if it be known, for example, that the lime will bear two and a half parts of sand, then the mortar may be composed of one part of this lime, two parts of sand, and half a part of factitious trass. This small quantity of trass will not much augment the expense, and will always correct the bad effects resulting from portions of the lime having been too much burned, or impaired by exposure to the air. The further the hydraulic limes are from the qualities I have above supposed, the greater should be the proportions of natural or artificial trass.

The question, however, is, to know what should be done in a country where there is no hydraulic lime, or where it is of an inferior quality. It is on this point that I differ entirely from Mr. Vicat. This engineer contends that it is best to make factitious hydraulic cement by the process he points out; while I think there will, in general, be more economy, and better and more uniform results, by making hydraulic mortars at once from fat lime, sand, and artificial trass. It appears to me that the general bearing of the very numerous experiments I have presented, leaves no room to doubt as to this matter.

I will add, that, from time immemorial, in countries affording natural hydraulic limes, they have been used with great advantage. Wherever they were not to be had, hydraulic mortars were made, directly, of fat lime and cement. I have, several times, had occasion to demolish works in water, of which the mortars had been made in this manner. It appears then, that, in fact, I only propose to continue a method long in use, with this difference, that in lieu of using every kind of cement indiscriminately, I give the means of distinguishing the good from the bad, and of making such as will give results equal to those furnished by natural puzzalona or trass.

To ascertain which are proper cements to produce good hydraulic mortars, on being mixed with fat lime, the following means may be used. From a neighbouring brick kiln three bricks should be taken, one of which should be a lightly burned brick; another should be chosen from those which are considered to be burned in the best manner; and a third from those too much burned, but not vitrified in any degree. The brickmakers know well how to distinguish them by the sound and the colour. A fragment of each of these bricks should be separately reduced to a very fine powder, and passed through a very fine wire seive. The finer the dust, the better; in taking it between the fingers no grains should be felt, and it should be soft to the touch. Fat lime which has been reduced to paste for some time, should then be made into mortar with one of these cements—using one part of lime in paste, to two parts of cement. They must be well mixed together, adding the water, necessary to produce a pasty state. The mortar should then be placed in the bottom of a tumbler. If the mortar be stiff, the tumbler may at once be filled with water; if, on the other hand, the mortar has been made rather thin (which facilitates the mixing) it should he left long enough in the air to assume some consistence before the glass be filled. The same course should be followed with the two other cements, and all the glasses must be ticketed. It is necessary to add, in making the several mortars, such quantities of water as will bring all to the same consistence, nearly. After two or three days, the mortars should be touched lightly with the fingers, to ascertain whether they have begun to harden; and when this happens, they must be examined every day, noting that which hardens first, and the time at which each arrived at that degree of induration that on pressing it strongly with the thumb no impression was made. In order to judge more accurately of this state, the turbid water must be thrown off, and the surface of the mortar, which is always covered with a little semi-fluid matter, must be lightly cleaned with a rag. If the mortar is not yet hard enough to resist the thumb when strongly pressed, it must be again covered with water for subsequent examination. Should there be several brick yards at hand, using different clays, the same process should be applied to the brick dust from each. It will be useless to try dust from tiles, provided the clay is the same as that used for bricks, because the result would be substantially the same.

We have seen that the dust of bricks which have been burned in a current of air, hardened in the space of three or four days, while the dust of bricks burned out of a current of air, has generally taken from ten to twenty days, and sometimes even thirty days to harden, and has, nevertheless, made good mortars. I have also made the remark, that mortars of the hydraulic limes which harden very quickly, did not give great resistances; but those made of cements which have caused fat lime to harden promptly, have always given good mortars. We ought, therefore, to prefer those cements which cause fat lime to harden promptly. If any cement, after fifteen or twenty days, gives to fat lime only a weak consistence, it should not be employed.

In experimenting with the ashes and cinders of forges, the same process should be followed. If, of these substances, after a month's immersion, any should impart to fat lime but a feeble consistence, or remain entirely soft—in neither case should it be employed.

By means of a very simple chemical process, it may be ascertained before hand, whether bricks but little, or highly, burned, should be taken. Take a little of the crude clay, or a little of the brick dust, put it in a glass and pour over it a little diluted nitric or muriatic acid, or even strong vinegar; should there be no effervescence, it is proof that the bricks should be highly calcined to give good cement. Should there be considerable effervescence, it is because the clay contains a notable quantity of carbonate of lime. To determine nearly the quantity of lime, a little of the clay, having been dried in a gentle heat, must be weighed; it must then be diffused through a small quantity of water, and muriatic acid be poured on, little by little, as long as there is any effervescence; it should then be filtered, or gently decanted, the residue washed in a large quantity of water and again decanted. The residue being then dried in the same gentle heat as at first, must be again weighed; if the weight be less by one tenth, than at first, it is a proof that the clay contained that quantity, about, of carbonate of lime, which has been dissolved out by the acid. In this case bricks but lightly burned must be taken; and so much the less burned as the loss of the clay, by the acid, shall have been the greater. If the clay lose only four or five per cent. of its weight, the bricks which are called " well burned bricks," should be preferred. In addition to the chemical trial just described, it will always be proper to make the trial first explained—that being the most certain.

With brick dust, we may easily obtain mortars which, according to my mode of determining tenacity, will support from 220 lbs. to 330 lbs. before breaking, if composed of equal parts of lime, sand and brick dust. This force is sufficient for gross masonry: but, for important works, such as the floors of locks, foundations of dikes and dams, caps of arches, and for factitious stones, of which I shall speak in the sequel, it is necessary to have cements that will give mortars capable of supporting from 330 lbs. to 440 lbs.

To obtain cements or puzzalonas of the strength just mentioned, we proceed in the following manner. We choose clays soft to the touch, taking, in preference, those of which earthen ware, stone ware, delft ware and tobacco pipes are made, ascertaining, by the above chemical trials, whether there be any lime, and if so, the quantity. Of these clays we make balls of the size of an egg, which we calcine in a reverberatory furnace, heating gently at first, and, after about one hour, pushing the fire so as to keep the balls constantly at a low red heat; the balls, of which there will be ten or twelve, being placed within a large Hessian crucible having a hole in its bottom. To avoid exposing these clays to be struck by a current of cold air, as they would be if put on the bottom of the crucible, a piece of slate perforated with many small holes should be put across the middle of the crucible, (which is commonly of a conical form, narrowest at the bottom:) by this means the balls of clay will be in the centre of heat, and will be, during the calcination, always in contact with a current of atmospheric air. When the balls have been burned for three or four hours, according to the quantity of lime contained in them, one of these balls will be taken out, and

marked with the number of hours it has been under calcination; at the end
of every succeeding hour another ball will be withdrawn and marked in
like manner. All the balls being withdrawn, they will be reduced to fine
powder, and a mortar will be made of each, exactly in the same way as
was pointed out for mortars made of brick-dust. We shall ascertain, in
this way, the time of burning required by the clay, to give to fat lime the
most prompt induration, and we shall have an idea of the difficulty to be
overcome in reducing the cement to powder. To operate on a large scale
proceed as follows.

In countries where wood only is to be burned, a furnace may be made
like that in the plate I, Fig. 2. If the clay to be used be greasy, the expense
of tempering it may be saved. It will be cut from the bank into pieces, of
the form and dimensions of common bricks. These will be dried in the
air like bricks, and then be placed on their edges on the hearth of the furnace, laying them obliquely with respect to its axis, and at a little distance
asunder; the second layer will be placed on the first, crossing them. A
fire will then be made in the two arches below the hearth, gentle at first,
and gradually increased. It is apparent that the clay will, in this way, be
calcined in a current of air, through the holes in the hearth. These bricks
will be heated less intensely than the balls that were in the reverberatory
furnace, and it will therefore be requisite to leave them exposed to the fire
for a longer period. After twelve or eighteen hours calcination, one brick
will be withdrawn. If the clay is coloured with iron, the colour will now be
compared with the colour of that specimen of the first trial which gave the
most prompt induration to fat lime. If the colours are exactly alike, it is a
proof that the clays in the furnace have received sufficient calcination, and
the fire will be stopped; but if the colours are different, the heat will be
continued, and another comparison will be made, after another lapse of
time; and so on until a colour is obtained which indicates the proper degree
of burning.

If the clay contain little or no iron, or if the furnace trial showed that
the colour varied but little with considerable variations in the intensity of
heat, then, having withdrawn, successively, several bricks, reduce them to
fine powder, and make several mortars by mixing this powder with fat lime
—noting the time required to harden, and taking all the precautions directed for the proof essay. In the first batches burned on a large scale,
considerable pains will undoubtedly be required to determine the time requisite for the best degree of calcination; but when this point is once ascertained, there will be no longer any difficulty, and the operation may be
confided to ordinary workmen.

In countries where the fuel must be coal or peat, it will be preferable to
use a conical kiln for burning the clay. I will observe here, that Mr. Chaptal in calcining the clays of the south, in a conical kiln, placed them, by
accident it appears, in the most advantageous position; that is to say, they
were so placed as to cause them to be calcined in a current of atmospheric
air. If this celebrated chemist had noticed the great action that lime exercises
on the calcination of clays; and that it is necessary to heat but little when
the clay contains as much as one tenth, and to heat much when it contains
little or no lime; he would have completely resolved the important question of the perfection of artificial puzzalonas. In many of the northern Departments, conical furnaces are used for burning lime. Plate I, Fig. 3, represents one of those furnaces which I saw in the neighborhood of Paris. The
following is the mode to be adapted in burning clays therein. Instead of

-the form of bricks, the clay will be cut from the bank with a shovel, into nearly cubical pieces. A workman will then with his hands, flatten the angles, giving to each piece a rounded form of the size of an apple, which will not require much labour. These balls will be left to dry in the air. Preparatory to placing the balls in the kiln, an arch of dry stone masonry, will be turned from the centre pier to the sides of the kiln, at the height of the top of the four doors. The centre pier serves, besides, to direct the contents of the kiln towards the doors. The dry stone arch will be so constructed as to leave passages for the air. A rather thick layer of coal or turf will be put upon the arch, and on this a layer of balls of clay, thus filling the kiln with successive layers of fuel and balls of clay. When the kiln is two-thirds full, the arches will be filled with fuel. The fire being lighted at the four openings, will gain the whole interior of the kiln, and the clays will be thus calcined in a current of air. After some time—demolishing a portion of the dry stone arch, a few balls of clay will be withdrawn, with which the different essays that I have pointed out, in speaking of the other furnace, will be made. The dry stone arch will permit the fuel to be renewed under the clay, until the balls of clay near the bottom, and which are the least burned, have received the requisite calcination. In proportion as the combustible is consumed, the mass of balls of clay will subside, and new layers of balls and of fuel will be supplied above. When the trials have shown the clay below to be sufficiently burned, the arch will be taken out. The lower balls will fall towards the openings, and will be removed with tongs. The others will descend, also, as the fuel burns away. As fast as clay is withdrawn from below, fuel and clay will be added above, so as to make the burning continual. If some balls are found not sufficiently burned, they will be put aside, and when enough are collected, will be reburned by being mixed with less fuel. A kiln built expressly for making puzzalona, might be of smaller dimensions than that represented in Fig. 3. Perhaps two openings would suffice; replacing in this case the pier in the middle by a wall of the same height, sloping both ways, and presenting an arch towards each of the openings.* This kind of kiln would be of great advantage in the calcination of hydraulic lime, as it would supply fresh quick lime during all the season of operation—an important object, as we have seen by preceding experiments. There would also be a more uniform burning than in the kilns ordinarily constructed in Alsace, where the lime is burned in a very unequal manner. I am persuaded that in places where coal can be procured at a moderate price, great advantages may be derived from conical furnaces; which will serve, at the same time, for the calcination of hydraulic lime, and of clays of which it is designed to make artificial puzzalona.

* In situations where calcined clay is hard to pulverize, and there is no machinery to apply to this object, the crude clay should be dried in the air, and being reduced to powder, should be burned in a reverberatory furnace of which the hearth is laid at the greatest angle that the clay dust will lie without sliding. On this inclined hearth a layer of dry powder will be placed of the thickness of six to eight inches. The front of the furnace should have a horizontal portion, on which to make a fire of wood. The inclination of the hearth will cause the heat and flame in passing upward towards a chimney in the part opposite to the fire, to heat the powdered clay. From time to time, the heat will be suspended in order to stir the clay with a rake. In this way it will be calcined in a current of air, and the operation of pulverising the cement, which is both tedious and expensive, when there is at command no proper machinery worked by water, will be avoided. AU.

In countries where there is neither coal nor turf, it seems to me that the conical furnace might still be used for calcining clays. It will suffice to take dry wood, and in preference round sticks, which should be cut into lengths of four inches: these little pieces should be mixed with the clay balls, and the operation of burning should be like that with coal. I do not doubt that a good result would be obtained.

Clays which are greasy to the touch are easily formed into balls, or shaped like bricks, without any preparation; but it is possible, it may be necessary to temper such clay as is used in brick making, this being generally more meagre.

When very greasy clays, containing no lime, are used, it will sometimes be difficult to reduce the cement to powder without machinery. In such cases, clays should be preferred which are not too greasy and which contain about five per cent. of lime: these clays are, moreover, more common than others. It is not to give energy to the cements that we should prefer earths containing a little lime: we have seen that opposite effects are sometimes produced. But the presence of this substance has two considerable advantages; the first is that the clay requires less burning to yield good puzzalona, whence results an economy as to the fuel: the second is that the clay containing lime is more easily reduced to powder. Thus it might be well to mix a little lime with clays which contain none, or to mix clays which contain no lime with clays that contain too much: but as these operations require a good deal of work, it will be necessary to calculate the relative expense of the several modes, namely, burning the clays hard, and pulverizing them, though with difficulty—mixing a little lime with the clay—or mixing clays together. The relative expense will depend on the price of fuel, and the means at command for breaking down the clay. A pestle mill, or mill with large stones, like those used in pulverizing plaster of Paris, would, it appears to me, be most convenient.

The name *puzzalona* expresses that this substance is obtained from the village of Pouzzol in Italy—that of *trass*, has no etymology. In the notice which I published in 1825, I proposed to give the name hydraulic cements to substances substituted for trass and puzzalona. This denomination appears to me to be convenient, and I shall generally employ it. I have entered into many details as to the fabrication of these productions because they are of great importance in constructions. I proceed to report sundry experiments that I made with hydraulic mortars.

CHAPTER VII.

Various Experiments on Mortars placed under water.

Much importance has been attached to the manner of slaking lime. Mr. Lafaye published in 1777, a memoir in which he gives, as a secret recovered from the Romans, the mode of slaking lime by plunging it into water for a few seconds, and then withdrawing it to slake and fall to powder in the air. This powdered lime is preserved in a covered place. Other Engineers have asserted that there is great advantage in stifling lime as it slakes; that is to say, covering it with sand before it begins to slake, in order to retain the vapours liberated during the process. Mr. Fleuret attributes great efficacy to this vapour, for he says "This vapour awakens and excites the appetite of the workmen, whence I conclude that it contains principles proper to the regeneration of lime and consequently to the hardening of mortars. But it is proved that nothing escapes but the vapour of water accompanied by some particles of lime. I made, on this point, the experiments contained in the following table.

Table No. XXV.

No. of the mortars.	Composition of the mortars.		No. of days required to harden in water.	Weight supported before breaking.
			days.	lbs.
1	Obernai lime slaked to powder with 1-5 of its volume of water, being left in the air . . . Sand	$\frac{1}{2}\big\}3$	15	176
2	Lime the same, slaked to powder with 1-5 of its volume of water, being covered with sand . . . Sand	$\frac{1}{2}\big\}3$	15	176
3	Lime the same, slaked by being plunged in water for 50 seconds . Sand	$\frac{1}{2}\big\}3$	15	154

Observations on the Experiments of Table No. XXV.

To make the three experiments above, I took a piece of Obernai lime which I divided into three portions. The first portion was slaked by throwing on one fifth of its volume of water, leaving the lime at rest in the air for twelve hours before making it into the mortar No. 1. The hardening was slow because the experiment was made in November.

No. 2 was slaked in the same manner with this difference, that I covered the lime with the sand as soon as I had thrown on the water. This, also, was left to itself for twelve hours before making it into mortar. These two experiments gave, we see, the same results.

The third experiment differs from the first in this, that to slake the lime, I plunged it into water for fifty seconds—afterwards treating it in the same manner as No. 1. The result was less by 22 lbs. It is singular that I got the same results, as will be seen further on, by making similar mortars and leaving them in the air, instead of placing them under water. The result, it seems to me, is owing to the lime, immersed for fifty seconds, absorbing too much water, which is hurtful, as the experiments in the following table will show. I purposed repeating the trial, by varying the time during which the lime should be immersed, but I had not an opportunity.

We have seen, in tables Nos. IV, V and VII, that the Obernai and Metz lime soon lose a great part of their properties, when they have been slaked to dry powder and left exposed for some time to the air. It is true that a piece of Obernai lime gave me, in this way, the most favourable result of table No. VI, but only in the first month after slaking: for, afterward, this lime rapidly lost its quality. We ought then, by no means to apply the process of Mr. Lafaye to hydraulic limes, unless assured of a different result from mine, which, I think, need not be looked for.

As to fat limes, table No XIV shows that when they were slaked to powder, and left in this state, in the air, for a couple of months, I obtained, by mixing this lime with trass, results sensibly better than when I used lime just slaked. I think, therefore, that it is best to slake fat limes to powder and to leave them for a month or two in this state in the air, before using them in mixture with hydraulic cements; but the process of Mr. Lafaye may be much simplified, by throwing on the lime a quarter, or a third, of its volume of water: it was in this way that I operated; avoiding, thereby, the embarrassment of panniers or baskets. We have seen, above, that lime slaked to powder has the property of absorbing oxygen; and it is to that property I attribute the benefit derived from leaving lime exposed to the air after being slaked to powder. Table No. XV offers a similar result; but as the proportions were not the same, I do not know which of the two modes is preferable—slaking fat lime to powder, or reducing it at once to paste.* We see that in both cases, there is an advantage in not making the mortars immediately. If time had been allowed me I should have repeated these experiments; making the proportions the same. It sometimes happens that hydraulic lime has been wet, either in the lime house from carelessness, or out of doors, when slaked and covered with sand. I accordingly made the following experiments with lime slaked with more than the usual quantity of water—making mortars therewith at different periods.

Table No. XXVI.

Composition of the mortar.	Made immediately.		After 12 hours.		After 24 hours.		After 36 hours.		After 48 hours.		After 60 hours.		After 72 hours.		After 84 hours.	
	H	W	H	W	H	W	H	W	H	W	H	W	H	W	H	W
	d.	lb.	d.	lb.	d.	lb.	d.	lb.	d.	lb.	d.	lb.	d.	lb.	d.	lb.
Obernai lime slaked to humid powder with a volume of water equal to the volume of lime measured in powder . . 1 ⎱ S Sand . . 2 ⎰	15	242	16	209	20	165	22	132	24	121	26	97	30	77	32	65

Observations on the experiments of Table No. XXVI.

To make the above experiments I took Obernai lime fresh from the kiln, and slaked it by throwing on a bulk of water equal to the bulk of lime: thus slaked, it was in the state of powder, but on pressing it between the fingers it was felt to be a little moist. I made at once, a mortar, taking one part of this lime in powder, and two parts of sand; and I put it in water, after having left it for twelve hours in the air: I made other mortars in the same way, every twelve hours, and at the end of a year, I broke them all. The table shows that after twelve hours the mortar had already lost much of its force, since the second mortar supported 33 lbs. less than the first. That which was made after twenty-four hours lost 77 lbs., and at the end of thirty-six hours, this lime gave a mortar that had lost almost half its force. The table shows that the strength of these mortars went on diminishing in a very rapid manner, to the last, which being made after eighty-four hours, supported only 66 lbs., in lieu of the 242 lbs. which the same lime sustained at first. We see also, that the rate of hardening decreased in a very rapid manner. These experiments show how dangerous

* Comparing the series of Nos. 1 and 3 of table No. XV, we see that at the end of six months, lime slaked to powder supported 44 lbs. more than that slaked to paste. but in the following mortars, the advantage was only 11 lbs. which is but trifling.
Au.

it would be to slake hydraulic lime with too much water, and how important it is to keep it from the rain. In the experiments I have made, I almost always slaked hydraulic lime with one-fifth of its volume of water,
and fat lime with one-fourth; because, as we have seen in the first table,
the latter absorbs more water than hydraulic lime, before being reduced to
paste. But in slaking on a large scale, the workmen always waste a portion
of the water on the ground: there will therefore be no disadvantage in slaking
hydraulic lime with one-fourth, and common lime with one-third of its bulk
of water.

The experiments in the above table explain why mortar No. 3 of table
No. XXV gave a result inferior to the others: the reason is, probably, because
during the fifty seconds that the lime was plunged in water it absorbed too
great a quantity; and as it remained twelve hours exposed to the air, it lost
part of its strength. I will now give some experiments that I made in
in order to ascertain the influence of different quantities of trass on the
qualities of mortars.

Table No. XXVII.

No. of mortars.	Composition of the mortars.		No. of days required to harden in water.	Weight supported before breaking.
			days.	lbs.
1	Fat lime slaked to powder and measured in powder . . . . 1 Sand . . . . 1 } 2¼ Trass . . . . ¼		19	103
2	Lime the same . . . . 1 Sand . . . . 1 } 2½ Trass . . . . ½		15	163
3	Lime the same . . . . 1 Sand . . . . 1 } 2¾ Trass . . . . ¾		10	216
4	Lime the same . . . . 1 Sand . . . . 1 } 3 Trass 1		8	301

Observations on the experiments of Table No. XXVII.

We see that in the above experiments I first used a very small quantity
of trass, and that I augmented it little by little. No. 2, containing very
little trass, gave a result superior to many mortars made of natural or artificial hydraulic limes: such a mortar would not be dear, and might be employed with advantage in gross masonry.

I made no experiments to determine the quantity of sand or factitious
puzzalona that would suit the hydraulic and fat lime, of the neighborhood
of Strasburg, because I think these experiments should not be made on a
small scale. We have seen that the same quarry furnishes limestone giving different results. A multitude of essays, on several pieces of lime
calcined to different degrees, would have been necessary, which would
have demanded much time. Instead of following this course, I proposed,
(after getting some facts as to proportions from the above experiments) to
take mortar already made at the works, the lime being there slaked in large
quantities at a time: repeating this several times, I should have determined
the quantity of sand and hydraulic cement which it would be proper to
mix with the lime used at the works: but I quitted Strasburg before it was

in my power to make these experiments. There was used at that place, as I have before stated, one part of quick lime (measured as quick lime) to two and a half of sand: the mortar was good; as there was occasion to ascertain in several partial demolitions.

Mr. Raucourt has advanced the opinion that sands require different quantities of lime according to their degree of coarseness; and to know the quantity of lime, it will suffice to measure the void spaces between the particles of sand, these void spaces being the measure of the lime. Accordingly, he filled a vessel, successively, with several kinds of sand and determined the quantity of water which could be poured on each without overflowing the vessel, whence he obtained for each the quantity of lime that should be added. But experiments should be made to ascertain whether the best mortar is obtained when these voids in the sand are just filled with lime; this Mr. Raucourt has not ascertained.

Before the publication of Mr. Raucourt's work, Captain Henry Soleirol of the Engineers, had engaged in researches of the same sort. Capt Soleirol, also, thinks that no more lime should be added than will fill these void spaces in the sand. But his experiments presented anomalies difficult to explain; and they are not sufficient to cause us to admit the principle, in anticipation. This theory is ingenious, but it wants, as yet, the support of facts. The subject is important and deserves to occupy the leisure of Engineers.

The next table presents several experiments made with fat lime in reference to the manipulation of mortars.

Table No. XXVIII.

No. of the mortars.	Composition of the mortars.	No. of days required to harden in water.	Weight supported before breaking.
		days.	lbs.
1	Mortar in equal parts of fat lime, sand and trass, put in water immediately	18	290
2	Same mortar put in water after having been left twelve hours without being reworked	13	328
3	Same mortar reworked, after twelve hours, without water—and put in water twelve hours afterward	13	330
4	Same mortar reworked, after twelve hours, with a little water, and put in water twelve hours afterward	15	326
5	Same mortar, put in water after twenty-four hours—without being reworked	12	308
6	Same mortar reworked after twenty-four hours with a little water, and put in water twelve hours afterward	15	363
7	Same mortar, put in water after thirty-six hours without being reworked	12	319
8	Same mortar, reworked after thirty-six hours with a little water, and put in water twelve hours afterward	15	363
9	Same mortar, put in water after forty-eight hours without being reworked	12	319
10	Same mortar, reworked with a little water, after forty-eight hours, and put in water twelve afterward	15	330
11	Same mortar put in water after sixty hours without being reworked	12	308
12	Mortar of one part of Obernai lime and two parts of sand, put in water immediately	15	154
13	Same mortar put in water after twelve hours exposure without being reworked	15	165
14	Same mortar, reworked with a little water after twelve hours, and put in water twelve hours afterward	12	198
15	Mortar of Obernai lime, sand and trass in equal parts, put immediately in water	4	405
16	Same mortar reworked with a little water after twelve hours, and put in water twelve hours afterward	3	528

Observations on the experiments of Table No. XXVIII.

It often happens that a good deal of mortar is prepared and that bad weather for a day or two prevents the workmen from using it. If it be hydraulic mortar, it becomes hard in the interval of a day, and often of a night, and it would be impossible to use it in that state. By reworking it for a long time, it might be brought to the proper consistence without any addition of water, but this is expensive: it is better to bring it to proper consistence by reworking it for a short time with a little water. Many Engineers think that mortar is improved by being worked several times a day: they consequently often make mortars several days before hand—work it well at first, and permitting it to stiffen, bring it again to proper condition by reworking, because, say they, *good mortars must be tempered with the sweat of the Labourer*: but the sweat of the Labourer costs money, which it is important to save. These considerations induced me to make the above experiments.

The first eleven mortars were composed of fat lime, sand and trass in equal portions. No. 1 was put in water immediately, while No. 2 was left twelve hours in the air, and then put in water without being reworked. This last we see gave a resistance sensibly greater than the first. Nos. 3, 4 and 5 remained twenty-four hours in the air before being put in water; No. 3 was reworked, twelve times, without water, No. 4 was reworked with water, and No. 5 was not reworked. It is important to remark that the results of No. 3 and 4 are very nearly the same as No. 2—No. 5 supported a weight sensibly less than No. 4.

After twenty four hours, it was not possible to rework these mortars without adding a little water. In consequence, Nos. 6 and 7 were put in water after thirty-six hours: with this difference between them, that No. 6 was reworked with a little water, while No. 7 was not reworked, No. 6, we see, gave a result decidedly better than No. 7.

Nos. 8, 9, 10 and 11, were made in the same way, and gave better results with those mortars that had been reworked with a little water, than with those that had not been reworked; at the end of sixty hours the resistance began to diminish.

If we compare Nos. 4 and 5, 6 and 7, 8 and 9, 10 and 11, which were left in the air, we shall see that those which were reworked with a little water, gave greater resistance than those which were not reworked.

If we compare Nos. 2 and 3, we see that this last mortar gained very little by being reworked, although it was worked over twelve different times. An excess of trituration, therefore, seems useless; for three or four pounds, more or less, of resistance, is almost nothing, when the mortars support 330 lbs.

Nos. 12, 13 and 14, were made with hydraulic lime and sand. The first two gave about an equal resistance; No. 14, which was reworked with a little water, was much the best of the three.

Lastly, Nos. 15 and 16, were composed of Obernai lime, sand and trass; No. 15 was put immediately in water. No. 16 was not put in until it had been worked with a little water. The latter gave a result much superior to the former.

I ought to mention that when the mortars had taken a slight consistence in the air, I always compressed them gently with the trowel before putting them in water; but Nos. 1 and 15 having been plunged into water as soon as made, were not compressed, while Nos. 4 and 16 were. I cannot think that so slight a compression has made so great a difference. We see besides that there is but little difference between Nos. 12 and 13, although this last had been compressed, while No. 14, which had been reworked with water, afforded a resistance much greater.

The mortars Nos. 12, 13 and 14, ought not to be compared with Nos. 15 and 16, first, because the last two contain trass, and, secondly, because the two limes were of different burnings. It results from the table, that when we have hydraulic mortar, composed of fat lime, sand and trass, or of hydraulic lime and sand, or mixed with trass; in either case, there is no disadvantage in reworking with a little water, when, from any circumstances, it has become too dry to be used. There is even an advantage in doing it; thus, in making mortar at night, and in the morning giving it a little water, and, by a little work, bringing it to its first condition, the mortar can only be improved thereby; but an excess of trituration is useless—not augmenting the strength of the mortar in comparison with the increase of expense. The following table contains several other experiments which I made on mortars.

Table No. XXIX.

No. of the mortars	Composition of the mortars.	No. of days required to harden in water.	Weights supported before breaking.
		Days.	lbs.
1	Mortar of one part of fat lime and two parts of trass	4	462
2	Same mortar with the same trass wet	4	451
3	Same mortar with the same trass not so fine as No. 1	6	231
4	Mortar made of 1 part of Obernai lime and 2 parts of sand, put in the water at the end of 12 hours, without being reworked	10	231
5	Same mortar, reworked after 12 hours, and put in water 12 hours afterward	10	220
6	Mortar of 1 part of Obernai lime and 2 parts of sand tempered thin	10	176
7	Same mortar—tempered stiff	10	161
8	Mortar of 1 part of fat lime half burnt and 2 parts of sand		
9	Mortar of 1 part of Obernai lime and 2 parts of sand	12	110
10	Same mortar with the sand broken fine	10	253
11	Mortar of 1 part of Obernai lime and 2 parts of earthy sand	15	132
12	Same mortar, with the same sand after being washed	8	231

Observations on the experiments of Table No. XXIX.

The first experiment was made with ordinary trass which had been sifted through a fine hair seive; it was thus that I used it in all my experiments. No. 2 was made of the same trass which I had left during a month at the bottom of a vessel wherein it was covered with water. Several constructors think it necessary to keep trass from moisture; this experiment proves there is nothing to fear from water. There is no disadvantage in leaving the pieces of trass, or of burnt clay of which artificial trass is made, exposed. But, when in a state of powder, it is necessary to keep it covered from winds.

No. 3 was made of the same trass which had been passed through a much coarser seive. The result, as we see, was inferior, by one half, which is not surprising, as I shall show in the sequel. It appears that it is important that trass and hydraulic cements be finely pulverized: there should be no perceptible asperities on taking the substance between the fingers. The two experiments Nos. 4 and 5, have the same object as the preceding table; they were made from lime of another burning. No. 4 was put in water after twelve hours exposure in the air, without being reworked. No. 5 was reworked without water after twelve hours, and put in water twelve hours afterwards. If there is any advantage, it is rather in favor of the mortar which was not reworked; but such slight differences may be regarded as nothing. We can conclude only, that when hydraulic mortars have been well mixed, which is the case when they appear homogeneous to the eye, nothing will be gained by any further labour. But we have seen by the preceding experiments, that if, after having left mortars at rest for some time, they be worked up anew with a little added water, increased force will be given to them.

Nos. 6 and 7 were made with the same Obernai lime. Both were left in the air for twelve hours before being put in water, and all other circumstances were the same. The only difference being, that No. 6 was made into thin, and No. 7 into stiff mortar. There is a sensible difference in the resistances: and that both are feeble, must be ascribed to their being both made of a piece of inferior lime. The result is in opposition to the opinion of Mr. Vicat, for at the conclusion of a note that he wrote on the first experiments that I published, he says: "Mr. Treussart affirms, as respects the manipulation, that mortars tempered to ordinary consistency, that is to say, soft, are better than stiff mortars. This implies a contradiction, not only of facts generally observed up to this time, but also, in a measure, of the observations of the author himself."

I announced these results in 1823, because they are important in the manipulation of mortars, and were furnished by my experiments. I am fully aware they are in opposition to the opinion generally received; but I do not see in what they are opposed to my own observations, nor does Mr. Vicat inform us. They, on the contrary, coincide with all that precedes.

We have seen, in fact, that mortars gain sensibly, after they have somewhat hardened, by reworking them with a little water. We have also seen, at the commencement of this memoir, that fat quick lime, reduced to thin paste with water, is capable, for a long time, of absorbing fresh quantities of water. Is it not probable then that it is the same with hydraulic lime? When it has been reduced in paste to the consistence of common mortar, it is possible that it may not yet have absorbed all the water necessary to convert it into the best mortar. It is possible that a mass of mortar put in water, may absorb but a small quantity in consequence of its prompt induration. If so, it is not astonishing that a new quantity of water added to a mortar, after it has absorbed the first—or that a mortar made more fluid at first, should give the best results. The question is important, because it is much easier to mix mortars when they are thin than when they are stiff; and there results, consequently, a considerable saving. I was bound to give the results obtained with Obernai lime, in order to draw attention to them, and engage constructors using those sorts of lime, to experiment on the subject. All the mortars made at Strasburg, whether for works in water or air, were made of the consistence of common mortars, and very often, when, from any cause, they had somewhat stiffened, they were worked up anew with a little water, and we always had very good results.

Experiment No. 8 was made to verify an important fact announced by Mr. Minard, Engineer of Roads and Bridges. He states that by burning the lime feebly, so as to leave a portion of the carbonic acid in the lime stone after burning, a very good hydraulic lime will be obtained. I, in consequence, repeated his experiment, taking a piece of fat lime stone and placing it in the kiln above the tiles, so as to burn it but partially. I satisfied myself, by testing with muriatic acid, that, after this feeble burning, the piece of lime still contained much carbonic acid: but it had also lost so great a portion, that on throwing water on it, it was reduced to powder. I made mortar with this lime—mixing it with sand, and put it in water; but we see that I obtained no result: at the end of a year the mortar was entirely soft.

Experiment No. 9 was made with the same lime and sand as experiment No. 10; the only difference being that No. 9 was made with common sand in its natural state, and No. 10 with the same sand after it had been broken up very fine. Both mortars were composed of one part of lime in paste to two and a half parts of sand. Many constructors think that coarse sand is preferable for gross masonry. We see, however, that the resistance I obtained with common sand, not coarse, was only 110 lbs., while that given by mortar made of the same sand after it had been pulverized, was 253 lbs. I confess that this result surprised me greatly. When I made these two mortars, which were put in water, I made two others of the same kind which I left in the air. We shall see, in the second section, that the mortar made of common sand broke under a weight of 187 lbs., while that which was made of the pulverized sand supported 275 lbs., although it was cracked. Commonly, the mortars put in water have given me, when made of hydraulic lime, better results than those left in the air. I am induced, therefore, to think that No. 9 gave a result so feeble in consequence of some circumstance that escaped notice. It is possible that the mortar was cracked without my perceiving it; and it, therefore, as yet, appears to me doubtful whether there can be so great an advantage, as I find in these two experiments, in making mortar of fine sand; although it seems certain that there is an advantage in the case of hydraulic limes, in making mortar of fine sand. Mr. Vicat obtained a similar result, as we see by his table No. XVI.

No. 11 was made of one part of fat lime in paste to two parts of an unwashed, earthy sand used at Phalsburg. No. 12 was made of the same lime and the same sand cleared of the earthy matter by washing. The washed sand gave me a result almost double that afforded by the earthy sand. It is therefore very important to use clean sand.

We find in vol. VII, of the *Annales des Mines* a discussion between Mr. Vicat and Mr. Berthier, as to the cause of the solidification of mortars. Mr. Vicat attributed it to the chemical action exercised by the lime on the siliceous matter. Dr. John, on the contrary, had established in principle, that the substances mixed with lime to make mortars, and which he denominates alloys, *(alliages,)* are altogether passive. He relates that, according to his experiments, caustic lime attaches neither quartz, nor any other stony substance. Mr. Berthier, who has examined this question, says, "I think, with Mr. John, that the alloys perform no chemical part in mortars; these alloys appear to me to have the effect, 1st, of diminishing the consumption of lime; 2d, of regulating the shrinkage, by moderating it, making it uniform and preventing cracks; 3d, probably, of facilitating dessication and the regeneration of carbonate of lime, and hastening the induration; 4th, of augmenting the solidity of mortars." According to Mr. Berthier, the molecules of the alloy contract with the molecules of the lime an adherence more or less strong. If this adherence be less than that which unites the molecules of lime to each other, the mortar will not be more solid than was the pure hydrate: it will, however, cost less, it will harden quicker, and will be less subject to crack in drying, which is of itself a great advantage. But if the force of adhesion of the lime be less than the force with which it adheres to the alloy, we may conceive that the mortar may acquire more tenacity than the pure hydrate; and this is, probably, what takes place in mortars.

Other philosophers, and several engineers, have thought that the solidification of mortars was owing to the lime passing again to the state of carbonate, by absorbing carbonic acid from the air. This opinion cannot, however, be sustained; for we know that carbonic acid penetrates only very slowly into the portion of hydrate of lime which is exposed to the air. Very large masses of mortar, plunged into water, will sometimes acquire complete hardness in three or four days, while other mortars containing the same quantity of lime, and placed in the same circumstances, often take more than a month to indurate. Mr. Darcet analysed the mortar from the Bastile, and found the lime had only half the carbonic acid required to saturate it. Mr. John analysed several ancient mortars that were very hard, and found a much smaller proportion of carbonic acid. Besides, it by no means follows that all the carbonic acid found in old mortars, has been absorbed by the lime: for we know from experience that it is difficult to disengage all the carbonic acid from lime by calcination. The lime we use in our constructions often contains a great deal; and it is not, therefore, surprising that the analyses of old mortars show a great difference in this respect. The following, moreover, is a proof that the absorption of carbonic acid has no influence on the induration of mortars, at least in the beginning. I took hydraulic lime and reduced it to the state of hydrate with distilled water, making a rather thick paste, which I placed at the bottom of a phial; I then filled the phial with distilled water and corked it tightly; and when the lime was so much stiffened as not to run, I inverted the bottle, (still corked,) placing the mouth in a vessel full of water. I repeated the experiment with mortar made of hydraulic lime and sand, and with another mortar of fat lime and trass. These three substances hardened as quickly as if they had been put in water which was in contact with the air. Being deprived of all communication with the air, we cannot ascribe the hardening to carbonic acid. The surface of several old mortars exposed to the air has been observed to have passed to the state of carbonate; but only for a small depth, and it requires several centuries to produce even this change. The induration of mortars cannot, therefore, be attributed to the regeneration of carbonate of lime.

The reasons given by Mr. Vicat, and Mr. Berthier, on the question whether there is, or is not, a combination of lime with the substances united with it to form mortars, not appearing to me to be conclusive, I shall offer my own opinion on this subject, so important as regards the theory,—presenting some facts in support of my views.

To account for the solidification of mortars in water, it seems to be necessary to divide them into two distinct classes; those composed of hydraulic lime and sand, and those composed of fat lime and puzzalona, or some analagous substance. As to mortars made of hydraulic lime and sand, it is not at all necessary to suppose that there is a chemical combination between those two substances, for we have seen by the first tables that the hydraulic limes, alone, when they are reduced to paste, harden promptly in water without it being necessary to mix any substance with them. We might be led to believe that there was a combination between hydraulic lime and sand by experiments Nos. 9 and 10, of table No. XXIX, which prove that the strongest resistance is given by fine sand; but, on the other hand, the facts cited by Mr. John, who found that sand was not attached by quick lime, and the reasons given by Mr. Berthier, lead to the belief that there is no such combination. To explain the hardening of mortars made of hydraulic lime, it is not necessary to suppose that it combines with the sand, since this lime hardens when alone in the water. It remains then to explain why hydraulic lime, itself, should harden in water. I will observe, on this point, that this particular lime is a combination of lime and a certain quantity of argil, by means of calcination; it is a substance, therefore, altogether different from lime, and it has acquired new properties that the lime had not: lime dissolves in water, while good hydraulic lime does not.

We know that when we mix, in certain proportions, soda, or potash, which are opaque, and soluble in water, with silex, which is also opaque, and heat the mixture, we obtain a new substance, which is transparent and insoluble in water, and which is called glass. It is not, therefore, astonishing that lime mixed with a little clay and heated, should produce a new substance that will harden in water, while lime alone will remain soft. Although we give to this compound the name of hydraulic lime, it ought, in fact, to be regarded as a substance altogether different from lime; it is a new body with new properties.

As to hydraulic mortars made of fat lime and puzzalona, or other analagous substance, I do not see that the hardening in water can be explained without supposing a combination between the fat lime and the puzzalona; for this lime, put alone in water, or mixed with sand, remains always soft. To prove the truth of this explanation, I made the following experiment: I took a mortar composed of one part of lime made from white marble, and two parts of puzzalona, which mortar had been one year in water. From the centre of this mortar I took a piece which I reduced to very fine powder, putting the powder in a vessel which I then filled with distilled water. But we know that if fat lime be put in water, the water will dissolve $\frac{1}{400}$ of its weight in a few minutes. Nevertheless, after twenty-four hours, the distilled water had no portion of the lime. I satisfied myself, on the other hand, that the lime of the mortar had not passed to the state of carbonate: because, on throwing muriatic acid on the powdered mortar, there was very little effervescence. The lime had not therefore passed to the state of carbonate, and still it would not dissolve in water, which could only proceed from its state of combination with the puzzalona.

I communicated this fact nearly two years ago to Mr. Berthier, giving him a little of the pulverized mortar which I used in my experiment, and he obtained the same result that I did. I will add that I made some hydraulic mortar by mixing one part of fat lime measured in paste, with two parts of puzzalona; one portion of this mortar I placed at the bottom of a glass, and covered it immediately with water; the other portion was also placed in the bottom of a glass, but was not covered with water till after the lapse of twelve hours. A strong pellicle of carbonate of lime formed all over the surface of the water which had been put on the fresh made mortar, while in the case of the mortar that had been twelve hours in the air before being covered, there was only a light pellicle of carbonate of lime on portions of the surface of the water; more than half the surface of the water was without any pellicle. This experiment proves that lime combines very promptly with puzzalona.

The hardening of hydraulic mortars in water may be explained, then, in the following manner: if the mortar be made of hydraulic lime and sand, this last substance appears to be in a passive state; the induration of mortar takes place because hydraulic lime hardens of itself in water—this being a property resulting from the state of combination of a small quantity of clay with the lime. If the proportion of lime be too much forced, a good hydraulic lime will no longer be obtained. A similar effect occurs in making glass: if the quantity of soda or potash be too much forced, the result is nearly a deliquescent compound. When hydraulic lime is made of fat lime and puzzalona, the hardening takes place because there is brought about a combination of fat lime and puzzalona in the moist way. In this case—that the combination may work well, it is requisite that the puzzalona be in greater proportion than the lime.

There is always a reduction of volume, in making mortars, on the mingling of the constituents. I have endeavored to measure this diminution by experiments on a large scale. First, four heaps, composed each, of 10.60 cubic feet of Obernai quick lime, and 21.20 cubic feet of sand—making altogether 127.20 cubic feet, became reduced by manipulation to 101.71 cubic feet of mortar of ordinary consistence: the volume diminished therefore in the ratio of 1.00 to 0.80—that is to say, was lessened 0.20. In a second experiment, fifty eight heaps,* composed each of 10.602 cubic feet of quick lime, and 26.505 cubic feet of sand, forming together a volume of 2152.21 cubic feet, produced 1779.955 cubic feet of mortar. The primitive volume diminished, therefore, in the ratio of 1.00 to 0.822—that is to say, was lessened 0.178. According to the first experiment, the reduction was one fifth: and in the second, where there was more sand, it was about one sixth. These facts will be useful in making analyses, to determine prices.

Mr. Lacordaire, Engineer of Roads and Bridges, engaged on the canal of Bourgogne, has announced that he has obtained good hydraulic mortars by the following means. He burnt hydraulic lime stone but partially, and slaked it by immersion. The portions the most burned fell to powder; and the lime thus furnished he used by mixing it with sand, and with the portion of the lime stone that did not slake; which portion he pulverized and used as a cement. There has been established, at Pouilly, a manufactory of this substance, to which the name of Pouilly cement has been given; and as a cement, it is mixed with fat lime. We see that Mr. Lacordaire has applied to hydraulic lime, a process analagous to that which Mr. Minard proposed for fat lime stone, and which in our trials gave no results, as may be seen page 104.

I procured two specimens of the hydraulic lime stone of Pouilly, and also a piece of the half burnt lime of which the cement of that name is made. One of these lime stones is a distinct blue, and the other of an ash colour. The piece of half burnt lime was of a brown colour, and had been out of the kiln about six months. I made with this half burnt lime the following essays: I detached a piece on which I poured water; there was no heat given out, and it did not fall to powder. I then put a piece in muriatic acid diluted with a little water; there was considerable disengagement of carbonic acid, and it dissolved, leaving a residue of about one fifth, which was clay mixed with a little red oxide of iron. I reduced the piece still left, to a very fine powder, and made therewith the following experiments: I first mixed one part of fat lime measured in paste, with two parts of this powder. After having well mixed the whole with a little water, to bring it to the consistence of sirup, I placed it in the bottom of a glass. One hour afterward I was obliged to cover it with water, because it became consistent. Twelve hours after being covered with water, it was completely hard. I made a second experiment by reducing the powder, alone, to paste with water, and in an hour after being placed in the bottom of a glass, it was covered with water; at the end of twelve hours the induration of this, also, was complete. Lastly, I made a third experiment with one part of fat lime and two parts of this powder, as in the first essay; but I added no more water than was requisite to reduce the mixture to a thick paste, and I left it in the air; it hardened with as much promptitude as plaster of Paris: and fifteen days afterwards it appeared to possess very great hardness. It will be possible, perhaps, to substitute this substance for plaster advantageously.

*In the original, it is 52 heaps, which must be a misprint, as it requires 58 heaps to make up the quantity of 2152.21 cubic feet.—*Trans.*

It results from the essays just given, that this matter reduced to paste with a little water, hardens in water, and in the air, with great promptitude; and that, employed in powder with fat lime, in the manner of puzzalonas, an equally prompt hardening is obtained. It appears to me that the name *cement* given to this substance is not suitable; for it is, really, a sub-carbonate of hydraulic lime, that is to say, an hydraulic lime but little burnt, and containing, consequently, much carbonic acid. I may here observe that if we mix one part of fat lime with two parts of good hydraulic lime reduced to powder, this mixture will, equally, harden in water, without our being authorized to say that this powdered hydraulic lime is *cement*. This name belongs only to the powder of burnt clays; it is possible, however, that usage will preserve to this substance the name of cement, since it is used in the same manner as cement.

The fine observation of Mr. Lacordaire opens a new field as to hydraulic mortars. It will be very important to ascertain the tenacity of this substance; for we have seen by the Boulogne pebbles, and by several other mortars, that those which harden very quickly do not offer a great resistance. We have seen by table No. III, that several hydraulic limes, well burned and reduced to paste with water, have given, alone, greater resistance than when mixed with sand. The great promptitude of induration of these slightly burned limes merits particular attention. To judge accurately of this new mode of employing hydraulic limes, it will be necessary to make comparative experiments, first of the same lime stones, both slightly burned and thoroughly burned, made into paste with water; afterward by mixing them with a great quantity of sand; lastly, the lime but slightly burned should be used as cement with fat lime and with hydraulic lime, and with each of these kinds of lime united to sand. The hardening of the several mixtures should be compared; and at the end of a year they should be submitted to rupture, to determine their tenacity. Supposing that one part of fat lime, mixed with two parts of lightly burned hydraulic lime used as cement, should give a resistance equal to that afforded by mortar composed of the same hydraulic lime well burned and two parts of sand, it will then be necessary to examine which of these two processes is the cheapest.

In the first case lime only, which is a dear substance, is used; but the hydraulic lime, which composes two-thirds of the mortar, being much less burned, requires less fuel, at the same time that it requires a good deal of labour to pulverize it. We see, then, that it is by comparing the expense, with the resistance, of mortars, that we can fix upon the process to be adopted. There are circumstances, undoubtedly, where it is important to secure a speedy induration; but in ordinary cases, there is no inconvenience in waiting eight or ten days to allow the concrete, or mortar, to take sufficient hardness. It is to be presumed that we shall, ere long, have experiments which will show us whether this new mode of employing hydraulic lime presents advantageous results, as respects the tenacity of mortars. In those places where good hydraulic lime is found, it is very important that the experiments, of which I have spoken, should be made.

I have said that the half burned lime which I used as cement, had been calcined for six months; and that I obtained, nevertheless a prompt induration. That might be owing to its being still a stone, and that the air could not penetrate to the interior. It will be important to ascertain whether this lime will preserve its energy thus long, when reduced to powder. It will be equally necessary to know if it be indifferent whether this lime be plunged in water as soon as it is burned; or if it be preferable to half burn the whole kiln, so that it shall receive no water until it comes to be mixed into mortar with thorough burned lime.

We find in volume VII of the *Journal des Mines*, the analysis, made by Dr. John, of several old mortars; and by Mr. Berthier of several lime stones. I will terminate this chapter by the exposition of these analyses in the following tables.

Analysis by Dr. John of several Mortars.

	Mortars in air.						Hydraulic mortars.		
	1	2	3	4	5	6	7	8	9
Carbonic acid	0.0600	0.0575	0.0175	0.0500	0.0900	0.1200	0.0050	0.0225	0.0225
Lime in the state of carbonate	0.0800	0.0781	0.0260	0.0663	0.1194	0.1591	0.0070	0.0295	0.0298
Lime combined with other substances	0.0170	0.0431	0.0665	0.0207	0.0322	0.0809	0.0305	0.0395	0.2977
Combined silex	0.0100	0.0115	0.0375	0.0125	0.0025	0.0025	0.0200	0.0035	0.0800
Quartz and sand	0.8000	0.8010	0.7850	0.8375	0.6884	0.5600	0.7750	0.8950	0.3500
Alumine—oxide of iron					0.0275	0.0275			
Water . .	0.0330	0.0088	0.0675	0.0130	0.0400	0.0500	0.1625	0.0100	0.2400
	1.0000	1.0000	1.0000	1.0000	1.0000	1.0000	1.0000	1.0000	1.0000

1. Mortar one hundred years old, from the exterior joints of St. Peter's, at Berlin.

2. Mortar a hundred years old from the interior joints of the same church.

3. Mortars six hundred years old, from a covered (*encombrée*) foundation of the same church.

4. Mortar six hundred years old, from the walls of the Cathedral of Brandeburg.

5. Roman mortar, from the wall of a tower built at Cologne under Agrippa in the first century of the Christian era.

6. Roman mortar from a tower built by Agrippa.

It appears that in these last two mortars the portion of lime not saturated with carbonic acid is combined with the alumine.

7. Mortar three hundred years old, from the outside wall of the old castle of Berlin.

8. Old Roman, hydraulic mortar.

9. Mortar from Treves four years old.

We see by the above table that none of these mortars contain, by a notable quantity, the portion of carbonic acid required to saturate the lime; since according to the analysis of page 1, lime-stone contains, ordinarily, 33 per cent of carbonic acid. Mortar No. 5, for example, which was nearly two thousand years old, contained only about 13 per cent; and it is to be noticed, as I have already said, that the lime, as we use it in our constructions, is never completely deprived of this acid. We notice also that the hydraulic mortars are those which contain the least carbonate of lime. And lastly that a part of the lime is found united chemically with other substances, such as silex alumine, and iron, and perhaps with all three at the same time. These substances appear to be combined with the lime by calcination.

Lime produced by different calcined limestones, yielding common lime according to the analysis of Mr. Berthier.

	Fat Lime.						Meagre Lime.	
	1	2	3	4	5	6	7	8
Lime . .	0.964	0.954	0.972	0.935	0.916	0.860	0.780	0.600
Magnesia .	0.018	0.018	0.000	0.010	0.015	0.090	0.200	0.262
Clay . .	0.018	0.028	0.028	0.040	0.069	0.050	0.020	0.000
Oxide of iron &c.				0.015				0.138
	1.000	1.000	1.000	1.000	1.000	1.000	1.000	1.000

1. Limestone of the fresh water formation of Chateau—Landon near Nemours; compact, yellowish, a little cellular, sonorous: yields very fat lime.

2. Limestone of Saint-Jaques; compact, yellow, texture somewhat saccharoidal; it forms the base of the Jura mountains; makes a very greasy lime which hardens but slowly.

3. Lower marine limestone (*calcaire grossier*) of Paris: gives very greasy lime.

4. Limestone which forms the roof of the iron mine of La Voulte (Ardiche;) compact, yellowish white: containing shells which prove it to be contemporaneous with the Jura limestone, specific gravity 2.67: gives very good fat lime.

5. Limestone of Lagneux (Ain:) compact, of a light yellowish gray; affording fat lime which is much used at Lyons.

6. Fresh water limestone of Vichey (Allier:) compact, cellular, yellowish white, gives very good lime, but not very greasy.

7. Limestone of the neighbourhood of Paris, which appears to belong to the fresh water formation: compact, yellowish; gives meagre lime, but not hydraulic.

8. Secondary limestone of Villefranche (Aveyron:) lameller, of an ochery colour, the lime obtained in an experiment on a small scale was very meagre without being hydraulic.

Limes produced by different limestones, yielding hydraulic lime according to the analysis of Mr. Berthier.

	Moderately Hydraulic.					Very Hydraulic.					
	1	2	3	4	5	6	7	8	9	10	11
Lime .	0.870	0.830	0.840	0.820	0.820	0.745	0.688	0.740	0.683	0.700	0.746
Magnesia	0.040		0.025	0.015	0.015	0.035	0.060	0.020	0.020	0.010	0.160
Clay .	0.090	0.070	0.135	0.165	0.165	0.220	0.252	0.170	0.240	0.290	0.078
Oxide of iron, &c. .		0.100						0.070	0.057		0.016
	1.000	1.000	1.000	1.000	1.000	1.000	1.000	1.000	1.000	1.000	1.000

1. Limestone of Vougny (Loire;) sub lamellar, yellowish, filled with ammonites and other shells; yields very good lime which sets in water.

2. Limestone of Saint-Germain (Ain;) compact, deep gray, veined with white carbonate of lime; lamellar, and penetrated with gryphites, &c., at Lyons this lime is used for hydraulic works.

3. Limestone of Chaunay near Macon; compact, fine grained, yellowish white, it is of the secondary formation: this lime is hydraulic.

4. Limestone of Digne (Jura;) compact, penetrated with plates of calc-spar (*lamelleo de calcaire*) and containing a great number of gryphites, of a deep gray, this lime is hydraulic.

4. Limestone which accompanies the preceding, and which possesses the same properties; compact, of a grain almost earthy; of a clear gray.

6. Secondary limestone of Nimes (Gard;) compact, yellowish gray; affords a hydraulic lime which is there considered of excellent quality.

7. Lezoux lime (Puy-de-Dome;) made of a fresh water calcareous marle; it is said to be excellent, they are in the habit of slaking it by leaving it in heaps in the air, after having moistened it: it produces a copious jelly with acids.

8. Compact limestone of an unknown locality: gives very good hydraulic lime.

9. Secondary limestone of Metz (Moselle;) compact, of a grain almost earthy, of a bluish gray more or less deep: the lime it affords is known to be very hydraulic.

10. Calcareous marle of Senonches, near Dreux (Eure-et-Loir;) compact very tender, may be diffused through water like clay, but does not fall to powder when burnt. This substance is not like the limestones which have an earthy fracture, a mixture of carbonate of lime and clay. It leaves in acids a mealy residue, soft to the touch, which contains only a trace of alumine, which dissolves in liquid caustic potash even when cold, and which comports itself in all respects like silex which has been separated from combination: nevertheless it is certain that this substance exists in the Senonches lime only in the state of mixture: because, by operating with great care, we find by analysis, that the proportion of carbonic acid is exactly that which is necessary to saturate the lime. I have, before, in some varieties of carbonate of magnesia (*magnésie carbonatée,*) encountered silex soluble in alkalis, although not in combination, but have never found it in carbonate of lime. The Senonches lime is very well known: it is much used at Paris: it hardens more promptly, and acquires greater hardness than Metz lime: it dissolves in acids without leaving the least residue. (What Mr. Berthier says here of this lime is very remarkable and deserves to fix attention on this particular kind of lime.)

11. A mixture of four parts of chalk from Meudon and one part of Pas-sy clay (in volume,) which Mr. Saint-Leger uses to make the artificial hydraulic lime of Paris.

If we compare the common limes of the first table, above, with the hydraulic limes of the second, we shall see, 1st. that the latter contains, in general, much more clay than the former: 2d., that several limes contain more than two-tenths of magnesia, without being hydraulic, while they become eminently so, when they contain the same quantity of clay: 3d., that almost all the common limes contain a small portion of clay. We see that No. 5 of the common limes contains, within one thousandth as much clay as No. 2, of limes moderately hydraulic: it is probable that these two limes have about the same degree of hydraulic property, but that it is weak. It would be interesting to know the resistance of the mortars made of all the limes contained in the above two tables. It is only by determining the tenacity of mortars made of limes of which the composition is well known that we can adjust the composition and proportion of clay so as to produce the best hydraulic limes.

CHAPTER VIII.

Of Sand, and Hydraulic Sand (Arénes.)

Sands are classed relatively to their constituent parts: thus there are siliceous sands, granitic, calcareous sands, &c., some sands result from the slow decomposition of rocks of the same nature. Sometimes they are mixed; and it often happens that they contain several metallic substances—principally iron.

The different revolutions that the earth has undergone have caused considerable deposits of sand in places where there are now no water courses; and even at great elevations. On certain coasts there are extensive collections of sand, which the French calls *dunes;* these are heaped up by the winds. Rivers transport a great deal of sand, and their shores are some times covered with it. Sands are often mixed with vegetable earth. In this case they are not proper for mortar. To be suitable to this end, they should be almost perfectly free from earthy matter. When on the subject of mortars exposed in the air, I shall point out a very simple means, that I have used for several years, of freeing sands from the earth they contain.

Constructors distinguish sands into *river-sand, sea-sand* and *pit-sand.* This last is found in the great deposits mentioned above: it bears the name of *fossil sand,* also: its grain is generally more angular than that of *sea sand* or *river sand.* All these sands contain the same elements. Siliceous, or granitic sand, or a mixture of the two, are most common: calcareous sands are most rare.

Vitruvius, and others after him, thought that *fossil* or *pit* sand was the best for making mortar. Belidor thought, on the contrary, that *river sand* was preferable. Mr. Rondelet has since made experiments which appear to establish that *pit sand* is better than *river sand.*

I purposed examining whether, in fact, there was much difference, in making mortars of one sand rather than of another: but I quitted Strasburg before I could apply myself to the subject. Nevertheless, some facts, of which I shall speak when on the subject of mortars exposed to the air, lead me to believe that the divergence of opinions, as to which are the best sands, results from the experiments having been made with sand more or less fine, or more or less earthy. The experiments cited page 105, show that earth mixed with sand is very injurious to mortars. But the authors quoted above do not say whether, before making these experiments with pit and river sand, they took care to wash both of them. If they did not wash them, the superiority which they found to belong to either, may have been, on one hand, due to the greater freedom from earthy matters of the better sand of the two, and on the other, to the greater fineness of the particles. My results were obtained with granite sand, and it remains to be ascertained whether they would have been the same with other kinds of sand. The question is important, and should be examined with care

A species of fossil sand has lately been discovered, which is very remarkable: the knowledge of this singular substance is due to Mr. Girard de Caudemberg, Engineer of Roads and Bridges. This Engineer published, in 1827, a very interesting notice of this subject, which cannot fail to produce important results. I will state succinctly the principal facts contained in this notice, and I will add some observations that have been made since.

"There exists" says Mr. Girard," in the valley of the river Isle, fossil sands of which the colour varies from redish brown to yellowish red and even ochre yellow. They are called 'arénes,* which denomination we shall preserve in this notice, to distinguish them from common sands. These sands are often used alone, as mortar, in walls of enclosures and of houses; and as they have the property of making a paste with water, and as they shrink less than clay, they are very proper for this kind of construction: they represent in this case a pisé, which acquires hardness and resists inclemencies. But the proprietors of the mills on the river Isle, in the department Gironde, discovered by accident a quality in the arenes much more important and worthy of serious attention; they use it with common lime more or less fat, to form mortars which set under water and acquire great hardness."

Mr. Girard says that for want of hydraulic lime, he made several Locks with mortar composed of common lime and arenes. He states that he obtained very good results; and that the following year it was necessary to use the pick to break up the concrete that had been made with these arenes.

The examination of the arenes showed Mr. Girard that they were all composed of sand and clay in various proportions. By means of washing and decantation he separated the clay from the sand, and in eight kinds of arenes he found the proportions of clay varied from ten to seventy per cent. He ascertained that those arenes which were meagre, were hydraulic only in a very feeble degree. The sand of the arenes is sometimes coarse and sometimes fine: it is occasionally calcareous, but more frequently siliceous or mixed. Some of the arenes are red, others brown, yellow and sometimes white.

The arenes are generally found on the summit of the hillocks which form the basins of rivers and brooks: they are rarely found in valleys. The deposits of the substance are superimposed on masses of argillaceous tufa (tuf argileux,) or calcareous rocks; they have all the characters of an alluvial deposit. The beds are often separated by pebbles. Rolled pebbles are, moreover, often seen disseminated here and there in the mass. Some of the beds are more than fifty feet thick. Mr. Girard says it appears to him that the environs of Bordeaux, and the valleys of the Aube and upper Seine, contain a great deal of it; and that it exists in a multitude of localities.

Mr. Girard had occasion to ascertain that the arenes were employed in many ancient constructions, and he cites, among others, the thick revetments of a remnant of fortification at Mucidan (Dordogne) which dates back several centuries, and it appears that the very old constructions at Nimes were made with arenes.

Mr. Girard says he has assured himself by experiments that in preserving for a year under water, mortars containing equal proportions of crude energetic arenes, and the same arenes calcined, that there was no appreciable difference in their consistence; but that the torrefaction of the arenes had the advantage of hastening in a remarkable manner, the setting or induration of the concrete.

* It appears that the word arène was known to several Constructors, for Mr. Sganzin says page 25, in speaking of Sands: "They call arènes those of which the particles are finer and more regular." And this is all he says. Au.

Mr. Avril and Mr. Payen discovered, about the same time, in Bretagne, the properties of puzzalona, in gray wacke, and in decomposed granite, though to a degree quite feeble. They remarked, besides, that natural puzzalonas acquire a new degree of energy by a slight calcination.

Captain Leblanc of the Engineers, employed at Peronne, gave on the 30th November 1827, an interesting memoir on the arenes which are found in great quantity in the neighbourhood of that place. I will transcribe the commencement of the memoir. "In the numerous demolitions, made in 1825 and more especially in 1826, preparatory to the repair of the crown work of Paris, it was remarked that the ancient mortars (from 150 to 600 years old) were generally very hard. It was particularly noticed, at the time of the demolition of the piers of bridge forty-one, which was situated in quick sand, below the level of the waters, that the mortar was harder than elsewhere. To these facts the only exception was in the demolition of scarp thirty-three at the close of the year 1826. The mortar of this masonry was still soft. On examining the mortars which were hard, it was perceived that the sand therein was very fine, and that these mortars, from their aspect, seemed to have been made of the sand of the country, rejected in the official instructions, because too earthy. (This sand is used in all the constructions of the town.) Another consideration led to the belief that the sand of the country had been used: for all this masonry appeared to be very carelessly put together; the mortar, badly made, showed every where, lumps as large as a hazle nut, of lime not mixed with sand and still soft; although all the surrounding mortar was very hard. It was to be presumed that when applying so little care to all parts of the workmanship, the constructors had taken no greater, as to the choice of sand: and that they used that which was nearest at hand—namely the sand of the country. We have said that the mortar of scarp thirty-three was found still soft after two hundred years: it seemed on examination to be meagre; and, although the sand seemed to be the sand of the country, the mortar did not look like the other; under these circumstances, this example suspended, for the time, the conclusions that had already been drawn as to the advantage of using the Peronne sands."

The author states that on recommencing labours in 1827, he made six cubes of mortar, of which three were composed of sand recommended in official instructions, and the other three of the clayey sand whereof the good masonry appeared to have been made. One cube of each kind of mortar was left in the air, one put in a humid place, and one in water.

It was in this interval, as Capt. LeBlanc states, that the notice of Mr. Girard appeared. What was said in that notice showed that the clayey sand of the neighbourhood of Peronne was a true arene. The mortar made of common lime and this arene had completely hardened in the water at the expiration of a month; so as to receive no impression when borne upon strongly by the thumb. A mortar made at the same time of the same lime and of the sand recommended officially, and usually employed, remained entirely soft at the end of several months. By heating the arenes, Capt. LeBlanc ascertained that the hardening took place much more promptly, for the mortars made of the crude arenes required a month to harden, whereas those made of arenes that had been heated, hardened in eight or ten days. This officer undertook some experiments to determine the degree of calcination proper to impart the quality of most prompt hardening, and to ascertain whether the effect of calcination would be to augment in a sensible manner, the strength of mortars, but his experiments are not yet finished. The discovery of arenes in the environs of Peronne, is, at all events, a great advantage for the works in progress at that place. Masonry in the air may be executed with crude arenes; and if it appear that calcination augments both the promptitude of hardening and the solidity of mortars, this operation might be resorted to in all cases of constructions in water.

The arenes of the environs of Peronne are found on the tops of the hillocks which border the valley of the Somme, like those of the valley of the Isle, and they lie upon a calcareous mass. Towards the bottom of the river banks, the arenes are mixed with fine sand, and moderately fine sand, and sometimes, with coarse grains. It is only towards the tops of the hillocks that they are found composed entirely of fine sand. The inhabitants call it clay. It is found, also, on hills quite elevated. Capt. LeBlanc states that the arenes which contain only very fine sand are less hydraulic than those which lie a little lower and which contain a mixture of fine and moderately fine sand; that in those places where the ground rises gently from the river, the banks of sand are always mixed with, and sometimes separated by rolled or broken pebbles, which is another point of resemblance with the arenes of the valley of the Isle, as described by Mr. Girard. The colour of these arenes is obscurely reddish, a good deal resembling bistre: they present the appearance of an ochrey earth.

Capt. LeBlanc adds that since the discovery of the arenes of Peronne, they have been found at Bapaume, at Douai, on the road from Bethune to Arras, and that this substance appears to be very common in the valley of the Somme, and in Flanders. At Bapaume, the workmen have known for a long time that this clay was hydraulic: the millers of the neighbourhood having executed works in the water therewith, with very good results. In the month of July last, Captain LeBlanc informed me that there had been found in the neighborhood of Ham, an arene pronounced to be more hydraulic than that of Peronne, and that it was used a long time ago in the fortifications of the castle.

I procured some of the arenes from Ham: they sent me two kinds; one yellow and the other greenish. We shall see in the sequel that they are clays. I satisfied myself that they contained no lime. I made two kinds of mortar therewith, taking one part of lime in paste to two parts of the arenes, and put them under water. I made a similar mortar with puzzalona. The puzzalona mortar hardened completely in six days: the two mortars made of arenes had not fully hardened at the end of three months. These experiments were made last December, which retarded the induration no doubt; but being placed in a chamber where the temperature was about ten degrees, (cen?) (50 Far.,) I was astonished at the slowness of the induration.

I calcined some of the greenish arene, keeping part at a low red heat for half an hour in a crucible; another part during one hour; and a third portion during two hours. I then made three mortars like the above, with these three calcined arenes. The two mortars of the arenes, calcined, one for half an hour, and the other for an hour, hardened in a month. That calcined for two hours, required nearly two months to attain the same degree of hardness. It is true that I did not calcine this substance in a current of air; but I was surprised that, being calcined, it did not harden sooner. It will be important to make many experiments on different arenes, crude, and calcined in various degrees, so as to know the greatest promptitude of induration that can be secured, and the tenacity of mortars both in air and water.

Two specimens of mortar taken from the Castle of Ham were sent to me: one of these mortars was made in 1601, and the other in 1802; they were both of very strong consistence. I found, nevertheless, that they did not offer the same degree of hardness as mortars made of trass and hydraulic cement; but these arenes will be not the less advantageous in constructions in water and in air, on account of the great economy that attends their use. In places where good arenes are at hand, they should, in cases where a prompt hardening is required, in caps of arches. &c., always be employed mixed with hydraulic cement.

I had occasion to notice, a short time since, between the park of Versailles and Saint Cyr, a hillock of clayey sand which looked to me like the sand from Ham: some was yellow and some red; the colours being well separated. I made with these two clayey sands, two mortars composed of one part of fat lime and two parts of these sands, and placed them in water. They were not indurated at the end of four months, but it was perceptible to the touch, that they had taken a degree of consistency.

At Paris they build the walls of houses with plaster, and cellar walls with mortar. I have had occasion to observe latterly, that several of these mortars were made of clayey sand which appeared to me to be a species of arene: it contained a little lime, and some of it is yellow, and some greenish, like that from Ham. I learned that this sand was brought from the neighborhood of the ancient garden of Tivoli, and that it appears to have been employed at Paris for a long time to improve mortars. I made two mortars of these two clayey sands, adopting the same proportions as with the sands from Saint Cyr, and placed them in water. The results were similar to those given by the clayey sands from Saint Cyr. From what has been said, we see that these clayey sands are arenes of little energy: they do not appear to me to be proper for mortars that are to be placed in water; but the hydraulic property they possess, feeble as it is, will give, for works in the air, much better mortar than ordinary sand. From what has been stated above, it appears probable that there exist several banks of arenes in the neighborhood of the Capital; and it is probable some may be found more energetic than those I tried; it will therefore be important to make researches, adopting the same process as is recommended page 92, for cements.

If we mix clay with fat lime, the resulting mortar will take no consistence when put under water. It is necessary that clays be more or less calcined to become hydraulic. Mr. Girard seems to think that the arenes have been submitted to the action of fire, and that perhaps they have a volcanic origin; but this second assertion does not seem to be a necessary consequence of the first; all that we may affirm is, that the arenes are clays which have sustained the action of fire. On the other hand, the small rounded stones and pebbles found in some of these deposits, prove that they are, also, alluvial. It is not easy to meet important facts without seeking to account for them, although at the risk of deceiving ourselves.

The flattening of the poles of the earth, and the swelling out of the equator, demonstrate that our globe has been in a soft state. Some philosophers maintain that the earth was in a state, primitively, of fusion; these are called *Vulcanists*. Others contend that the softness of the earth was an effect of water; these are called *Neptunists*. The opinion of the *Vul-*

canists is a very ancient one, and prevailed for a long time; but the great number of shells, the remains of marine animals, and other objects, encountered at very elevated positions, superseded the opinion of the *Vulcanists* with that of the *Neptunists*. Later still, new observations, and amongst others, the great heat of certain thermal waters; the elevated temperature which is found at the bottom of very deep mines; the sudden formation of some islands which have been thrown up from the bottom of the sea, and several other facts, have brought back the old opinion that our globe was primitively in a state of incandescence; and there are, at this day, several philosophers who think that the earth is cooled only at the surface, that it is still in a state of incandescence in the interior, and that volcanoes communicate with this vast focus of heat. But whatever may be the opinion adopted as to the primitive condition of our globe, it cannot be doubted that it has sustained several successive modifications by fire and water. The hypothesis that the globe was at first in a state of incandescence, and that it has since sustained revolutions by the operations of water, is that which appears to me to accord best with various observed facts. The presence of arenes over a considerable extent of France, in places where no traces of extinct volcanoes are to be found, is an important circumstance for geologists. It is curious to see the study of hydraulic mortars furnish new arguments in favor of the theory of the *Vulcanists:* but, as often noticed, all the sciences have some points of contact.

The experiments that I shall give in the second section, on mortars made of fat lime and sand, and exposed to the air, will show how important it is to search after good arenes in the environs of our public works; because it is a means of procuring good mortars at a very cheap rate, and because it is the only means of procuring them cheaply, in countries where there are no hydraulic limes.

CHAPTER IX.

On Concrete. Circumstances in which it is advantageous to use it.

In Belidor's time many foundations were made by stones thrown into the water, putting over at the same time with the stones, mortar susceptible of hardening in water. This mortar took the name of beton; and this manner of founding was called founding *a pierre perdue*. This method was exposed to the great disadvantage of putting too much mortar in some places, and not enough in others; because, when founding in a great depth, it was not possible to see how to distribute the mortar. Now a days, a practice is adopted of breaking up the stones to the size of an egg, and mixing them, above water, with mortar possessing the property of indurating in water, and then lowering the mixture to the spot where it is required. We have seen that the name of hydraulic mortar is given to that which possesses the property of setting in water, and the name of concrete is now confined to the mixture of this mortar with these broken stones. Concrete is therefore nothing else than the masonry made of small materials; and by making, on the surface, this mixture of hydraulic mortar and broken stones, the great advantage of having a homogeneous mass is secured. If the hydraulic mortar be of good quality, the masonry thus formed is very hard: the quality of the concrete depending, principally, on that of the hydraulic mortar.

The method of mixing small stones with hydraulic mortar in order to form concrete in water, appears to have been employed by the Romans. At page fifty-three, a passage is cited from Vitruvius, in which he says that very solid constructions are made in water, by mixing together puzzolana, lime and stones, (some authors translate it *small stones.*) I do not know whether any Roman works, made in water, of small stones, have been discovered; but some are found out of water, which are evidently the same as our modern concrete. It appears that for a long time the ancient method was abandoned; and that it has been resumed, after perceiving the disadvantages of founding with *pierre perdue.*

If good hydraulic mortar be used, without any admixture of stones, the foundation will be not less solid, but much more costly. The stones are added to the mortar in order to lessen, considerably, the expense. To diminish it still more, a certain quantity of gravel is added, occupying a portion of the interstices between the stones. In countries where stones are not to be had at a reasonable rate, broken bricks may be substituted. And in countries where gravel, only, can be had at a cheap rate—both stones and bricks being dear—the concrete may be formed by mixing this gravel with hydraulic mortar. Wherever masonry and concrete are carried on at the same time, all fragments of stones, bricks, and tiles should be saved: these materials may be usefully employed in the concrete, and with great economy; as they will prevent the necessity of purchasing stones or bricks for the purpose of being broken into small fragments for concrete.

When hydraulic works are founded in shallow water, they are often made of masonry of stone and mortar. For this purpose a dam is built around the spot, the water is pumped out, and the masonry goes on as if upon the surface of the dry ground. But when the depth of water is from six to ten feet, the difficulty of keeping the water out is very great; especially in sandy grounds. Much expense is incurred in pumping out the water; the water often forces itself through the masonry; and the mortar is, thereby, drenched, and sometimes far the greater part washed out, which might occasion formidable accidents in the constructions. Lastly, when the depth of water exceeds ten feet—and it is often necessary to found in much greater depth, as in sixteen, twenty, and twenty-six feet—it then becomes impossible to keep the water free, because of the great quantity that enters through every part, preventing, of course, the execution of the work by such means. In this case the foundation is made either in a caisson, or with concrete. The first consists in making a large chest, perfectly tight in the bottom and sides: the masonry is built therein, and in proportion as the load of masonry sinks the caisson, the buoyancy of this last is increased, by adding buoyant bodies, until the masonry is laid in proper quantity; when the caisson is grounded on the exact spot for the foundation. This means is often expensive on account of the construction of the caisson, which requires much care, and is subject to several inconveniences. To found with concrete, the place on which the work is to be laid is surrounded with sheet piles of suitable strength, driven to a depth a little greater than the level at which the work is to be commenced. The earth within the enclosure is withdrawn to the proper depth, then the concrete is deposited in small quantities and in layers. When the concrete has been brought to the level, or nearly to the level, of the surface of the water, further progress is arrested; and it is left until it is sufficiently hardened to sustain the superstructure. If the hydraulic mortar is of good quality, the masonry may be commenced on this concrete foundation, after ten or twelve days of repose. If, for particular reasons, the foundation was not brought quite to the surface, the water may be drawn off down to the surface of the concrete, in order to lay thereon the first courses of masonry. If the ground is consistent, and the concrete is to be carried only to a small depth, the sheet piling may be dispensed with; it being sufficient to dig out the earth in a proper form and to the proper depth. Lastly, if the ground be bad, and the foundation deep, then, after having driven the sheet piles, and taken out but little earth as a commencement of the excavation, it will be necessary to support the upper part of the sheet piles, to prevent their yielding to the pressure of the earth. An important thing, while the concrete is being sent down, is to prevent, as much as possible, any decided current of water within the enclosure, as this would wash away part of the mortar. Especial care must be taken to make, in the piles, at the level of the surface of the water, an opening, so that the water within shall always be maintained at the same level as the water without; otherwise the difference of level would occasion veins of water through the concrete, which would be very injurious. There might happen to be considerable springs of water in the spot where the foundation is to be made, which would drench the concrete and prevent its setting; in this case the means the most simple of remedying the difficulty, it appears to me, would be the stretching a strong tarred canvass over the springs. There are several modes of transmitting the concrete through the water; one is an inclined trough which conducts it to within a short distance of the bottom; but this means has the disadvantage of making it necessary to divide the concrete into small portions, in order that it may run in the trough, whereby it becomes much washed in the transit. There is the further disadvantage of being obliged, often, to change the place of the trough. Belidor proposed to send down the hydraulic mortar in a box managed with cords, one of which being attached to the bottom, served to upset the box when it had descended low enough. A more convenient mode, though nearly the same, was used at Strasburg; it was as follows: A sort of spoon was made, of strong sheet iron, 20 inches long, and sixteen inches wide; the bottom of the spoon was flat; on the sides and at the back, the iron was turned up square, to the height of six inches, but not in front; the front edge was merely curved upward a little. The spoon was fixed on the sides to an iron handle, having a ring in the middle. This ring was suspended on an iron hook, which was fastened by a socket to a wooden handle; so that the spoon was movable around the point of suspension at the end of the socket, but maintained itself in a horizontal position when filled with concrete. By means of the long wooden handle it was let down to the bottom; when, on pulling a string attached to the back of the spoon, it was upset, the concrete fell out, and the spoon was withdrawn to be again used in the same way. This instrument is very convenient, permitting the distribution of the concrete with facility whenever it may be wanted. It was contrived by Captain Bizos, of the Engineers. When the excavation is large, several workmen are employed, each with a spoon like that described. In No. 4, of the *Memorial de l'Officier du Génie*, will be found the details of the foundation of a baterdeau, with concrete. I will here, however, state succinctly the manner in which the concrete is placed in the situation designed for it, and the precautions necessary to be taken.

When concrete which has been permitted to stiffen somewhat in the air, is deposited in water, it soon softens. A layer is deposited of twelve to sixteen inches in thickness; some time after having softened, it begins to recover consistency. At the end of twelve hours it is to be lightly compressed, and afterward more strongly, by a flat rammer. Whatever precautions may be taken, there is always a portion of the concrete washed out, which forms a layer of soft matter on top of the last stratum. If this soft matter be of some thickness, it will prevent the layers of cement from uniting together; it should therefore be removed, which may be done in several ways. If the foundation be laid in a river, or upon its margin, a couple of labourers are sent out an hour before the general labours begin, who gently sweep the surface of the beton with hair brooms, thus mixing up this soft matter with the water; they then open small gates which have been prepared a little below the surface, in the upper and lower sides of the enclosure. A current is thus established at the surface of the water within the enclosure, and the turbid water passes off—the sweeping being continued till the water becomes quite clear. The concrete which has begun to harden the preceding night, will not at all suffer by this operation, if it be performed gently. If the situation be such that a current cannot be established, then the soft matter is swept into one corner of the enclosure, and is taken out by drags. If the mass of concrete has not much height, the above operation may be dispensed with; but if its height be as much as six or eight feet, it will be proper to resort to the process two or three times during the execution of the work.

Constructors have considerably differed as to the proportions of stones chip and gravel which should be mixed with the hydraulic mortar. I will give the proportions of the materials forming the concrete used at Strasburg.

The first care is to perfect the mortar which is to serve as the basis of the concrete; for on this depends its quality. The hydraulic lime and the cement that are to be employed, will therefore be tested by the processes I have pointed out. If the hydraulic lime be good, a mortar will be made of this lime and sand, as I have explained in page 9. I stated that the lime should be slaked at night, by measuring, in a bottomless box, of the capacity of about twelve cubic feet, the quick lime, sand, and other matters: that after having slaked the hydraulic lime with about a quarter of its volume of water to reduce it to powder, it should be covered with the sand and the puzzolana. The experiments I have given show that it is advantageous to let the hydraulic lime repose during twelve hours at least, after being slaked to powder and covered with sand, but that it should not be left in this state more than from ten to fifteen days, before being made into mortar.

If the hydraulic mortar is to be made of fat lime and hydraulic cement, we have seen that there will be an advantage in slaking the fat lime one or two months before hand, with about one third of its volume of water. When the lime has been slaked in this manner, it will be put in a covered place, and at the expiration of the time mentioned, it will be measured either in powder or paste, and mixed with the quantities of sand and hydraulic cement that shall have been found necessary to compose the mortar. If pressed for time, the mortar may be made with lime fresh from the kiln—and it may even be made with lime that has been for a long time melted into cream—but with less advantage.

I suppose then, that hydraulic lime is to be used, and that it has been slaked towards evening, with a quarter of its volume of water, as directed above; the next morning, or several days after, as the case may be, one of the heaps is passed, dry, a couple of times under the Rab; the quantity of water is then added that is necessary to bring it, with thorough mixing, to the ordinary consistence; and if there be no pressing need, it is made into a heap till evening. It is then worked anew with a little more water, and again brought to the ordinary consistence: it is then spread out in an even layer of four to six inches thick, and is covered as uniformly as possible with the stone chips and gravel; the whole will then be several times turned with the shovel until the stones, gravel, and mortar are well mixed together. The concrete being thus made, will be poured into a heap, and left until it has acquired a degree of stiffness permitting it to be broken up in large pieces.* It is in this state when it is put in the spoon to be lowered down to the bottom, as described above. We have seen, by the experiments of table No. XXVIII, that hydraulic mortars gain sensibly when they are left until they have somewhat stiffened. The time required to come to this state depends on the season: if it be very hot weather, the concrete acquires the due consistence in about twelve hours; generally twenty-four hours are required, and sometimes thirty-six hours.

If the concrete be made of fat lime, sand and hydraulic cement—after having slaked the lime to powder and left it at rest in the air for some time, the mortar will be made as with hydraulic lime, and it will be treated in the same way, to form concrete. We see then, that there is no difference in the manner of using these two kinds of lime, except that with hydraulic lime, to obtain the best results, it is necessary to make the mortar soon after the lime is brought from the kiln; while with fat lime, it is best that the lime be left a month or two in the air after having been slaked.

The quantity of stone-chips and gravel to be mixed with the mortar, has varied much according to different constructors. As I have before said, the object of these matters is to lessen the expense; and such a quantity should be put in as that all the fragments shall be tied together by an adequate quantity of mortar. The first concretes made at Strasburg were composed as follows:

Hydraulic lime measured before being slaked   -   -   0.75
Sand - - -   - -   -   - 1.50
Gravel   -   -   -.   -   - 0.50
Stone-chips   -   - -   -   - 1.00

This concrete was designed for foundations of revetments and other works of that kind.

To make floors of Locks and other hydraulic works, the concrete was composed thus:

Hydraulic lime measured before being slaked   0.75⎫ The resulting
Sand - - - - - -   - 0.75⎪ bulk of
Trass, or hydraulic cement   - - - 0.75⎬ beton
Gravel - - - -   -   - 0.50⎪ was
Stone-chips - - -   -   - 1.00⎭ 300

————————
3.75

Experience afterwards taught us that we could make the mortars with one part of Obernai lime measured as quick lime, and two parts and a half of sand, without making it too meagre. As to the other materials, several cubes of concrete of about twenty inches length of side, and containing

---

* In the last *Devis Instructif du Genie*, it is said, page 63, that after having mixed the mortar of the concrete with the stone chips, all will be made into a heap to be used immediately; and in note 53, referring thereto, it is said that this is the process that was followed at Strasburg. This is a mistake; at Strasburg the concrete was always left at rest in the air until it had acquired enough consistence to be attacked with the pick, and it was never used immediately after being made.   Au.

various proportions of stone-chips and gravel, were made, and put under water in a ditch; and at the end of a year they were broken, with iron masses, to determine the quantity of stone-chips and gravel that might be added without disadvantage. After the experience of these trials, the mortar was made of one part of Obernai quick lime, and two parts and a half of sand only, or of sand mixed with hydraulic cement in various proportions, according to the importance of the work. Thus ordinary mortar, whether for the concrete of coarse (gros) works, or for gross masonry, was composed of 0.30 of Obernai quick lime and 0.75 of sand. For works more important, the mortar was composed of 0.30 of Obernai quick lime, 0.30 of hydraulic cement, and 0.45 of sand. Sometimes it was made of 0.30 of Obernai quick lime, 0.20 of hydraulic cement, and 0.55 of sand. There was almost always added to this mortar from 0.60 to 0.75 of stone-chips and gravel—nearly in the proportion stated above; that is to say 0.25 of gravel and 0.50 of stone-chips; and it was found that the mortar could bear this quantity without disadvantage. The heaps of beton were thus made up of about 1.80 of materials, which, on being mixed, sustained a diminution of from $\frac{1}{6}$ to $\frac{1}{8}$, according to the proportions used.*

Each heap of concrete, containing about 64 cubic feet of materials, requires four men to make the mortar, mix therewith the stone fragments, and deposite the concrete in the water. If the work requires ten heaps to be made in a day, forty men will be necessary. There will also be required, for such an operation, two intelligent men to slake the lime, and proportion the materials; two workmen, also, will be employed in breaking the stone; and a carpenter will be needed to mend tools, repair scaffoldings, &c., and, lastly, two or three workmen will be wanted for unforeseen calls. There would be great economy in making the mortar by means of the machine described in page 10.

Mr. Vicat thinks that concrete should not be left to take any consistency in the air. According to this Engineer, it should be deposited while it is yet ductile. In the observations made by him upon the pamphlet which I published in 1824, he says: "Mr. Treussart has occupied himself with the management and manipulation of concrete: he is of opinion that concrete which has acquired a degree of stiffness in the air becomes harder in water than when it is immersed of the ordinary consistence, that is to say, soft. That is true; but only when the cohesion of the concrete is preserved, after the immersion, by the aid of some envelope; and this Engineer was wrong in practising the defective method indicated by Belidor, namely, leaving the concrete at rest in the air until it had acquired such hardness as to be attacked only with the pick, and then to place it in water, where it softened, and loses, afterward, all consistence. I have found that, after eight months, the absolute hardness of a concrete made of puzzolana, immersed according to Belidor's method, was, on an average, to that of the same concrete immersed in a stiff though ductile state, as 15 is to 100."

It would not be difficult to bring forward a great number of facts, com-

* The above proportions expressed in other terms, are,

Hydraulic lime as before	-	0.60	0.60	0.60
Sand - - -		1.50	0.90	1.10
Hydraulic cement -	-		0.60	0.40
Stone-chips -		1.00	1.00	1.00
Gravel - - -		0.50	0.50	0.50

Tr.

pletely overturning what is here advanced by Mr. Vicat. In 1818 the baterdeau of Fort Mutin at Strasburg was constructed on a mass of concrete of more than 260 cubic yards. In making the concrete the process given above was followed; and the process of Belidor was pursued in depositing it. Eight days, only, after it had been deposited, the masonry was begun, and was pushed with much activity to completion. This baterdeau sustained, only six months after it was commenced, one of the highest floods of the River Ill, without the occurrence of any kind of accident.

If the concrete became soft, and lost all consistency, as Mr. Vicat supposes, how was it possible to construct the masonry thereon after only eight days? The concrete would have yielded to the weight of the baterdeau if it had not been of strong consistency; and cracks would have appeared at the junction of the old masonry. The baterdeau would have been carried off by the first flood of the Ill, if the concrete had not been very hard. At a later day, we successively built upon foundations of concrete a scouring sluice with five passages, in the great ditch of the Town: then an escape sluice and several other works, and lastly a *canal à poutrelle* in the great ditch, to lead the water to a mill—all the bottom of this canal being of concrete. All these concretes set in a short time, to great hardness; and during the same season, the masonry was constructed on these foundations, without any accident resulting.

Mr. Vicat says that the absolute hardness of a concrete immersed in Belidor's mode is, on the average, compared with that immersed while firm and ductile, as 15 to 100. We have seen by the experiments of table No. XXVIII. that mortar which had been reworked, sometime after it was made, and which had been at rest afterward, before plunging it in water, gave a better result than when immediately immersed. Mr. Vicat admits it to be true, when the cohesion is preserved by the aid of an envelope. I can conceive that this Engineer might have obtained the result he announces, if he destroyed the cohesion of the concrete that he submerged in Belidor's mode; that is to say, if he reduced it to small fragments; but that was not the way we operated at Strasburg. When the heaps had taken some degree of hardness, they were not broken up into small pieces, but they were broken by the pick into large pieces which were transmitted down through the water by means of the spoon above described. On breaking up the heap of concrete into large pieces, there remained some small fragments, though not in considerable quantity, when the concrete had adequately stiffened. These were made anew, into paste with water, and added to the heap of concrete then being made; or transmitted by the spoon and deposited on the concrete under water. I do not therefore think that Belidor's process has any disadvantage: and the considerable works carried on in this way at Strasburg, afforded very good results. The concrete hardened very promptly—Mr. Vicat's operation to the contrary notwithstanding. I do not say there would be great disadvantage in immersing the substance as soon as made; but I believe it would be more exposed to be washed. The process of Belidor was followed at Strasburg, because the experiments which have been cited had taught me that mortars which were destined to be put in water, were better when worked up of the ordinary consistence than when worked up stiff, and that there was a sensible saving in the manipulation. But, in this soft state, the mortar would have been much washed, if put at once into water; for which reason it was left to harden somewhat, according to the advice of Belidor.

It often happens that the floors of sluices, and foundations of hydraulic works, may be built, without being troubled with water. In such cases these floors and these foundations are ordinarily built of stone, resting on grillages: but wood does not unite with masonry, and the mortar often unites badly with the stones: whenever these constructions have to support a considerable pressure of water, leaks will, therefore, be the consequence. In such instances, where floors of locks and foundations of dams can be constructed without the presence of water, I think it would be preferable to make them of concrete: the expense of grillages would be saved, and they almost always cause leaks. It would be necessary, after the concrete is laid, to cover it with a few inches of water, or with a layer of moist earth: because, in general, hydraulic mortars take a stronger consistence under water, or in humid ground, than when they remain exposed to the air, and especially during summer.

If we notice the retained waters at mills and locks, we see that when the walls are constructed of large cut stones, the water often escapes through the joints, carrying away the mortar, causing a considerable loss of water by leakage, and finally involving the destruction of the works. I am pursuaded that there would often be economy, and always great advantage, in making the side walls of Locks of concrete, instead of stones or bricks, or perhaps the concrete might be restricted to those parts where leaks are most apt to appear.

The use of concrete is very advantageous in the foundations of constructions in water, because it avoids the necessity of drawing off the water, always very expensive, and which has the great disadvantage, by the differences of pressure which result, of giving rise to veins which dilute or wash away the mortar. We have not as yet derived all the advantages that concrete will afford. I am pursuaded that ere long, when it shall be required to construct the piers of a bridge; or a revetment, in a river of from seven feet to twenty feet depth, the method of caissons will be abandoned. The following process, it appears to me, might be followed with advantage.

After having surrounded the space in which the foundation is to be laid with a row of jointed piles in contact, or a row of strong sheet piling; it will be easy to drag out the bottom to the depth of about seven feet, and to fill the excavation with concrete up to the level of the bottom of the river, or a little below, if it be supposed that the works will cause the bottom of the river to be somewhat lowered. When the concrete has been placed, and while it is yet somewhat soft, a second range of sheet piling should be driven into the concrete itself, parallel to and three and a half to five feet distant from the first row. These sheet piles should be driven only about eight inches into the concrete. It will be easy to connect the second row of sheet piles firmly to the first row by means of ties and braces. When this is done, the concrete will be left to take a suitable hardness, and then the space between the rows of piles will be filled with good puddling earth. There will thus be obtained a coffer dam reposing upon concrete; and all the water may be withdrawn from within the inner piling, without leaving any leaks, provided the concrete has hardened sufficiently to resist the pressure of water. It will therefore be easy to build with masonry, upon all that part of the concrete which is within the enclosure.

If it should happen, in consequence of the depth of water, that there was reason to fear the whole bottom of concrete might be raised; this might be easily guarded against by placing wooden trestles on the concrete—these trestles supporting timbers bearing a platform and the necessary load of stones: when the masonry—begun between the trestles, should be sufficiently advanced, this scaffolding with its load would be removed. The masonry being raised above the surface of the water, the inner row of sheet piles may be easily removed and also the earth of the dam. As to the exterior row of piles, or sheet piles; if they have been driven in as deep as six or eight feet, it would be somewhat difficult to remove them. To lessen this difficulty, it would be well, before depositing the concrete, to stretch some canvass along the lower part of the inside of this outer row of piles, to prevent the concrete from introducing itself into the joints; or lastly, this outer row may be sawed off level with the bottom.

We see that by this method we are obliged to make the foundation rather larger than would be otherwise necessary; but this is no disadvantage to the work as it will increase the stability. If the nature of the ground be such as to require piles under the foundation, they will be driven as in the ordinary method. There will be the advantage of not being obliged to drive them very equally, nor to saw them off at the same level exactly, as is necessary when founding with a caisson. In founding with concrete, it will suffice to drive the piles to the same level within a few inches. When the concrete is sent down, it will spread itself at the same time, on the ground, and around the heads of the piles, to which it will exactly mould itself. If the mass of concrete is from five to seven feet deep, it will form, as it were, an artificial rock resting on piles, and capable of sustaining an immense load of masonry without the slightest injury.

I was under the necessity of studying the project of which I have given above the principal dispositions merely, because we had in view, early in 1825, a bridge on piers of masonry across the Ill, which river is from six to ten feet deep; and, being subject to floods, would have offered great difficulties. I am well convinced that the method I have summarily indicated would have had great advantages over the various modes in use, including the method with caissons; which cost a good deal in the first place, and demand great care in cutting off the piles exactly at a level, and in properly grounding the caisson thereon. Besides it is almost always requisite to surround the foot of the caisson with loose stones, which considerably restrict the passage for the water between the piers, thereby augmenting its velocity, and consequently increasing its wearing action on the bottom. By the method I have suggested, all these inconveniences are avoided: and it is equally applicable to sluices, dry docks, and all other hydraulic structures that are to be made in depths exceeding 20 feet, and where it would become very difficult and expensive to get a foundation by making coffer dams and pumping out the water.

When it is required to build in stagnant water, or where there is a gentle current only, and the materials for a very good concrete are at hand, the whole foundation may then be made of concrete to within a short distance of low water level. It will not be necessary, in this case, to give so great a breadth to the foundation, as in the preceding case; the inner row of sheet piles might be smaller; and they might be separated from the outer row only by the breadth of an ordinary offset in the foundations. No puddling would be needed; all the space within the inner row would be filled with concrete up to low water level nearly, where the stone masonry would be begun. The pier being finished, the two rows of sheet piles would be removed as in the preceding case. When the pier is to be built, thus, of concrete up to low water, the current must be feeble, and the materials whereof to compose the concrete, very good. In cases where one of these conditions is wanting, it will therefore be most safe to use the first method, which brings the concrete no higher than the bed of the river, finishing the rest with masonry, for I doubt if a concrete can be made which will resist the continued action of a current of water, as effectually as masonry made of good stone.

CHAPTER X.

Summary of the First Section.

From the facts presented in the foregoing articles, may be deduced the following conclusions.

There are two modes of making hydraulic mortar; first, by making it of lime that is naturally or artificially hydraulic, and of sand; and secondly, by making a mixture of common lime and puzzolana, or of some analagous substance.

In countries where there are good natural hydraulic limes, it is very advantageous to employ them; and in such cases no use should be made of fat lime. In gross masonry, they may be used with sand alone; but when it is required to construct the foundations of sluices, roofs of arches, and other similar works, it is advantageous to add to the mortar, a little hydraulic cement.

In a country where there is no hydraulic lime, in lieu of making it by calcining lime with a little clay, it is more advantageous, and more economical, to make hydraulic mortar by mixing, directly, fat lime with hydraulic cement and sand. The advantage is the greater in countries where there is no chalk, and where it would be necessary to submit the lime stone designed to be made hydraulic, to two successive burnings—burning it the second time with a small quantity of clay.

Fat lime becomes hydraulic by being burned to the proper degree with a little crude clay; this result is not obtained if the clay has been previously calcined. Fat lime also gives a good hydraulic mortar, when it is united in the moist way with a mixture of equal parts of puzzolana and sand, and when the proportion of these substances is at least double that of the lime.

Silex, when it is very finely divided and disseminated in lime stone, produces good hydraulic lime, as is proved by the Senonches lime: when fat lime and finely divided silex are burned together, a hydraulic result, though feeble, is obtained. Iron and the oxide of manganese communicate to lime no hydraulic property: iron in the state of brown or red oxide, prevents the lime from heating much in process of slaking. It does not appear that alumine or magnesia, cause lime to become hydraulic; but when these substances are mixed with silex, good results are obtained. The best process for converting fat lime into hydraulic lime, is to burn it with a small quantity of crude clay; the proportion of $\frac{1}{5}$th of clay, seems the most suitable; and it appears that the best clay is that which contains as much silex as alumine.

The quality of hydraulic lime is improved by mixing with the clay that is to be burned with the lime, a small quantity of water containing soda; a better result is obtained with potash; but this means would be too embarrassing, and would occasion an excess of expense which might not be in proportion to the advantage, were the operations on a large scale.

Hydraulic lime bears less sand than is commonly thought; there are few of these limes which can be mixed with more than $2\frac{1}{4}$ parts of sand, without sensibly diminishing the resistance of the mortars. Fat lime may take a greater quantity of mixed sand and puzzolana to form hydraulic mortar.

Puzzolanas, or hydraulic cements, which are energetic, apply equally to hydraulic lime and fat lime. In mixing hydraulic lime, or fat lime, with sand and puzzolana, or other analagous substance, in equal parts, a better result is often obtained than by mixing these limes with puzzolana alone. When very hydraulic lime is used, the addition of sand permits a sensible diminution of the quantity of puzzolana, natural or artificial, required to obtain a prompt induration and great resistance. With fat lime there always results a very good mortar, on mixing it, in equal parts, with sand and natural or artificial puzzolana; and if it sometimes happens that a mortar a little superior is obtained with lime and this last substance, without the sand, the advantage is not so great as to compensate for the greater economy of using sand also.

Hydraulic limes are difficult to burn to the proper degree. When they are not sufficiently burned, they slake badly; and the resulting mortar has not all the tenacity it ought to have.* A degree of heat a little greater than it should be, causes, with these limes, a beginning of vitrification; they then slake slowly; the mortar they form loses its force, it swells after having been used, and may occasion considerable injury to the works. Hydraulic limes should be used soon after leaving the kiln; they should not be slaked with much water, like fat limes, nor be left in a state of cream, like them, because, in a very short time they would become very hard, and it would be impossible to make use of them. Whether slaked with a small quantity of water to reduce them to dry powder, or left to slake in the air, they, in general, very soon lose a part of their hydraulic properties, and finally pass to the state of common limes. It is likely that this effect is due to the absorption of oxygen by the hydrate. It would appear that hydraulic limes containing the oxide of maganese preserve their energy better when they have been left to slake in the air than when they have been slaked to powder by water. Notwithstanding the precautions that hydraulic limes demand, it is important to employ them whenever natural limes of this sort, of good quality, can be obtained, because they supply a very good mortar at a cheap rate. We should carefully study the exact point of burning, and should satisfy ourselves, as to whether or not they soon lose their hydraulic property, on exposure to the air, when slaked to dry powder, or when air slaked; without these precautions, we may expose important works to failure, by making very bad mortar out of very good lime. Common lime has not, like hydraulic lime, the inconvenience of losing a part of its qualities, by a degree of heat a little greater than that which is most suitable. A very violent fire is required to produce this result. Whether slaked with much water so as to be made into a fluid paste and run into vats, or with a little, only, so as to be reduced to dry powder; or if spontaneously slaked in the air; or if used immediately as it comes from the kiln, a good hydraulic mortar is always obtained by mixing fat lime, in equal parts, with sand and natural or artificial puzzolana. By air slaking the result is the least good.

*This is understood as applying only to hydraulic lime stones which have been burned sufficiently to be employed as lime; as to those which have been burned but very little, to be employed as cements, according to the process of Mr. Lacordaire, I have no experience that will enable me to pronounce as to the tenacity of the mortars they afford.   Au.

It appears that by slaking in the air, the lime absorbs a considerable quantity of carbonic acid; and the mortar which results is filled with white points, which are particles of carbonate of lime, that cannot be made to disappear, whatever pains may be taken in the mixing process.

The best mode of slaking hydraulic lime is to sprinkle it, as it comes from the kiln, with about one fourth of its bulk of water. A measure containing about one third of a cubic metre (a cube of about three feet three inches on each side) permits the mixture of the materials that are to compose the mortar, to be easily made. Before sprinkling the lime, it is to be surrounded with the mortars that are to be mixed with it, and when it is slaked and gives out no more vapours, it is to be covered with these mortars. The lime is left in this state for twelve hours at least, and for eight or ten days at most. The quantity of water necessary to bring the mortar to the ordinary consistence is afterward added. Care must be taken to make the mortar no faster than it is needed. The heap of lime surrounded by the sand and other materials should be covered from the rain.

With common lime the process will be a little difficult; being slaked as it comes from the kiln, with one-third of its volume of water, the lime, in a state of powder, should be put under cover, and left in this state for one or two months. At the end of this period it should be measured in paste and mixed with the sand and cement in due proportion, adding the quantity of water necessary to bring it to the consistence of ordinary mortar. This process is the one which gives the best results; but if this be inconvenient the lime may be used as it comes from the kiln, or after it has been lying, wet in vats for any length of time.

A great deal of trituration is useless, either with hydraulic or with common limes. It is enough if the mortar be homogeneous, which is the case when a heap of about thirty-five cubic feet has been passed under the Rab five or six times by four men. Mortar made of ordinary consistence, and even rather thin, is easier to mix thoroughly, and gives better results than when it has been mixed in a stiff state. If it becomes a little dry before being used, there is no objection to working it anew, with the addition of a little water. It might be left from night till morning, to be then passed twice under the rab: the mortar acquires more consistence by moistening it a little. It might be remixed in this way during a couple of days without losing its force.

In mortars made of hydraulic lime, the sand appears to be in a passive state; in hydraulic mortars made with fat lime, the puzzolana or other analogous substance, enters into combination with the lime; and it appears to be that combination which gives to the mortar the property of hardening in water. Fine sand is preferable to coarse for hydraulic mortars; that which is earthy diminishes the force of the mortar considerably.

When one part of quick hydraulic lime is mixed with two parts of sand, the resulting mortar is diminished about one fifth; the diminution is only about one sixth if the mixture be one part lime and two and a half sand.

All clays calcined to the proper degree, and reduced to powder, are susceptible of giving factitious puzzolanas—better or worse, according to the composition. The clays most proper to make good puzzolanas are those which are greasy to the touch—such as are commonly used for making Dutch ware, stone ware, earthen ware and tobacco pipes. Clays which contain one fourth of alumine are greasy to the touch; those which contain from one third to one half, give very good results. The substance of which it is most important to observe the presence in clays, is lime. If this substance exists in the clay in the proportion of one tenth, or more, and the clay be exposed to too great a heat, a cement will be obtained which will not possess the property of causing lime to harden in water; but if it be moderately burned, a good result will be secured. The more lime there is in the clay, the less it should be burned.* When no lime is present, it is generally necessary to burn the clay as much as a well burned brick; some clays demand a degree of heat a little greater, according to their proportions of alumine and silex. Even when the clay contains no lime, it should not be too much burned; otherwise it will lose part of its hydraulic property. When it contains up to one-tenth of lime, it requires a less degree of heat than is needed to produce a well burned brick. When it contains more than one tenth, the heat required to burn tiles is sufficient. The clay is supposed to be moulded before burning, into bricks of ordinary dimensions.

When the clays contain only four or five per cent. of lime, some having been properly burned, seem to be benefitted thereby, and others, not; which appears to depend on the proportions in which the silex and alumine exist in the clay. Lime cannot therefore be considered as augmenting, in a sensible degree, the energy of puzzolana; but it has the advantage of bringing the clays more promptly to the proper state of calcination, and making them easier to pulverize: in these respects, therefore, the presence of a little lime tends to economy. Clays which contain about one-third of alumine, and four or five per cent. of lime, appear to be most favourable to the production of puzzolana, provided they be burned to a degree a little below that required to give a well burned brick.

Cement suitable for making a good mortar for heavy masonry, may be made out of ordinary bricks. The dust of tiles, has no advantage over that of bricks, as a cement. The important point is to know the true degree of calcination which the clay requires. Bricks should not be taken indiscriminately from the kiln, but those should be selected which have been found on trial to afford the best hydraulic cement.

Iron gives no energy to Puzzolana; it even seems to be more injurious than beneficial: for ochreous earths did not give good results while with clays entirely without iron, very good were obtained.

Carbonate of magnesia, which is often mixed with clays in small proportion, has no influence when the burning is carried only to the degree proper to yield good hydraulic cements.

Soda does not appear to have a sensible influence in improving hydraulic cements or artificial puzzolanas, but potash has a marked effect. When the clays which it is desired to convert into hydraulic cement, have imbibed a solution of potash, standing at 5° of the *pese acid*, equal in bulk to one-fourth of that of the clay, the cement is sensibly increased in energy; but the advantage to be derived does not appear to me to be so great as to recommend this means in practice. With such clays as I have designated, artificial puzzolanas are obtained, which are in no degree inferior to the natural productions; and by these means, proportioning the cement properly, mortars may be obtained of very great hardness.

Nitrous clays appear to be good for the purpose of being transformed into hydraulic cements: clays containing a little saltpetre (Nitrate of potash) should not, therefore, be rejected.

* When I speak of lime contained in the clay, it is meant that the lime is in the state of carbonate.   Au.

When the clays that are to be calcined have had a little of the solution of soda, potash, or saltpetre, at 5° of the *pese acid*, added to them, they do not easily lose their hydraulic property by too high a degree of calcination.* This mode would be embarrassing and occasion some expense; but common salt (muriate of soda) might be substituted, and would be but little expensive or troublesome. It appears probable that a like result would be obtained with sea water: because we have seen, page 68, that the Dutch make artificial trass of clay which they draw from the bottom of the sea; and which they sell as natural trass.

When the clays to be transformed are calcined with a current of atmospheric air, the mortars harden in the water much more promptly than when the clays are burned out of a current of air. I cannot assert that the resistance of such mortars is much greater, though it appears to me to be probable. As it is important to obtain, in many circumstances, mortars which harden promptly in the water: the clays on these occasions should be calcined in a current of air, in such furnaces as I have described.

Ashes, and the scoria of forges, belong to the class of artificial puzzolanas: there are some which give very good, and others which give very bad results.

Basalt, when calcined to a proper degree, affords good artificial puzzolanas.

Amongst mortars composed of hydraulic lime and sand, those which harden most promptly in water do not always give the greatest resistance: but those do, generally, which are composed of fat lime and puzzolana either natural or artificial. The most certain means of knowing whether hydraulic lime is of good quality, is to reduce it to paste with water, and to plunge it in this state, into water, to see if it hardens speedily: or, otherwise, to mix one part of the lime in paste, with two of sand. To learn the quality of hydraulic cements, or natural puzzolanas, it is proper to make a little mortar, using two parts of cement, and one of fat lime measured in paste, and place it under water.

All hydraulic mortars harden quicker in summer than in winter. If the mortar, made for trial in summer, is composed of hydraulic lime and sand, or if it be composed of hydraulic lime alone, a very good result will be certain, if at the end of eight or ten days the hardening be such that no impression can be made on the essay by pressing strongly with the finger. If this result is obtained only after the lapse of fifteen or twenty days, it is a proof that the lime is only moderately hydraulic.

With mortar made of hydraulic cement and fat lime, a similar induration should be obtained in from three to five days, if the cement be of the first quality, and if it has been calcined in a current of air. Should the hardening take place only at the end of twelve or fifteen days, with cement calcined in a current of air, it may still be employed with advantage. But if the cement has not been calcined with a free current, instead of hardening in from three to five days, it will require from twelve to fifteen, and still give a very good resistance. It may be estimated that, in winter, the induration will demand nearly twice as much time as in summer, without any diminution of the strength of the mortar.

Arenes are clays which have been subjected to the action of fire: they are therefore true natural puzzolanas. It appears that France contains this substance in many places; and it will be found in many more, as research-

* This is the effect, when the clays contain no lime; but I do not know whether it would be the same, if lime were present. Au.

es shall be multiplied. It is with arenes as with natural puzzolanas and trass: all have not, by any means, the same energy: but those which are feeble may be advantageously employed in mortars to be exposed to the air, while those which have more energy may replace hydraulic cements in constructions under water, in the case of ordinary works, and where no circumstances demand a prompt induration.

The use of energetic arenes affords good mortar for masonry in water and in air, at a very cheap rate.

Concrete is nothing else than masonry made of hydraulic mortar and small stones. The use of concrete is of great advantage in founding under water at depths which occasion great expense if pumped dry. Foundations in concrete require little or no pumping: they are capable of supporting the heaviest loads.

The goodness of the concrete depends on the quality of the hydraulic mortar. It appears that the ancients sometimes constructed with this sub- stance: its use since has been much neglected. All the advantages possi- ble, have not yet been derived from this mode of construction; its advan- tages will be better appreciated when its use shall be more extended; and when the manner of perfecting hydraulic mortars shall be better under- stood.

CHAPTER XI.

Of Mortars made of Lime, Sand and Puzzolana.

If it is of great consequence, in making mortars that are always to remain under water, to be able to make them of good quality; it is of no less consequence to know how to prepare those which are to remain exposed to the air, in such a way that the masonry shall be lasting. People have been struck with the solidity of the remains of Roman masonry, while masonry which we ourselves have erected has often been of very limited duration. All have concurred in attributing the difference to the superiority of Roman mortars. To explain this superiority, it has been supposed that the Romans were possessed of a peculiar manner of slaking lime. Mr. Lafaye published in 1777, a method of slaking, which consisted, as described in our first section, in plunging the lime in the water for a few seconds—the lime being placed in baskets, and then to allow it to slake in the air. He gave this process as a secret recovered from the Romans; and he pretended that by this process as good mortar was obtained as theirs. This made much noise at the time; but it was soon ascertained that although there was some advantage in this mode of slaking lime, it was far from giving the mortars the superior quality the author claimed. Afterward, Mr. Loriot announced that mortar like that of the Romans might be obtained by mixing a certain quantity of powdered quick lime with lime slaked and reduced to paste in the common mode; but experience did not confirm this method of M. Loriot.

Others, to explain the goodness of Roman mortars, have attributed it to the time that has elapsed since the works were executed, whence has come the saying that " mortar is still new that is not one hundred years old," (*le mortar que n'a pas cent ans est encore un enfant.*) But then, it is asked, how comes it that so much masonry perishes before it is an hundred years old, while, in the same climate, some is found which has passed through near twenty centuries without repairs, and far the greater part is still standing? Those who pretend that a great lapse of time is necessary to the induration of mortars, think that the lime absorbs carbonic acid (although situated in the heart of the masonry) and thus passes to the state of carbonate; but several facts contradict this opinion: for there are certain limes which afford very good mortar in a very short time, while others never indurate, as is often seen in demolitions. On the other hand we have seen, in the first section, that according to the analysis of several ancient mortars, many were found which had very great hardness, and which nevertheless contained only a small quantity of carbonic acid; and we know that the lime used in building is never wholly deprived of it. We cannot admit, then, that carbonic acid penetrates far into the interior of masonry; and it is proved, by multiplied observations, that moisture remains during a very long time in the interior of certain walls. Dr. John reports, on this subject, that about ten years ago, they demolished the piers of the Tower of St. Peter's, at Berlin; this tower had been built eighty years, and the pillars were twenty seven feet thick; the mortar on the outside was dry and hard, but that in the middle was as fresh as if it had been lately placed there. I can state that in 1822, that the lower part of a bastion at Strasburg, being under repair, the mortar was found to be as fresh as if just laid, and nevertheless, this bastion was erected in 1666; the revetment was only about seven feet thick, but the moisture of the earth resting against it, prevented the lower part from drying. Similar facts are observed in constructions still more ancient. It results from what has been advanced, that the good quality of the mortars of several ancient structures is not due to the manner of slaking the lime, as Mr. Lafaye supposed, nor to the process of making mortar supposed by Mr. Loriot, nor to the time that has elapsed since they were built. The experiments which follow will confirm this remark; which is in accordance also with general opinion at the present day. The great number of hydraulic works which were to be repaired or rebuilt at Strasburg, induced me to direct my first researches to the object of obtaining good mortars for the water; and it was only when these were well advanced that I began to study mortars for the air. I quitted the place before finishing my experiments. The experiments that I made, though few, appear to me, however, to throw some light on the theory of mortars in the air, and to explain in a satisfactory manner, whence was derived the good quality of the mortars found in many ancient works. It will be useful I think to report them.

It is the opinion of a great many constructors that when common, or fat lime is to be used, it is necessary to have it lie wet in vats or pits for a long time: it is asserted, that the older it is the better it is. The experiments of the following table have for object to verify this important point.

Table No. XXX.

No. of the mortar.	Composition of the mortars.		Weights supported before breaking.
1	Fat lime which had been lying a long time wet—measured in paste	1 ⎰ 3	0
	Sand	2 ⎱	
2	Same lime	1 ⎰ 3½	0
	Sand	2½ ⎱	
3	Same lime	1 ⎰ 3½	0
	Sand	2½ ⎱	
4	Same lime	1 ⎰ 3¾	0
	Sand	2¾ ⎱	
5	Same lime	1 ⎰ 4	0
	Sand	3 ⎱	

Observations on the Experiments of Table No. XXX.

To make these experiments, I took fat lime which had been slaked and lying wet in a pit for five years—a portion of the same having been used in the construction of the theatre of Strasburg. The mortars were all made in the same manner, and broken in the same way as the hydraulic mortars; they were left in the air in a cellar for one year before cutting them down to their ultimate dimensions and submitting them to the test: the proportions of sand varied from two up to three parts of sand for one of lime measured in paste. The resulting mortars had no consistency, and crumbled between the fingers with the greatest ease. I confess I was much surprised at the result, for the sand which I used was the same as that used in the mortars of the first section; and, as I have said, was a granitic sand very slightly earthy. I made another experiment with the same lime, and the same sand washed to free it of the small quantity of earth which it contained, but I obtained no better result. I also repeated this essay with another sand, also washed, varying the quantity of water used in making the mortar, but always with results similar to those of the above table, that is to say, mortars without any consistency.

These bad results cannot be attributed to the quality of the lime, for it has been shown by the analysis in page forty-one, to be the product of a calcarious carbonate containing only a very small quantity of iron: this is the lime that has been used for a long time both for the public and private edifices of Strasburg. The theatre, as I have observed, was built of this lime: this beautiful structure does not promise, therefore, to be of long duration.

At the same time that I made the experiments of the preceding table with lime and sand, I made corresponding ones with the same lime and trass, and also with lime, sand and trass. The following table gives the results.

Table No. XXXI.

No. of the mortar.	Composition of the mortars.			Weights supported before breaking.	Weights supported before breaking.
				lbs.	lbs.
1	Fat lime which had been lying a long time wet, measured in paste	1	} 3	242	440
	Trass	2			
2	Same lime	1	} 3¼	264	484
	Trass	2¼			
3	Same lime	1	} 3	286	517
	Trass	2½			
4	Same lime	1	} 3¾	341	528
	Trass	2¾			
5	Same lime	1	} 4	297	462
	Trass	3			
6	Same lime	1		286	143
	Sand	1	} 3		
	Trass	1			
7	Same lime	1		297	165
	Sand	1¼	} 3¼		
	Trass	1⅛			
8	Same lime	1		319	187
	Sand	1¼	} 3½		
	Trass	1¼			
9	Same lime	1		330	209
	Sand	1⅜	} 3⅝		
	Trass	1¼			
10	Same lime	1		330	209
	Sand	1½	} 4		
	Trass	1½			

Observations on the experiments of Table No. XXXI.

All the above mortars were composed of the same old lime as those of the preceding table. The experiments were made in duplicate: those in the first column were prepared in August, 1823, and were left during a year in the air, in a cellar; those of the second column were made in the month of October, 1824, and were left during a year in the air in a chamber where there was no fire. We see that the results are very different: 1st, the five mortars in the first column made of lime and trass only, gave much weaker resistances than the similar mortars in the second column, while it is the inverse with mortars made of lime, sand and trass: 2d, in the first column, the mortars made of lime, sand and trass, gave, in general, better results than the corresponding mortars made of lime and trass only, while it is the inverse in the experiments of the second column.

I am unable to account for the differences shown by these two series of experiments; I cannot say whether, or in what degree, it is to be attributed to their being made at different seasons, and placed in different atmospheres. It is not easy to ascribe such great variations to these two causes; I should rather be inclined to believe that the trass which I used in 1824 was not the same as that used in 1823, and that this has occasioned these opposite results. I purposed repeating these experiments, but my departure from Strasburg in 1825 prevented.

The mortars of the first column of table No. XXXI; were made at the same time as those of table No. XXX; and when, in 1824, I made the experiments of the second column, I also made five mortars like those of No. XXX. and placed them in a chamber—the preceding having been deposited in a cellar. These five mortars, composed of old lime and sand only, remained, like the analogous mortars, without consistence, and were unable to bear any weight.

Seeing that I could get no results with the old moist lime and sand, I made some essays agreeably to the process of Mr. Loriot; they are given in the following table.

Table No. XXXII.

No. of the mortar.	Composition of the mortars.		Weight supported before breaking.
1	Fat lime which had been lying a long time wet, measured in paste	1 } 3	0
	Sand	2 }	
2	Lime the same	1-2 }	0
	Unslaked fat lime reduced to powder	1-2 } 1 } 3	
	Sand	2 }	
3	Lime the same	2-3 }	0
	Unslaked fat lime, &c.	1-3 } 1 } 3	
	Sand	1 }	
4	Lime the same	3-4 }	0
	Unslaked fat lime, &c.	1-4 } 1 } 3	
	Sand	2 }	
5	Lime the same	4-5 }	0
	Unslaked fat lime, &c.	1-5 } 1 } 3	
	Sand	2 }	

Observations on the experiments of Table No. XXXII.

The process of Mr. Loriot consists in mixing a certain quantity of quick lime reduced to powder, with lime which has been lying for some time slaked and wet; and following his method, I varied the quantities of the two kinds of lime, and yet we see, that I obtained no results. The mortar dries quickly, it is true, on account of the presence of the quick lime, but this is not a true induration. The property of drying quickly is what, no doubt, led Mr. Loriot into error. We see, then, that this mode, offered by the author as yielding very good mortars, gives, in fact, only very bad. It is not surprising, after seeing the above results, that the attempt to repoint the platform of the observatory by this method did not succeed.

Having no good results with the old lime, nor with Mr. Loriot's process, I quitted the erroneous methods of others, and made the following experiments.

Table No. XXXIII.

No. of the mortars.	Composition of the mortars.	Made immediately.	After 15 days.	After 1 month.	After 2 months.	After 3 months.	After 4 months.	After 5 months.	After 6 months.	After 7 months.	After 8 months.	After 9 months.	After 10 months.	After 11 months.	After 12 months.
		lbs.	lbs.	lbs.	lbs.	lbs.	lbs.	lbs.	lbs.	lbs.	lbs.	lbs.	lbs.	lbs.	lbs.
1	Fat lime slaked in thick paste 1, Sand 2½ } 3½	99	50	44	33	33	33	33	33	22	22	22	22	22	22
2	Same lime 1, Sand 1¼, Trass 1¼ } 3½	319	308	308	297	319	308	319	308	319	352	363	341	319	308
3	Fat lime slaked in thin paste 1, Sand 2½ } 3½								33	22	22	22	22	22	22
4	Same lime 1, Sand 1¼, Trass 1¼ } 3½								308	297	308	286	297	286	275
5	Fat lime slaked to dry powder and measured in paste 1, Sand 2½ } 3½									0	0	0	0	0	0
6	Same lime 1, Sand 1¼, Trass 1¼ } 3½									286	297	330	297	308	

Observations on the experiments of Table No. XXXIII.

These experiments were made at the same time as those of table No. XV, of the first section, and with the same fat lime. I slaked a part as it came from the kiln, giving it only the quantity of water necessary to reduce it to thick paste, and I made therewith the experiments comprised under Nos. 1 and 2. I slaked a part into thin paste, and made with it the experiments under Nos. 3 and 4, and I also slaked a part into dry powder, by giving it a quarter of its volume of water, and with this I made the two series, Nos. 5 and 6. All these experiments comprise the interval of a year, and the several epochs at which they were respectively made are given in the table. The figures of the table give the number of pounds that the mortars supported before breaking.

The series of mortar No. 1, is composed of one part fat lime slaked to thick paste, and two parts and a half of sand. We see that the mortar made immediately, acquired a hardness which is not, in fact, very great, but which is passable. The mortars made after fifteen days had nearly one half less consistency; at the end of two months it had two thirds less, and the mortars made after six months had not strength enough to support the weight of the scale pan, &c., which was twenty-two pounds. This result is very remarkable. If we compare it with table No. XXX, of which the mortars being made of lime that had been lying slaked and wet for five years, had no strength, we cannot but think that slaking fat lime into vats and letting it lie there in a wet state, is a mistaken practice. The practice may have been induced from the considerable increase of bulk it gives to fat lime; but the trials I have made show it to be a very bad process, at least with the limes I used.

The series of mortar No. 2, was made of one part of lime in paste, to two and a half parts of sand and trass in equal proportion. The result was very good. It will be noticed that it was best after the 8th, 9th and 10th month. The experiments above having been commenced the middle of November, the greatest resistances correspond to the months of July, August and September. The mortars were deposited in a cellar; but the cellar was one to which external differences of temperature were soon transmitted. In summer, therefore, these mortars were exposed to an atmosphere humid and mild.

The series No. 3 differs from the first only in the lime having been slaked to a thin, instead of a thick paste. The lime was left six months before making any mortar with it. We see that the results were the same, that is to say, were equally bad with those of the first series.

The fourth series differs from the second only in being made of lime slaked thin, while the second series was slaked to a thick paste. I only began to make the mortars after six months had elapsed. We see that the results are good, but rather inferior to those given by lime slaked to a thick paste.

Series No. 5 was made of the same lime, slaked to dry powder. This series was not commenced till six months after the slaking of the lime. The mortars I obtained had no consistency, and crumbled easily between the fingers. The mortars of the first and third series, made at the same period, bad as they were, gave resistance enough to be submitted to fracture. The lime of series No. 5, was slaked by a process analogous to that of Mr. Lafaye, which consists, as I have stated, in plunging the lime for a few seconds into water, then withdrawing it, allowing it to slake of itself, and keeping it for some time before using it; to avoid the embarrassment of the baskets proposed by Mr. Lafaye, I contented myself with throwing on the lime the quantity of water necessary to reduce it to powder, which, in fact, amounts to the same thing. I however obtained no result. It is possible that Mr. Lafaye made his experiments a short time after the slaking of the lime, and comparing them with others made of lime slaked and lying wet for a long time, he found the first to be the best; but it was probably because the lime he employed, like that in the above table, required to be used immediately after being slaked. It appears to me that Mr. Lafaye was deceived in attributing his success to the mode of slaking which he followed.

The experiments of table No. VI were also made with lime slaked to dry powder, mixed with sand and trass. I did not commence these trials till after six months, and I was only able to continue them four months, for want of time. The results are about the same as those of the fourth series, and a little inferior to those of the second.

In the first four series, the proportions were one part of lime in paste, to two and a half parts of sand and trass. To obtain results with the last two series in which the lime was slaked to powder, that might be compared with these, I took care, when making the mortars of the last two series, to reduce this powder to paste, and to measure it in this state.

If we compare the above table with table No. XV, whereof the mortars were made of the same lime, we shall see that in general the mortars left in the air gave results a little weaker than those put in water.

Table No. XXX has shown the bad quality of mortars made by mixing sand with fat lime that had been slaked and wet for some years. The following are corresponding experiments made with the same lime just from the kiln.

Table No. XXXIV.

No. of the mortars	Composition of the mortars.		Weights supported before breaking.
			lbs.
1	Fat lime slaked as it came from the kiln and measured in paste immediately . . . . 1 } 3 Sand . . . . 2 }		68
2	Same lime . . . . . . 1 } 3½ Sand . . . . 2¼ }		57
3	Same lime . . . . . . 1 } 3½ Sand . . . . 2½ }		44
4	Same lime . . . . . . 1 } 3½ Sand . . . . 2¼ }		10
5	Same lime . . . . . . 1 } 4 Sand . . . . 3 }		0

Observations on the experiments of Table No. XXXIV.

The experiments of table No. XXXIV, were made with lime just from the kiln. The mortars were made immediately, and with a view to ascertain the quantity of sand which this lime would bear. The results shew that the greatest resistance corresponded to one part of lime measured in paste, and two parts of sand, and that the resistances diminished in proportion as the sand was increased. No. 4 had so little strength that it was unable to support the weight of the scale pan; and No. 5 crumbled readily between the fingers. The proportion in general use is one part of fat lime measured in paste, to two parts of sand. Some constructors think that more sand is requisite, but the trials in table No. XXXIV, do not at all confirm this opinion. I regret not having begun by putting a smaller proportion of sand; these experiments should be repeated.

The experiments of tables Nos. XXX and XXXIV are the same, with this difference, that in table No. XXX, lime which had been slaked and lying wet for some years, was made use of, while, in table No. XXXIV, the mortars were made of lime as soon as it was taken out of the kiln. In table No. XXX, with the old lime, I could get no results, whatever were the proportions; while with the same sort of lime fresh from the kiln, the mortars gave some resistance. I do not know how to account for the mortar No. 3, above, being more than one half weaker than mortar No. 1, of table No. XXXIII, which was made and proportioned in the same manner. The differences may be owing to the degree of burning of the lime. It appears to me that fat lime loses quality by being worked up with too much water; but I made no experiments to determine the quantity of water proper to be put in these kinds of mortar; these experiments are yet to be made. It results, nevertheless, from the experiments given in the first section, and from those given above, that lime, whether common or hydraulic, does not bear as much sand as is commonly thought; but it appears to be able to bear more trass, whether alone or mixed with sand; which may be attributed to the combination that takes place, in the moist way, between the trass or puzzolana, and the lime. I purposed making some essays with a view to ascertain the quantities of sand and factitious puzzolana that ought to be mixed with fat lime to give mortars of good resistance; but these proportions can only be fixed after numerous trials, and almost all my leisure had been absorbed by my researches as to factitious puzzolana. I should want, before undertaking the experiments on the proportions of mortars, to have some fixed data, so as to avoid too great a number of useless trials. This is a labour that remains to be undertaken; and it will, no doubt, give different results, according to localities, and according to the quality of lime and factitious puzzolana employed. On summing up, it will be perceived that by whatever manner I operated, only indifferent results were obtained by mixing fat lime with sand; while I obtained very good results by mixing one part of fat lime, measured in paste, with two and a half to three parts of sand and trass taken in equal quantities; as may be seen at the end of table No. XXXI, and in the series No. 2, of table No. XXXIII. It will no doubt be objected to me that several demolitions have been made of masonry built of fat lime; and that the mortars have been found very hard. I will answer this objection; but I am first obliged to present several other experiments.

CHAPTER XII.

Of mortars made of Hydraulic lime and sand, or of Hydraulic lime and Puzzolana.

After I had become acquainted with the good qualities of the Obernai hydraulic lime, I used it not only for works in water, but also for masonry in the air. It required some patience to change the habits of the workmen, and to bring them to the use of other means than those they had been accustomed to apply to the slaking and management of fat lime; but I was ably seconded by Lieut. Col. Finot of the Engineers, who was charged with the immediate superintendence at Strasburg; and, thanks to his efforts, all the persons employed soon became familiar with the manner of treating hydraulic lime, and excellent results were obtained.

In the observations made by Mr. Vicat on the pamphlet published by me in 1824, he thus expresses himself: "Mr. Treussart pretends that hydraulic limes are only made in order to obtain mortars which will harden in water: so far from that being the case, it may, on the contrary, be said, that hydraulic limes (when the country does not furnish them naturally) are made only because mortars composed of these limes and common sand are, at the same time, the most economical and the best, that have yet been discovered, to brave the inclemences of the weather, resist the alternations of hot and cold, wet and dry, &c."

It is true that at page 46 of my pamphlet I said "The author observes that hydraulic limes are made only to compose mortars which have the property of hardening in water. Since this result is obtained, directly, with fat lime and factitious trass, and the results thus obtained are the best, he thinks this mode the most advantageous." This passage cited independently, might lead to error: but, as in all that preceded, the question was, only, as to works in water, it means that when there are works to be built in water, it is necessary to produce hydraulic mortars; and that when there is not, on the spot, natural hydraulic lime, it is preferable on all accounts, to make hydraulic mortar of fat lime and factitious trass, instead of making artificial hydraulic lime according to the process of Mr. Vicat. I did not in the pamphlet of 1824, give details as to the manner of employing hydraulic lime in the air, because I had not then facts enough to warrant it; but I did not say that they might not be employed with advantage in constructions in the air: very far from that—for my experience having taught me, on several occasions, how dangerous it is to use in the air hydraulic lime that has been too much burned (and I may add that it is as dangerous in the water) I said, speaking of hydraulic limes, at page 5 of the pamphlet, that, "if they are used in the air when too much burned, they may occasion very serious accidents, because they dilate considerably, and may heave up very large stones; it is therefore important to employ this lime only when it is calcined just enough." We see therefore that I was far from thinking that we should not use hydraulic limes in the air: but that I thought it my duty to notify that they must not be made use of when too much burned, because of the serious accidents that might result. If this observation had been attended to, the works of the *Vésére* would not have sustained the serious accidents that obliged them to rebuild several Locks. At Strasburg, care was taken to reject such pieces as were too much burned; and although it often happened that mortar of the ordinary consistency, made of lime just from the kiln, was used, no serious accident befel.

All the officers of the Corps of Engineers are acquainted with Metz, and know the good quality of its hydraulic lime—there used in air as well as in water. I have, myself, used the lime under several circumstances; and, as I observed in the first section, there was built at Strasburg, under my direction from 1816 to 1825, more than a million of masonry, both in air and water, of hydraulic lime. Mr. Vicat was, therefore, altogether deceived as to the sense of the phrase which he quoted; he, moreover, has himself said nearly the same thing: for, in commencing the second section of his work, he says, page 31, "hydraulic mortars, as the name indicates, are designed for masonry to be placed in water: they are also called betons." Were this phrase cited alone, we might apply to Mr. Vicat the reproach he directs to me. I do not think that Mr. Vicat wished us to understand that this lime should not be used in the air; because every body knows that it may. Not only do I think that hydraulic mortars are the best to be used in constructions in the air; but—much more than that, my labours have led me to think that, with fat limes, moderately good mortars cannot be made, in whatever manner treated, if no hydraulic cement be added to them: which is saying, in a word, that the sole means of obtaining good mortars in the air, is to use only hydraulic mortars. The only essential point in which I differ from Mr. Vicat is, that I think—as in mortars for the water, it is preferable to make the hydraulic mortar, directly, with fat lime and factitious puzzolana or other like substance, instead of making hydraulic lime by the process he has indicated, when in a country where there is none naturally good. This method has, besides, the advantage that in countries where the lime is only moderately hydraulic, the mortar may be sensibly meliorated by adding a small quantity of hydraulic cement and a greater quantity of sand, (which would be but a small expense;) while according to the process of Mr. Vicat, it would cost as much to improve, suitably, the moderately hydraulic lime thus at command, as to produce the entire conversion of fat lime into hydraulic lime.

I shall give, in the following tables, results which I obtained with different hydraulic limes from the environs of Strasburg, Metz, and other places.

Table No. XXXV.

No. of the mortars.	Composition of the mortars.		made immediately	After 15 days	After 1 month	After 2 months	After 3 months	After 4 months
			lbs.	lbs.	lbs.	lbs.	lbs.	lbs.
1	Yellow Obernai lime slaked to powder and measured in powder 1 / Sand 2	} 3	99	110	132	99	77	66
2	Same lime 1 / Sand 1 / Trass 1	} 3	231	242	262	246	246	220
3	Same lime air slaked and measured in powder 1 / Sand 2	} 3		77	44	55	44	44
4	Same lime 1 / Sand 1 / Trass 1	} 3			231	253	262	253
5	Metz lime slaked to powder and measured in powder 1 / Sand 2	} 3	114		88	44		
6	Same lime 1 / Sand 1 / Trass 1	} 3	268		231	220		
7	Same lime air slaked and measured in powder 1 / Sand 2	} 3			66	40		
8	Same lime 1 / Sand 1 / Trass 1	} 3			242	253		
9	Another Obernai lime slaked to powder and measured in powder 1 / Sand 2	} 3	220	121	88	77	66	
10	Same lime 1 / Sand 1 / Trass 1	} 3	264	264	286	297	275	
11	Same lime air slaked and measured in powder 1 / Sand 2	} 3		88		55		
12	Paris hydraulic lime slaked to powder and measured in powder 1 / Sand 2	} 3	187		121			
13	Common lime reburnt with 2-10 of Holsheim clay, slaked to powder and measured in powder 1 / Sand 2	} 3	176		110	88	55	44

Observations on the experiments of Table No. **XXXV.**

All the experiments of this table were made with lime that had been slaked to powder with one-fifth of its volume of water: and the proportions were, one part of lime in powder to two parts of sand.

The first four mortars of the series were made of the same Obernai lime as those of table No. VI which were put into water. No. 1 was composed of lime and sand. If we compare its resistance with that of the like mortar of table No. VI, we shall see, 1st. that the piece of lime which, with sand, produced mortars of feeble consistence in the water, has also given feeble results in the air (it appears that the piece of lime was but slightly hydraulic:) 2d. that the tenacity of the mortars has, alike in both cases, augmented for a certain length of time, after which it rapidly decreased: 3rd. that the mortars left in the air, have generally given a weaker resistance than those placed in water.

Series No. 2 was made of lime, sand and trass, in equal parts. The result we see is much meliorated. The resistance went on increasing like the similar mortar of table No. VI. These mortars, also, exhibited less tenacity than those under water.

Series No. 3 was made of the same lime left to slake spontaneously. The proportion was one of lime, in powder, to two of sand. It was not till after fifteen days that I could procure enough lime in powder to commence the experiment. If the results be compared with No. 1, we shall see that lime air-slaked gave resistances much inferior to those obtained with lime slaked by water to powder—as was the case with mortars put under water.

Series No. 4 was made of air-slaked lime, sand and trass, in equal parts. These results being compared with those of the 2nd. series, we see but slight difference: if compared with the like mortars put under water of table No. VI, we see that they are sensibly inferior.

The series No. 5, 6, 7 and 8 shows similar experiments with Metz lime; these mortars are made of the same lime as those of table No. VII, which were deposited in water. The results given by the Metz lime are weak; but it is probable that with this lime, as with others of the like nature, very different results are afforded by different pieces from the same quarry. I am not entitled to say that the Metz lime is inferior to the Obernai lime, not having made experiments enough with the former to be able to compare. The observations made on the first four series of table No. XXXV, apply, generally, to the mortars made of Metz lime.

Series Nos. 9, 10 and 11 were made of the same Obernai lime, as the mortars of table No V which were put under water: the results are good. No. 9 shows that if not made up till it has been slaked fifteen days, this lime loses nearly one half of its force: and that it loses more and more as this period is extended. If we compare the mortar made immediately, with its analogous experiment in table No. V, we shall see that the mortar left in the air supported 44 lbs. less than the mortar left in water. With the other mortars the differences are not so great.

In comparing series No. 10 above, with the corresponding series in table No. V, we find that the mortar made immediately, gave a resistance only about one-half of that of the similar mortar of Table No V; while the mortar No. 2 of the present table, made of another lime, supported a weight rather greater than the similar mortar of table No. VI, which had been put in water. I cannot explain this anomaly. The other mortars of this series, made at different periods, were inferior, or at most only equal to the corresponding mortars that had been put in water.

The series No. 11 comprises only two experiments with lime left to slake spontaneously: these two experiments consumed all the lime. The results are weaker than the corresponding ones of series No. 9 of which the lime had been slaked to powder with water, agreeing in this respect with the comparison of No. 1 and 3 above.

Series No. 12 comprises two experiments only, made of artificial hydraulic lime manufactured at Meudon, by Mr. Saint Leger. Having but a small quantity of lime, I was unable to make a greater number of experiments. The resistance of mortar made immediately, is good: that made at the end of a month has lost nearly half its force. Two mortars made of the same lime and put into water, are given at No. 1 of table No. X. On comparing them we see that the mortar made at once and left in the air, supported the same weight as that put in water. Mortar made of this lime after being slaked a month, gave when exposed to the air, a resistance of 121 lbs. and when plunged into water, only 88 lbs.

Series No. 13 is of mortar made of an artificial hydraulic lime composed of fat lime and Holsheim clay. The result is nearly the same as that of series No. 12. We see that the strength of the mortar diminished rapidly by the exposure of this lime to the air; and that at the end of four months it had lost three-quarters of its strength.

I made but few experiments with artificial hydraulic limes in the air, but those which I did make, show that they differ in nothing from natural hydraulic limes. They show, also, that in the air, as well as in water, better mortars are generally obtained with fat lime, sand, and substances analogous to puzzolana, than with hydraulic lime and sand.

On comparing the above mortars, left in the air, with the same mortars put in water, we are led to the following conclusions: when mortars are made of hydraulic lime and sand, to be used in masonry exposed to the air, it is of great importance to use the lime soon after it is burned: otherwise it loses a great portion of its force, as it does under water. When we are obliged to wait some days before using it, it should be slaked to dry powder, by throwing on a quarter of its volume of water, and be immediately covered with the quantity of sand that is proper to mix with it to make mortar. These kinds of lime should not be left to slake spontaneously, because they require a considerable time to become reduced to powder, and in general, lose a great part of their energy. Before deciding on adopting the process of air-slaking for hydraulic limes, we should previously convince ourselves by experiment, that the particular limes are exceptions to the general rule; that is to say, that they do not lose a great part of their energy by being left to slake in this manner. If the hydraulic lime we have at command has no great force, we may, nevertheless, make very good mortar by mixing sand, and a quantity of some substance analogous to puzzolana with the lime. For example, with calcined clay-dust of good quality, we may have a mortar of great hardness (even when the lime has very little hydraulic property, or is nothing but fat lime) by mixing lime, sand, and clay-dust, in equal parts: but a less proportion of clay-dust may suffice, with a greater degree of hydraulic strength in the lime, or if the work consist of gross masonry.

Comparing mortars made of the same constituents, and in the same manner —some having been left in the air, and others put under water, we see that the latter, in general, have given the greater resistances. Humidity is, therefore, favourable to hydraulic mortars. In the case of masonry made of fat lime, it has always been recommended, if earth was to be laid against it, that it should be left to dry for some time, before backing it with earth; and with the same object it has been directed to wait a year before pointing the work. We see that with hydraulic mortars used in the air, it will be better to act differently. As the masonry rises, it will be best to throw the earth against it. The pointing should be finished at the same time as the masonry, this being the better and more economical mode. During warm weather, the top of the wall should be copiously watered, at the close of the day, and whenever the masons break off during the day. This was always done at Strasburg, and was found to be a good practice.

I shall give in the following table several experiments that I made with various kinds of lime, in order to know their quality and the quantity of sand that might be mixed with them.

Table No. XXXVI.

No. of the Mortars.	Composition of the mortars.			Weights supported before breaking.
				lbs.
1	Yellow Obernai lime slaked to powder and measured in powder	1	} 3	196
	Sand	2		
2	Same lime	1	} 3½	161
	Sand	2½		
3	Same lime	1	} 4	99
	Sand	3		
4	Yellow Obernai lime measured in paste	1	} 3	301
	Sand	2		
5	Same lime	1	} 3½	275
	Sand	2½		
6	Same lime	1	} 4	242
	Sand	3		
7	Another Obernai lime measured in paste	1	} 3	220
	Sand	2		
8	Same lime	1	} 3½	165
	Sand	2½		
9	Same lime	1	} 3½	143
	Sand	2½		
10	Same lime	1	} 3¾	88
	Sand	2¾		
11	Same lime	1	} 4	66
	Sand	3		
12	Yellow lime of Bouxviller measured in paste	1	} 3	231
	Sand	2		
13	Same lime	1	} 3¼	242
	Sand	2¼		
14	Same lime	1	} 3½	253
	Sand	2½		
15	Same lime	1	} 3¾	231
	Sand	2¾		
16	Same lime	1	} 4	187
	Sand	3		
17	Oberbronn lime measured in paste	1	} 3	297
	Sand	2		
18	Same lime	1	} 3½	165
	Sand	2½		
19	Yellow Obernai lime alone—reduced to paste			323

Observations on the Experiments of Table No. XXXVI.

The first three numbers were made of the yellow Obernai lime, slaked to powder soon after leaving the kiln. The proportions were one part of lime to the several quantities of sand stated in the table. We see that the strongest result corresponds with the least quantity of sand. Different circumstances having taught me that hydraulic lime would not bear as much sand as is commonly thought, I proportioned the following mortars with lime measured in paste.

Nos. 4, 5 and 6, were made at the works, and consequently with mixed pieces of lime; the proportions are shown in the table. The best result answers to one of lime and two of sand, and it will be remarked that these three mortars are superior to the first three, which I attribute principally to a smaller quantity of sand.

The numbers from 7 to 11, were made of lime from another burning: the sand was augmented each succeeding trial by a quarter of the bulk of lime, while in the preceding experiments it had been augmented by a half. The best result corresponds with one part of lime in paste to two parts of sand; it is possible that a smaller proportion of sand would be still better, for we see that No. 19, which is lime reduced to paste without any sand, gave a stronger result; but as No. 19 was made of lime of another burning, I placed it at the end of the table that it might not lead to any false conclusions. I did not anticipate that there may be good hydraulic limes which will support only a very small quantity of sand; otherwise, I should have commenced the series with a much smaller proportion.

The numbers from 12 to 16, are mortars made of the hydraulic lime of Bouxviller, a small village situated at the foot of the Vosges, between Haguenau and Savern. This lime was treated in the same way as the Obernai lime that precedes it in the table. We see that the Bouxviller lime will bear more sand than that from Obernai, and that the best result corresponds to the proportion of one part lime measured in paste to two and a half parts of sand. The lime was of the same burning as that used in table No. III. Comparing the figures of the two tables, I was surprised to see that the same lime supported more sand in the air than in the water, which has happened very rarely in the course of my experiments; I am ignorant whether this is owing to some peculiar circumstance, or is a quality pertaining to certain hydraulic limes.

The experiments Nos. 17 and 18, were made with lime from Oberbronn, a village at the foot of the Vosges, to the left of the road from Haguenau to Bitche. I obtained a very good result with one part of this lime measured in paste and two parts of sand; but No. 18 shows that by putting two and a half parts of sand in the mortar, it lost nearly half its force. When making these two experiments with Oberbronn lime, I put, on one side, a fragment which I slaked with one-fifth of its volume of water, so as to reduce it to dry powder. I left it in this state, in the air, for fifteen days. I then made a mortar like No. 17. This mortar broke with the weight of 132 lbs., in lieu of the 297 lbs. which the mortar supported when made of lime just slaked. I obtained a similar result with the Bouxviller lime. All the limes, therefore, which I have used in my experiments in the air, and which are included in the preceding tables, require to be used a very short time after being burned: they lose, otherwise, a great portion of their energy; as is also the case when they are used in water.

No. 19 was made, as I have said, of Obernai lime, alone, reduced to paste with water. When I saw the hardness of this hydrate, my intention was to make similar trials with other limes, in order to know if the sand added in the composition of mortars, always, or only with some peculiar limes, diminished the resistance of the hydrates: but I was obliged to quit Strasburg before it was in my power to make the essays.

ARTICLE XIII.—*Various experiments with Mortars exposed to the Air.*

In this article I shall give several experiments which I made on mortars exposed to the air. Several are repetitions of those contained in article VII, of mortars placed in water.

Table No. XXXVII.

Composition of the mortar.	Made immediately.	After 12 hours.	After 24 hours.	After 36 hours.	After 48 hours.	After 60 hours.	After 72 hours.	After 84 hours.
	lbs.	lbs.	lbs.	lbs.	lbs.	lbs.	lbs.	lbs.
Obernai lime slaked to a moist powder, with a volume of water equal to the volume of lime . . . . 1 } 3 Sand . . . . . . 2 }	220	209	165*	132	132	110	92	68

Observations on the experiments of Table No. XXXVII.

The above experiments were made with the same lime, and in the same proportions, as those of table No. XXVI, of which the mortars were put in water. For the manner of operating, I refer, therefore, to the observations on table No. XXVI.

These air mortars behaved like those placed in water. The mortar made immediately, afforded, in the air, a resistance rather less than the corresponding mortar of table No. XXVI; the others gave results about the same in the two cases. It is therefore important not to slake hydraulic lime with too much water, whether it is to be used in the air or in water; and we perceive that the method proposed by Mr. Lafaye is very inconvenient for hydraulic lime, because it requires the quick lime to be broken into small pieces of nearly equal size, which is a long and expensive operation. Unless this be done, the small pieces will absorb too much water, and the large pieces too little.

Table No. XXXVIII.

No. of the mortars.	Composition of the mortars.	Weights supported before breaking.
		lbs.
1	Mortar made of equal parts of common lime, sand and trass	143
2	Same mortar, worked anew, without water, after 12 hours	154
3	Same mortar, worked anew with a little additional water, after 12 hours	209
4	Same mortar, do. after 24 hours	198
5	Same mortar, do. after 36 hours	165
6	Same mortar, do. after 48 hours	187
7	Mortar of 1 part of Obernai lime and 2 parts of sand	154
8	Same mortar, worked anew with a little additional water, after 12 hours	176

Observations on the experiments of Table No. XXXVIII.

These experiments were made with the same lime as, and in a similar manner to, those recorded in table No. XXVIII. The first six mortars correspond to Nos. 1, 3, 4, 6, 8, and 10, of that table, which were put under water. I made similar trials with lime and sand only; but, as I used lime which had been slaked for some time, I obtained only feeble results—the greater part of the mortars not supporting the weight of the scale pan.

If we compare No. 2 of the above table with No. 1, we see that the mor-

*This mortar was cracked, which may have lessened its resistance.—AUTHOR.

tar that was reworked without water, after twelve hours, gained but little upon that which had not been reworked; but that No. 3, which had been reworked with a little water, had gained a good deal. After twenty-four hours, the mortar No. 4 had become so dry that it was impossible to rework it without water; I was therefore obliged to moisten it a little, like No. 3. We see that the result was about the same as at the end of twelve hours. After thirty-six hours the hardness had become sensibly weaker, and at the end of forty-eight hours it had become stronger than at the end of thirty-six hours—an anomaly which I cannot explain.

Comparing the results of the above table with the corresponding ones of table No. XXVIII, we find that the resistances of the mortars left in the air are sensibly less than those placed in water. We see also that in both cases, I obtained no advantage of consequence, by reworking the mortars without additional water; but that there was a material augmentation of force, on reworking the mortars with a little water.

Nos. 7 and 8, of the above table, answer to Nos. 13 and 14 of table No. XXVIII, and were made of the same lime. There is in these mortars, also, much resemblance as to the effect of reworking upon mortars in air and in water; that is to say, the mortar which had been reworked with a little water after twelve hours, presented a greater resistance than that which had not. The resistances of these tables are generally rather weak, because of my using lime which had been slaked for about fifteen days.

At all works, it is often necessary to rework the mortars in the course of the day, especially in hot weather, when it dries very quickly and becomes too stiff to be used. During the hours of recess from labour, and when the works are interrupted by rain, the mortar will harden considerably. It would sometimes demand a great deal of labour to restore the mortar to a suitable consistency without water. My practice has always been to add a little water whenever the mortar had become, from any cause, too stiff, and required reworking. The preceding remarks show that no disadvantage attends this mode of operating. There is, no doubt, a limit, both as to the quantity of water to be added, and as to the time elapsed before reworking; and I purposed making other experiments in order to ascertain these limits, but I had not time. The experiments cited are nearly sufficient, and they prove that the opinion on which is founded the saying that *" mortar should be tempered with the sweat of the workmen,"* is a prejudice leading to considerable useless expense. The essential point is, that the lime, and the substances added to it, be intimately mixed; and this is most easily accomplished when the mortar is soft.

Table No. XXXIX.

No. of the mortars.	Composition of the mortars.	Weights supported before breaking.
		lbs.
1	{ Obernai lime slaked to powder, with 1-5 of its volume of water, leaving it in the air . . . . 1 } 3 { Sand . . . . 2 }	154
2	{ Same lime, slaked to powder with 1-5 of its volume of water, covering it with sand . . . 1 } 3 { Sand . . . . 2 }	154
3	{ Same lime, slaked by plunging it into water for fifty seconds . . . . . 1 } 3 { Sand . . . . 2 }	132

Observations on the experiments of Table No. XXXIX.

These experiments are the repetition of those described in table No. XXV, and they were made of the same lime. The results are similar to those given by mortars put under water; only they are a little weaker. The comparison of Nos. 1 and 2 shows that there is no advantage, when slaking lime, to cover it with sand. This is called *stifling* the lime; and several constructors think that the vapour which rises, on slaking, possesses valuable properties.

Mortar No. 3 of table No. XXXIX was made of the same lime as No. 3 of table No. XXV, and I used, in slaking the lime, the process recommended by Mr. Lafaye, which consists in dipping the quick lime into water. The resistance was less than No. 1, which was slaked by throwing on a little water. This appears to me to be owing to the pieces of lime absorbing too much water from being in small pieces; and as the lime remained twelve hours in this state, it lost a part of its force—for it follows, from tables Nos. XXVI and XXVII, that lime, slaked to a humid powder has already lost a part of its energy, when it has lain twelve hours exposed to the air.

Table No. XL.

No. of the mortars	Composition of the mortar.		Weight supported before breaking.
			lbs.
1	{ Common lime measured in paste { Pulverized bricks lightly burned .	1 } $3\frac{1}{2}$ $2\frac{1}{2}$ }	297
2	{ Same lime . . . { Pulverized bricks well burned .	1 } $3\frac{1}{2}$ $2\frac{1}{2}$ }	143
3	{ Same lime . . . . { Pulverized tiles lightly burned .	1 } $3\frac{1}{2}$ $2\frac{1}{2}$ }	253
4	{ Same lime . . . . { Pulverized tiles well burned .	1 } $3\frac{1}{2}$ $2\frac{1}{2}$ }	99
	{ Same lime . . . { Pulverized tiles lightly burned—recal- { cined for six hours. .	1 } $3\frac{1}{2}$ $2\frac{1}{2}$ }	0

Observations on the experiments of Table No. XL.

The above experiments are of the same kind as those made with mortars put under water, and reported in table No. XVI. These air-mortars gave similar results with those put in water; that is to say, those made of pulverized bricks, or tiles, but lightly calcined, gave much better resistances than those made of more highly burned bricks or tiles. We see that the dust of No. 5, which had been recalcined by being kept red hot for six hours, gave with the same lime, a mortar that had no strength. The dusts used in these trials, like those of table No. XVI, contained a notable quantity of lime. The resistances of the mortars left in the air, were, in this instance also, rather less than those of the mortars put in water.

Table No. XLI.

No. of the mortar.	Composition of the mortar.		Weight supported before breaking.
			lbs.
1	Common lime measured in paste .... 1 } 3½ Brick dust . . . . 2½ }		132
2	Same lime . . . . 1 } Brick dust, same as No. 1, recalcined for } 3½ half an hour . . . 2½ }		165
3	Same lime . . . 1 } Brick dust same as No. 1, recalcined for } 3½ one hour . . . . 2½ }		275
4	Same lime . . . . 1 } Brick dust, same as No. 1, recalcined for } 3½ two hours . . . . 2½ }		308

Observations on the experiments of Table No. XLI.

These experiments correspond with those of table No. XVII, that is to say, having used brick dusts which gave resistances the feebler the more they were burned, as those of tables Nos. XVI and XI,—other brick-dusts were found, as those of tables Nos. XVII and XLI, which gave results exactly opposite. The mortars of the two tables XVII and XLI, gave in air and in water, results so much the stronger as the cements had been the more burned. In speaking of tables Nos. XVI and XVII, I said, that the differences were owing to the cements of table No. XVI, containing much lime, while those of table No. XVII, contained little. But the cements of tables Nos. XL and XLI, were the same as those of tables Nos. XVI and XVII, and the results in the air were just like those in the water. The comparison of these four tables leads to an important conclusion; namely, that clay-dusts which give results with fat lime, when placed under water, will also give good results, when exposed to the air: and if the results be bad in the first case, they will be equally so in the second. Whence it follows that to know whether clay dust which is to be used in air mortar, will give good results, it should be tried with fat lime in water; following the process pointed out in the first section. We may be certain that cements which have not the property of causing fat lime to harden in water, will give, in the air, no better results than the same lime mixed up with sand alone. On the other hand, the more hydraulic the cements are, the better, for all uses in the air. The trials of which we have spoken, should not be neglected, for they are of great importance, as regards the solidity of masonry exposed to the air.

Table No. XLII.

No. of the series.	Composition of the mortars.	Weight supported before breaking.
		lbs.
1	Obernai lime alone, reduced to paste	323
2	Verdt lime alone, reduced to paste	99
3	Metz lime alone reduced to paste	119
4	Lime from the Boulogne pebbles	99
5	Mortar composed of one part of fat lime that had been long lying slaked and wet, measured in paste—and two parts of puzzolana	429
6	Mortar made of one part of same lime do. and two parts of trass	451
7	Mortar do. do. do. and two parts of Sufflenheim cement	429
8	Mortar do. do. do. one of sand and one of Sufflenheim cement	363
9	Mortar do. do. do. and two pars of forge scoriæ	55
10	Mortar do. do. do. one of sand and one of Paris cement	0
11	Mortar made of one part of fresh lime measured in paste and two parts of common sand	77
12	Mortar do. do. do. and two parts of common sand pulverized	121
13	Mortar made of one part of Obernai lime measured in paste and two and a half parts of common sand	187
14	Mortar of one part of same lime do. and two and a half of sand, pulverized	275*
15	Mortar of one part of quick-lime but little burned, measured in paste, and two parts of sand	—22
16	Mortar made of one part of Lixen lime measured in paste and two parts of earthy sand	—22
17	Mortar of one part of same lime do. and two parts of River sand	143
18	Mortar of one part of do. do. and two parts of earthy sand, washed	176
19	Mortar of one part of Dosenheim lime and two parts of earthy sand	—22
20	Mortar of one part of same lime and two parts of river sand	132
21	Mortar of one part of do. and two parts of earthy sand washed	176

Observations on the experiments of Table No. XLII.

This table contains a variety of experiments, which I will explain. Nos. 1, 2, 3 and 4 were made of lime slaked soon after being burned, and by the necessary quantity of water, reduced at once to paste. These hydrates of lime like the mortars which precede them, were placed in a cellar, and tested at the end of a year. The hydrate of Obernai lime, No. 1, was very good. No. 2, a hydrate of Verdt lime, gave so feeble a result as to surprise me, after that which I had obtained by placing a hydrate of the same lime in water—table No. III shows that the resistance of this hydrate was 484 lbs. As the specimens were from different burnings, I presume that in this last trial, I used a piece but feebly hydraulic. The Metz lime

*This mortar being a little cracked, its resistance was diminished.

No. 3, gave a feeble result, also. I have already said that I made but few experiments with this lime, and it is possible that the small quantity that was sent me was, by accident, but feebly hydraulic. No. 4 was from the Boulogne pebbles, and was treated the same way as the preceding. The resistance was feeble, and, we have seen (table No. VIII) that, with a single exception of a trial made with this lime highly calcined, all the mortars it has furnished, have supported but small weights. The above lime, No. 4, had received only the ordinary calcination.

Nos. 5, 6, 7, 8, 9 and 10 were made of fat lime that had been lying slaked, and wet, for five years, since the erection of the Theatre. The proportions were one part of this lime in paste, to two parts of the several substances mentioned in the table. The mortar No. 5, composed of this lime and puzzolana, gave a very good result. No. 6 made, in the same manner, of trass, gave a resistance a little better still. Mortar No. 7 made of the hydraulic cement of Sufflenheim, gave a resistance equal to that afforded by puzzolana. Mortar No. 8 made of equal parts of lime, sand and Sufflenheim cement, supported a weight rather less than No. 7, in which there was no sand. No. 9 was made in the same manner as the preceding mortars, using the scoria of forges. I satisfied myself that these scoria contained little or no clay; and it is to this that I attribute the bad result. I said in the first section, that with the Tournay ashes, and the ashes of the forges of Boulogne, very good mortars were made; owing to this, that the sea-coal, burned in the forges of those places, contained a considerable quantity of clay, which was calcined in a current of air, by the combustion of the carbon of the coal. The scoria of forges, and the ashes of furnaces, should not, therefore, be used in mortars in the air, before ascertaining whether these matters have the property of causing lime to indurate under water.

No. 10 is a mortar composed of one part of fat lime measured in paste, one part of sand, and one of Paris cement. This cement was from the manufactory of Mr. Saint Leger, and was the same as that used for the mortars put into water. We saw, at page 83, that two mortars made of this cement had promptly hardened in water, but that both were cracked. The mortar made of one part lime and two parts of cement supported 187 lbs., and that made of lime, sand and cement, supported only 99 lbs. I was much surprised at the bad result of the mortar No. 10 in table No. XLII; it had so little consistence that it crumbled easily between the fingers. I attribute the bad effect to the great quantity of lime that Mr. Saint Leger mixed with the clay, in making the cement. It might be that the cement was too much burned. Some separate trials lead me to think that cements made of clays containing about one tenth of lime, are less proper for mortars in the air than for mortars in water: it appears also that they allow but little sand in the composition of the mortar. I intended making some experiments to settle this matter but had not time. My departure from Strasburg also prevented my making, with the several clays of the environs of that place, experiments in the air, analogous to those which I made with the clays, under water. My various essays, however, induced me to think that in making artificial puzzolanas for mortars intended to be exposed to the air, the presence of lime in the clays to be calcined, is still more hurtful than when the mortars are to be used under water. Clay, therefore, should be chosen which contains no lime or very little.

Nos. 11 and 12 were made of fat lime reduced to paste shortly after burning. No. 11 was made of one part of this lime measured in paste, and two parts of common sand. No. 12 differs only in having the sand pulverized. We see that the result was much better with the fine sand. Nos. 13 and 14 were similar experiments made of Obernai lime. With the fine sand, the resistance was, in this case also, much the greatest, although the mortar was so cracked as necessarily to diminish its force. We have seen in table No. XXIX, that mortars in water gave similar results. We ought to conclude, therefore, that whether for mortars in air or in water, fine sand is the best, notwithstanding the opinion to the contrary of most constructors.

Old mortars are often found which are very hard, and which contain a great quantity of gravel as large as a pea. This fact is sometimes cited to prove that it is best to use coarse sand in gross masonry, but the reasoning is not just. These kinds of mortars are really concretes: the gravel they contain can have no influence on the goodness of the mortar. But if this gravel is mixed with fine sand (as is often the case) and the lime is hydraulic, then a very good mortar is obtained—the strength of the mortar depending on the strength of the lime.

No. 15 was made of lime which had been placed above the tiles in the kiln, and was, therefore, but slightly burnt: it was the same lime as was used in making the mortar to be put in water, No. 8 of table No. XXIX. Only bad mortars were obtained by this means, either in the air or in water.

Nos. 16, 17 and 18 were made of three different kinds of sand and a lime moderately hydraulic, obtained from the village of Lixen, near Phalsburg. No. 16 was made of one part of this lime, measured in paste, and two parts of a very earthy pit sand, which is found in the neighbourhood. The resulting mortar had so little consistency, that it could not bear the weight of the scale pan. No. 17 was mixed in the same proportions with river sand from Zorn, near Saverne; the resistance was passable. The same proportions were observed, in mixing No. 18, with the same sand as was used in No. 16, after being freed, by washing, from earthy matter. We see that this mortar was good, and superior to the mortar made of river sand.

Nos. 19, 20 and 21 were repetitions of three preceding experiments: using, however, another lime, also moderately hydraulic, obtained from the village of Dosenheim. The mortars made of Dosenheim lime, like those made of Lixen lime, prove that earthy sands afford only very bad mortars; but that, being washed, they are superior to river sands. I was led, in 1823, to make these experiments, because there was to be had near Phalsburg only pit sand which was half earth. Whenever there was any work to be executed requiring some care, the people of that place were obliged to get river sand from the river Zorn on the other sides of the Vosges. This brought the price to about $0.03½ per cubic foot—so high as to prevent its being procured for the masonry of revetments: it resulted that the masonry of that place, made of mortar in which the earthy sand of the neighbourhood was used, has needed considerable repairs, and in making the necessary reconstructions, it was very apparent that the degradations had been owing to the bad quality of the mortar.

After getting the results of these last experiments, I used no sand at Phalsburg except washed pit sand. It required 70.68 cubic feet of the earthy sand to yield 35.34 cubic feet of the washed sand: 0.62 of a day's work sufficed for the washing: it would, therefore cost less than one half of the expense of bringing the river sand.

The sand may be washed on a large scale in the following manner; a basin being made of masonry from seven to ten feet wide, and from twelve to sixteen long, the height of the walls should be about two and a half feet, with the exception of one end, which should be only one foot two inches high; the bottom should be paved with flat stones; the basin should be built near a stream of water, or if that be not practicable, a well should be sunk near it. A layer of sand of about one foot thick, should be placed in the basin, and a plank one foot four inches wide placed on edge, on the low wall, raising it to the height of the other walls—the plank being fitted into grooves made in the side walls to receive it. The basin must then be filled with water from a brook, or from a pump in a well, as the case may be; and the sand must be well stirred up with *rabs* by two or three labourers. Allowing the time found to be necessary for the sand to precipitate, the plank must be suddenly withdrawn, and a great part of the water will pass off at once, loaded with earthy matter. This operation must be repeated until the water passes off but slightly turbid: the sand may then be taken out and left to dry, and the washing be applied to another portion.

For economy, the basin may be constructed of planks, as was done at Phalsburg. It was six feet eight inches long, four feet four inches broad, and two feet two inches deep. There was left in front an opening of only fourteen inches deep by ten inches broad. But this opening was too small for the water to run off rapidly. It is best to place a movable plank of some breadth across the whole front of the basin, so that the water may pass off very quickly.

The last experiments of table No. XLII, show how important it is to use clean sands in making mortars: but before washing off the earthy matter, it is proper to be satisfied, by the means I have pointed out, that the sands are not arenes.

CHAPTER XIV.

Observations on Mortars exposed to the Air.

It results from the experiments given in chapters XI, XII, and XIII, that in exposing to the air mortars made of sand, and lime which had been laying a long time slaked and wet, I obtained no satisfactory result; while I obtained tolerable results with sand, and the same lime recently slaked. The resistances of these last mortars were 68, 77, and 99 lbs., while the others were unable to support the scale pan, whatever may have been the process of fabrication. I ought not, however, from this to take up a general conclusion, and counsel against slaking and running lime into vats to preserve it; because I have not made experiments enough to pronounce positively on the subject—which is one of great importance. It is necessary to repeat these trials in different countries, so as to operate on various kinds of lime, before proscribing this method; which, while it may be a bad method for certain kinds of lime, may be very good for other kinds. I do not know for how long a time the method of running lime into vats has been followed. It may have been introduced in consequence of the considerable increase of bulk which it gives. I do not know that it was followed by the ancients. Vitruvius has left a work on architecture, in which he has given many details as to the manner the Romans carried on their works. We find in this author, as rendered from the Latin by Perrault, the architect, the following passage extracted from Book II, chapter V: " When the lime has been slaked, it must be mixed with sand, in such proportions that there shall be three parts of pit sand, or two parts of river sand to one of lime: because this is the most just proportion of the mixture, which will be much better still, if there be added to the sea or river sand a third part of sifted tile dust."

We see nothing in this passage that indicates the mode of slaking; but it is certain that the Romans made great use of hydraulic lime, as there are many remains of their works in countries where this lime abounds: such are the constructions they have left us on the banks of the Moselle, and in several parts of France. But these limes could not be slaked and left in the above manner, (as they would harden in the water;) and, if it had been the practice to slake them differently from fat lime, Vitruvius would no doubt have mentioned it. It appears probable to me, therefore, that the Romans used fat lime as they did hydraulic lime, that is to say, immediately after the burning. This is the more likely, as Vitruvius directs, in the process of stucco making, that only lime that had been long slaked should be used. The following are his remarks on this subject. Book VII, chapter II. " Having examined all that appertains to pavements, the manner of making stucco must be explained. The principal matter in this is, that the lime should be slaked for a long time, so that if there should be some particles less burned than the rest, they may, having time thus given them, be as thoroughly slaked, and as easily tempered, as that which was thoroughly calcined: for, in lime which is used as it comes from the kiln, and before it is sufficiently slaked, there is a quantity of minute stones imperfectly burned, which act on the plaster like blisters, because these particles slaking more slowly than the rest of the lime, break the plaster and mar all the polish." It appears to me that the precaution of slaking the lime a long time before hand, is here recommended as an exception, and that in the mortars intended for masonry, the Romans used all limes soon after they left the kiln. It is remarkable that the same author directs, in the first passage cited, mixing with the mortar a portion of sifted tile dust, observing that it will much improve the mortar.

We have seen that my experiments were very unfavorable to the process indicated by Mr. Loriot and Mr. Lafaye: they were in error in recommending them as, in principle, recovered from the Romans. Moreover, these processes have, for a long time, justly fallen into disrepute.

As to the opinion that the hardness of mortar is due to the regeneration of carbonic acid, I have shown that according to the analysis of Mr. Darcet and Dr. John, several ancient mortars, although very hard, contained but a small portion of the carbonic acid necessary to the saturation of the lime. It has been stated that the Italians sell little caskets and snuff boxes which they make of ancient Roman mortars: but it has been noticed that they use for these purposes only the exterior parts of the mortar in which the lime had passed to the state of carbonate, while the interior often afforded but a weak consistence.

In examining Roman mortars; it is observed that they are often of great hardness, although it is evident that the mixture had been made with very little care. We must therefore attribute the hardness of these ancient mortars to other causes; for, as I have said, all these mortars are not by many degrees equally hard.

To explain the hardness of Roman mortars, it will suffice, I think, to cast the eyes over tables Nos. XXXVI, XL, XLI, and XLII. Table No. XXXVI contains mortars made of hydraulic lime and sand. These mortars exposed to the air for one year only, show great tenacity. Tables Nos. XL, XLI, and XLII, contain, also, very good mortars made of fat lime, puz zolana, trass, and several kinds of cement. The use of cement goes back to high antiquity, for Roman and Egyptian structures often contain it. Those who wish to solve this question, without recourse to the quality of the lime, or to cements, object that there are ancient remains which appear to have been made of fat lime, since they are seen in countries where no puzzolana or hydraulic limes are to be found, and they have not the aspect of mortars made with cements. I will observe, touching this point, that if we examine the two tables in page 111, which contain the analyses of several lime stones, we shall see that many limes which are ranked with fat limes contain, nevertheless, small quantities of clay. Although they may not contain enough clay to harden under water, they ought to afford much better mortars in the air than those limes which contain none. Again, hydraulic limestones are often found disseminated amongst the strata of fat lime stones. And, lastly, the important observation of Mr. Girard, on the hydraulic proportions of *arenes* explains easily how very good mortars may have been made of fat lime. I will observe, in addition, that the Romans, in all the countries they occupied, executed a great many works, of which only those made of good mortars survive to the present day. Saint Augustine complains of the manner in which mortars were made in his day: and the same complaints are found in Pliny; who says, chapter XXII, " that which causes the ruin of the greater part of the edifices of this city (Rome) is, that the workmen employ, from fraud, in the construction of the walls, lime which has lost its quality."* We see, therefore, that all the Roman mortars were not good.

For my part, I am convinced, that if those ancient constructions that have reached our times, be examined with attention, it will be ascertained that they were made either with hydraulic lime and sand, or with fat lime and sand mixed with cement, or with arenes: in a word, that these mortars had all the elements of good hydraulic mortars.

We are in the habit of composing our mortars of fat lime and sand; the preceding experiments show that we are wrong: our mortars have, consequently, little durability. We shall not obtain durable masonry in the air, until we make use, therein, of hydraulic mortars. In countries where good natural hydraulic lime is to be had, no other kind should be used for any purpose whatever. For ordinary masonry, the mortar should, in that case, be made of lime and sand only. In countries where there are no natural hydraulic limes, but where there are arenes, the mortar should be made of fat lime and these arenes: in both these cases the mortars would be cheap. In countries where neither arenes nor hydraulic limes are to be procured, it will be necessary to incur a little additional expense, and make use of fat lime, sand, and hydraulic cement. To combine economy and solidity at the same time as much as possible, the proportions, in cases where there are to be one part of fat lime and two of sand and cement, the mixture may be made as follows, viz: one part of fat lime measured in paste, one and a half of sand, and a half of hydraulic cement; (according to similar proportions made with trass, as shown in table No. XXVII,) we should have, by this means a very good mortar. The proportions of hydraulic cement, stated above, should be used in all common masonry: in works demanding more care, the mortar should be composed of lime, sand, and cement, in equal

---

*We might infer, from this passage, that Pliny complained because the lime was not used soon after its calcination. AUTHOR.

parts. I have said, that the proportions indicated for common masonry, should augment the expense but little: but were the augmentation more considerable, it is certainly much more economical to incur at once, all the expense necessary to produce a permanent work, than to build at a cost rather less in the first instance, and to be obliged to reconstruct the work entirely, after no great lapse of time. A government should construct for posterity: and I do not doubt that this end would be attained by making all masonry with hydraulic mortar, in the manner I have pointed out.

Officers of engineers often have to construct arched rooms, passages, &c., that are to be always covered with earth. The mortar of these constructions is generally composed of fat lime and sand. To resist filtration and humidity, it is customary to place a cap, or masonry roof, made of hydraulic mortar, over these arches: but experience shows that these caps do not fulfill their object, and that they often afford a passage to the water, especially when made of bad cements. I cited an example at page 84, and I might cite many others. Even when the caps are made of good mortar, it may happen that there is humidity in the casemates, and that the arches leak: for we have seen at page 134 that mortars made of fat lime do not dry completely, even in a century, when the walls are thick. And this result is the more certain when the masonry is covered with earth as in casemates. The walls against which the earth lies, almost always allow the water to transude, although the cap may be impermeable. Besides, from the considerable load that these arches often sustain, the masonry that has been made of mortar slow to harden, will settle, causing cracks and leaks in the caps. The only means of obviating these disadvantages, is to construct all the masonry of the casemates with hydraulic mortar. We shall thus secure the great advantage of a prompt induration: the subsidence will consequently be less sensible, and cracks less apt to occur; the walls will no longer allow moisture to transude, and even should there be some cracks in the caps, the water will, with difficulty, find its way through arches made with hydraulic mortar.

The manipulation of mortars designed for exposure in the air, should be the same as that described in the first section for mortars designed for water.

CHAPTER XV.
On factitious Stones and Concretes, exposed to the Air.

Mr. Fleuret, formerly Professor of Architecture in the Royal Military School, of whom I have before had occasion to speak, published in 1807, a work on the art of composing factitious stones. The following passages are to be found in page 12: "The art of building with factitious stones is very old; it was in use with the Babylonians, and the early Egyptians, amongst the Greeks and Romans, and it is still pursued in Barbary, and amongst the nations of Malabar.

"According to Pliny, the columns which adorn the peristyle of the Egyptian labyrinth, were of artificial stones, and this vast edifice has existed three thousand six hundred years. The pyramid of Nynus is formed of a single block. The enormous stones composing the great and strong walls raised in the empire of Morocco, as is reported by the Abbe de Marsi, from writers whom he quotes; the square stone that formed the tomb of Porsenna, spoken of by Varro and Pliny, which was thirty feet wide by five feet high, were composed in the same manner as the pyramid of Nynus, and lead us to believe that these monuments owe their existence and their preservation to a process as easy as it is simple, and which unites the advantage of solidity with economy.

"All factitious stones of a volume thus considerable, were made by encasement, and the process of massivation; that is to say, that in the great walls built thereof, these stones were formed the one upon the other, by beating the materials, with rammers, into spaces formed by planks, as I shall explain."

Mr. Rondelet states, in his preface, that the columns of the choir of the church of Véselay, in Bourgogne, were ascertained to be factitious stones by Marshal Vauban, and the pillars of the church of Saint Amand, in Flanders, were made in the same manner.

I have had no opportunity to ascertain whether blocks of stone of extraordinary dimensions, were factitious; this question could not be well settled, except by examination of the masses themselves. It is possible that several of the large blocks mentioned were factitious: but it is not easy to believe, in a wall formed of large pieces placed one upon another, that these large pieces are factitious, for it seems to me that it would be much more difficult to construct a wall of that sort, than to make the whole wall of one piece, whereby the moving and transportation of masses of an enormous weight would be avoided. I do not at all doubt that artificial stones of large dimensions may be made, for all depends on making a good mortar: nevertheless it seems proper not to admit such facts as are cited above without a thorough examination.

The Italians, at Alexandria, make very good factitious stones with the Casal lime, and employ them in angles; they are four feet eight inches long, by two feet eight inches wide, and two feet eight inches high; they are buried under ground for two or three years, and there acquire great hardness. These stones are made in the following manner. For one cubic yard they take 0.24 of Casal lime measured in paste, and 0.90 of sand. These are well mixed together, adding the water necessary to form a paste, and there is then added 0.20 of pebbles, (cailloux;) these factitious stones are therefore real concretes. Their goodness depends on the quality of the mortar applied to making them. Mr. Fleuret proposes to make the mortar for these factitious stones in the following manner.

He slakes the lime by immersion, according to the process of Mr. Lafaye, to which he attaches great efficacy. When slaked to dry powder, it is to be deposited in a dry situation, enclosed in casks covered with straw mats loaded with stones. He recommends that, each time the cask is resorted to for lime, a part only of the mat should be raised, and that it be replaced as soon as possible, in order to guard gainst the contact of the air, which he says is very hurtful. He makes a perfect mixture of sand and clay dust, in the proportion of two measures of sand to one of dust; or, which is better, he mixes sand and dust in equal parts. He then takes two measures of the mixture of sand and dust, and one measure of lime after being tempered with water, and makes them into a heap. He then works them dry, moistening them little by little as they mingle. Lastly, they are taken to a trough, where they are beaten by rammers of wood armed with iron, which are suspended from the ends of poles acting with a spring, like the spring pole of a turner's lathe. Mr. Fleuret says the mortar is improved by wetting it in the trough with a little lime slaked thin, and used in the proportion of one-sixth of the mortar. He censures the practice of reworking the mortar with fresh portions of water, which he says weakens it much.

The author adds that hard stone pulverized, may be substituted for sand,

and that scoriæ, iron scales, and sea coal ashes, furnished by forges, are still better than pulverized stones and clay dust. These are, in brief, the means pointed out by M. Fleuret, for making the mortar he designs for factitious stones. The mortars being made after this process, they are placed in moulds where they are beaten and strongly compressed. Mr. Fleuret has made much use of factitious stone in making water conduits, pump tubes, troughs, &c.

Mr. Fleuret established a manufactory of factitious stones at Pont-a-Mousson. We might suppose that, having at his command the good hydraulic lime of Metz, he would obtain good results; but, as I have said, in the first section, when we attempted to apply this process to making factitious conduits at Phalsburg, and caps of arches at Landau and Strasburg—using the lime of the country, we did not succeed. What I have before stated shows that it is less the manipulation than the choice of materials which affords good mortar, and consequently good factitious stones. But Mr. Fleuret has not given us the means of ascertaining the quality of the materials: and it follows that in pursuing the path he has pointed out, we are exposed to bad results, as happened in the above cases.

According to the experiments I have made, the best process for making mortars to be used in forming factitious stones is, if we use hydraulic lime, to slake it to powder with about one quarter of its volume of water, and to cover it with the materials that are to be mixed with it. I have several times remarked on the importance of making the mortar soon after the slaking of the lime. We ought not therefore to slake more lime at one time, than will suffice for eight or ten days. If the lime be eminently hydraulic, sand only need be added; and, of sand, that which is fine should be much preferred. If only a mixed sand can be had, it should be passed through a fine sieve; if it be too coarse, it should be pulverized; and if it be earthy, it should be washed by the process I have given.

If the lime be only moderately hydraulic, it will be necessary to make the mortars by adding to the lime equal parts of clean fine sand and cement.

If we happen to be in a country where the only lime is fat lime, we have seen, by table No. XXXIII, that it is quite immaterial whether this lime be used as soon as it is burned, or after having been slaked for some time, to paste or powder. Care should be taken to use only hydraulic lime made of clay, which contained but little lime. The mortar will be made by mixing the lime with the quantities of clean fine sand and hydraulic cement which shall have been found by trial to be the proportion best suited to the lime. In general, the proportion of one part of fat lime measured in paste, to two, or two and a half, of the other ingredients, will afford a very good mortar. There will be no disadvantage in wetting the mortar sufficiently to cause it to work easily, nor in reworking the mortar with a little additional water, should it become too dry. An excess of trituration is useless; it is sufficient if all the materials be well mixed. All my experiments show that iron does not improve mortar. The scoriæ, and the ashes of forges should not therefore be used without our being satisfied before hand, by the means I have pointed out, that they are hydraulic.

When the hydraulic mortar of which the stones are to be formed, has been made as above, it should be placed in moulds, if the stones are to be of small dimensions, and should be loaded with weights, or submitted to heavy pressure, until it has acquired sufficient consistence to be withdrawn from the moulds without breaking. The stones are then to be deposited in a moist place for about one year.

When factitious stones are made for water conduits, or other objects that are to be buried under ground, there is no objection to using red cements, such as are generally made from brick earths; but this colour would be disagreeable to the eye; and in case the objects are to be exposed to view, cements derived from clays that do not take this colour from burning should be used; such, for example, as are used in making tobacco pipes, stone ware and crockery. With the same view, cement derived from slate may be used.

There is no doubt in my mind that with good mortar, factitious stones may be made which will afford, at the end of a year, a resistance approaching that of ordinary bricks, and that the strength will go on increasing with time. We find in the Annales de Chimie, Vol. XXXVII, that "Mr. Monge, in visiting the ruins of Cesaria, remarked, in a temple consecrated to Augustus, that the pillars had wasted away to a great depth, but that the mortar projected. He tried in vain to break off a piece. The mortar was of very fine and equal grain; it appeared to be composed of fine sand and very little lime, very well mixed." It has been remarked that in the ancient Roman constructions which still exist in the Northern districts, the mortar has perfectly resisted the inclemencies of the seasons. I made at Strasburg large cubes of hydraulic mortar, which I withdrew from the water after about one year, and left exposed to the air during several summers and winters without their sustaining any injury. In the 7th No. of the *Memorial de l'Officier du Genie*, it may be seen that I proposed in 1819, to cover with factitious stone the floor of a sluice *de chasse*, which was 100 feet wide and was composed of five passages. The foundation was of concrete, and it was covered with a layer eight inches thick of good hydraulic mortar, which became united to the concrete, formed a factitious stone, showing, the next year, great solidity. It has now been made ten years, and it has sustained no injury. This means may be used with great advantage in countries where there is no good stone for cutting, or where such stone is dear.

In countries where free stone is not to be obtained, it is very advantageous to be able to compose factitious stones to form the angles, copings, casements of doors and windows, cornices, gutters, water conduits, &c.; this mode of fabrication might even be applied advantageously to objects of the largest dimensions. It often happens that for bridges across the ditches of fortifications, pieces are needed of about three feet in thickness: where stones are not to be had of suitable quality, these pieces may be easily made on the spot in a single piece of factitious stone: under similar circumstances, piers of sluices, columns, and obelisks may, also, be made; but in the cases of such large masses, it will not be easy to bury them in the first instance, and afterwards place them in the proper situations. It will be best, therefore, to construct them on the spot. It does not seem to me to be indispensable to make plank moulds to give them their proper shape: forms such as are used to direct the construction of walls, would suffice. It would only be necessary to take care, when the mortar had been made of ordinary consistency, that it should stiffen a little before being used, so that on being spread with the trowel it would retain the form given it, and at the same time be so ductile as to spread easily and unite itself well with the previous layer. As this mortar dries very quickly, there is no danger that the work of the morning will give way under the pressure of that of the afternoon. After having finished the day's work, care should be taken to cover the top of the wall with wet straw matting, so as to maintain a favourable humidity; in the morning the surface of the mortar should be rammed with a small flat rammer, and be made slightly wet, so as to be somewhat softened and brought into proper state to unite with the succeeding layer. As the work rises, care must be taken to surround it with straw, or some similar substance, which must be kept always moist during the first summer. If the work have but little altitude, earth may be banked against it. In all constructions of this kind, it is proper to make the work with a little excess of dimensions, so that the following year some tenth of an inch of the outside, which, having dried too quickly, will be less hard than the interior, may be cut away; pressure should always be applied, in any way most convenient, where the nature of the structure will permit it.

If it be thought proper, these factitious stones may be coloured at the time they are made, by mixing in the mortar composing the surface, some suitable metallic oxide.

If the factitious stones are to be of large dimensions, gravel or small stones may then, for the sake of economy, be mixed with the mortar: in such cases the resulting mass will be concrete. This substance was used by the Romans: several of their works are found in which the faces of the walls are of stones, and all the interior of a mixture of mortar and pebbles. Mr. Fleuret having enumerated, as stated in the beginning of this chapter, the great monuments supposed to have been made of factitious stones, says "There are even great walls constituting the enclosure of towns, large aqueducts, and piers of bridges, still remaining, nearly entire, from the time of the Romans, of which the faces are made of very small stones, and the heart of the wall of pebbles mixed with stones larger or smaller, thrown at hazard between these light facings. This masonry made of fragments, and rammed in an encasement, becomes but a single mass, and is rendered so compact by continuity, that in a short time the walls becomes indestructible."

I do not think that this masonry was made in encasements; the facing walls were substitutes therefor; and had there been no facings, the concrete, as I have before observed, might have been built up without moulds. But we see by the quotation, that the Romans made much use, in constructions in the air, of small materials mixed with their mortar, and it is this kind of construction which, as I have said, we now call concrete. I have stated, in the first section, that in repairing, in 1816, one of the dams which sustained the navigable canal of Strasburg in its passage across the ditches of the fortification, I found that the facings alone were of free stone, and that all the interior was of concrete, of great hardness, which led me to presume it had been made of hydraulic lime, and induced me to make researches, whereby I became possessed of the qualities of Obernai lime, and afterward of many other hydraulic limes in the neighbourhood.

In constructing, with concrete, the interior of baterdeaux that have sufficient thickness, we may be certain of their great durability. In rubble or regular masonry, the mortar does not always unite itself perfectly to the stone—so that if there be a head of water, it will at least find a passage between the joints. This cannot happen in masonry made of small materials, as concrete, because all these small stones are separated from each other by a portion of the mortar which will oppose filtration. In the two baterdeaux of Strasburg which I have cited, the facings were displaced; but the central mass of concrete prevented a single drop of water from passing, notwithstanding the bad condition of the facings.

Mr. Rondelet says at page 116 of his work "There is found near Metz in France, a very hard stone with which they make lime of very superior quality; this lime, newly slaked and mixed with gravel, affords a concrete or species of mortar, of which the consistence is so great that arches may be constructed of it, without bricks or stones; these arches form a single piece as hard as stone.

Lieut. Col. Finot has constructed at Strasburg, within two years, an arch of concrete of about thirteen feet four inches diameter, which has succeeded well: the piers are of masonry. A similar arch has been coustructed at Schelestadt. This kind of arch offers great advantage in many circumstances.

When the arches are to be underground; this will be the best means of preventing filtration; but that the underground room may be perfectly dry it will be necessary to make the piers and end walls also of concrete.

It often happens that there are casemates and cellars which in time of floods, fill with water. This may be prevented by putting a structure of concrete upon the bottom: and if the water filters through the walls, by reinforcing them with a plaster of concrete. By these means we turned to profit, at Strasburg, several casemates, of which the floor was below the level of the water in the river, and in the ditches, in time of floods.

We are frequently obliged to carry a canal over a stream of water, and vice versa. In such cases aqueducts are built. It is here particularly, as in aqueducts in general, that concrete is indispensable. If it be thought proper to build the arches of stones or bricks, it is indispensable, in order to resist filtration, to make all the masonry above the arches, of concrete. In countries where proper materials for making the arches cannot be obtained at a reasonable rate, it will be advantageous to make the arches of concrete, in which case the aqueduct will be formed of a single piece. Arches of large dimensions may be constructed in this way, either for aqueducts or for ordinary bridges.

It is necessary sometimes to enlarge a wharf, in cases where the river cannot be restricted; and it is done by making all the courses of masonry, projecting, or corbel, courses—a very expensive construction, on account of the large dimensions which the stones must have. The same result may be obtained with concrete, which will form but a single piece of great solidity, at small comparative cost. By similar means *machicoulis*, which are sometimes necessary to protect the entrance to forts, may be made.

Researches are now being made as to the means of preserving grain in *Silos*. It is requisite to success, that the grain be preserved from the contact of the air, and from humidity. Both these conditions will be secured at the same time, by making the *Silos* of concrete. After the grain is deposited therein, it may be hermetically sealed by closing the mouth with the same substance. *Silos* may be of great advantage in provisioning fortified places: and it is important that attention be directed towards them.

In some departments in the north of France, no good building stones are to be found, and revetment walls are there constructed of fragments of chalk, there being a facing of bricks to preserve the chalk from contact of the air. But in several of these places the bricks are of bad quality, and this facing scales off, requiring considerable, and perpetual, outlays for repairs. In such circumstances it would be, I think, advantageous and economical, to build the revetment entirely of concrete. It should be composed of hydraulic mortar in which would be mixed gravel, fragments of chalk, bricks or any similar matters, in the proportions indicated in the first section. Taking care to apply on the outside a thick plaster of the same kind of mortar. The plaster should be applied at the time the concrete is laid, so that it may unite with it perfectly. By this means the chalk will be preserved from contact of air. As the wall rises, humid earth should be placed against the back of it, and the front should be covered with straw-mats or a thick layer of straw, which should be kept wet during all the first summer. In countries where good *arenes* are to be had, revetments in concrete would not be dear; and, besides the advantage of avoiding considerable expense in repairs, it would be more difficult to make breaches in revetments of concrete than in those constructed of stone.

I will observe that in the construction of revetments, which have, commonly, about thirty-three feet in height, and sustain a great mass of earth, the bad quality of the mortar often makes a much greater thickness of masonry necessary than if the mortar were good. By making, as I have proposed, all the masonry of hydraulic mortar, the expense will be augmented a little; but on the other hand it will be possible to diminish the thickness of the walls, which will be a compensation. By making the revetments of concrete they will be of a single piece, and the thickness may be sensibly reduced; which will amount to a great saving wherever good arenes are at hand. Nothing would prevent these revetments being made with counterforts or with relieving arches.

In the south of France particularly, are to be seen revetments of great exterior slope. This mode of construction, permits the thickness of masonry to be considerably reduced: but it cannot be adopted in the north, because of the humidity which favours the development of vegetation in the joints, causing the ruin of the masonry. By constructing these revetments with concrete, taking care to apply a strong exterior coat of plaster immediately, and to unite it perfectly with the beton, there will be nothing to fear from vegetation, and the talus of the wall will allow its thickness to be considerably lessened. This will be worthy of trial at those places in the north where the materials are not generally good, and where arenes are to be obtained.

When repairing revetments from which portions had scaled off, from the effect of vegetation, I had occasion to remark that sometimes the lime seemed to have disappeared from the mortar almost entirely; to such a degree that it was thought the lime had been fraudulently reduced in quantity in making the mortar. Examining these separated parts of the wall, I remarked that all the joints of the stones were filled with roots which had penetrated to a great depth. There remained hardly any thing but sand in the joints of the stones. I was led to believe from this that fat lime is absorbed by vegetation. I saw no such effect in masonry made of good hydraulic mortar. It is possible that the hardness of these mortars resists the development of vegetation; or that this kind of lime is less favourable than fat lime. In making revetments of concrete, giving them a good coat of plaster made of hydraulic mortar, of which the surface should be made very smooth, it seems to me that there would be nothing to fear from vegetation.

In the northern department of which I have spoken, the buildings are not more solid than the revetments. They are obliged to make them of bricks which are at the same time of bad quality and very dear. In many southern districts houses are made of *Pisé*. This kind of construction is not in my opinion solid enough for military establishments; and I doubt if it would succeed in the humid climate of the north: but I see nothing to prevent these buildings being made of concrete. I have shown that with hydraulic mortar we obtain a strength approaching that of common bricks. The walls of houses constructed of concrete containing this kind of mortar would possess great solidity, and wherever arenes were at command and building materials bad, would be erected with great comparative advantage. The angles of the building, and the casements of doors and windows, should be made of factitious stone, and the walls should be covered with a coat of hydraulic mortar, coloured to resemble stone. The precautions indicated above, against too rapid drying, should not be omitted. It would be easy to make a trial of this kind, on some small building, or a guard room, kitchen, &c.

We often have to construct bomb proof buildings, for powder magazines, barracks and other establishments. In countries where the mortars are of bad quality, I am of opinion that it would be wrong to make them of concrete. When made of stones, or bricks, I have already said, that it seems to me necessary to use hydraulic mortar. I will add that when it is thought proper to make the arches of stones or bricks, I regard as indispensable, after the centre has been struck, to make all the masonry above these arches of concrete; this being, in my opinion, the only means of securing their future impermeability. This mass of concrete might, in fact, enable us to dispense with a plastered cap; but, for greater security, it will be best to put on a coat of plaster of about one inch in thickness. It is very important when these caps are in progress, to shield them from the sun. They are sometimes covered with a sail cloth; but this does not preserve them from hot air which causes them to dry too quickly. It would be better and cheaper, to cover them, as they advance, with moistened straw. When the caps have acquired sufficient consistence, they should be polished, and again covered with straw, which should be kept moist all summer. If the arches are to be covered with earth, this earth, at least in part, should be put on as soon as the caps have been polished.

There is still another use to which concrete may be applied with great advantage, namely in the abutments of suspended bridges. When there is not rock to which to attach the chains, it is necessary to build abutments; but these chains acting in an angle of about 45°, a great part of the tension is in a horizontal direction. If the mass of the abutment is of cut stone; or rubble masonry, the mortar not fastening the stones together strongly, this force may disjoin them horizontally. This lately happened to the suspended bridge built opposite the *Invalids* at Paris. I do not doubt that the masses of masonry forming the abutments would have been competent to resist a much greater force than they were subject to, if those abutments had been of a single piece each: but as they were constructed of cut stone and rubble masonry, and there had not been time for the mortar to dry thoroughly, the masonry separated into two parts near the middle of the abutment, so that the hand might be introduced between them. This I consider the explanation of the accident which made it necessary to demolish the bridge before it had been entirely uncentered. If the masses to which the chains were fastened had been of concrete, they would have formed a single, homogeneous, inseparable mass; it would have been necessary for the chains to have drawn it off entirely, or to have broken it, while, in the actual case, it was only necessary to disjoin stones that had but recently been united by mortar. When bridges of this kind are built it seems to me proper to make the abutments, to which the chains are to be attached, of concrete: and they should be erected a year in advance so that the substance may acquire sufficient solidity.

The beginning of autumn is the most favorable season for making concretes that are to be exposed to the air.

I will conclude by observing that the expense necessary to the composition of good mortars for concretes, must be encountered. In countries where the arenes are not very hydraulic, they may be mixed with hydraulic cement in proportions depending on the energy of the materials. As I have said above, it is more economical to encounter the requisite expense of good masonry, at once, than to execute it cheaply of bad materials.

I have thought it proper to enter into some details as to the advantageous use to be made of concrete in places where building materials are of bad quality; and to indicate some new modes of construction to be substituted for those now in use.

CHAPTER XVI.

Summary of the Second Section.

The experiments reported in the second section of this memoir, lead me to the following conclusions, as to mortars exposed in the air.

When I made mortar by using fat lime that had been lying slaked and moist for a considerable time, and sand only, I could obtain no satisfactory result, whatever were the proportions. In making mortars with sand, and fat lime just from the kiln, I could obtain only mediocre results. The lime I used was got from a carbonate of lime containing only a minute quantity of iron. It will be important to ascertain, whether, as I anticipate, similar results will be produced in other countries. Should the experiments in other places afford similar results, it will be necessary to abandon the practice of keeping fat limes lying slaked and wet for a long period, and to adopt that of using them fresh from the kiln.

The process of slaking lime announced by Mr. Lafaye, and that given by Mr. Loriot, afford no sensible amelioration with fat lime.

Hydraulic limes mixed with sand, produced very good mortars in the air, as well as in water. These limes must be used soon after the calcination, as they lose a great part of their energy. Mortars made of hydraulic limes afford a greater resistance when they are mixed with sand and hydraulic cement, than when mixed with sand only. Hydraulic cements, or other analogous matters, mixed with limes, restore the energy of those which had been too long exposed to the air; and augment the energy of those which are but moderately hydraulic.

Hydraulic mortars made of fat lime, sand, and hydraulic cements, or other analogous matters, are excellent when used in the air. When sand and cement, in equal parts, are added to lime, it is almost a matter of indifference whether the lime be used fresh from the kiln, or slaked to powder with a little water, and for some time exposed to the air in this state, or, having been slaked and lying wet for a considerable time. But if only a small quantity of cement is to be added to the mortar, it will be best to use the fat lime shortly after its calcination.

In countries where good natural hydraulic limes are to be had, they may be used with sand only, in making mortars for exposure to the air. When such limes are not to be found, instead of making artificial hydraulic limes, it will be preferable, as in the case of water mortars, to make the hydraulic mortar directly, by mixing fat lime with sand and hydraulic cement. The proportion of cement to be mixed in the mortar will depend on its quality, and the nature of the works to which it is to be applied.

Clay dust containing about one-fifth of lime appears to be less proper for mortars that are to be exposed to the air, than for those to be placed in water: but a few hundredths of lime, far from injuring, have an advantageous effect in saving fuel, and facilitating the pulverization of burnt clays. Clay dust, and other analogous matters, should always be made very fine.

Arenes mixed with fat lime afford hydraulic mortars, which are very good in the air. When the arenes are feeble, they should be mixed with a little hydraulic cement.

When *clay dust, ashes, scoriæ of forges,* and *arenes,* have only weak hydraulic properties, they give to air-mortars but feeble tenacity. Before using these matters in the air, therefore, they should be tried by mixing them with fat lime, and plunging them in water, according to the process given in the first section. It is the more important to make such trials, because these substances are very dear, and some varieties of them produce no better effect than so much sand.

Fat lime and hydraulic lime do not seem able to bear as much sand as is commonly thought. Fine sand affords much better results than coarse, both in air-mortars and in water-mortars. Earthy sands must be avoided. In places where earthy sands, only, can be procured, they must be washed: but before resorting to this operation, we should be satisfied that these sands are not arenes. Should they prove to be arenes, they must be used in the state in which they are found.

The process given in the first section for the manipulation of water-mortars applies equally to air-mortars. No ill consequences need be apprehended from wetting the mortars to the degree requisite to their being worked with ease; nor, when they have become too stiff, from exposure to the air, from adding a little water, on reworking them. An excess of trituration, beyond what is required to mix the ingredients thoroughly, is altogether useless.

It does not appear that the Romans had any particular process for making their mortars. No masonry has survived to our day but such as was made of hydraulic lime, or of fat lime and hydraulic cements, or arenes (I speak here of masonry made of small materials.) An inspection of their mortars shows that they were often made with little care, proving that their good quality is to be attributed solely to the quality of the lime, or of the substances mixed with it.

If, in general, no better results are obtained with fat lime, than those obtained by me, the practice of making mortars of fat lime and sand only, should be abandoned. A small quantity of hydraulic cement, or of some substance of similar nature, should always be mixed in the mortar; that is to say, all air-mortars should be hydraulic mortars. The expense will be a little greater it is true, but there will be full compensation in the duration of the masonry. There is no economy in putting up cheap masonry which will require to be rebuilt at the end of a few years; and will need costly repairs, annually: it is much better, and really more economical, to encounter, at once, the expense which will secure to the work an indefinite duration, and exemption from all but trivial repairs.

Hydraulic mortars, whether made of hydraulic lime and sand, or of fat lime and hydraulic cement, or other similar substance, resist the inclemences of the seasons well, which makes them proper to form factitious stones. The art of making factitious stones is nothing more than the art of making good hydraulic mortars. This kind of stone may be easily made to possess, at the end of a year, a tenacity about equal to that of ordinary bricks, and this tenacity will go on augmenting, for several years. The solidity of hydraulic mortars is favoured, and of course the solidity of factitious stones also, by keeping them moist during the first year. They should, therefore, be buried under ground, or placed in water, if their dimensions will allow; and when too large to be ·thus disposed of, they should be formed on the spot they are to occupy, and be enveloped in some material which may be kept wet. It would be proper to make their dimensions a little in excess, in order to bring them, subsequently, to their true dimensions, by cutting away the surface that had been in contact with the air. In order to avoid disagreeable colours, cements should be taken, which are but little coloured by the oxide of iron.

In countries where building materials are of bad quality, and where energetic arenes, or good hydraulic limes, are to be had, concrete may be advantageously employed, in the construction of revetments, underground rooms, aqueducts, and various buildings: this mode may also be employed, even where no arenes or hydraulic limes are to be found, provided the materials for making cements, can be procured at a moderate price.

It will be important, wherever works in masonry are to be carried on, to make experiments in order to ascertain, 1st, the quality of the several kinds of lime to be found in the neighbourhood; 2nd, whether it be best to use fat lime fresh from the kiln, or to slake it into vats, and allow it to lie for some time wet, as is commonly done; 3rd, the proportion of sand that gives the best mortar; and 4th, the quality of various arenes and cements to be found in the vicinity.

To make these various experiments, both for water-mortars and air-mortars, I think the essays should be submitted to trial, after about one year, with a machine like that used by me, and of which a drawing is added. It would be advantageous to make, in all places, the trials with prisms of mortar of the same dimensions, in order to compare the various results, and to ascertain the relative qualities of the materials, in different districts or countries. The great number of experiments I had to make, was the reason why I used prisms too small. I think that quadrangular prisms 14 inches long by 4 inches, (0.35m × 0.10m × 0.10m) would be of suitable size.

To this end the mortar should be moulded in boxes 14 inches long by 4.80 in. wide by 4.80 high: after a year, four-tenths of an inch should be cut from each face, and the prism be placed in two stirrups of iron, like those in the plate—the stirrups being twelve inches clear distance apart, and be broken in the manner pointed out in the first section. Similar prisms should be made of the best brick earth in the vicinity, which, after being burned, should be cut down to the same dimensions as the mortar prisms; these brick prisms being broken, the average weight sustained by them will serve to appreciate the resistance of the mortar prisms. Stone prisms should also be subjected to the same trial: these, when of good stone, will show a strength much beyond that of the best bricks: I doubt if mortars can be brought to afford a resistance equal to hard stone: but the strength of bricks may be easily attained, and that will give good masonry.

I must urge upon Engineers to study, in their several localities, the meterials most proper to make good mortars. The fabrication of mortars has been, for a long period, abandoned to a routine which has produced perishable masonry, requiring frequent repairs; and thus consuming funds which might have been applied to the construction of new work or the amelioracion of the old. Engineers should not consider it beneath them to be occupied in this kind of research: and they should leave behind them at each place, a relation of the experiments they have made, and the results they have obtained. These operations require minute attention, certainly, but this will be recompenced by works of long duration.

SECT. III.—EXTRACTS FROM

"RESEARCHES AS TO LIME BURNING."

BY M. PETOT,
Engineer of Roads and Bridges.*

————

CHAPTER XVII.

————

On the Preparation of Factitious Puzzolana, and particularly of that
afforded by Gneiss Sand.

————

§ 1. *On different kinds of Puzzolana.*

The important part that puzzolanas play in the improvement of hydraulic mortars, sufficiently explains the interest that belongs to an examination of this subject. As yet we know of no other means of forming mortars susceptible of hardening in water: and even since hydraulic limes have become the subject of particular study, that of puzzolanas has not been the less attended to, because hydraulic limes are not to be found in every locality, nor is it always possible, or economical, to manufacture them; and because in many circumstances they give mediocre results only, unless mixed with a certain dose of puzzolana.

Puzzolanas may be arranged in two principal classes, namely, natural puzzolanas, and artificial puzzolanas. Among the first, the most energetic are, generally, volcanic matters of a composition analogous to clays. These were discovered first in Italy, where their use goes back to time immemorial. Afterwards they were found in countries possessing extinct volcanoes, as Auvergne, Vivarais, Guadaloupe, &c. The matters which furnished them have sustained, by igneous action, a change in the primitive mode of combination in their elements; but as the intensity of this action was not every where the same, there resulted products of various degrees of cohesion: and it is not difficult to conceive that great differences may exist in their qualities, although none may exist in their chemical composition.

*Paris, from the Royal press, 1833.
22

It may, nevertheless, be possible that a puzzolana is no more than of medium quality, merely because, as is said in common parlance, it is still *too young*. In cases where there was at first too much cohesion, certain influences may, in the course of time, bring about a state of disaggregation. This phenomenon is not without example in nature: the greater part of the feldspathic rocks are in these circumstances, and produce a second variety of puzzolanas. Such, particularly, are the graywackes of Carhaix, the arenes of Perigord, and our gneiss sands. The geological position of these substances, at least of the gneiss which we have before us at Brest, does not admit the supposition of any igneous action. This disaggregation goes on little by little, and we take, as it were, nature in the act, for between the upper parts of the quarries which are in a state of sand, and those which are still in the condition of hard rocks, it is not rare to find a series of layers of every intermediate grade of cohesion.

These recent puzzolanas are but slightly energetic: but by torrifying them, they are rendered, if not equal to the first, at least applicable to almost all the same uses: they thereby pass into the class of artificial puzzolanas.

In the same class we must also arrange, after they have been highly calcined, compact schists, and even basalts. Calcination was, in fact, the means applied to these substances by M. Gratien Lepère, and the Swedish engineer Baggé. Lastly, all clays, considered either as proceeding from the decomposition of rocks, or as forming particular earths, lead to the same result by the application of heat.

Few localities are without clays; whence the general use, from very remote periods, of the dust of bricks or tiles, as cement. We may now substitute, with economy, the sands of graywacke, of gneiss, and of arenes; but these latter substances are less common. By their use the subject does not change its aspect; there is merely an enlargement of its boundaries.

In all puzzolanas, natural or factitious, the elements of clay, namely, silex and alumine, determine the hydraulic qualities: moreover, silex alone, in jelly, or lightly calcined, but in a state of extreme division, gives, by its mixture with fat lime, a good hydraulic mortar; while it is not the same with alumine; we may, therefore, say, definitively, that silex is the base of all puzzolanas; and that, reciprocally, all substances containing silex in a state of feeble cohesion are apt to become puzzolanas.

§ 2. *On several methods employed in the preparation of Factitious Puzzolanas.*

The study of the quality and use of natural puzzolanas not having immediate connexion with the question before us, we shall restrict our remarks to artificial puzzolanas. And we shall first refer to the several methods applied to their preparation.

The material to which recourse is had, may be submitted to heat, first, in the state of powder; and second, in the state of fragments, either brick shaped, or of irregular forms. In the first case, all refractory, ochreous, or calcareous, clays may afford good puzzolanas by a torrefaction of a few minutes. It will be sufficient to spread the powder in a thin layer on an iron plate, and keep it incandescent from five to twenty-five minutes. M. Vicat, to whom we are indebted for the knowledge of this method, adds, however, that it has not been applied on a large scale, and that it offers some difficulties. M. Girard de Caudembourg assures us, from his own experiments, that when the arene sands have been lightly torrefied, the time required to set under water is shortened, but the hardness of the mortars is not increased. This consequence, founded on a particular case of calcination, does not prove that it is true in general of arenes, more than of graywacke or gneiss.

In the second case the materials are employed either pure, that is to say, in the state nature supplies them, or previously mixed with certain substances designed to facilitate the chemical reaction. This premised, we see, according to Gen. Treussart, that calcareous clay brought to the same degree of calcination as lightly burned bricks, gives good results; and that from this degree up to that of the highest calcination, its energy rapidly diminishes, and at last becomes null; that for ochreous clays, on the contrary, the calcination of lightly burned bricks gives very mediocre results; but that these results are progressively ameliorated up to the degree of burning required to produce good bricks, beyond which it decreases indefinitely; that, lastly, refractory clays also give excellent puzzolanas at the degree of burning which makes good bricks, but they resist better than the ochreous clays the effect of a higher calcination, and do not sensibly lose quality up to a calcination equalling that of common lime. It is, consequently, to be supposed that they attain their maximum less quickly; and such is, without doubt, the reason why Chaptal—submitting to the same mode of calcination refractory clay, sometimes pure, and sometimes mixed with the sulphate of iron, which gave the equivalent of an ochreous clay, found different results, and concluded that the oxide of iron was an element essential, generally, to the success of the operation.

Clays, at the same time ochreous and calcareous, but containing at least a tenth of their weight of lime, like clays simply calcareous, require only a slight calcination. (Treussart.) We may thus, by a slight burning, obtain good puzzolana with an ochreous clay, by impregnating it with a certain quantity of lime, according to the recommendation of Inspector General Bruyère. We might also, with equal success, replace the lime by potash or soda; and such, for example, is what is called *aquafortis cement*, a residue left in the preparation, by means of clay and nitrate of potash, of nitric acid.

At the works on the canal from Nantes to Brest, graywacke, in irregular pieces, was submitted to a degree of heat like that required to furnish good bricks. And, according to M. Vicat, blue schist requires to be heated till it swells up, (*boursoufle*,) and basalt till it melts, (*le basalt doit couler.*)

For the burning of all these materials in fragments, lime kilns or brick kilns may be used. Unfortunately, the uniformity of the burning not being perfect in any of these kilns, fragments are mixed together, some of which are too much, and some too little, burned; and, consequently, there is a mixture of good and bad puzzolana, affording a mediocre result, or at least a result quite inferior to what may be obtained in the laboratory.

If to this be added, the expense necessary to pulverize and sift these same fragments, it will be perceived how important it is to be able to apply on a large scale M. Vicat's method; for with that method nothing is easier than to arrive at a uniform degree of calcination; after which the products need no manipulation. Such was the object in view in constructing the furnace described below. The abundance of the gneiss sand in the quarries of the port of Brest enabled us to avoid the expense of a preliminary pulverization, and at the same time we were enabled to turn to profit the immense quantity of wood chips furnished by the naval constructions.

Note.   Then follows in the original:
Description of a furnace for factitious puzzolanas.
Details relative to the various parts of the furnace.
Progress of burning.
Quantity of products obtained.

The furnace being a reverberatory, the cement was spread out upon the hearth in undulating zones, rather thicker near the front than in the rear, or on the sides, and the aperture was closed for twenty to twenty-five minutes. At the end of this time the surface submitted to the flame was renewed, by turning over the substance.   Waiting about another twenty minutes, the calcination was sufficient, and the matter was drawn away to give place immediately to another portion.   The author then proceeds:

The quantity of puzzolana prepared in this way varied as the furnace was more or less hot; but it became constant after the fifth or sixth day, and amounted regularly to 120 cubic feet in 24 hours. The number of burnings in the same interval was 34; which gave for each burning 3.53 cubic feet of puzzolana and 42 minutes of time.

The first days the furnace was in operation, we withdrew as much as 177 cubic feet in 24 hours. But experience was not slow in demonstrating that too much in quantity was injurious to the quality; and, which is remarkable, this imperfectly burned sand was less energetic than the crude sand. It was not less important to prove, on the other hand, what would happen in prolonging the calcination beyond 42 minutes. To this end, two new essays were made, the one with two hours', and the other with three hours' burning; and we found that under these circumstances, the energy of the puzzolana suffered a little as respects the rapidity of the setting, but remained about the same, as to resistance to rupture, at the end of fifteen months.

It was important to have, as a term of comparison, some trials of the gneiss burned in the state of fragments, according to the process antecedently used. For that purpose we took, at hazard, a considerable stock of powder reduced from fragments burned during twelve to fifteen hours in a lime kiln; and other powder reduced from fragments burned above the lime, in another lime kiln. With the first, the results were inferior to those with the crude sand; with the second, they were sensibly better than the crude sand, but weaker, notwithstanding, than the sand calcined in the reverberatory furnace.

§ 3. *Comparative experiments with the Puzzolana of Gneiss, taken in different conditions.*

The experiments here mentioned are united in the two following tables.

173

Table No. XLIII.—*First series of experiments.*

No.	Composition of the mortars.	Time required to set.	Resistance to rupture per 0.394 inch (centimetre) square.	Age of the mortars when broken.	Remarks.
		d's.	lbs.	mo's.	
1	One of lime in paste with two of crude gneiss sand	20	2.35	8	Immersed in sea-water. The time of setting, a little uncertain on account of the surface swelling up.
2	Same with two and a half	20	3.23	do.	
3	Same with two of sand slightly calcined	35	2.04	do.	
4	Same with one of sand do. and one of quartzose sand	?	<0.77	do.	
5	Same with two and a half of gneiss sand calcined for 42 minutes	7	5.37	do.	The resistances to rupture were calculated generally after the formula of Galileo, $2Pc = Rab^2$ wherein P indicates the weight that caused the rupture; c the distance of the point of support of the mortar to the point of application of the load; a, the breadth of the prism, and b, its depth.
6	Same with two do.	7½	5.37	do.	
7	Same with one and a half do.	8	4.03	do.	
8	Same with one do. and one of quartzose sand	20	<0.99	do.	
9	Same with two of pulverised fragments having been heated from twelve to fifteen hours in a lime kiln	34	2.11	do.	
10	Same with one and a half of the same puzzolana	?	<0.97	do.	
11	Same with one of do. and one of quartzose sand	?	<0.75	do.	All the mortars comprised in this table were immediately immersed in sea water.
12	Same with two of pulverized fragments heated more highly than the above	8	3.43	do.	
13	Same with two of do. from another fragment,	7	4.69	do.	

Table No. XLIV.—*Second series of experiments.*

No.	Composition of the mortars.	Time required to set.	Resistance to rupture per 0.394 inch (centimetre) square.	Age of the mortar when broken.	Remarks.
		d's.	lbs.	m's	
14	One of lime in paste with two of gneiss sand calcined for forty-two minutes	8	5.19	15	Tempered stiff and immersed immediately in fresh water.
15	Same with two of sand calcined during two hours	12	5.70	do	
16	Same with two of sand calcined during three hours	20	5.76	do	
17	Like No. 14, but tempered very soft and immersed immediately in fresh water	24	3.04	do	

No.	Composition of the mortars.	Time required to set.	Resistance to rupture per 0.394 inch (centimetre) square.	Age of the mortar when broken.	Remarks.
			lb s.	mo's	
18	Like No. 15 but a little less soft than No. 17	16	3.96	15	
19	Like No. 16 and about the same consistence as No. 18	20	4.70	do.	It is remarkable that under fresh water the mortars have not the same tendency to swell up as in sea-water.
20	Like No. 14 but allowed to dry for 18 hours before the immersion	12	6.60	do.	
21	Like No. 15 and with the same precaution as No. 20	11	7.17	do.	
22	Like No. 16 and with the same precaution as Nos. 20 and 21	13	6.60	do.	

§ 4. *On the influence of the inert portions of gneiss sand.*

The trials Nos. 4, 8 and 11 indicate that the puzzolana of gneiss will not bear any addition of quartzose sand: all the other numbers indicate that when calcined properly it gives mortars that set very soon under salt water or fresh water, but that it acquires in the end, only a moderate hardness. In fact, it can be arranged only in the class of puzzolanas *simply energetic.*

All these results appear to us to be affected by one and the same cause, the presence of inert matter. We know that gneiss, like granite, is formed of quartz in grains, mica and feldspar: but the quartz totally resists spontaneous decomposition; the mica resists it in part, because it is that substance which is seen in the sand of the quarry in countless brilliant spangles: the feldspar alone undergoes chemical alteration, and furnishes the active element of puzzolana. The energy of this puzzolana depends then on the relative quantities of feldspar on the one hand, and of quartz and mica on the other. Several attempts at a separation have given us a mean proportion of about one quarter for the quartz. The mica is much more abundant but difficult to separate. On collecting, by means of a very fine seive, the most pulverulent portions of a well burned sand, it appeared to be extremely charged with mica; and on tempering it with lime in paste, it gave a mortar which did not indurate in water till the end of 24 days; while with the same sand not sifted, the setting of the mortar occurred at the end of the 7th day.

We will add that the proportions of constituents may vary, from one quarry to another, or even in different veins of the same quarry. It was thus, probably, that on one occasion, the calcined sand, taken at hazard from the store house, gave us—*time of setting, five days—resistance to rupture per 0.394 inch, (centimetre) square—11.22 lbs.—age of the mortar when broken* $5\frac{1}{2}$ *months.*

The energy of the products obtained from the reverberatory furnace appears then to depend quite as much on the substance used as on the degree of calcination given to it.

§ 5. *Trials of the same reverberatory furnace in the calcination of plastic clays.*

What we have thus far said of the gneiss sand is applicable, for the greater part, we do not doubt, to graywacke sands and to arenes; but circumstances have not permitted us to verify it.

Plastic clays have the advantage of these feldspathic rocks, in not being mixed with matter essentially inert; in this respect they offer more chances of being converted into very energetic puzzolanas. But can they be treated with success in the reverberatory furnace? We wish to clear up this question, by some trials, of which we will proceed to give an account.

We made use of the common clay of Brest, which is ochreous and eminently plastic. After having cut it into small slices by means of a wire, and having dried these little slices in the air, they were reduced to powder, or rather they were ground, in an apparatus, of which a description would be useless at this time, but which may be said to be founded on the same principle as a *coffee-mill*. The clay brought to this state was introduced into the furnace, as the gneiss sand had been, and was heated with the same kind of fuel, first for forty-two minutes, then for two hours, and afterward for three hours. We had thus three kinds of puzzolana, which, used in the fabrication of mortars, gave:

The 1st. *an imperfect hardening—a tendency to form paste with water;*

The 2nd. *hardened in twenty days—resistance to rupture after fifteen months,* 3.17 *lbs;*

The 3rd, *hardened in eleven days, resistance to rupture after fifteen months,* 6.86 *lbs.*

At the same time we found:

That with puzzolana from well burned square tiles, the hardening took place in 7 days; and the resistance to rupture, after eight months, was 14.30 *lbs: that with puzzolana from Italy, the hardening took place in seven days, and the resistance to rupture, after eight months was* 16.35 *lbs.*

Whence we see that the degree of heat afforded by our reverberatory furnace is insufficient to give to plastic clays all the energy of which they are susceptible. It might be otherwise if we were to use a better fuel: but it is not the less demonstrated that, as regards calcination, we cannot place gneiss sands and plastic clays in the same list. As to these last, one consideration is striking; which is, that if the calcination be not perfectly uniform, all those portions which retain a tendency to form paste with water, will become an obstacle to the setting of the mortar, and a permanent cause of alteration. The gneiss sands, on the contrary, act even in their natural state, like puzzolana; and, in the most unfavourable case, give a mixture of portions, only more or less active.

§ 6. *On calcination on a small scale, upon thin iron plates.*

The results we have just been exposing do not at all conform to the manner in which the preparation of factitious puzzolanas, by heating pulverulent substances on plates of sheet iron, has been considered. *An incan-*

descence for a few minutes—a very moderate burning, compared to what is required in the burning of lime on a large scale, or even in the burning of bricks, carries with it the idea of a degree of heat easy to attain; and, consequently, of the necessity of a particular influence exerted by the contact of atmospheric air. It will not, therefore, be without interest to rectify this opinion by new experiments, which, besides, lead to some other remarks.

On exposing iron plates to the fire in a common fire place, the degree of heat obtained is too feeble: for the clay in powder, heated in this way during 10, 20, 30, 45, and 60 minutes, gave a puzzolana still forming paste with water, excepting the last, which was passible. Under the same circumstances, limestone reduced to powder, did not lose beyond 6 or 8 per cent. of its weight. In order to obtain greater heat, and to operate with more promptitude, we placed plates of sheet iron in a small forge over a fire of charcoal, we then found, for 100 grammes of powdered hydraulic limestone containing 33 per cent. of carbonic acid, duration of calcination—10 minutes—15 minutes—20 minutes—45 minutes: corresponding loss of weight —8.33 gms.—30.00 gms.—32.85 gms.—33.00 gms.

The last three specimens, sprinkled with water, slaked and swelled like ordinary lime just from the kiln. In a few minutes, therefore, the same effects are produced by ignition on a plate of sheet iron, as after several days of burning in a kiln.

To ascertain what would happen on replacing the powdered limestone by powdered clay, we made two series of experiments, one on gneiss sand, and the other on an ochreous clay: mortars were made of the resulting puzzolanas; and we deduced from the experiments the two following tables.

Table XLV. *Gneiss Sand.*

Duration of the calcination.	0	3½′	5′	7½′	10′	15′	20′	40′	60′	120′	B. It was not always possible to ascertain exactly the loss of weight, on account of the adherence of the sand to the iron.
Loss of weight on 100 grammes		gms. 6.20	g. 6.30	g. ?	g. 7.30	g. ?	g. 7.15	g. ?	g. ?	g. ?	
Order in which the hardening under water occurred	4	3	1	1	1	2	3	4	5	5	The hardness was measured by the weight necessary to force into the mortar a wire 0.047 of an inch in diameter.
Hardness after two months.	Soft and without consistence	gms. 400	g. 800	g. 800	g. 800	g 800	g. 500	g. 300	g. 250	g. 180	

Table No. XLVI. *Powdered ochreous clay.*

Duration of the calcination.	5′	7′	10′	15′	20′	25′	30′	40′	60′	120	The first two specimens were heated more violently than common. The clay adhered to the sheet-iron.
Loss of weight on 100 grammes.	?	?	gms. 9.50	g. 9.65	g. 1160	g. ?	g. 12.20	g. 12.50	g. ?	g. ?	
Order in which the hardening under water occured	4	3	3	2	1	1	2	4	5	6	All the puzzolanas mentioned in these two tables, were of a decided red, except the first, which had the natural colour of the sand.
Hardness after 2 months.	gs. 900	g. 1000	g. 1000	g. 1100	g. 1500	g. 1500	g. 1200	g. 600	g. 500	g. 200	

These tables show that the degree of heat necessary to convert ochreous clay into good puzzolana differs but little from that necessary to the complete calcination of lime, and may, consequently, be assimilated to that required to produce good bricks: that for the gneiss sand, as we have already shown, a much lighter calcination will suffice, and which, on a large scale, should not exceed the calcination given to slightly burned bricks. Nothing as yet shows the truth of the hypothesis, that the contact of the air exercises a particular influence on the calcination of any argillaceous substances whatever, on plates of iron. It is objected, it is true, that the same substances calcined in close vessels do not give the same results; but there is nothing in that which should surprise us, as we will attempt to prove.

§ 7. *On calcination in Close Vessels.*

We operated in a melting furnace with crucibles of about 4¼ quarts: instead, however, of four hours' fire required for melting trass, we limited our fire to two hours. The first crucible containing gneiss sand, contained, besides, several small fragments of hydraulic limestone, weighing about ⅓ of a pound each, and so disposed, that after the exposure to the fire, we could ascertain, by their aid, as by a pyrometer, the relative intensities of the heat in different parts of the mass. We here see what happened.

1st. In the high and central parts of the crucible, the gneiss sand neither changed colour nor consistence: and the calcareous pieces lost only five or six hundredths of their weight.

2nd. In the enveloping layer, the sand, slightly agglutinated, had taken a pale gray slate colour; and the calcareous pieces, rather more burned than the preceding, gave a pellicle of lime which slaked in contact with the air.

3rd. In the more exterior layer, the sand had the consistence of the scoria of forges, and a decided slate colour. The calcareous fragments were found in the state of perfect lime, but without any indication of supercalcination, or any adherence to the matter surrounding them.

A second crucible, filled with ochreous clay, in powder, which had been dried at a low red heat, gave products altogether analogous; that is to say, gave three distinct species: one of the ordinary red colour, another of a deep purple, and a third of a slate colour.

In the transition from one to the other of these principal products, there

23

necessarily existed a great many shades, difficult, certainly, to isolate, but which did not the less correspond to so many particular degrees of calcination. We may then conclude,

1st. That it is nearly impossible to obtain a homogeneous torrefaction in close vessels.

2nd. That if the substances employed are ochreous, their fusibility will manifest itself at a degree of heat less than that which is necessary for the calcination of lime; which does not happen when in contact with the air on plates of iron.

3rd. That consequently, in these two modes of preparation of puzzolana, the same degrees of heat do not correspond to the same chemical reaction.

4th. That, therefore, not having any thing but the appearance of the substances, to guide us in the choice of terms of comparison, we are liable to oppose to the best puzzolana prepared in contact with the air, another prepared in a close vessel, in which the chemical reaction of the elements is in a very different state of advancement: and this, whether the clay were ochreous, or simply composed of silex and alumine.

Thus then, as has been already seen, it might happen that two mortars made of different puzzolanas, would acquire, after a certain time, the same hardness without having had, nevertheless, the same promptness of induration. Thus we may say, further, that the variable proportion of alumine soluble in hydrochloric acid, is not a consequence of such or such a mode of calcination, but rather of the difficulty of seizing terms of comparison perfectly exact.

§ 8. *On the decrease of the energy of Puzzolanas as they approach the point of vitrification.*

The phenomena which will be developed in the following chapter, taught us the importance of ascertaining whether the diminution in the energy of puzzolanas was progressive as the substances approached the term of vitrification. With this view we collected the preceding puzzolanas, prepared in close vessels, and bearing traces more or less evident, of vitrification. Making mortars of these, we remarked in the first place, that a very small addition of water sufficed to soften them in a singular manner. Be that as it may, the specimens obtained in stiff paste, were immersed the same day; the others were not immersed till the next day, in order to give them time to dry. After fifteen days none of them had acquired any kind of consistence; all being merely inert matter. With time, these results might change, no doubt, but they will not be the less inferior to those of § 6.*

If, instead of substances containing the oxide of iron, we had employed those containing lime, potash, or soda, it may be presumed it would have been the same; because the substances we have named all act as fluxes with silex. Thus, therefore, in whatever manner the solidification of mortars may be explained, it is necessary to admit, that puzzolanas require to be deprived of water by heat, and not to have too great cohesion given to

---

*After a month, these mortars had not improved perceptibly. The specimens made of the puzzolana the most highly calcined were as soft as on the first day. Au.

them. Whence it results that the most proper degree of calcination cannot be the same for all puzzolanas, but should vary, more or less, according as the substance employed contains more or less water, and a flux more or less energetic.

§ 9. *The relation between the quality of Puzzolanas and some of their physical properties.*

In indicating the conditions necessary to obtain good puzzolanas, M. Vicat says, (*Résumé sur les mortiers*, page 33,) that the matter ought to have the minimum of specific gravity, and the maximum of absorbent power. If this were rigorously true, it would be an argument against the hypothesis of a chemical reaction in the solidification of puzzolana mortars. We believed it would be interesting to verify this opinion; and to that end, we made the several experiments exhibited in the following tables.

Table No. XLVII.

Gneiss sand, in several states of calcination.	Weight of substance submitted to experiment.	Weight of substance after 18 days' exposure in a dry place.	Weight of substance after 3 days' exposure in a humid place.	Weight of substance after 7 days' exposure in a humid place.	Maximum increase of weight for 100 parts of the substance.
	Grms.	Grms.	Grms.	Grms.	Grms.
Crude sand highly dried	41.90	42·00	42.30	42.30	0.95
Calcined for 3½ minutes	35.75	35.83	36.05	36.05	0.84
Do. 5 do.	35.50	35.60	35.80	35.80	0.84
Do. 7½ do.	36.00	36.10	36.30	36.29	0.83
Do. 10 do.	34.50	34.60	34.75	34.75	0.72
Do. 15 do.	33.75	33.86	34.05	34.04	0.80
Do. 20 do.	34.70	34.80	34.95	34.95	0.75
Do. 40 do.	32.45	32.54	32.67	32.65	0.61
Do. 60 do.	32.30	32.39	32.52	32.50	0.68
Do. 120 do.	30·25	30.44	30.55	30.55	0.66
Calcined in a close vessel, a little melted, (un peu frittée)	55.00		55.20	55.15	0.36
Do. do. more melted	51.70		51.80	51.75	0.20
Do. do. still more melted	49.90		50.00	50.00	0.20

Table No. XLVIII.

Ochreous clay in several states of calcination.	Weight of substance submitted to experiment.	Weight of substance after 18 days' exposure in a dry place.	Weight of substance after 3 days' exposure in a humid place.	Same after 7 days' exposure.	Same after 9 days' expo sure	Maximum increase of weight for 100 parts of the substance.
	Grms.	Grms.	Grms.	Grms.	Grms.	Grms.
Calcined during 5 minutes .	26.55	26.59	26.85	26.95	26.94	1.50
Do. 7 do. .	27.00	27.17	27.45	27.54	27.54	2.00
Do. 10 do. .	32.45	32.49	32.90	33.05	33.04	1.85
Do. 15 do. .	32.15	32.20	32.65	32.74	32.72	1.77
Do. 20 do. .	29.20	29.22	29.58	29.63	29.65	1.52
Do. 25 do. .	31·70	31.75	32.03	32.12	32.15	1.40
Do. 30 do. .	29.65	29.70	29.95	30.03	30.05	1.33
Do. 40 do. .	29.25	29.26	29.50	29.57	29.57	1.08
Do. 60 do. .	36.70	36.74	37.05	37.20	37.20	1.36
Do. 120 do. .	19.00	19.04	19.20	19.25	19.25	1.31
Calcined in a close vessel, a little melted, (un peu fríttée) .	54.65		54.74	54.80	54.76	0.27
Do. do. more calcined	55.40		55.53	55.60	55.50	0.36

These two tables show, 1st, that puzzolanas exposed in a dry place have a very weak absorbent power; 2d, that this absorbent power augments, in a very sensible manner, in a wet place, a circumstance which renders the condensation of gas, admitted by some persons, but little probable; 3d, that this power is at its maximum before the gneiss sand or the clay had acquired the most advantageous degree of calcination; 4th, that it is not equal, by a considerable difference, in the two kinds of puzzolana, and in this respect it gives a tolerably correct idea of the relative energies; 5th, and lastly, that the vapour of water thus condensed does not enter into combination with the fixed matter, for it escapes, though in a small quantity, by a simple hygrometric variation in the atmosphere.

Experiments show that in taking bricks in several states of calcination, and immersing them in water, the proportion of liquid absorbed is greater for bricks but slightly burned, than for bricks more burned; that is to say, it is greater for bricks which give only a mediocre puzzolana, than for those which give a good puzzolana. The same experiments will also show that dry clay, before reaching the term of good burning, augments its volume in passing through the term of half burning; and that in this last state, the density of the brick is less than in the preceding. The maximum of energy, therefore, neither corresponds to the maximum of density, nor to the maximum of absorbent power.

CHAPTER XVIII.

On the Preparation—the Preservation—and the Use of Plastic Cements.

§ 10. *On Lime Stones which serve for the preparation of Plastic Cements.*

When a lime stone contains about twenty per cent., or more, of its weight of clay, it may furnish the substance known under the names of *plas-*

tic cément—Parker's cement—Roman cement. This substance has the property of hardening very soon, like plaster of Paris; but it has also the further property of indurating under water, like the hydraulic limes. These plastic cements present characters so peculiar, in their preparation and in their use—they have, besides, acquired so high an interest in France since the creation of the establishment of Pouilly, that we have thought proper to appropriate to them a special article, the better to insist on several observations of which the importance will be easily seen.

Until within a few years, plastic cement was a production exclusively English. It was principally near the Thames that the stone, proper for its fabrication, was found. In 1802, similar stone was found on the sea shore, at Boulogne, but in rolled pebbles, and in too small quantity to become an object of regular preparation. It exists also at Baye, near Nevers, according to M. Vicat; in Russia, according to Messrs. Lamé and Clappeyron, and, no doubt, in many other localities; but up to the present time the researches of M. Lacordaire, at Pouilly, are the only ones which have produced very positive results, on a large scale, in France.

The stone from which the English cement is derived, appertains to the upper steps of the secondary, lias formation. It is ordinarily found in rounded masses in the middle of marley strata. That of Pouilly appertains to the same geological formation: such a coincidence leads us to conclude that this kind of formation is most favourable to new investigations However that may be, the following are analyses of plastic cements already known:

English cement—carbonic acid deducted	55.4 of lime,	44.6 of clay.
Cement of Boulogne pebbles	54.0 do.	46.0 do.
Pouilly cement—first variety	42.86 do.	57.14 do.
The same—second do.	36.37 do.	63.63 do.
Russian cement	62.00 do.	38.00 do.
Cement of Baye	21.62 do.	78.38 do.

§ 11. *Mode of preparation followed by Parker.*

It was in 1796 that Parker first indicated the means of converting into cement, the very argillaceous lime stones found in roundish masses, and called *septaria.* His process consisted, essentially, in pushing the calcination of the stone to vitrification: and he took out, for his process, a patent in which are the following details:

"The stones are first broken into small fragments: then burned in a kiln as is commonly done with lime, at a heat sufficient to vitrify them; afterward reduced to powder by a mechanical or other operation. The powder thus obtained is the base of the cement. To compose this cement in the most advantageous manner, two parts of water are mixed with five parts of powder, and stirred and beaten to effect a mixture. The cement thus made ought to set or harden in ten or twenty minutes either in air or in water." (Extract of a report of M. Mallet to the *Société d'Encouragement.*)

Parker not having succeeded in his enterprise, and his process having been abandoned, it was generally supposed that he was mistaken, founding the opinion on what happens with fat lime too highly calcined. But here analogy fails, as we shall soon show by experiment.

§ 12. *Mode of preparation followed by the successors of Parker.*

The plastic cement which now circulates in trade should not be designated by the name of Parker's cement, for there is a capital difference in the preparation. We are ignorant whether the successors of Parker have given a description of their process; but it is easy to judge of the means by the end. Their cement, in fact, treated with muriatic acid, causes a notable quantity of carbonic acid gas to escape. It has besides an ochreous colour resembling that of the natural stone, and differing much from that which may be given it by vitrification. There is no doubt, therefore, that the cement is formed of the septaria *incompletely calcined.*

As to the method followed by M. Lacordaire, M. Mallet, at page 12 of the report already cited, says:

" The stone is explored by blasting with powder in pits and galleries, at a mean depth of about 262 feet. The selection of stone is made above ground, where it is broken into pieces the size of the fist, and carried to the kiln, which is of the kind called *fours contans ou à feu continu* (continual fire.) The stone, when burned and brought to the state of lime, is ground under a pair of cast iron cylinders weighing about 5300 lbs. . . .

. . . The cement is afterwards passed through sieves formed of iron wire separated 0.06 of an inch; by this first operation, a cement is obtained which is called No. 2. This is then passed through a bolting machine also formed of iron wire, but with finer meshes; and it is then called No. 1."

M. Mallet no where says that the cement is incompletely calcined; but it would be a mistake to suppose otherwise. It is, besides, easy to prove it; for the cement tried with acids, permits, as in the English cement, a notable quantity of carbonic acid to escape.

§ 13. *As to what occurs to Plastic Cements at the point of complete calcination.*

We see from what precedes, that it is equally possible to obtain plastic cements by super-calcination and by incomplete calcination.* But the fact most worthy of remark is, that at the point of *complete calcination*, not only the stone does not slake, but if it be treated like ordinary cement, it gives a substance nearly inert. All this is the reverse of fat lime; and it is impossible to confound one substance with the other.

This instant of inertia of plastic cements, between the points of incomplete calcination and supercalcination, seems to us a capital fact in the study of the substances. It explains how a suitable lime stone might escape

---

*The existence, at the same time, of two means of preparing plastic cement, and the obscurity in which the method of Parker remained, has occasioned more than one mistake. M. Hassenfratz, for example, says in his treatise on mortars, page 195, " The calcination of this stone (Boulogne pebbles) is the same as that of ordinary lime; if it is too much heated, it vitrifies and is no longer proper for making cement." And further on (page 197) he adds, " At London they calcine, in conical furnaces with a central fire of sea coal, the lime stone of which they make Roman cement: but the management of the fire demands much attention, because when the heat is not properly adjusted, the cement sustains an incipient fusion, and is no longer proper for any use." He had, notwithstanding, said (p. 126) that the Boulogne pebbles, strongly calcined, and for a long time, gave a lime which hardens easily, and that this hardening became equal to that of stone, at least; but when it is only calcined to the same degree as fat lime, the cement does not harden with the same facility, nor so much. AUTHOR.

discovery and be rejected as unsuitable, from a simple fault of calcination, which would not be a fault with fat lime, or with hydraulic lime. In this category we may cite the trials of Gen. Treussart of the Boulogne pebbles. He calcined the stone in the middle of the common lime in an Alsace lime kiln: he was thus led to anomalies which we now easily comprehend.

Note. The author then refers to Nos. 1, 4, 6, 7, 9, and 12, of table No. VIII, p. 33, of the preceding work of Gen. Treussart.

M. Vicat, effecting the calcination by the same means, no doubt, found that the cement of Baye did not harden till after three days' immersion. This would not be a long time for hydraulic lime, but it is unreasonably long for a plastic cement, which the Baye lime stone, from its composition, may be considered to be. The proportion of clay is so great in this cement, that we think it must contain a notable quantity of silex in grains; otherwise, it does not comprise a larger proportion of lime than the artificial mixtures of M. Bruyère, and like them would afford only a puzzolana and not a plastic cement.

§ 14. *Experiments on the English Cement, and on the English Cement Stone.*

We will now detail the experiments that have led us to a knowledge of these alternations of good and bad quality in plastic cements—beginning with the English cement.

1st. The English stone that we had at command was of a yellowish colour, and very compact texture. After having broken it into small pieces, and placed it in a crucible, we heated it in a laboratory furnace furnished with its dome, up to the complete disengagement of the carbonic acid—as proved by pieces taken from the upper part of the crucible. But owing to the inequality of calcination in a vertical direction, a great number of fragments were found, agglutinated, fritty, and blackened. They were separated with care, and gave by trituration, a powder of blackish gray. Not knowing, at that time, the process of Parker, we thought that all the super-calcined stone must be good for nothing: and it was only to acquire a direct proof thereof that we tempered this powder with water. After a few minutes, to our surprise, the first specimen had hardened. A second specimen prepared and put under water, showed that the induration was comple in less than fifteen minutes.

All the stone that was in the upper part of the crucible had escaped any sensible change of colour: pounded and sifted, it was of an earthy yellow; a mortar of stiff clayey consistence was made of it, and immediately placed under water without any envelope. It did not fall to pieces in the water, but, twenty days after, it remained in the same state, that is to say, like a substance wholly inert. A small portion of the same mortar, exposed to the air, had set in one hour and twenty-five minutes, and fifty days after had acquired great hardness.

Another portion of this same yellow powder was mixed with an equal volume of fat lime, to ascertain whether it would act like puzzolana. This mortar, examined for fifteen successive days, comported itself like the unmixed cement; but after about a month, it had set.

2d. The English cement on which we experimented was derived from a stock collected in July, 1824, for the naval works; it had therefore been on hand five years and a half. It was damaged; but we shall show further on that a very feeble heat sufficed to impart much energy to it—causing it to set in fourteen minutes. We filled a crucible with this cement and heated it: the unequal action of the heat enabled us to divide the cement into three portions, in appearance very distinct.

The first part, treated with muriatic acid, liberated no gas; a perceptible change of colour, and a slight agglutination, attested that there had been a commencement of super-calcination. A mortar was made of it, and immediately immersed: The setting was not complete till after six and a half hours.

In the next portion the beginning of super-calcination was more manifest; it should have been triturated and sifted anew, and this operation having been omitted, we think that a diminution of energy was the consequence. However this may have been, after its immersion the edges crumbled off, but the setting was complete in three hours and forty minutes.

Lastly, the third portion, which was from the bottom of the crucible, was *fritty* and *drossy*; it gave a powder of a slate blue colour. A little of it was made into mortar, and made to fill the bottom of a glass: this being put under water appeared hard in thirty-three minutes. A second larger specimen was immersed, not being supported on the sides: the edges did not crumble in the least, and at the end of forty-eight minutes it had well set.

§ 15. *Similar experiments with the Pouilly Cement.*

Not having the Pouilly cement at command, we were not able to operate throughout as in the other case: but this circumstance need not, we think, be much regretted, since the cement in powder, with which we were supplied, still retained much carbonic acid, and would enable us to ascertain, equally, the effects of complete calcination and of super-calcination.

The Pouilly cement, revived by a new calcination of a few minutes, like the English cement, sets in the air in five minutes. A crucible filled with cement, already deteriorated, was calcined in a heat not very great: cement taken from the top of the crucible, had not lost its carbonic acid, and set under water in eight minutes and a half: the remainder was divided into two specimens which indurated in the air, one in eleven minutes, and the other in sixteen minutes. These cements, at the moment of setting, disengaged heat in a remarkable manner.

Another crucible filled with the same, having been heated more violently, the first portions of powder, tested by muriatic acid, retained hardly any traces of gas; they afforded a mortar, which, exposed to the air, disengaged a little heat, and hardened in thirty-six minutes. At this moment it was immersed, but soon split to pieces, softened, and preserved its consistency only in a few places. After fifty days, it was found totally reduced, and decomposed into friable lumps.

The remainder of the contents of the crucible was divided into two portions. The first, containing much that was agglutinated, required to be pulverized again; it gave a mortar that hardened in the air in twenty-one minutes, and preserved its form, well, after immersion. The second, completely converted into scoria, became, in powder, of a blue purple: converted into mortar, it hardened in the air in twenty-six minutes, and did not lose its consistency in water.

§ 16. *Indications, touching the preceding experiments, given by the proof of Rupture.*

It became interesting to complete these experiments, trying the proof, or test, of rupture; and such is the object of the following table: but we have some previous observations to make.

Plastic cements acquire a strong consistence in a short time. For example, the experiments of M. Leroux at Cherbourg, reported in the memoir of M. Mallet already quoted, were made after about fifty days, and gave very satisfactory results. We have operated with a shorter interval: but it is possible that two mortars may be equal at the end of the year, and not at any briefer period, especially when one is immersed, the other exposed to the air, and when the volumes are very small. But we could not avoid this last inconvenience, because, from being obliged to separate the products into several portions, the bulk of each particular kind was necessarily small. For each specimen we never had more than fifteen cubic inches of mortar: the numbers that we are to submit must therefore be received with caution, and only as stating the hydraulic qualities of the substances.

Table No. XLIX.

No.	Substances employed.	Time required to harden.	Resistance to rupture per 0.394 inch (centimetre) square.	Age of the mortars.	Observations.
			lbs.	Days.	
1	English stone completely decarbonated . .			20	Could not be tested.
2	The same stone, with fat lime		1.10	50	Immersed.
3	The same, super-calcined	15' in water.	6.39	50	Do.
4	English stone, carbonated	14' in the air.	15.75	35	Exposed to the air.
5	The same . . .	14' in water.	7.24	35	Immersed.
6	The same reburnt up to super-calcination . .	6 h. and 30'			Put in a glass.
7	The same, super-calcinated more strongly . . .	3 h. and 40'	2.69	35	Immersed.
8	The same, super-calcinated to the state of scoriæ .	48'	5.17	36	Do.
9	Pouilly cement carbonated	5' in the air.	3.46	34	Do.
10	Do. . . .	16'	1.93	34	Do.
11	Do. . .	11'	4.22	34	Do.
12	The same, completely decarbonated . . .	36' in the air.		30	Fell to pieces under [water.
13	The same, perceptibly fritty	21 in water.	19.07	34	Immersed.
14	The same, in scoriæ .	26'	3.15	34	Do.

§ 17. *On the alteration of Plastic Cements.*

The English cement delivered at the Port of Brest, in 1824, was preserved in well closed barrels: that which came to us from Pouilly was in a double cask, with an interval of about two inches filled with absorbent powder of common lime or powdered charcoal: this last method is very expensive no doubt, but it is preferable to the first, when the cement is to remain a long time in store. Whatever may be the process, however, the substance, whether it retains a portion of carbonic acid, or has been super-calcinated, will always lose part of its energy.

In fact, the English cement, which in the first place, set under water in twenty-two minutes, required twenty-one hours to set, after it was five years old, without the barrels having been opened or exposed in any humid place. The Pouilly cement which may be made so energetic as to harden in the air in five minutes, required forty-eight minutes as a mean term of the several trials to which we submitted it, after being four months in store. Further, the barrel having been first opened, and then closed less exactly, sufficed to cause the outside layers of cement to afford a mortar the edges of which crumbled under water, and which had not hardened at the end of four hours.

As to the super-calcined cement, that which would harden, in the first instance, in fifteen minutes, was so altered by thirty-nine days' exposure to the air, that it had acquired only a half-consistence during three days that we successively examined it.

Under such circumstances, we may easily see that the mortars are not susceptible of acquiring great hardness. It is true that the diminution in this respect, is not proportioned to the diminution in the energy of setting; but it does not the less follow, that those plastic cements of which the use is deferred, lose the quality the most characteristic, if not the most precious; and that notwithstanding the precaution used in barreling the substance, the evil can only be retarded. Connected with this, if we consider the liability to negligence in the process of calcination and pulverization, we can comprehend how it is that the use of plastic cements has fallen more than once into disfavor; why the manufacturers have been accused of mixing inert matter with their products in order to augment the bulk; and why the great price of these substances, joined to the uncertainty as to their qualities, has deterred many constructors from their use.

§ 18. *On the chemical phenomenon that accompany the alteration of Plastic Cements.*

We were at first of opinion, from such considerations as are above stated, that it would be preferable to export, instead of the cement, the cement stone before calcination, as is done with plaster of Paris. An augmentation of weight of twenty or thirty per cent. might be compensated by the suppression of the barreling and all other means of preservation. But although we might act thus in certain places, we could not in all places: and there would be no guarantee that the best mode of preparation would be followed every where; or that the quantity of cement needed, would be worth the trouble of calcination.

Examining then, what occurs in the alteration of plastic cements, we in the first place, ascertained that the super-calcined cement, when exposed to the air for thirty-nine days, had absorbed carbonic acid, and we concluded, *a fortiori*, it would be the same with the cement incompletely calcined, because the combination of lime and clay does not, therein, take so much cohesion; but we have not been able to satisfy ourselves that this gas, often found in cement the quality of which is good, should be hurtful when found under other circumstances; we have considered, as much more probable, that its presence is indifferent in all cases; and that the cements were good only because the lime and the elements of the clay existed therein in a proper state of combination.

We ascertained, afterward, that cements, while they enjoy all their energy, are not soluble in water; or at least the oxalate of ammonia gives to the water in which they have been immersed, scarcely the lightest cloud. The deteriorated cements, on the contrary, give a precipitate quite abundant, and susceptible of being collected.

We noticed, lastly, that the super-calcined cement and the Pouilly cement, which are of a deep colour, become whiter as they deteriorate; and the white parts give to the water in which they are immersed, a cream which is incapable of solidifying.

From these indications we have concluded that the deterioration of cements is accompanied by a chemical disunion between the lime and the clay composing them; that no doubt the lapse of time between the preparation and the use of the cement, may permit a spontaneous decomposition, but that water, either alone or aided by carbonic acid, is the most active cause; and that we may, therefore, restore to these elements all their primitive energy, by submitting them to a new calcination sufficient to drive off the absorbed water, and re-establish the combination between the lime and the clay.

These are the theoretic inductions which determined our researches as to the possibility of making use of damaged cements. Experience has fully confirmed them, as will be seen in due time.

§ 19. *On the revivification of deteriorated cements.*

Pouilly cement that hardened in the air in twenty three minutes was heated to a low red heat during twenty five minutes, on a plate of iron. After this operation, being tested with muriatic acid, it showed the presence of carbonic acid, as before: converted into mortar it became hot and solidified almost instantly. The setting was perfect in less than five minutes.

Cement of the same kind, heated more violently, and in a crucible, was divided into three portions: the first hardened under water in eight and a half minutes, the second in the air in sixteen minutes; and the third, in eleven minutes. All three, tried by muriatic acid, disengaged much carbonic acid.

English cement, setting under water in twenty one hours, was made red hot on a plate of iron for twenty eight minutes: this operation did not deprive it of its carbonic acid: tempered and immersed, it hardened in thirty-one minutes.

Cement of the same kind heated for about one hour was divided into two parts: the first, retaining still a little carbonic acid, hardened in the air in fourteen minutes, and the second, which was nearly in the same state, hardened under water in fourteen minutes.

English cement supercalcined, exposed to the air during thirty nine days, and which had become incapable of setting under water in two days, was heated on a piece of sheet iron to a red heat for thirty minutes. It retained all the carbonic acid it had absorbed: being tempered and immersed it set completely in thirty-one minutes.

Wishing to apply this operation on a large scale we exposed entire barrels of the deteriorated cement in the reverberatory furnace, in the same way we had exposed the gneiss sand. After this new torrefaction, the English cement which had refused to indurate in less than twenty-one hours, would now set equally hard in twenty-three minutes, at most, either in the air or in the water. In similar circumstances the Pouilly cement which did not harden in less than two or three hours, was brought to give very good results in seven or eight minutes.

There is no doubt then, that at a small expense, and by the aid of a feeble heat, the injury sustained by plastic cements, from remaining too long in store rooms, or exposed in damp places, may be repaired.

§ 20. *On the recovery of cement mortars already hardened.*

The experiments we have just given caused us to conceive the hope of restoring cements which had hardened after being accidentally moistened and even of restoring mortars themselves. We ascertained that the thing is, in fact possible, but at a much higher temperature.

Mortar made of Pouilly cement, one month old, and already offering a resistance to rupture of about 13 lbs. per 0.394 inch (centimetre) square, was reduced to powder. A portion of this powder made red hot for twenty minutes, gave a mortar which did not become hot and did not harden. Another portion was heated in a crucible for almost one hour: the first layers of cement had visibly changed colour, but had not lost their carbonic acid: they gave a mortar that acted like inert matter. The last layers, on the contrary, were completely decarbonated; a mortar was made of this which increased in temperature sensibly after three minutes' exposure to the air, and hardened after ten minutes; but being then immersed, it split and softened.

Some of the same powder heated more highly in a crucible, and giving some indication of supercalcination, was tempered with water, but, from inadvertency, into too soft a paste. The setting was nevertheless complete after four hours in the air, and it sustained itself well in the water.

Another crucible heated more highly still, gave a mortar which, exposed in the air, took immediately a remarkable consistency; at the end of six minutes, the trial wire gave almost no depression on the surface. There was no heat disengaged at the time of setting.

A last crucible, heated in the same manner, gave also a supercalcined cement which hardened in eight minutes without any disengagement of heat. This specimen and the preceding were immersed immediately; the water did not alter them.

If it be desired to reproduce these results on a large scale, it must not be done in a kiln built to burn puzzolanas, but in a lime kiln; taking care to place the mortar or blocks of hardened cement at the bottom of the charge, in order to obtain the proper degree of supercalcination. We should add, however, that we have not employed this mode of restoration.

§ 21. *Indications touching the preceding experiments, given by the proof of rupture.*

As in §16, we have united, in the following table, the resistances to rupture of the specimens of mortar of which we have been speaking in the preceding paragraphs.

Table L.

No.	Substances employed.	Time required to harden.	Resistance to rupture per 0.394 in. (centimetre) square.	Age of the mortar.	Remarks.
			lbs.	ds.	
1	Pouilly cement .	23' in the air	20.25	35	Left in the air.
2	do. restored on a plate of sheet iron .	5'	3.46	34	Immersed.
3	do. do. in a crucible	11'	4.23	34	do.
4	do. do. by supercalcination .	5'	11.53	26	Left in the air.
5	English cement deteriorated	21 hours	3.27	35	Immersed.
6	do. restored on a plate of sheet iron .	31'	4.32	35	do.
7	do. do. in a crucible . .	14' in the air	15.75	35	Left in the air.
8	do. . .	14' in the water	7.22	35	Immersed.
9	Mortar restored by supercalcination .	4 hours	3.60	26	do.
10	do. more highly calcined	6' in the air	4.26	26	do.
11	do. . .	8'	13.26	26	Left in the air.

§ 22. *Influence of the age of Mortars.*

The two tables we have given of experiments, show a notable difference between mortar immersed and mortar exposed to the air—unfavourable to the former in all cases but No. 13 of the first table. They also show differences between the specimens immersed, which, judging from the time required to harden, were equal in quality. Has the age of the mortar an influence on these results? This we were desirous of ascertaining, at least in part, by some trials which are given in the following table.

Table LI.

No.	Substances employed.	Time required to harden.	Age of the mortar at the first trial.	Resistance to rupture per 0.394 inch (centimetre) square.	Age of the mortar at the second trial.		Resistance to rupture per 0.394 inch (centimetre) square.
			ds.	lbs.	mos.	ds.	lbs.
1	Pouilly cement with one half volume of water. . .	46'	22	7.35	1	19	8.01
2	do. .	46	27	9.72	4	11	14.36
3	do. .	51	34	17.70	1	19	16.92
4	do. .	42	42	14.64	4	11	14.71
5	do. .	52	49	13.03	4	11	24.11
6	do. .	54	51	15.29	4	11	19.59
7	do. .	47	60	19.11	4	11	19.76

All these specimens were made, the same day, with cement from the same barrel, tempered with an equal quantity of water, and immersed immediately after the instant of setting in the air; they were all of the size of a common brick. Notwithstanding these similar circumstances, the mortars did not comport in the same manner; and they converged more or less rapidly to the resistance they would have acquired at some future period, as, for example, at the end of one or two years.

§ 23. *On the mixture of sand and puzzolana with plastic cements.*

Thus far we have employed pure cement, in order to avoid bringing in new cases of irregularity; but it is not less necessary to know to what extent the substances will support a mixture of sands or puzzolanas: and consequently, to know whether it be possible so to add these substances as to have mortars equally good and more economical. With these objects we prepared several specimens which were submitted to rupture after about fifty-four days. This, as has been said above, is no doubt too short a time: but the numbers obtained agree in demonstrating that though sands and puzzolanas, in no way augment the quality of cement-mortars, they may be used without detriment in small proportion; as may be judged by the following table.

Table LII.

Substances employed.		Time required to harden	Age of the mortar at time of trial	Resistances to rupture.
		min.	days.	lbs.
One of Pouilly cement with	one-half of quartzose sand	48	54	14.64
do.	one-half of gneiss sand	43	do.	17.57
do.	one-half of coarse quartzose sand .	50	do.	12.31
do.	one-half of Italian puzzolana in gravel .	58	do.	14.55
do.	one-half of quartzose sand	44	do.	11.36
do.	one-half of do. and one-half of puzzolana. .	57	do.	13.04
do.	one of gneiss sand .	47	do.	13.58
do.	one of coarse quartzose sand .	1 h. 2m	do.	9.89
do.	one of puzzolana sifted very fine . .	49	do.	14.74
do.	one and a half of quartzose sand .	47	do.	8.29
do. .	one and a half of gneiss sand . .	1h. 7m.	do.	7.61
do.	two of quartzose sand	1h. 18m.	do.	5.86

As to the ability of these cements to resist frost we have no precise information to impart. We can only say that we applied the process of Mr. Biard to a specimen of pure Pouilly cement which had hardened in the air and was five months old. It deteriorated sensibly from the beginning of the experiment; and at the end of the seventh day we found 1.43 gr. loss from the original weight of 210 grs. Several kinds of bricks tried at the same time, as well as a specimen of mortar made of puzzolana from Italy, did not lose, by a great deal, as large a proportion of their substance. It is to be feared, therefore, that mortar of the Pouilly cement is not frost proof: and this will become a great objection, if, as has been proposed, this cement is used in making casts of moulded objects, statues, bas-reliefs, vases, &c., to be exposed to the ordinary inclemencies of the weather.

§ 24. *Classification of plastic cements with respect to limes and to puzzolanas.*

As we said in the beginning of this chapter, the limestones that afford plastic-cements contain a large proportion of clay: larger than hydraulic limestones, and less than calcareous puzzolanas. Establishing then the continued series of combinations which may be formed of pure lime and pure clay, we shall be led, as in the following classification, to three distinct products.

Table LIII.

Lime.	Clay.	Resulting products.	Distinctive characters of the products.
100	0	Very fat lime	Incapable of hardening in water.
90	10	Lime a little hydraulic	Will slake, when properly calcined, like pure lime—and will besides harden alone under water.
80	20	do. quite hydraulic	
70	30	do. do.	
60	40	Plastic cement	Will not slake with any degree of calcination—and will harden alone under water.
50	50	do.	
40	60	do.	
30	70	Calcareous puzzolana according to Mr. Bruyére	Will not harden under water without the addition of fat lime or of hydraulic lime.
20	80	do.	
10	90	do.	
0	100	Puzzolana of pure clay	The same.

The distinctive characters given in the table, show, as the proportions vary, the effects of a predominance of lime or clay. But the plastic cements have two maxima of energy, one at the point of incomplete calcination, and the other at the point of supercalcination: do they enjoy this singular property, exclusively? It is important to ascertain this.

1st. Pure lime stone incompletely calcined, slakes with difficulty, and even requires to be pulverised like plastic cement. According to Mr. Minard, if it be tempered with water and immersed, it comports in the beginning like a very energetic substance; and after four days, according to Mr. Vicat, it is impossible to make an impression with the finger. But beyond this, the solidification does not advance.

On the other hand Hassenfratz (at page 203 of his *Traité des mortiers*) says he has noticed that the fat lime of Moustier, supercalcined, gives, after being pulverised and tempered, a mortar which *sets strongly in water.* Mr. Vicat, also, announced in 1818 that common fat lime supercalcined, in contact with a mixture of charcoal and seacoal, became incapable of slaking, and gave, on pulverizing and moistening it, *a paste which hardened under water.*

It is hardly necessary to say that at the term of complete calcination, fat limes are entirely incapable of acquiring, alone, under water, any consistency. However feeble, therefore, may be the hydraulic property of fat lime at the points of incomplete and supercalcination, it is not the less true that it does exist, as in plastic cements.

2nd. Before Mr. Lacordaire had engaged in the Pouilly enterprise described §12, he had ascertained that a limestone but little hydraulic, from which all the carbonic acid had not been expelled by calcination, afforded a true cement; and he applied this observation to profit, in the works of the canal *de Bourgogne*, which he had in charge. With this view he used the ordinary kilns of the country, reducing to three days, the burning which was commonly extended to six or eight days: he afterwards slaked the lime by immersion, separating the subcarbonated portions, which he incorporated in the mortar, after having reduced them mechanically to powder.

We were of opinion that the common limestone of Pouilly, alternating with the variegated marles, contained, like the marles, the claystone (septaria) of which Parker's cement is made, and that if Mr. Lacordaire preferred extracting these materials by subterranean galleries, rather than by open quarries, it was, no doubt, because he found, below, richer deposits and a better choice of materials. But one of our friends, Mr. Avril, an Engineer, to whom we had communicated our researches, profited by his being at Pouilly to examine this point with much care. He has announced that, in fact, the common limestone of Pouilly properly treated, and retaining about fifteen per cent. of carbonic acid, sets under water in five minutes, and does not yield in any thing to plastic cements; that therefore, the preference accorded to septaria, could not be explained except on the supposition that it was easier, with it, to secure the degree of calcination necessary, and because the limits of greatest energy were more extended. He also discovered that the hydraulic limestone of Pouilly, *suitably supercalcined*, enjoyed the same properties as when in the state of subcarbonate.

Some direct experiments on a few fragments of a hydraulic lime stone from Pompean, *(Ille-et-Vilaine,)* and from Doué *(Maine-et-Loire,)* lead us to believe that these properties are common to all limestones of analogous composition.

3rd. The good puzzolanas produced, on the one hand, by a torrefaction of some minutes on plates of iron, and on the other, by ochreous and refractory bricks, well burned, seem at first to establish two maxima of energy for clays also; but the experiments of the 17th chapter, (§6 and §7) demonstrated that these two degrees of heat are in fact but one and the same, and that these substances become so much the more inert as the term of vitrification is approached.

As to clays containing at least a tenth of lime, they require, according to M. Treussart, that the degree of calcination should correspond with that of a slightly burned brick; beyond which they become of a quality more and more deteriorated. Is it still the same, at the transition from puzzolanas to plastic cements, when the proportion of lime is from twenty to thirty per cent.? We are unable to say. But it is possible that the influence of lime is then prominent enough to give rise to two maxima of energy.

§ 25. *Geometrical representation of the influence of Heat on the several compounds of Lime and Clay.*

In order the better to exhibit the influence of heat on the several compounds of clay and lime, we will attempt to represent it geometrically. To do so, let us conceive that from a fixed point two lines are drawn at right angles to each other, of which the horizontal one shall be taken as the axis of the abscissas, and the vertical one, the axis of the ordinates. Then suppose that on the axis of the abscissas we take, from the point of intersection, lengths proportionate to some of the principal degrees of torrefaction; that, for example, we choose for the first the degree of moderate burning of bricks; for the second, the degree of thorough burning of bricks; for the third, the degree of complete calcination of fat lime; and lastly, for the fourth, the degree of super-calcination of the same lime. If, then, the ordinates be raised on the points of division, and we consider the compounds of lime and clay to be submitted to the corresponding degrees of heat, we might lay off on these ordinates, lengths proportionate to the hydraulic energy of each particular product; and afterward, through the extremities of these lengths, pass a continuous curve, which will be the curve of energy of the compound, whether hydraulic lime, plastic cement, puzzolana, or even fat lime.

In this manner we have constructed the figures 4, 5, 6, 7 and 8, of plate II. Let us go into some particulars respecting them.

1st. Fig. 4 represents the curve of energy of fat lime. This curve has one ordinate null at the abscissa No. 3, which is the term of complete calcination; but at the abscissas 2 and 4, the ordinates have some magnitude, for they correspond to a hydraulic power, feeble it is true, but real.

2d. Fig. 5 represents the curve of energy of hydraulic lime. At the abscissa No. 3, the ordinate will vary much according to the portion of clay contained; but is greater than zero and less than the ordinates Nos. 2 and 4, because on one hand the lime is hydraulic by supposition, and on the other hand we obtain an instantaneous induration, and an improvement in the hardness of mortars, as in plastic cements.

3d. Fig. 6 represents the curve of energy of plastic cements. In some the ordinate No. 3 is nearly null: is it the same in all? we think not. We know in fact that the best hydraulic limes are not those which contain the most clay; that, for example, in the manufacture of artificial hydraulic lime, the proportions of twenty to twenty-five per cent. of clay are recommended as being most suitable. Accordingly, the ordinate No. 3, which is null for fat limes, will augment progressively up to lime containing twenty-five per cent. of clay, then descending in a continuous manner for the limes with thirty per cent. of clay, for the plastic cements with forty, fifty and sixty per cent., finishing by becoming null. We give this explanation as a simple theoretical induction only.

4th. Fig. 7 represents the curve of energy of calcareous clays employed as puzzolanas. The maximum of this curve is at the abscissa No. 1—the term of bricks but little burned. The clays which, from the proportion of lime, approach most nearly to plastic cement, enjoy, perhaps, a second maximum of energy: but we have traced it only by a dotted line.

5th. Fig. 8 represents the curve of energy of clays not calcareous. This curve has only one maximum, which is at No. 2—the term of bricks well burned.

To resume—we see that each of the compounds of lime and clay is characterised by certain properties which vary, more or less, according to the predominance of one or the other of these constituents; that clays have only one maximum of energy, but that limes have two, and that, therefore, plastic cements only offer a particular case of a general phenomenon.

CHAPTER XIX.

On the change in Hydraulic Limes, and on the solidification of Mortars in general.

---

§ 26. *Influence of spontaneous slaking on Lime in general.*

As lime is not always used immediately on leaving the kiln, it is important to know what modifications time will bring about in its properties; and what precautions are necessary for its preservation, or in its use, after it may have become deteriorated.

When quick lime is abandoned to the contact of air, it absorbs moisture and carbonic acid from the atmosphere, and a certain quantity of oxygen also, according to Gen. Treussart. At the same time it splits and falls to powder; this being what is called *spontaneous slaking*, or *air slaking*.

For a long time it was thought that lime thus slaked was good for nothing; but this was improperly generalizing a consequence which is true only with one particular kind of lime. In fact, M. Vicat has ascertained, 1st, that fat limes do not deteriorate, and that they even give superior results to those obtained by slaking in the ordinary mode of immersion: 2d, that for hydraulic limes, on the contrary, spontaneous slaking is the more disadvantageous as the energy of the lime is originally the greater.

We owe to Gen. Treussart the proof of this last observation; obtained while he was in search of the relation between the degrees of alteration in the air; and time of exposure to the air. The following are some of his results.

Table No. LIV.

	Made Immediately.	After 15 days.	After 1 month.	After 2 months.	After 3 months.
	lbs.	lbs.	lbs.	lbs.	lbs.
Obernai hydraulic lime with two parts of sand	121	77	44	33	<22

These specimens were all kept under water. We see, therefore, that all delay in the use of hydraulic lime tends to convert it into common lime, and that in large works a circumstance of this kind might be of serious consequence.

§ 27. *On the manner of preserving Hydraulic Limes.*

In the deterioration of hydraulic limes it is necessary to consider the influence of the water applied in slaking, and the influence of the contact of air. While the quantity of water absorbed does not exceed a quarter of the weight of lime, this last will remain in dry powder; it cannot solidify; and experience demonstrates that it may then be preserved without change, provided it be carefully covered from the contact of the air, in very tight barrels for example, like plastic cement. But if this powder, which is easily obtained by immersing the lime for twenty or thirty seconds in water, is exposed to the air, it comports nearly as in the case of air slaking; it becomes common lime. At works where there must be large supplies, it is hardly possible, however, to put the lime in casks, because they would be expensive from their number, and embarrassing from their bulk. A middle course remains, which consists in storing the quick lime in very close sheds, and enveloping it, on all sides, with a layer of lime already reduced to powder, in any way: an obstacle will thus be opposed to the circulation of air, and the interior parts of the mass will be preserved from its influence.

If this process is not perfect, it is at least economical: and although all the layers of powder which serve as an envelope will be unfit to be used as hydraulic lime, it still may be used in a way that will soon be pointed out.

§ 28. *On the use of Puzzolanas in correcting the deterioration of Hydraulic Lime.*

In order to cause fat lime to harden under water, it is mixed with puzzolana; but deteriorated hydraulic limes, as we have said, act like fat lime: if this assimilation be exact, then the same process ought to be applied to both. This is, in fact, what happens; and it is observed that the amount of alteration has no sensible influence on the hardness acquired after about one year. Gen. Treussart was the first who insisted on this important fact; the following are some of his experiments.

Table No. LV.

	Made immediately.	After 1 month.	After 2 months.	After 3 months.	After 4 months.
	lbs.	lbs.	lbs.	lbs.	lbs.
Obernai hydraulic lime slaked spontaneously and mixed with one of sand and one of trass	209	389	352	308	495

Table No. LVI.

	Made immediately.	After 15 days.	After 25 days.	After 35 days.	After 45 days.	After 2 months.
	lbs.	lbs.	lbs.	lbs.	lbs.	lbs.
Obernai hydraulic lime slaked by immersion and mixed with one of sand and one of trass . . .	493	330	297	286	304	399

Hydraulic limes employed while fresh, will, according to M. Vicat, support puzzolanas the more advantageously, as the limes are the less energetic; and on the other hand, they deteriorate so much the more rapidly as they are the more energetic: we may thence conclude that if a hydraulic lime has been exposed to any cause of deterioration, it is prudent to mix with it, a certain dose of puzzolana, without any regard to its primitive degree of energy. Artificial hydraulic limes should be treated in the same way.

§ 29. *On the preservation of Puzzolanas.*

As to factitious puzzolanas, it may readily be conceived that their preservation requires but little care, for we know that from their situation in nature, the natural puzzolanas are exposed to all the vicissitudes of the seasons without any apparent loss of energy after a great lapse of time. We will say, however, that a newly made and perfectly dry puzzolana, from its possessing a higher degree of absorbent power, must have a favourable influence on the setting of the mortars. The mortars are often, in fact, tempered too soft; and, to lime already slaked to cream, the workmen add more water to lessen their labour; this excess of water being absorbed in part by the puzzolana, the mortar preserves a strong consistence, favourable to the reaction of its elements. In this respect it is therefore advantageous to keep the puzzolanas in dry situations, or at least if they have been moistened, to dry them in the air, or in the sun, before using them.

§ 30. *On the Solidification of Fat Lime.*

The preparation and the preservation of lime, puzzolana, and plastic cements, are connected so intimately with a knowledge of their properties, that we think it will be useful to add to the indications already given, some developments relative to the theory of mortars in general.*

Proceeding from the simple to the compound, let us explain what relates to common, or fat, lime. When it is plunged into water, it absorbs rapidly, and solidifies, a quantity of water equal nearly to 0.22 of its weight. Withdrawn, then, and left in contact with the air, it slakes with disengagement of heat, and is reduced to dry and impalpable powder. In this state it is capable of absorbing much water still, but without sensible disengagement of heat, and there results a paste more or less stiff. The first portions of the fluid, form, with the lime, a true chemical combination, known by the name of *hydrate of lime:* the other portions of water are, simply, *interposed.* Thus, lime in stiff paste will throw out, on working it, so much water that it is unnecessary to add more on making the mortar. The hydrate of lime, on the other hand, can only be decomposed at a high temperature.

This hydrate being a dry powder, its molecules are too far apart to be able mutually to approach each other, and to pass into the state of a compact mass; it is only after being brought to the state of paste that the hydrate is in a condition to be used. That being premised, it is well known that fat lime, if kept from contact with the air, may be preserved an indefinite time in paste; that this same lime at the ordinary temperature, or at a higher temperature, in paste, or dissolved in water, is without any chemical action on quartzose sand, whether the sand be in fine powder

*In a manuscript note communicated to M. Vicat early in 1826, and mentioned in his last work on mortars, we have already stated some of the propositions which follow.
AUTHOR.

or not; that the mortars which result from the mixture of these two substances, remain soft, like lime alone, as has been ascertained by Dr. John, on examining thick masonry two hundred years old. But if the lime in paste, or the mortar, be left in contact with the air, it will solidify; and if the air be replaced by pure carbonic acid gas, the solidification will take place with great rapidity. In both these last cases the carbonic acid is absorbed by the lime, and this absorption will go on till the acid is to the base, in the ratio, approximately, of 43 to 57, as in the natural subcarbonate of lime. But it is worthy of remark that the proportion of water appropriated to the conversion of lime into a hydrate, is not rejected: the carbonate is not, therefore, *regenerated*, as before the calcination; and it is, in fact, a double salt, which might be called the *hydro-carbonate* of lime.

We see then that for the solidification of fat lime, 1st, the proportion of water must be greater than in the dry hydrate: 2d, there should be contact of the air, or, better still, of pure carbonic acid gas. 3d, the mixture of quartzose sand, without the contact of the air, would not have the least influence. Hence comes the superiority that lime slaked spontaneously, and consequently already somewhat carbonated, imparts to mortars. Hence also the impossibility that these mortars should harden under water, since water, in general, contains only inappreciable quantities of carbonic acid in solution.

The solidification, as Mr. Vicat remarks, spreads from the surface towards the centre of the specimen: but the quantity of gas that can pass through the voids of mortar beyond a short distance, is too small for its direct influence to be sensible: if then, there is not a total cessation of absorption, it must be admitted that the transmission must go on by the play of affinities—by the tendency that the several concentric layers of lime have to an equilibrium of saturation, like the transmission of heat in solid bodies. It must also be admitted that the equilibrium is the more difficult to attain, as the parts requiring saturation are more remote from the surface, and the dose of acid already received, is the greater, so that the thickness of mortars is injurious to their solidification: that in equal times, the increase in hardness will be far from being equal, and will progressively become less and less, and, lastly, though it may be exact to say that mortars made of fat lime improve as they grow old, still the improvement may not be at all sensible at the expiration of periods of only a few years each.

§ 31. *On the distinctive characters of Meagre lime and Hydraulic lime.*

Natural limestones often contain earthy or metallic oxides, which by calcination combine with the lime. Whence result modifications in its properties. Thus it is known that lime will remain a fat lime so long as the foreign substances do not form a tenth of its weight; but beyond that it becomes meagre, that is to say, it swells much less on slaking; and, if amongst these foreign bodies, silex should predominate, the paste, with, or without, sand, will acquire the property of hardening in water. It was for a long time thought that other foreign bodies acted like silex; but the method of investigation followed by Mr. Berthier, leaves no doubt in this respect. We will give a summary of his results.

Comparing, first, the quality of various limes with their chemical composition, Mr. Berthier found:

Fat lime from Chateau-Landon to contain 96.4 pure lime—1.80 of magnesia—1.80 of clay (silex and alumine.)

Meagre lime from Coulommiers 78.00 pure lime—20.00 of magnesia—2.00 of clay (silex and alumine.)

Lime moderately hydraulic from Saint-Germain—89.00 of pure lime—1.00 of magnesia—10.00 of clay (silex and alumine.)

Lime very hydraulic from Senonches—70.00 of pure lime—1.00 of magnesia—29.00 of silex. To these analyses we will add:

Meagre lime of Brest—82.30 of lime—10.00 of oxide of iron—7.70 of clay.

We see from these analyses that silex, whether pure or mixed with alumine, renders lime hydraulic; and that magnesia, or the oxide of iron, renders it meagre and not hydraulic. Mr. Berthier found the same consequences when proceeding synthetically: he ascertained that silex in jelly, calcined with pure lime, gave an hydraulic product; that alumine, magnesia, oxide of iron, and oxide of manganese, calcined, one by one, with pure lime, gave a meagre lime only: that alumine or magnesia mixed with silex increased the hydraulic property, and, lastly, that the proportions the most favourable for the mixture were equal parts of silex on the one hand and alumine or magnesia on the other.

A consequence results from these considerations which it is important to mention: it is this, that the process of Mr. Vicat for preparing artificial hydraulic lime, does not answer equally well on taking any limestone or clay that may present itself: that it is, with difficulty, applicable to meagre limes mixed with ochreous clays, and that this is the case at Brest, where, the matters being charged with oxide of iron, nothing passable was obtained, and we were obliged to resort to puzzolanas.

§ 32. *On the solidification of hydraulic lime.*

Hydraulic lime slaked in the ordinary manner solidifies a certain quantity of water as fat lime does; and forms, with an excess of water, a paste, more or less stiff. If left exposed to the air, it absorbs less carbonic acid than fat lime; and, like fat lime, it retains the water it had solidified.

According to Mr. Vicat there are in 100 parts of fat lime = 100.00

Absorbed carbonic acid	76.00
Retained water	17.00

And in 100 parts of hydraulic lime which contains a fifth of its weight of clay:

Absorbed carbonic acid	54.00
Retained water	15.00

But this last result may be put under the following form:

Pure lime	100.00
Clay	25.00
Carbonic acid	67.50
Water	18.70

It differs therefore, in this respect, very little from fat lime, so that it is equally a *hydro-carbonate* of lime, the clay appearing not to enter into the combination.

On the other hand, when the paste remains immersed in water, the aid of the carbonic acid is no longer possible, and that of the silex becomes indispensible to solidification. It remains to seek the cause of this phenomenon.

1st. Pure lime is soluble in five or six hundred times its weight of water, and the product is called *lime water*.

2nd. Pure lime combined by calcination with gelatinous silex is only partially soluble in water, and leaves a residue, composed of sixty-five parts of silex and thirty-five parts of lime, which is known under the name of *neutral silicate of lime*.

3rd. Pure lime combined in the same manner with alumine, magnesia, oxide of iron, or oxide of manganese, although it has lost the property of swelling much, or slaking, is still soluble in water, and the residue contains nothing but pure alumine, or magnesia, or the oxide of iron or manganese.

4th. In order that a lime may be hydraulic, it will suffice that it possesses six or seven per cent. of silex, a quantity that can render only a very small dose of lime insoluble.

5th. Plastic cements, at the point of complete calcination, may be assimilated to ordinary lime—they are but slightly hydraulic, although they contain a considerable portion of silex.

We see then that the combination of silex with lime has, alone, the advantage of resisting the attacks of water: that if alumine and some other oxides raise the hydraulic energies, it arises probably from this, that the obstacle they interpose to the swelling of the lime tends to the concentration of the molecules, thereby helping their predisposition to submit to the influence of the silicate of lime: and that free lime, notwithstanding its solubility, ought always to predominate in the immersed paste.

The question being thus stated, it is necessary to explain two effects; the insolubility, and the hardness, acquired by mortars under water.

In the first place, it cannot be admitted that the silicate of lime solidifies separately, and that it envelopes the hydrate as a gangue; for the last would not be less soluble, and the hardness acquired would be proportionate to the quantity of silicate, which, in general, is not true. Every thing leads to the opinion rather, that the molecules of silicate are so many centres of attraction, with respect to the soluble molecules, and that, within the sphere of activity of each of these centres, there is an arrangement which may be assimilated to a true *crystallization*.

On this hypothesis, we conceive, the most proper proportion of silicate, is that which leaves around each molecule thereof, a layer of hydrate equal in thickness to the radius of the sphere of attraction: that below this term, that is to say, in measure as the silicate becomes more abundant, the layers of interposed hydrate are submitted to attractions which interfere with and disturb, instead of mutually aiding, each other, that above this term, that is to say when the silicate is in too small a quantity, the layers of hydrate may still solidify, not so soon, nor wholly by the direct action of the silicate, but by the influence of the particles nearest the silicate, which, in measure as they solidify, react in their turn upon others: as in saline solutions, a crystal already formed may be the proximate cause of crystallization.

It may in the same manner, be conceived that hydraulic mortars have need of moisture rather than dryness, because the water preserving to the molecules a certain mobility, permits their arranging themselves in juxtaposition by the proper facets. It must not however be concluded that soft mortars would be preferable to mortars in stiff paste: because the water augmenting too much the distance of the molecules, would throw them beyond the sphere of mutual attraction: hence one of the causes why hydraulic mortars are generally less hard on the surface than in their central parts, while it is the reverse with all mortars made of fat lime and hardened in the air.

§ 33. *On the influence of the dissolving action of water.*

This fact has relation to another cause on which it is important to insist.

When hydraulic mortar is immersed in the bottom of any vessel, two opposite molecular forces are set in action: on the one hand, the action of the silicate of lime on the hydrate, and on the other, the solvent force of the water with respect to this same hydrate. The water being supposed tranquil, the lower portions of it dissolve the lime: but as this water becomes more dense it remains at the bottom, without power of removal; and the lime thus dissolved cannot be transferred to the upper portions of fluid except by the play of affinities—by a transmission analogous to that of carbonic acid in the interior of mortars made of fat lime. However that may be, the portion of water in immediate contact with the mortar losing its solvent power in proportion as it approaches the term of saturation, an equilibrium will soon be established between the two opposite molecular forces, and then all solution will cease. But if the superficial layer of mortar has lost a small portion only of its hydrate, this equilibrium, will, as regards the progress of solidification of the mortar, be only instantaneous: this layer might in fact continue to take cohesion from the influence of the under layers of mortar not attacked by the water.

If, on the other hand, the liquid be agitated, in order to render the saturation uniform throughout the mass of fluid—or rather, if the mortar be immersed in running water, it may happen that the exterior layers of mortar will, little by little, lose all, or the greater part, of their hydrate; but this effect not being brought about instantly, the interior layers would be protected for a time sufficient for them to harden beyond its solvent power before becoming, in their turn, exposed to the action of the water. We can conceive, therefore, that mortars may wash away for a certain depth: and that thickness may be an indispensable condition to the success of the solidifying process.

§ 34. *Influence of Quartzose Sands.*

As the practice is to use hydraulic limes, not pure, but mixed with sands, it is important to study the influence of these sands on the induration of mortars. We shall speak here only of quartzose sands, which are the most common.

It is demonstrated by experiments that caustic lime, cold or hot, is without any action on quartz in discernible particles: if, then, it adds to the quality of hydraulic mortars, it can only be because, 1st. it augments the density of the mass, and thus prevents its being brought to the state of soft mortar by being too easily permeable to water: or, 2nd. because its adherence to the lime, however feeble it may be supposed to be in the first instance, is an accelerating cause of crystallization. That this should be so, it is not necessary to suppose that the sand exercises a chemical action on the lime: because we know, for example, that in the preparation of rock-candy, and of verdigris or acetate of copper, &c. it is only necessary to stretch threads, or place sticks of wood, in the solutions, to determine the crystals to group around them like clusters of grapes, while none show themselves any where else. Sands in this, do no more than aid the tendency of hydraulic limes to take cohesion; and their influence is null when this tendency does not exist, as for example in fat lime. If the experiments with this last lime be attentively examined, it will be seen that they harden better alone than when mixed with sand: that the particles of hydro-carbonate have greater cohesion amongst themselves than adhesion to sand; whence it naturally follows that sands which divide the mass most thoroughly, that is to say, the finest sands, are the worst, because in an equal section the extent of surfaces in contact is the greatest. The contrary takes place in hydraulic limes, according to Mr. Vicat. If some experiments of General Treussart do not accord with these ideas, it seems to be owing to the too great quantity of sand used in his mortars.

§ 35. *On the solidification of deteriorated hydraulic limes.*

We have seen, at the commencement of this article, that hydraulic limes slaked spontaneously in the air, and not used for some time, lost their energy, more and more. We will add an analogous fact that we have had occasion to observe; it is that the hydraulic lime of Doué preserved for two years in flagons, well stoppered, so as to prevent any change of air, or the absorption of humidity, remained in fragments it is true; but these fragments had lost the power of slaking, and also of setting under water, after having been tempered like plaster. What has occurred in this case? This we have to explain.

It is well known that the limestone affording hydraulic lime, when treated, before calcination, with muriatic acid, leaves generally an insoluble residue composed of silex and alumine; but that immediately after calcination, the same stone, now become quick lime, is completely soluble, which shows the existence of a chemical combination: this being premised—we have taken hydraulic lime which had been slaked in air for two months; treated it with muriatic acid in excess, and it gave a considerable gelatinous residue: we have treated hydraulic lime preserved for two years in the same way, and the gelatinous residue was so abundant that we were forced to believe there could be no silex dissolved with the lime. But however that might be, is it not evident that the silicate of lime is decomposed, at least in part? that, therefore, in the case of the deterioration of hydraulic limes, the silex having taken cohesion, is only to be considered as being mixed intimately with the lime, and consequently can do no more than perform the office of puzzolana mixed in small doses with fat lime. Hence the great inferiority of the results, and the necessity of remedying them by the method of General Treussart.

§ 36. *On the solidification of Puzzolana Mortars.*

Let us pass now to the case of puzzolana mortars. According to what has been said before, an indispensable condition to the solidification of lime under water, is, that a small portion of this same lime be first rendered insoluble—each of the insoluble particles becoming the centre of attraction with respect to the surrounding layers of hydrate. Is this condition fulfilled on mixing fat lime with puzzolana? This is put beyond doubt by Mr. Vicat showing that puzzolanas have the property of precipitating lime from its solution in water, and that their energy is proportionate to the quantity of lime water they can thus precipitate. Whatever may be the cause of this property, whether it does, or does not, belong to a chemical combination between the lime and puzzolana—a combination difficult to conceive on account of the state of cohesion of the silex—a cohesion assuredly much greater than in deteriorated hydraulic lime, it is not less true that this fact suffices to establish a satisfactory analogy between the solidification of puzzolana mortars, and those made of hydraulic lime. It may be inferred from thence that the mixture of puzzolana with slightly hydraulic lime will give good results, because in such limes the proportion of hydrate would not be superabundant; with limes very hydraulic, it may be inferred, on the contrary, that this mixture would become injurious, because the proportion of lime would be too small, and there would result a kind of plastic cement, at the term of complete calcination.

The puzzolanas are mixed like sands, in the proportion of one and a half to two and a half in volume, to one of lime in paste. This proportion supposes, no doubt, much more silex, than is required to constitute hydraulic limes; but it must be remarked that in these limes, all the particles act in the most favourable circumstances possible, while in the above mixtures, they are collected in grains of some size, acting only by their surfaces, and their action being weakened by the cohesion that they already possess in a high degree.

§ 37. On the solidification of Plastic Cements.

Let us, in the last place, see to what degree the principles previously admitted will serve to explain the solidification of plastic cements, in the most general case; that is to say, as was explained at the end of chapter XVIII, section 25.

1st. In fat limes imperfectly calcined or super-calcined, the particles carbonated or super-calcined, requiring to be worked to make a paste with water, and being convertible into hydrate only with difficulty, it may be conceived to be not impossible that they play the same part as lime rendered insoluble by silex or by puzzolana, and that thus the commencement of hydraulic quality is obtained.

2d. In hydraulic limes imperfectly calcined, the particles of carbonate act in the same manner, but with this advantage that their influence on the solidification is increased by that of the silicate of lime which is present.

In the same lime stones carried to the second maximum of energy, the particles of carbonate are replaced by the equally insoluble super-calcined particles.

3d. In the septaria furnishing the ordinary plastic cement, the clay is too abundant to leave, at the term of complete calcination, the proportion of hydrate of lime necessary to a good solidification: the imperfect calcination, then, has for object to render the silex only partially soluble in acids so that it may the more resemble the mode of action of puzzolanas.

Lastly, at the term of super-calcination, the clay of these same lime stones passes to a state of less energetic puzzolana than at the term of complete calcination, and thereby leaves a greater proportion of lime susceptible of conversion into hydrate.

———

The developments into which we have entered relative to the solidification of mortars in general, are far, no doubt, from exhausting the subject; and require to be sustained by numerous experiments. We are fully aware of this; but our object not being to present a treatise on mortars, we have restricted ourselves to so much as is useful in understanding the operations of lime burning, which we have described.

Sect. IV.—SOME RESEARCHES RELATIVE TO LIME AND MORTARS.

BY M. COURTOIS,
Engineer of Roads and Bridges.[*]

———

(From the Annales des Ponts et Chaussées, Paris, 1834.)

———

The art of making good mortars is every day becoming better appreciated, from the influence it exercises in the economy and on the duration of constructions. If, in every great work, the constructors would make known the researches they have instituted, and the conclusions to which they have been led, we should soon know the resources presented by each locality, and be every where able, progressively, to improve the manufacture of mortars.

Having had occasion at various times to make numerous essays on lime and hydraulic mortars, and on the means of making them economically, I think I am fulfilling a duty in presenting a summary of the principal re-.sults.

My investigations have had particularly in view the qualities of the mixtures, or combinations of lime and clay, comprised between hydraulic lime and cement; but in order not to leave any void in the scale of various proportions to be tried, I thought it best to try all combinations possible with 100 parts of the mixture.

I shall examine successively,

1st. The elements of these combinations, viz. limestones, clayey earth, and marl; I shall give the analysis of each, and examine their respective properties.

2nd. The combinations made with the most simple proportions, and which, for greater clearness in the tables, I shall call combinations of the first order: these will be mixtures of 1, 2, 3, 4, &c., parts of clay, with 9, 8, 7, 6, &c., parts of lime.

3rd. The combinations of the second order, or hydraulic pastes, result-

———

[*] The object of these researches was to give to fat lime the hydraulic quality necessary, and to mortars a determinate resistance, at a small expense.

ing from the preceding compounds, mixed, in their turn, with various proportions of fat lime.

4th. Combinations of the third order, or mortars resulting from the mixture of the preceding hydraulic pastes with twice their volume of sand.

I shall give, moreover, the experiments made with each hydraulic paste, and each mortar, to determine the hardness, after various periods of immersion, and to determine at the same time the resistance to rupture of each of the combinations.

I shall afterward examine the natural substances analogous to these several artificial combinations: indicating how they may be known, and showing the abundance of these hydraulic substances in nature.

Following my observations on the resistance of artificial hydraulic pastes, I shall give analogous experiments applied to the comparison of a great number of natural hydraulic pastes, and mortars made of these pastes.

CHAPTER XX.

Artificial combinations of Lime and Clay.

Lime. Without going into details as to the chemical properties of lime, it may suffice to say that this substance forms the base of limestones, and gypsum, or plaster of Paris; and that it combines, at a high temperature, with silex, forming what is called a silicate of lime. In the humid way, it appears to combine with clay, either crude or calcined, affording a hydrosilicate with a base of lime and alumine.

Lime, as it is used in making mortars, is obtained by the calcination of limestones, which are carbonates or subcarbonates more or less pure, found in all the formations; it is obtained also from some animal productions, as shells of oysters, and other shells.

The effect of calcination is to drive out the water and carbonic acid. By breaking the stone into pieces about one and a half inch square and passing a current of steam through the ignited mass, a cubic metre (35.32 cubic feet) of lime stone may be converted into lime, in a kiln with a continual fire, by burning about seven cubic feet of sea-coal:* in cold and moist seasons the consumption of coal is augmented; and amounts, sometimes, to a third of the volume of the stone.

If the limestone be argillaceous, the fire should be managed cautiously, and be less violent than to calcine a nearly pure carbonate of lime; for when the fire is too high, the lime and clay fuse, and give a vitreous matter inert, or without causticity, which is a double silicate of lime and alumine.

Whenever a piece of limestone is cooled before the calcination is completed, it becomes necessary to wet it before putting it again in the kiln;

----

* On the canal of Ardennes, where I caused large quantities of lime to be burned, the lime burners threw into the kiln one measure of sea-coal to five, six and even seven measures of limestone; it should be observed, however, that the stone was a chlorite-chalk, easier to convert into lime than limestones generally.

At Theil in the department of Ardèche, whence the best hydraulic lime that I know of is derived, they consume but one sixth of a measure of sea-coal in burning one measure of lime. AUTHOR.

without this precaution, it would be very difficult to reduce it completely to lime.

After calcination, lime has a great affinity for water, and augments in volume, by absorbing it. If a certain quantity of water be thrown on lime recently calcined, it heats, splits open, and is reduced to powder, or paste, according to the quantity of water absorbed; during this operation, a little water is carried off by the heat; but, when the lime is obtained from a nearly pure limestone, the volume of paste after slaking, is, sensibly, equal to the volume of water absorbed.*

Clay. Clays are composed of silex and alumine in variable proportions, often mixed with quartzose sand, oxide of iron, magnesia and lime. When the clays contain no sand, they are fine and soft to the touch; and form with water an unctuous paste susceptible of being moulded into any form.

The clays which I chiefly used are those of which the analyses are given in columns 1, 2, 3, and 4, of table LVII.

Combinations of Lime and Clay. If crude clay be mixed with various proportions of lime, pastes are formed which have much more consistence than clay alone: this paste, put under water, acquires at the end of three days, a certain hardness which it preserves, afterward, indefinitely; it attains its maximum of resistance, when one part of lime is mixed with nine parts of clay; this paste, after three days, resists the pressure of the thumb.

When a mixture of lime and clay, exposed for some days to the air, has lost a part of its water, without having been dried too rapidly, it may be afterward immersed without sustaining any alteration, provided the volume of lime be not greater than one third that of the clay; the proportion of lime might be less but should not be greater. A mortar of this sort might be used in the construction of cisterns, reservoirs, and other works, where an insoluble, rather than a strong, mortar is needed. I regret not being able to state the actual resistance of mortars made of lime and crude clay, but at the period I was occupied with these first researches, the hardening under water was the property to which I confined my attention.

The quality of augmenting the resistance of lime, which crude clay possesses appears to have been known for a long time in *Champagne,* where all the wooden houses are covered, exteriorly, with a plaster composed of lime and a white argillaceous and calcareous earth. The floors are also made with a plaster of the same nature, and when not dried too rapidly, they resist perfectly.

This property explains how it is that sand, mixed with a certain quantity of crude clay, forms a mortar with lime, which acquires a degree of hardness under water that does not, however, increase after some days.†

If fat lime, and clay containing little or no calcareous matter, be mixed, 1, 2, 3, 4, 5, 6, 7, 8 and 9, parts of clay, respectively, with 9, 8, 7, 6, 5, 4, 3, 2 and 1 parts of lime, a series of eleven compounds will be formed, of

---

*In a considerable number of experiments that I had occasion to make in 1823, I always obtained the above relation between the bulk of the slaked lime, and the absorbed water; the quantities of lime on which I experimented, varied from three and a half to ten and a half cubic feet. Au.

†The sands now referred to must not be confounded with those which contain, in their interstices, mud or slime more or less charged with animal or vegetable matter; when this last kind of sand is used, the lime forms, with the animal or vegetable substance, a soap, more or less soluble, which opposes the hardening of the mortars. Sands of this kind, if not washed free from these matters before they are used, always give very bad results.
AUTHOR.

which the first term will be pure lime, and the last, pure clay; if the last ten compounds be calcined, substances will result possessing the properties about to be described.

Hydraulic lime. The first two mixtures will give hydraulic lime, as Mr. Vicat has long since made known.

The lime of the first compound is moderately hydraulic, hardens slowly in water, and takes, in time, the consistence of hard soap.

The lime of the second, acquires, after three days immersion, the hardness of chalk: after 20 days immersion, it permits a stem 0.08 inch in diameter, loaded with 2.20 lbs. falling from a height of two inches, to penetrate 0.12 inch: and after two months immersion, it shows no sensible impression from the shock of the stem.

On mixing the lime of the first two compounds with fat lime, they divide with this last their hydraulic properties; but these properties decrease quite rapidly. Hydraulic lime containing 0.20 of clay, mixed with an equal volume of fat lime, acquires at the end of two months the hardness of lime containing 0.10 of clay. By this kind of mixture, the energy of lime, slightly hydraulic, is sensibly augmented; a lime which would take only a feeble consistence when alone in water, acquired, by mixture with one quarter, or only one fifth, of very hydraulic lime, the properties of limes that are moderately hydraulic.

Lime-cement. The four following compounds, containing 3, 4, 5, and 6 parts of clay united with 7, 6, 5, and 4 parts of lime, give, by calcination, substances that slake slowly, disengaging but little heat; but when pulverized and made into paste, increase in volume, and acquire, promptly, great hardness under water. Their augmentation of volume continues some time after they have commenced hardening; for if a glass be filled therewith, it splits in all directions, but the cracks do not become apparent till a month or two after it has acquired a hardness equal to that of chalk. This augmentation of volume, which breaks the glass in which the experiment is made, is however but slight; for when the paste is made into the form of bricks, it is rare that it presents fissures. Each of these compounds mixed with an equal volume of sand, and even with a double volume, gives a hydraulic mortar which, after six hours immersion, resists the pressure of the thumb: and after eight days, perfectly resists the shock of the stem above spoken of.

Besides the properties mentioned, the same compounds communicate to fat lime their hydraulic qualities; imparting all the energy of lime eminently hydraulic.

If 1, 2, 3, 4, 5, 6, 7, 8 and 9 parts of the powder of each of these compounds be taken, and mixed respectively with 9, 8, 7, 6, 5, 4, 3, 2 and 1 parts of fat lime, different degrees of hydraulic property will be given to the latter: with five parts of powder, a lime eminently hydraulic will be obtained: two parts of powder will suffice to make eight parts of lime hydraulic; but, one part of powder will communicate only a feeble degree of hydraulic property to nine parts of lime; after eight days' immersion, this last mixture will hardly have the consistence of moist soap.

If, an hour after the mixture, all the pastes made of the lime and powder, above mentioned, be immersed, they will set under water in six days for the least hydraulic; after that time, the hardest will resist the pressure of the thumb. Each of these pastes mixed with a volume of sand equal to the volume of paste at least, and to twice the volume of paste at most, will give a mortar which will harden in water a little less rapidly than the paste without the sand.

The compound of five parts of lime and five parts of clay is that which gives the most energetic powder.

According to the proportions of lime and powder, the paste is more or less gritty or more or less unctuous, but all harden in a short time after immersion: for example the powder derived from the compound of four parts of lime and six parts of clay gave results sensibly the same as those derived from a compound of six parts of lime and four parts of clay.

The compounds of which we have been speaking enjoy, therefore, the properties of lime and cement, at the same time. When mixed, alone, with sand, they serve to make mortars—acting, in this respect, like lime; when, on the other hand, they give hydraulic properties to lime, they, in that respect, act like cement: this double property has induced me to designate them by the term *lime-cement*.

Hydraulic Cement.—The terms of the series composed of 7, 8, and 9 parts of clay, respectively mixed with 3, 2 and 1 parts of lime, give, by calcination, substances that do not slake: their colour is more or less reddish, according to the greater or less quantity of oxide of iron in the clay. These matters being pulverized and made into paste, form a mortar, more or less meagre, which hardens under water in the space of ten days.

The powders of these compounds, mixed with various proportions of fat lime, give hydraulic pastes which harden under water in a few days.

These compounds being true cements, enjoying the property of hardening when alone under water, it seems convenient to designate them as *hydraulic cements* in order to distinguish them from *common cement* which, when alone, will take no consistence under water.

Common cement.—Clay, as has been long known, gives, by calcination and pulverization, a cement that being mixed with fat lime in various proportions, forms a mortar that hardens slowly under water, but which in time acquires a degree of hardness superior to that of hydraulic lime, either alone or mixed with sand, as we shall have occasion to show when on the subject of resistance to rupture of hydraulic paste and mortar.

Mode of mixing.—All the mixtures or combinations spoken of were made at the moment of slaking the lime*, or a short time afterwards.

When lime has been slaked for several days, the pastes and mortars split under water, take but little consistence, and seem to abandon their lime; which does not occur, or is much less sensible, when lime newly slaked is used: I content myself with stating the fact, without pretending to explain it.

When the lime is immersed while hot, an analogous effect is observed; but then it is caused by the swelling of a paste not saturated with water before the immersion.

The mixtures should, therefore, be made at the moment of slaking, but they should not be immersed for three or four hours afterward, if the volume is small, nor for twenty or thirty hours afterward when the bulk is considerable.

Mode of experimenting.—In the first experiments I had occasion to make, I mixed fat lime with a brick earth of which the analysis is given in the first column of table LVII.; this earth containing hardly $\frac{1}{80}$ of calcareous matter gave combinations possessing all the properties described above.

At this first period of the experiments—then less methodical than after-

* The slaking was always done by the ordinary process, that is to say by adding to the lime in a basin, the necessary quantity of water.—*Author.*

ward, I contented myself with putting into the glasses, volumes of paste occupying about a third of their capacity, and then pouring on water to fill the vessel. I subsequently measured the degree of advancement of the induration, by letting fall, from a height of two inches, a stem of iron $\frac{8}{100}$ of an inch in diameter, and loaded to weigh 2.2 lbs.

In a second series of experiments, I made use of argillaceous earth of which the analysis is given in the second column of the table LVII: this earth, as the analysis shows, contains nine per cent. of lime: it therefore gave pastes less resisting, and of a less prompt induration, than the preceding.

The volumes of paste were equal. To this end they were moulded in a hollow tin prism 1.8 inch long and 1.2 inch square: the substance thus moulded was, while still soft, forced out of the tin prism by a piece of wood of the same form and size, and placed at the bottom of a glass; each prism thus deposited at the bottom of a glass, remained half an hour exposed to the air and was then covered with water.

In mixing successively 9, 8, 7, 6, 5, 4, 3, 2, and 1 parts of the powder of the *ten combinations of the first order* with 1, 2, 3, 4, 5, 6, 7, 8, and 9 parts of fat lime, I obtained 100 combinations of the second order, or, in other words, one hundred different hydraulic pastes.

The figures of the two horizontal lines at the top of tables LIX. and LX., indicate the respective numbers, first, of the parts of the substances *a*, contained in the second column as combinations of the first order; second, of the parts of fat lime, which were mixed therewith to form the combinations of the second order.

The pastes of the same vertical column are, consequently, composed of the same number of parts of fat lime mixed successively with a certain number of parts of the several matters *a*, or combinations of the first order, mentioned in the second column of the table.

Hardening of Hydraulic Pastes.—To measure the degree of advancement of the induration of the several hydraulic pastes, I could not use the stem loaded with 2.2 lbs. of lead, because it would certainly have broken the prisms: I replaced it by another $\frac{48}{1000}$ of an inch in diameter, loaded with lead so as to weigh $\frac{3}{4}$ of a pound.

Fifteen days after the immersion, each prism, withdrawn from the water in which it had been immersed, was submitted to the shock of the stem just described, falling from the height of $\frac{8}{10}$ of an inch only; the number inscribed in each column of the table LIX, indicates the penetration for each prism.

Several prisms perfectly resisted the shock, and sustained no sensible penetration: others presented irregularities in their resistance without any apparent cause.

Two months after the immersion, the prisms were submitted to a second proof; the stem falling, then, from a height of $1\frac{8}{10}$ inch; the numbers expressive of the degree of penetration of the stem into each prism, are given in table LX.; as the effect of the shock should be double in the second proof what it was in the first, and as the degree of penetration had generally diminished, it results that in the space of forty days the resistance of all the hydraulic pastes was more than doubled.

After four months immersion, the stem, let fall from a height of $2\frac{4}{10}$ inches—the greatest height the instrument would allow, produced no sensible effect on the greater part of the prisms.

Resistance to rupture of hydraulic pastes.—At this period I thought it proper to measure the resistance to rupture. To obtain this resistance, I

27

operated with each hydraulic paste, on a prism 1.80 inch long, and 1.20 inch square, making use of an arrangement similar to that described by General Treussart in his work on mortars. Each prism passed through a small iron stirrup, and rested on two supports which were 1.20 inch apart; from the stirrup was suspended a scale-pan on which was placed, successively, greater and greater weights: that which caused the rupture was noted, and augmented by the weight of the stirrup and scale-pan, which was 12.10 lbs. The numbers indicating the weights that broke the prisms, are inserted in table LXI.

The results comprised in table LXI. present some anomalies, of which several were caused by voids that were found in a number of the prisms: others supported greater weights than was to be expected from their composition, without my being able to assign the cause.

The same table shows that lime moderately hydraulic, containing 0.10 of clay and 0.90 of lime, mixed in different proportions with fat lime, afforded prisms which supported from 29.0 lbs. to 66 lbs.

It also shows that very hydraulic lime, containing 0.20 of clay and 0.80 of lime, in the same circumstances, gave prisms that supported from 53 lbs. to 207 lbs.

That prisms of lime-cement mixed with different proportions of fat lime, supported from 53 lbs. to 440 lbs.

That prisms of hydraulic cement and fat lime, supported from 44 lbs. to 363 lbs.

That prisms of common cement and fat lime, sustained from 0.00 to 356 pounds.

A prism of common burnt brick, such as is used at *Rive-de-Gier*, having exactly the dimensions of the prisms of hydraulic paste, broke under a weight of 117 lbs.

Of the 100 prisms tried, 69 had strength superior to this well burned, but coarse grained, brick.

Resistance of mortars to rupture.—At the same time that the prisms of hydraulic paste were moulded, the same pastes were mixed with double the volume of sand, forming one hundred hydraulic compounds inserted in tables LIX, LX, and LXI. Combinations were thus formed of a third order, which we call mortars; these were moulded into prisms 4 inches in length by $1\frac{8}{10}$ inch square.

After four months immersion, the resistance to rupture of these mortar prisms was determined. To this end each prism was passed through a stirrup and made to rest on supports that were two inches apart: to the stirrup was appended a scale-pan in which weights were placed to cause the rupture: the weight which effected the rupture, increased by that of the scale-pan and stirrup, which was $12\frac{1}{10}$ lbs., was noted. The weights thus determined are inserted in table LXII.

These numbers are much weaker than might be expected from the resistances afforded by the hydraulic pastes (table LXI:) which deficiency in the resistances of these mortars, appears to be due to the quantity of sand, which was generally too great: in fact, *lime cements, and cements*, contain within themselves a certain quantity of matter not susceptible of slaking, and which, consequently, acts as sand: the portions of true hydraulic paste which should serve to bind together the sandy particles, were therefore in too small quantity in the greater number of the prisms.

I wished to leave the mortars immersed during at least one year, but time failed me.

A prism of common burnt brick, having exactly the dimensions of the prisms of mortar, broke under the weight of 240 lbs.

Of the 100 mortar prisms submitted to trial, there were but 5 that were superior to the brick prism.[*]

From what precedes, results the following classification of combinations, elementary in some sort, which may enter into the composition of mortar.[†]

1st. *Fat lime*—which does not contain clay, or in which the clay is less than the $\frac{1}{10}$.

2nd. *Hydraulic lime*—which contains that of $\frac{1}{5}$ of clay.

3rd. *Lime cement*—which contains from $\frac{1}{5}$ to $\frac{3}{5}$ of clay.

4th. *Hydraulic cement*—which contains from $\frac{2}{3}$ to $\frac{1}{10}$ of lime.

5th. *Common cement*—in which the lime is wanting, or exists in quantity less than $\frac{1}{10}$.

CHAPTER XXI.

Natural Combinations of Lime and Clay.

Limestones capable of affording hydraulic lime.—Lime, silex and alumine, the elements necessary to hydraulic lime, are substances that Nature affords in abundance in the secondary and tertiary formations: the crust of the globe is almost entirely formed of them: each of these substances alone, forms layers more or less thick, which often alternate with the others: this alternation is to be seen whenever, in the same formation, there is a change in the nature of the rock: thus, as is frequently seen, strata of clay, alternate with calcareous layers, and with strata of sand stone or free stone. When this happens it is rare that the stratum is entirely composed of the one substance; in the passage of the calcareous strata, for example, there are formed, first, calcareous strata containing a small quantity of clay, then, becoming more argillaceous, passing often to the state of marl, and at last, the clay is found almost alone, or without mixture of lime. When a succession of this nature is presented, it may be conceived not to be difficult to find a calcareous layer wherein the clay will exist in proportions suitable for hydraulic lime.

The preceding observation has often been useful to me in directing my search for natural hydraulic limes. In the Jura limestone formation (*formation Jurassique*,) for example, where such alternations are frequent, I have found hydraulic lime: 1st. near *Brabant* (Meuse,) in the oolitic beds which alternate with beds of clay: 2nd. near *Villers-le-Tourneur* (Ardennes,) in other oolitic layers, presenting the same alternations: 3rd. near Joinville (Haute-Maine.)

For a long time, a bed of gryphite lias, alternating with beds of clay, and which gives a lime slightly hydraulic, has been quarried near Lyons.

Near Macon, there exists a quarry of the same kind in the oolitic layers;

---

[*] When on the subject of natural *lime-cements* and of *common cements*, I shall refer to mortars that supported, after four months, a load almost twice as great as the greatest inserted in the table.—*Author.*

[†] In almost all localities, Nature offers the materials proper to form the different elements of mortar, in abundance; as will be shown in the following chapter.—*Author.*

the lime of Sury (Loire,) and that of Theil (Ardèche,) which are very hydraulic, are derived from some layers of lias found under analogous circumstances.

In the inferior layers of the chalk formation, where the same alternations are remarked, I very easily found hydraulic limes at different points on the limits of the formation, as Saint-Menehould, Rethel, and Vitry-le-Français.

In the tertiary formation, having noticed alternations of lime and clay near Hermonville (Maine,) near Valsery (Aisne) in the calcareous beds containing cerithiœ, and lastly, near Chateau-Thierry, in the strata of siliceous limestones, it was easy to point out the layers which it was proper to try, in searching for hydraulic lime.

The preceding observation is always true for the beds of the same formation; but it ceases to be exact at the point of passage of different formations. The chalk formation, for example, is often covered with the plastic clay which belongs to the tertiary: but these two layers appertain to two distinct formations; the first had existed for a long time before it was covered by the second; the calcareous matters not having been produced simultaneously, the two substances are simply juxtaposited, without alternation or mixture.

We may conclude, from what precedes, that whenever limestone is found alternating with clays or marls, one or several of the layers will give hydraulic lime. Five or six trials with small specimens will suffice to show which of the layers should be quarried.

I will terminate what relates to natural hydraulic limes by stating the process to which I submitted some of the limes, and the mortars into the composition of which they entered.

The experiments on the natural hydraulic pastes, and on the mortars made from them, were conducted under the same circumstances as the experiments mentioned in tables LXI and LXII, with the artificial combinations.

The prisms of hydraulic paste were $1\frac{8}{10}$ inch long and $1\frac{2}{10}$ inch square, and were placed on two supports which were $1\frac{3}{10}$ inch apart.

The prisms of mortar were four inches long and $1\frac{8}{10}$ inch square, and were placed on supports which were two inches apart.*

The same stirrup rested on the prism, and had suspended from it the scale pan, weighing, together with the stirrup, $12\frac{1}{10}$ lbs.

The lime derived from Theil (Ardèche) is the most powerfully hydraulic of any I have met with: it is obtained by burning a limestone of which the analysis will be found in the fourth column of table LVII.

---

*Knowing the resistance E of a prism of matter having the dimensions of those of the hydraulic paste, it is easy to determine the resistance E' of a prism of the same substance having the dimensions of the prisms of mortar; by using the formula $E = R \frac{ab^2}{c}$ in which a is the breadth of the prism, b its depth, and c the distance between the supports.

For other dimensions we have $E' = E \dfrac{\frac{a'(b'^2)}{c'}}{\frac{a(b^2)}{c}}$

And in substituting for a, b, c and a', b', c' the above values, we find $E' = 2.025 \ E.$ Author.

A prism of this lime having exactly the same dimensions as those of the hydraulic pastes in table LXI, broke under a weight of 229lbs; its resistance, after four months immersion, was, consequently, double that of a brick of the same dimensions.

In table LXIV, I have given the results of the proofs to which I submitted different prisms of mortars composed of Theil lime mixed with different quantities of sand: these mortars after one month broke under a weight varying from 59lbs. to 81lbs. Mortar composed of one part of lime and four parts of sand, broke under a weight of 59lbs., and that composed of one part of lime and one and a half part of sand, broke under a weight of 81lbs.

A prism of mortar composed of one part of Theil lime and two parts of sand, after four months immersion, broke under the weight of 469lbs.; the resistance of the mortar was, consequently, six times that of the same mortar one month old, and twice that of a brick.

In the environs of *Rine de Geir*, are the remains of a Roman aqueduct which conveyed a part of the waters of the Saint Etienne to Lyons; I extracted from these ruins a piece of mortar which appeared to be as hard as stone, and cut it carefully to the same dimensions as the prisms that had been tried: the prism of this mortar sustained a weight of 519lbs., only 50lbs. more than was borne by the prism made of Theil lime.

A prism of mortar composed of one part of lime from Vitry le Français, and two parts of sand, sustained, after four months immersion, a weight of 145lbs.

The lime from Sury (Loire,) which is generally regarded as very hydraulic, mixed with double its volume of sand, gave a prism of mortar which, after four months' immersion, broke under the weight of 64lbs. The resistance of this mortar was therefore hardly equal to the seventh of that of the mortar made of Theil lime. The small resistance of the mortar made of Sury lime, the hydraulic quality of which has been long known, resulted doubtless from some defect in the prism—perhaps an imperceptible crack.

Calcareous Stones and Earths which afford Lime-cements.

Every locality does not present the alternation of limestone and clay which facilitates the research for natural hydraulic limes; and it often happens that there is but one rock, and that, nearly homogeneous. Towards the middle of the chalk formation between Chalons and Troyes, the chalk is an almost pure calcareous carbonate, in which we seek in vain for a layer sufficiently argillaceous to afford hydraulic lime. The calcareous rocks, so abundant in the tertiary and secondary, are almost entirely wanting, or are only rarely found, in the lower formations. In these formations, there is no room for choice; it is necessary to use such limestone as can be found, and these rarely contain the proportion of clay that will yield hydraulic lime; but it is not rare to find, in these localities, substances which will give, by a moderate calcination, the *lime cements*. The greater part of the marls are of this sort, the clay and the lime composing them existing in variable proportions comprised within the limits affording *lime cements*: these substances are very common in France, and it will be as economical as advantageous, to give to fat lime the required degree of hydraulic property by mixing therewith marls calcined and pulverized.

When we are at liberty to choose, the marls that contain little or no sand should be preferred, so that the hydraulic paste which they assist in forming may bear the greater proportion of sand, and give a greater volume of mortar.

The calcination of marls requires a degree of heat less than that necessary to the calcination of limestone: when the fire is too great they vitrify, and form a double silicate with base of lime and alumine; when the fire is less ardent, they give a compact substance of which the fracture is slightly vitreous; this matter is difficult to pulverize, and gives a nearly inert cement; when the degree of heat is just sufficient, the fracture is dull, and the substance is generally easy to pulverise. Such wheels as are used in extensive works, for making mortar, will suffice to this end. When the degree of heat is insufficient, the cement is mixed with earthy portions which impair its energy.

It is difficult to give a general rule for the calcination of marls, because some require a degree of heat quite elevated. To ascertain, by an easy experiment, the degree of heat that each kind requires, the portion may be moulded into the form of a cylinder $4\frac{8}{10}$ inch in length by $1\frac{2}{10}$ inch in diameter, and exposed, one end in a violent fire, and the other on, or near, the outside of the fire; when the most highly heated end has begun to vitrify, the cylinder may be withdrawn from the fire and divided into four parts according to the apparent effects of the different degrees of calcination: by pulverizing each, it is easy to determine the degree of calcination which gives the most energetic cements: to prevent the cylinder breaking in the fire it is necessary to mould it around a wire.

It is requisite that the burned marl be pulverized, before the mixture with the lime; otherwise, the marl will absorb water, which will impair the energy of the powder, and prevent its intimate combination with the lime.

I had occasion to try several marls from the Departments of Loire, Ardennes, Maine and Rhone; they all gave good results. Parker's cement (English,) the Boulogne pebbles, and the Saint-Leger cement, are derived from marly stones which contain about as much clay as lime.

The Senonches lime comes from a marl containing more lime than clay: all these substances are, consequently, so many lime cements.

I made numerous experiments with three kinds of marl the analyses of which are inserted in table LVII, columns Nos. 6, 7 and 8.

The first comes from Saint-Just, department of Loire, the second from Aubigny in the same department, and the third from the Rhone at Lyons and at Givors.

The marl of Saint-Just contains only 36 parts of lime united with 41 parts of clay; this marl, calcined and pulverized, gives a very energetic lime cement.

The 5th and 6th experiments of table LXIII, prove that 8 and 7 parts of powdered marl united with 2 and 3 parts of lime, gave a hydraulic paste which, hardly two months old, sustained the weight of 361 and 312lbs.

The experiments 27, 28, and 29 of table LXIV, show that mortars four months old, composed of a hydraulic paste, half of which was made up of powdered marl from Saint-Just, mixed with twice its volume of sand, broke under the weight of 92lbs. The want of resistance in these mortars arises from the excess of sand. The Aubigny marl contains only twenty-five parts of lime to fifty-five parts of clay: this marl, calcined and pulverized, affords a lime-cement of moderate energy.

Experiments Nos. 11, 12, 13 and 14 of table LXIII show:

1st. That a prism of the powder, after four months immersion, broke under the weight of 154lbs.

2nd. That a prism of 9 parts of this powder, mixed with one part of fat lime broke under the weight of 141lbs.

3rd. That prisms of 8 and 7 parts of the powder, mixed with 2 and 3 parts of fat lime supported only 66 and 44lbs respectively.

The resistances of the prisms of mortar composed of powdered Aubigny marl, fat lime and sand, present much fewer irregularities than the prisms of paste.

Experiment No. 31 of table LXIV, shows that a prism of mortar made of one part of the powder and two parts of sand, immersed for four months, broke under a weight of 35lbs.; while experiment No. 34 proves that a prism of mortar composed of 4 parts of fat lime united to 6 parts of the powdered marl and 20 parts of sand, did not break till the load amounted to 174lbs.

The slight resistance of prism No. 31 results, evidently, from the excess of sand mixed with a powder whereof more than half already performed the office of sand, so that the prism contained hardly $\frac{1}{3}$ of powder susceptible of conversion into lime.

The Givors marl contains only 24 parts of lime united with 55 parts of clay, but, after burning, it is easier to pulverise than the marl of Aubigny, and gives a more energetic powder.

Experiment No. 3 of table LXIII, shows that a prism of this powder made into paste, after two months immersion, supported 222lbs.

Experiment No. 4 shows that another prism, of which the paste was composed of 4 parts of fat lime united to 6 parts of the powder, broke with the weight of 165lbs.

Experiment No. 26 of table LXIV, shows that a prism of mortar, one month old, composed of 1 part of powdered marl and three parts of sand, broke with the load of 37lbs.

Experiment No. 13 shows that a mortar composed of 1 part of the marl in powder and 2 parts of sand, broke under the weight of 51lbs., while experiment No. 23 shows that a mortar composed of two parts of powdered marl and 1 part of sand, sustained the load of 224lbs. Sand mixed with pastes made of powdered marl reduces their resistance, therefore, very much: this effect is less sensible with hydraulic pastes composed of fat lime and powdered marl, as seems to be proved by experiments No. 14, 15, 16, 17, 18, 19, 20, 21 and 22.

According to experiment No 22 of table LXIV, a mortar composed of 1 part of fat lime, 1 part of powdered marl and 2.40 of sand, broke with the load of 134lbs.

According to experiment No. 20, a mortar composed of 1 part of fat lime, 1 part of powdered marl, and 2.50 of sand, broke with the load of 136lbs.

And according to experiment No. 18, a mortar composed of 1 part of lime, 1 part of powdered marl, and 1.60 of sand, broke with the load of 139lbs.

These mortars being hardly a month old, the trials do not show sufficiently the influence of lime: I wished that more time should elapse, but being called away by particular circumstances, I preferred shortening the period to leaving out these trials.

Earths which will afford Hydraulic Cements.

The substances that I have designated *hydraulic cements*, and which are composed of 7, 8, and 9 parts of clay, respectively mixed with 3, 2 and 1 parts of lime, are true artificial puzzolanas; for analysis has shown that natural puzzolanas contain about $\frac{1}{11}$ of lime combined with silex and alumine. The greater part of argillaceous earths, and marls, effervescing with acids, and containing less than 40 per cent. of lime, may, when they do not contain too much sand, give by calcination and pulverization, natural hydraulic cements, susceptible of hardening under water. Each of these cements without any addition of lime, may, on being mixed with a quantity of sand equal to its volume, constitute a hydraulic mortar, but this mortar is much too meagre to be employed in masonry.

The yellow and white marls, which are very common in Champagne, give good hydraulic cements: I have found some of this kind on the little hills west of the town of Rethel; I have also encountered it at other points in the valleys of the Aisne and of the Maine. These earths mixed with a certain quantity of sand, serve to make bricks which are very light after being burned. When these bricks have not been exposed to a fire of such intensity as to cause a beginning of vitrification, they acquire great hardness under water: several millions of these bricks were made under my inspection, and used in the works of the canal of Ardennes. When the substance of the brick is vitrified, mortar adheres to it but feebly. To form good masses of masonry, bricks of which the substance is not vitrified and which have preserved the red colour, should be preferred; these are, in fact, unpulverized cement, having much affinity for lime, and to which mortars adhere strongly.

Clay, or argillaceous earth—Common Cement.—All clays, or argillaceous earth, not calcareous, burned more or less and pulverized, afford *common cement.* The cement commonly used is made from fragments of bricks or tiles. When the argillaceous earths of which cements are to be made, are exposed to a high degree of heat, they begin to melt and become fritty; in this state the pulverization becomes difficult, and the cement they afford is inert, and but little different from sand.

Of all the common cements that I had occasion to try, the most energetic was derived from the clay of Bédouan, in the department of Ardèche; the results of the analysis of this clay, are to be found in the third column of table LVII.

Experiment No. 15 of table No. LXIII shows that a prism of hydraulic paste, composed of 2 parts of lime and 5 parts of cement, after four months immersion, broke under a weight of 759 lbs.: an equal prism of Theil hydraulic lime, the best that I know, supported only 229 lbs.

Experiment No. 50 of table No. LXIV shows that a mortar composed of 1 part of the above hydraulic paste and 1 part of sand, after four months immersion, broke under a weight of 733 lbs.

Mortar composed of 1 part of Theil lime and 2 parts of sand, broke with a load of 469 lbs.; an equal prism of mortar obtained from a Roman aqueduct, about sixteen centuries old, broke under a load of 519 lbs.

These experiments prove that the hydraulic pastes and mortars which acquire in a short time the greatest strength, are those which are composed of a cement analogous to that furnished by the Bédouan clay.

I concluded the experiments on common cements by seeking to ascertain whether iron would augment the energy of the clay: to this end I mixed with clay different proportions of a ferruginous mineral (carbonate of iron mixed with carbonate of lime) and I pulverized the whole after burning.

The experiments from No. 17 to No. 25 in table LXIII, show the resistances of the hydraulic pastes made of clay-cements and the mineral: experiments from No. 41 to 49 of table No. LXIV, show the resistances of the mortars composed of this paste. It results from these two series of experiments that the mineral does not augment the energy of the cement, and that it even diminishes it, when the clay contains more than two-thirds of the substance.

CHAPTER XXII.

Summary and Conclusion.

From all that precedes, it results, that in going over the combinations that may be obtained by mixing clay not calcareous, and fat lime, in various proportions, we get, first, *hydraulic lime*, which contains as high as $\frac{1}{6}$ of clay; the combinations above this, containing from $\frac{1}{5}$ to $\frac{3}{5}$ of clay, possess at the same time the property of lime and of cement, and for this reason I have designated them as *lime cements;* lastly, the higher combinations, containing from $\frac{3}{5}$ to $\frac{9}{10}$ of clay, may have applied especially to them, the name of *hydraulic cement,* because of their being susceptible of forming hydraulic mortars, alone, or with the addition of a small quantity of lime.

Hydraulic lime.—The properties of hydraulic lime being well known, I have no further occupied myself therewith than was necessary to complete the general examination of the combinations of lime and clay, and to present some observations on the superposition of those calcareous rocks that contain the quantity of clay necessary to produce natural hydraulic limes.

Lime cements.—The combinations that I have called *lime-cements* having been but little examined hitherto, I have given to the study of their different properties, particular care. These combinations burned, pulverized, made into paste and immersed, harden under water very promptly; mixed with an equal volume of sand, or even with a double volume, they give a very good hydraulic mortar; mixed with fat lime at the moment of slaking, they give to this lime a hydraulic power depending on the proportions of the mixture: 2 parts of *lime cement* make 3 parts of fat lime very hydraulic; a still smaller quantity of *lime-cement* might suffice, and but rarely would more be necessary; unless it were thought proper to give to the paste a hydraulic energy superior to that of the best limes.

Very argillaceous limestones, and the greater part of the marls, which are very common in France, give, by moderate burning, natural *lime-cements;* we may therefore give to fat lime, a suitable degree of hydraulic energy, by mixing with it certain quantities of burnt and pulverized marl; the proportions should vary with the energy of the particular kind of pulverized marl at command; but it will be rarely necessary to exceed the proportion of two parts of powdered marl to three parts of fat lime.

At Lyons, and on the canal of Givors, use is made, for works under water, of the eminently hydraulic lime of Theil; but the marls found near these localities, of which I have ascertained the properties, might, on being mixed with fat lime, be substituted advantageously for Theil lime, of which the cubic metre (35.54 cubic feet) costs $8.55. Half of fat lime at $3.04, and half of powdered marl at $1.90, will give a very hydraulic paste, of which the cubic metre will cost only $2.47: the economy that will result from the use of this paste will be very sensible in the prolongation of the canal of Givors, of which the works will consume 10,000 cubic metres of the Theil lime.

In those localities where fuel is dear, and where there is not a supply of either natural hydraulic lime, or of marl susceptible of affording a *lime-cement*, it will be better to use an artificial *lime-cement*, than an artificial hydraulic lime; in fact, in a quantity of hydraulic lime obtained by mixture of fat lime and *lime-cement*, the last substance forming, at most, the half of the total volume, its use will reduce, in this ratio, the cost of burning, and of fabrication; on the other hand, fat lime and *lime-cements* will be more easy to preserve than hydraulic lime; and there will be, moreover, the advantage of varying the degree of hydraulic energy, and of retarding the conversion of fat lime into hydraulic lime until the moment it is to be applied.

Hydraulic cement.—The combinations to which I propose affixing the name of *hydraulic cement*, possess the property of giving, either alone, or mixed with an equal volume of sand, an hydraulic mortar more or less meagre. These cements united with fat lime, form pastes which harden under water, within the space of fifteen days. 1 part of cement suffices to render 2 parts of fat lime hydraulic.

The greater part of argillaceous and calcareous earths—very common every where—are proper to afford hydraulic cements, by burning and pulverization: the burning should be moderated, to prevent the matter from becoming fritty and inert.

When these argillaceous or calcareous earths contain a certain quantity of sand, they serve to make bricks, which are true hydraulic cements not pulverized; these bricks are very light after burning, and appear to want strength unless they have sustained a commencement of vitrification; but they adhere strongly to mortars, and when they are used under water, they soon acquire all requisite hardness; if, during the burning, these bricks are highly heated, they become fritty, often without changing form; but, in this state, they adhere but slightly to mortars, the cement of which they are composed having then become completely inert.

At the canal of Ardennes I had occasion to apply a portion of the preceding observations; because for the works of that part of the canal which lies in the valley of the Aisne there were no other materials than the argillo-calcareous earth covering the bottom of the valley, and the tender, chalky rocks that formed the slopes, together with earth and stones as tender as the chalk.

Different trials made on a small scale showed me, however, that, with care, bricks might be made of the earth from the valley: other trials brought to light, in the gray or chlorite chalk, strata affording hydraulic lime, so that in the course of the years 1826, 1827 and 1828, locks and other works were built with bricks made of the earth of the valley, hydraulic lime from the chalk, and masses of chalk, laid behind the facings of bricks.

Even in a chalky region, where no other materials of construction can be found than chalk, marls, and argillo-calcareous earths, and where, for this reason, the greater number of buildings are of wood, we may, therefore, erect works as solid as elsewhere.

Common cements.—As to *common cements*, I will limit myself to saying that they are the more energetic as they are derived from clays the more refractory: I will say further, that it appears evident to me, the resulting hydraulic pastes and mortars afford more resistance than the analogous mortars composed of hydraulic lime.

Lastly, I will deduce from the second portion of the facts reported by me, that in every locality where limestones, marls, or argillo-calcareous earths are to be found, hydraulic pastes and hydraulic mortars may be obtained at small expense; and that the resistances of one and the other may be caused to vary from 44 lbs. to 759 lbs. for prisms 2 inches long by $1\frac{8}{10}$ inch square.

Such are the observations I have had occasion to make: I know they are very incomplete, and that enough has not been done to show the influence of time on the resistance of pastes and hydraulic mortars: but if the results at which I have arrived are deemed worthy of the attention of constructors, I shall have attained the object, I proposed to myself.

Table No. LVII.

Analyses of several natural combinations of lime and clay, susceptible of giving after burning, hydraulic pastes, either alone or mixed with fat lime.

	Brick earth from Rive-de-gier.	White clay from Rive-de-Gier.	Clay from Bédoreau.	Limestone from Theil.	MARLS				Remarks.
					From Echaur.	From St. Just.	From Aubigny,	From Givors.	
	1	2	3	4	5	6	7	8	
Water	8.00	5.80	12.00	3.00	6.20	6.80	12.20	13.20	These analyses were made at the School of Mines of St. Etienne, by M. Socart, Chemist. I am indebted for them to Messrs Delséries and Clapeyron, Engineers of Mines.
Carbonate of lime		9.20		76.80	53.20	35.40	24.80	23.80	
Carbonate of magnesia		1.60		trace	2.00	1.20	0.00	0.80	
				79.80	61.40	43.40	37.00	37.80	
CLAY { Silex	57.80	60.00	52.00	14.40	22.00	26.00	38.40	39.60	
Alumine	19.60	14.80	28.00	2.80	7.20	15.00	11.60	7.00	
Lime	2.00		3.00	1.20	1.40	2.00	5.40	8.40	
Magnesia	0.00		1.00	0.40	0.00	1.20	0.00	1.60	
Oxide of iron	12.40	8.40	2.00	0.80	7.60	11.60	7.20	4.80	
Totals	99.80	99.80	98.00	99.40	99.20	99.20	99.60	89.60	

Table LVIII.

Analyses of natural combinations of lime and clay—extracted from the work of Gen. Treussart.

	Clays.			Hydraulic Lime.			Lime Cements.			Hydraulic Cements.		
	Pipe clay from Cologne.	From Frankfort.	From Suffenheim.	From Saint Germain.	From Metz.	From Senonches.	Parker's cement, (English.)	Boulogne pebbles.	Cement from Pouilly.	Puzzolana.	Trass.	Calcined Basalt from Haute Loire.
	9	10	11	12	13	14	15	16	17	18	19	20
Water	6.60	16.00	7.80							9.20	9.60	2.00
Lime				83.00	68.30	70.00	55.40	54.00	42.86	8.80	2.60	9.50
Clay — Silex	67.00	50.00	72.40							44.50	57.00	44.50
Alumine	24.00	32.70	11.80							15.00	12.00	16.75
Magnesia	1.20	1.50	2.00							4.70	1.00	
Peroxide of Iron	1.20		4.80							12.00	5.00	20.00
Potassa										1.40	7.00	
Soda										4.00	1.00	2.60
Oxide of Manganese												2.37
(clay)				clay 17.00	clay 31.70	clay 30	clay 44.60	clay 46.00	clay 57.14			
Totals	100.00	100.20	98.80	100.00	100.00	100.00	100.00	100.00	100.00	99.60	99.20	97.72

Table LIX.

Degree of penetration of a stem 0.047 inch in diameter, and ⅔ of a pound av. in weight, falling from a height of 0.787 inch upon prisms of artificial hydraulic paste, immersed for 15 days.

General Classification.	Substances (a) or combinations of the first order.	Substance (a) 10 / Fat lime 0	Combinations of the second order, or artificial hydraulic pastes, formed of a mixture of each substance (a) or combination of the first order, in various proportions with fat lime—the proportion being as follows, viz:								
			9 / 1	8 / 2	7 / 3	6 / 4	5 / 5	4 / 6	3 / 7	2 / 8	1 / 9
		inch	inch	inch	inch	inch	inch	inch	inch	inch	inch
Common cement	{ 10 of burnt clay / 0 of lime }	1.772	0.000	0.000	0.000	0.000	0.039	0.118	0.118	0.118	0.275
	{ 9 of burnt clay / 1 of lime }	0.039	0.000	0.000	0.000	0.078	0.078	0.118	0.078	0.590	0.512
Hydraulic cement	{ 8 of burnt clay / 2 of lime }	0.039	0.039	0.000	0.000	0.078	0.039	0.078	0.472	0.156	0.195
	{ 7 of burnt clay / 3 of lime }	0.039	0.039	0.039	0.078	0.156	0.039	0.078	0.156	0.236	0.275
	{ 6 of burnt clay / 4 of lime }	0.078	0.118	0.078	0.039	0.039	0.078	0.236	0.118	0.551	0.236
	{ 5 of burnt clay / 5 of lime }	0.000	0.000	0.000	0.078	0.078	0.039	0.118	0.118	0.118	0.118
Lime cement	{ 4 of burnt clay / 6 of lime }	0.000	0.639	0.039	0.118	0.118	0.039	0.195	0.195	0.195	0.275
	{ 3 of burnt clay / 7 of lime }	0.000	0.078	0.078	0.118	0.078	0.118	0.236	0.118	0.118	0.118
	{ 2 of burnt clay / 8 of lime }	0.118	0.078	0.156	0.156	0.156	0.236	0.473	0.195	0.275	0.195
Hydraulic lime	{ 1 of burnt clay / 9 of lime }	0.394	0.472	0.195	0.195	0.195	0.787	0.195	0.669	0.787	1.575
Fat lime	{ 0 of burnt clay / 10 of lime }	1.772									

Table LX.

Degree of penetration of a stem 0.047 inch in diameter, and $\frac{2}{3}$ of a pound avoirdupois in weight, falling from a height of 1.575 inch upon prisms of artificial hydraulic paste, immersed for two months.

Combinations of the second order, or artificial hydraulic pastes, formed of a mixture of each substance (a) or combination of the first order, in various proportions with fat lime—the proportions being as follows, viz:

(Column headings give the proportion of Substance (a) to Fat lime, e.g. "10/0" = 10 parts substance (a), 0 parts fat lime. All values in inches.)

General Classification	Substances (a) or combinations of the first order	Substance (a) / Fat lime 10/0	9/1	8/2	7/3	6/4	5/5	4/6	3/7	2/8	1/9
Common cement	10 of burnt clay, 0 of lime	1.772									0.275
Common cement	9 of clay, 1 of lime	0.078	0.000	0.000	0.069	0.039	0.078	0.118	0.118	0.156	0.118
Hydraulic cement	8 of clay, 2 of lime	0.078	0.159	0.000	0.000	0.039	0.039	0.039	0.039	0.078	0.118
Hydraulic cement	7 of clay, 3 of lime	0.039	0.019	0.000	0.000	0.000	0.019	0.019	0.039	0.078	0.275
Hydraulic cement	6 of clay, 4 of lime	0.039	0.039	0.000	0.019	0.019	0.019	0.039	0.078	0.118	0.118
Lime cement	5 of clay, 5 of lime	0.000	0.039	0.039	0.019	0.039	0.059	0.078	0.078	0.118	0.118
Lime cement	4 of clay, 6 of lime	0.000	0.000	0.000	0.019	0.019	0.039	0.039	0.039	0.078	0.078
Lime cement	3 of clay, 7 of lime	0.000	0.039	0.019	0.078	0.078	0.118	0.078	0.078	0.078	0.118
Hydraulic lime	2 of clay, 8 of lime	0.039	0.019	0.195	0.039	0.039	0.059	0.078	0.098	0.118	0.118
Hydraulic lime	1 of clay, 9 of lime	0.118	0.078	0.118	0.118	0.118	0.118	0.156	0.156	0.118	0.118
Fat lime	0 of clay, 10 of lime	1.772	0.156	0.118	0.118	0.236	0.393	0.276	0.315	0.315	0.315

Table LXI.

Weights that broke the prisms of artificial hydraulic paste—immersed for four months.

Combination of the second order, or artificial hydraulic pastes formed of a mixture of each substance (a) or combination of the first order in various proportions with fat lime—the proportions being as follows, viz:

General classification.	Substance (a) or combinations of the first order.	Substance (a) 10 / Fat lime 0	9 / 1	8 / 2	7 / 3	6 / 4	5 / 5	4 / 6	3 / 7	2 / 8	1 / 9
		lbs.	lbs.	lbs.	lbs.	lbs.	lbs.	lbs.	lbs.	lbs.	lbs.
Common cement	10 of burnt clay / 0 of lime	0	209	334	356	290	229	143	139	59	33
	9 of clay / 1 of lime	59	262	297	255	297	218	180	194	121	19
Hydraulic cements	8 of clay / 2 of lime	33	321	249	363	319	275	235	125	154	44
	7 of clay / 3 of lime	194	356	350	257	205	300	119	143	73	55
Lime cements	6 of clay / 4 of lime	152	249	229	255	255	185	141	130	68	53
	5 of clay / 5 of lime	438	235	387	185	180	341	194	132	99	48
	4 of clay / 6 of lime	396	183	275	172	200	119	121	108	99	64
	3 of clay / 7 of lime	194	178	304	156	147	136	77	161	123	79
Hydraulic cements	2 of clay / 8 of lime	139	207	114	134	152	0	81	106	84	53
	1 of clay / 9 of lime	70	75	86	97	51	44	40	33	33	29

Table LXII.

Weights which broke prisms of *mortar* or combinations of the third order—immersed during four months, and composed of the several artificial hydraulic pastes mentioned in the preceding table—mixed with double the volume of sand.

Combinations of the third order, or mortars made by mixing each of the hydraulic pastes of the second order mentioned below—with double its volume of sand NB. The several hydraulic pastes are composed as in the preceding tables, viz.

General classification.	Substances (a) or combinations of the first order.	Substance (a) Fat lime 10/0	9/1	8/2	7/3	6/4	5/5	4/6	3/7	2/8	1/9
		lbs.	lbs.	lbs.	lbs.	lbs.	lbs.	lbs.	lbs.	lbs.	lbs.
Common cement	10 of burnt clay / 0 of lime	0	161	99	183	169	185	132	123	79	75
	9 of clay / 1 of lime	48	147	163	143	183	185	205	114	117	55
Hydraulic cement	8 of clay / 2 of lime	73	128	167	174	161	326	198	134	183	141
	7 of clay / 3 of lime	95	187	147	128	200	123	167	106	119	44
	6 of clay / 4 of lime	75	222	209	198	169	224	158	114	141	55
Lime cement	5 of clay / 5 of lime	185	75	200	209	218	178	154	139	119	70
	4 of clay / 6 of lime	51	350	290	407	277	165	156	187	141	176
	3 of clay / 7 of lime	152	156	213	275	202	249	101	202	172	211
Hydraulic lime	2 of clay / 8 of lime	150	187	145	172	145	191	200	150	134	121
	1 of clay / 9 of lime	143	128	152	167	134	112	106	55	70	73

Table LXIII.

Resistance to rupture of prisms of paste of various natural hydraulic substances.

Nos. in the series.	Nature of the hydraulic paste.	Age of the paste or duration of immersion.	Fat lime and Hydraulic lime.	Hydraulic cement and lime cement.	Weight which caused rupture.
					lbs.
1	Theil lime	4 mo.	1	0	228
2	Pouilly cement	do.	0	1	431
3	Givors' marl alone	2 mo.	0	1	222
4	do. and fat lime	do.	4	6	165
5	St. Just marl, and fat lime	do.	2	8	361
6	do.	do.	3	7	312
7	do.	do.	6	4	167
8	do.	do.	7	3	132
9	do.	do.	8	2	88
10	do.	do.	9	1	77
11	Aubigny marl, alone	4 mo.	0	1	154
12	do. and fat lime	do.	1	9	141
13	do.	do.	2	8	66
14	do.	do.	3	7	44
15	Cement from Bédouan clay and fat lime	do.	2	5	759
16	Prism of burnt earth	do.			194
	Clay cements and a ferruginous cement burnt together and pulverized.				
17	9 of clay and 1 of the minerals	3 mo.	2	5	209
18	8 do. 2 do.	do.	2	5	218
19	7 do. 3 do.	do.	2	5	308
20	6 do. 4 do.	do.	2	5	114
21	5 do. 5 do.	do.	2	5	216
22	4 do. 6 do.	do.	2	5	273
23	3 do. 7 do.	do.	2	5	224
24	2 do. 8 do.	do.	2	5	136
25	1 do. 9 do.	do.	2	5	112

Table LXIV.

Resistance to rupture of prisms of different mortars—made with natural hydraulic pastes.

Nos. in the series.	Nature of the hydraulic paste used in making this mortar,	Age of the mortars or duration of immersion.	Fat limes and Hydraulic lime.	Hydraulic cement and lime cement.	Siliceous Sand from Givors.	Weights that caused the rupture.
	Hydraulic Limes.					lbs.
1	Lime from Chanay near Macon	4 mo.	1	0	2.00	39.6
2	do. Sury (Loire)	do.	1	0	2.00	66.0
3	do. Theil (Ardèche)	do.	1	0	2.00	469.0
4	do.	1 mo.	1	0	1.00	75.0
5	do.	do.	1	0	1·50	81.0
6	do.	do.	1	0	2.00	66.0

Table LXIV.—Continued.

Nos. in the series.	Nature of the hydraulic paste used in making the mortar.	Age of mortar or duration of immersion.	Fat lime and Hydraulic lime.	Hydraulic cement and lime cement.	Silicious sand from Givors.	Weights that caused the rupture.
	Hydraulic limes.					lbs.
7	Lime from Theil (Ardèche)	1 mo.	1	0	2.50	68.2
8	do.	do.	1	0	3.00	66.0
9	do.	do.	1	0	3.50	63.8
10	do.	do.	1	0	4.00	69.4
11	Saint-Leger cement, near Châlons-sur-Saône	4 mo.	0	1	2.00	160.6
12	Pouilly cement	do.	0	1	2.00	297.0
13	Marl from Givors, alone	1 mo.	0	1	2.00	50.6
14	do. and fat lime	do.	1	1	3.00	88.0
15	do.	do.	1	1	1.00	105.6
16	do.	do.	1	1	1.20	101.2
17	do.	do.	1	1	1.40	121.0
18	do.	do.	1	1	1.60	138.6
19	do.	do.	1	1	1.80	107.8
20	do.	do.	1	1	2.00	156.4
21	do.	do.	1	1	2.20	118.8
22	do.	do.	1	1	2.40	134.2
23	Marl from Givors, alone	do.	0	2	1.00	224.4
24	do.	do.	0	3	2.00	94.6
25	do.	do.	0	6	5.00	44.0
26	do.	do.	0	1	3.00	37.4
27	Marl from St. Just, and fat lime	4 mo.	4	6	20.00	143.0
28	do.	do.	5	5	20.00	92.4
29	do.	do.	6	4	20.00	77.0
30	Marl from Aubigny, alone,	do.	0	1	2.00	35.2
31	do. and fat lime	do.	1	9	20.00	70.4
32	do.	do.	2	8	20.00	74.8
33	do.	do.	3	7	20.00	125.4
34	do.	do.	4	6	20.00	173.8
35	do.	do.	5	5	20.00	94.6
36	do.	do.	6	4	20.00	70.4
37	do.	do.	7	3	20.00	101.2
38	do.	do.	8	2	20.00	37.4
39	do.	do.	9	1	20.00	52.8
40	do.	do.	5	5	15.00	121.0
	Lime cements and clay cements mixed with the ferruginous mineral.					
41	9 of clay and 1 of the mineral	do.	4	10	14.00	583.0
42	8 do. 2 do.	do.	4	10	14.00	294.8
43	7 do. 3 do.	do.	4	10	14.00	242.0
44	6 do. 4 do.	do.	4	10	14.00	134.0
45	5 do. 5 do.	do.	4	10	14.00	224.4
46	4 do. 6 do.	do.	4	10	14.00	319.0
47	3 do. 7 do.	do.	4	10	14.00	145.2
48	2 do. 8 do.	do.	4	10	14.00	127.6
49	1 do. 9 do.	do.	4	10	14.00	105.6
50	Fat lime and Bedouan clay	do.	4	10	14.00	732.6
51	Lime and clay from Rive-de-Geir	do.	4	10	14.00	642.4
52	Mortar from a Roman aqueduct	18 cen.				519.2
53	Prism of burnt earth					293.8

Sect. V.—BRIEF OBSERVATIONS ON COMMON MORTARS, HY-
DRAULIC MORTARS, AND CONCRETES,

WITH SOME EXPERIMENTS MADE THEREWITH AT FORT ADAMS, NEWPORT HARBOUR,
R. I. FROM 1825 TO 1838.

BY J. G. TOTTEN,

Lt. Col. of Eng. and Brevet Col. United States Army.

———

CHAPTER XXIII.

*On Lime, Hydraulic Cement, Sand, Mortar making, Strength of Mortars
and Grout.*

During the progress of operations under my direction in the construction
of Fort Adams, in Newport Harbour, Rhode Island, many experiments
were made with mortars exposed in the air; giving, in some cases, results
quite interesting.   The results are too limited in number and restricted in
variety, to justify the deduction of general principles; still they afford some
hints that may be deemed worthy of being followed up.

The following tables contain these results in a very condensed form;
but before giving the tables, it is proper to make some observations on the
materials employed—the manner of using them, and the modes adopted of
trying the relative strengths of the essays.

Lime.—Three kinds of lime were used, namely:

1st. "*Smithfield Lime.*"—From Smithfield, R. I. about fifteen miles from
Providence.   This is a very fat lime—slaking with great violence, when
properly burned, and affording a large bulk of slaked lime.

2d. "*Thomastown Lime.*"—From Thomastown (Maine.)   This is also a
fat lime, at least so far as it has been tried at Fort Adams: but it is probable that some of the many varieties—including those of the neighbouring
towns of Lincolnville, and Camden, may prove to be hydraulic.   The richer
varieties slake promptly, giving a large bulk of slaked lime.

3d. *Fort Adams Lime.*   This is made from a ledge of whitish transition limestone found within the domain of the Fort.   The stone is very
fine grained and compact, exceedingly difficult to break, and crossed in all
directions by three veins of whitish quartz.   The ledge is a bed, or large

nodule, in graywacke-slate. After calcination it yields, by sluggish slaking, a lime decidedly hydraulic. A little of this lime, after being slaked, was made into a cake of stiff hydrate; the excess of water being absorbed by bibulous paper: the cake was placed in the bottom of a tumbler and covered immediately with water. In about $7\frac{1}{2}$ days, a wire $\frac{1}{24}$ of an inch in diameter, loaded to weigh 1 lb., made no impression on this hydrate.

Three modes of slaking the lime were tried in these experiments, namely:

1st. *Slaking by Sprinkling.*—In this mode, water, in quantity sufficient to slake the lime to dry powder, but not enough to afford moist powder, was sprinkled upon the lime. The lime was not made into mortar until it had become cold.

2nd. *Slaking by Drowning.*—In this mode, water enough was given, in the first place, to reduce the lime to a cream of such consistency as to afford mortar of proper "*temper*" for common use without any further addition of water, provided the mortar was made up immediately. If the making the mortar was delayed, a further supply of water became necessary.

3d. *Air-slaking.*—In this mode, lime, reduced to pieces about the size of a walnut, was left in the air to slake spontaneously.

These were the processes by which the lime used in the experiments was slaked: but by neither of these, nor by any modification recommended by others, or that we, ourselves, could devise, were we able to free the hydrate from an infinity of small particles of lime, that being imperfectly, or not at all, slaked in the first instance, it was almost impossible, by any amount of labour afterward, to break down and mix with the rest. The mortar mill, hereafter described, reduced these refractory particles better than any of the ordinary modes of acting upon lime; but not sufficiently, without an unwarrantable amount of labour. All other means having failed, resort was had, at last, for the mortar for the masonry of the Fort, to grinding the dry lime to a very fine powder between millstones. Lime thus ground gives a perfectly homogeneous mortar: and some partial experiments lead to the opinion that the gain in the quantity of lime available for mixtures with sand, will, nearly if not quite, compensate for the expense of grinding. So far as the mortar thus made has been tried, the results were favourable: but the experiments on the quantity and quality of lime thus treated, though they justify confidence, are not, yet, so conclusive as to warrant any positive assertions.

Hydraulic Cement.—Three kinds of hydraulic cement were employed—namely, a kind that will be here designated as *hydraulic cement A*, which was supplied from the State of New York—another kind, called *hydraulic cement B*, supplied from a different manufactory in the same State—and "*Roman (or Parker's) cement,*" imported from England.

The experiments will show a material difference in the respective qualities of these hydraulic cements. According to them, cement A was the best, cement B the next best, and the "Roman cement" the worst; but it must be remarked that the last mentioned had, no doubt, greatly deteriorated, from imbibing moisture during a long voyage, and long keeping in store; while there is reason to suppose that the two first mentioned had been calcined within a few weeks. Between these two, there was also a marked difference; but though the superiority of cement A was probably in part intrinsic, it was, no doubt, in part, to be ascribed to its greater freshness. These cements, therefore, should, in our tables, be compared with themselves under various combinations with other ingredients, rather than with each other.

This is perhaps the best place to mention a very certain and satisfactory mode of testing the hydraulic quality of lime or cement. It is derived from Raucourt's work on mortars.

Of the lime or cement to be tried, a cake of quite stiff hydrate must be made of a size to lie, without touching the sides, in the bottom of a tumbler: any excess of water should be absorbed from the cake by bibulous paper, until it will just support a wire $\frac{1}{12}$ of an inch in diameter loaded to weigh $\frac{1}{4}$ of a pound—this wire should barely make its impression. Noting the hour and minute of the watch, the cake, thus prepared, should be placed in the tumbler, and covered immediately with water. If the specimen be very hydraulic, it will set almost instantly; if not very hydraulic, it may require days, and if but slightly hydraulic, it may require weeks to harden. In order to have some invariable measure of what we call *setting*, we have always used a wire $\frac{1}{24}$ of an inch in diameter, loaded to weigh 1 pound.

With these two simple instruments, and these simple appliances, the comparative hydraulic qualities of limes and cements may be detected infallibly. It may not be strictly accurate to say that those cements which indurate most promptly under water will afford the strongest mortars in the air; although that has, for the greater part, appeared to be the case, in our experiments; still it is highly probable that such cements will be found among the best; it is, at any rate, amongst such that we should look when in search of mortars of superior excellence; and it is undoubtedly true, that when hydraulic qualities exist in lime, although in feeble proportion, the lime is essentially benefited. A simple means of testing hydraulic quality is therefore of value.

Our experience has, however, taught us one important caution in the use of this test; which is, to leave the cement in the water for a day or two, although it may have set in a few minutes. A cement was under trial which, at the expiration of 7 minutes had set so as to bear the small wire with the weight of 1 pound—and at the expiration of 15 minutes, with the weight of 2 pounds. In about two hours, however, it was entirely soft again, having been broken down by the slaking of some free lime that happened to be present, and which had not had time to slake before the hydraulic ingredients had indurated. After about fifteen hours it was taken out of the water, restored to the condition of stiff mortar, and again immersed. It now hardened very slowly, and was six days acquiring the test hardness. Such cements require peculiar treatment. It is evident that there is great hydraulic energy wasted in the first instance of immersion; because the subsequent swelling of the lime, breaks down the indurated mass; and, removing the hydraulic particles beyond the sphere of mutual action, prevents any useful effect from the remaining hydraulic power. The slaking the lime should, therefore, be complete before the cement is immersed. The best mode of slaking this lime has not been ascertained. Perhaps it would be best to sprinkle a little water on cement of this kind, leaving it for a few hours in the state of moist powder—perhaps leaving it exposed to spontaneous slaking for the requisite time—and perhaps throwing on a small quantity of water, in order to slake the lime, and then exposing the cement to heat for a short time, so as to drive off the water absorbed by the hydraulic constituents. This last mode is suggested by the following facts.

Some hydraulic cement A, which had been in a cask more than one year, on first opening the cask, hardened under water in three hours. After two or three days, it required five hours to harden; and after ten days, about nine hours—the cask being kept covered by the head lying loosely upon it. A little of this cement that had been out of the cask for more than a week, on being heated (but not to a red heat) for a few minutes, set under water in three hours. Some of the same cement that had been in the office, enclosed in paper, for about three weeks, required six hours to harden in water, while a little of it, after being kept on a red hot iron plate for about fifteen minutes, hardened in water in 45 minutes.

This power of restoring the energy of deteriorated cements may have many important applications.

Sand.

Several kinds of sand were used in the experiments, namely:

Sand No. 1.—This is the kind habitually used at Fort Adams in stone masonry. It is entirely free from dirt, and the particles, though not very sharp, are angular. Separated mechanically, it was found to consist, in 100 parts, in bulk, of

particles from $\frac{1}{6}$ to $\frac{1}{12}$ of an inch in diameter—about					10.00
do.	$\frac{1}{12}$ to $\frac{1}{24}$	do.	do.	do.	5.00
do.	$\frac{1}{24}$ to $\frac{1}{48}$	do.	do.	do.	48.00
do.	$\frac{1}{48}$ to dust			do.	45.00
do.	dust mostly silicious—no dirt			do.	4.50

100 parts in bulk producing   do. 112.50

Sand No. 2.—Is the above sand freed from particles larger than $\frac{1}{12}$ of an inch.

Sand No. 3.—Is the above sand freed from particles larger than $\frac{1}{48}$ of an inch.

Sand No. 4.—Is sand No. 2, pounded very fine after being freed from dust by washing.

Mortar Making.

With a view to a thorough incorporation of the constituents, at a small expense, and in order, at the same time, to break down the refractory particles of lime before mentioned, a mortar mill was constructed at the commencement of the works at Fort Adams in 1825, which has been in operation ever since.

The mill consists of a very heavy wheel about eight feet in diameter (having a tire one foot broad) moving in a circular trough fifteen inches wide at the bottom—the diameter of the circle being about twenty-one feet. The lime is slaked under the wheel, and ground until, with suitable additions of water, it has become a homogeneous paste sufficiently dilute to make mortar of the ordinary consistency. The requisite quantity of sand is then gradually sprinkled in, as the wheel is in motion. The draught is easy to the horse until near the last; when, for a few minutes, as he is giving the last turns, after all the sand has been thrown in, it is rather heavy.

It was found convenient to use three barrels of lime to each batch of mortar.

The three mortar mills of Fort Adams were competent to supply in one day 3077 cubic feet of mortar, at a total expense of $0.087 per cubic foot, viz.

105 casks of lime, at $1.52 per cask,	$ 159.60
2094 bushels of sand, at $0.04 per bushel,	83.76
Carting sand to mill, $0.12 for 20 bushels,	12.56
3 horses and 3 drivers, at $1.50 per day,	4.50
6 labourers, at $1.00 per day,	6.00
1 cooper at $1.00 per day,	1.00
Other small expenses say	0 58
Total cost of 3077 cubic feet of mortar	$ 268.00

or $0.087 per cubic foot. It appears that the expense of *making* the mortar was $12.08, being about $\frac{1}{3}$ of a cent for a cubic foot.

The proportions in the above mortar are about 1 of lime in paste to $2\frac{1}{3}$ of sand—should the proportion of lime be greater, the mortar will, of course, cost more.

The above statement refers to mortar made without addition of any hydraulic substance. But such mortars are now never used at Fort Adams. Hydraulic cement, or burnt clay, or brick dust, or some other similar matter is added to every kind of mortar made at the work, in proportions varying with the purpose to which the mortar is to be applied. The poorest mortar we make contains 1 barrel of hydraulic cement to 3 barrels of unslaked lime and about 15 barrels of sand; the cement being added before the sand, and while the lime is being reduced under the wheel.

All the mortars used in the experiments in the tables, were made by hand with the trowel, with such exceptions, only, as are noticed.

Trials of the Strength of Mortars.

The strength of mortars as regards tenacity, was determined by measuring the force required to separate bricks that, having been joined by the mortar, had been left, for the desired length of time, in some place safe from frost or accident.

The bricks were joined in pairs, being crossed at right angles thus, so that, supposing each brick to be 4 inches wide, the surface of contact would be 16 square inches. The real surface, or surface of effectual contact, was, in every case, found by actual measurement. The mortar joint separating the bricks was made about $\frac{3}{4}$ of an inch thick: and, in order that this mortar should in all cases be equally consolidated, each pair of bricks was submitted to the pressure of 600 lbs. for 5 minutes, immediately after being joined.

An idea of the mode of separating the bricks may be got from fig. 9, Pl. II, where *a* and *b* represent two strong half-staples fastened to the floor: under these the ends of the lower brick are passed, while the ends of the upper brick are embraced by the piece of iron *c, c,* suspended from the steelyard *d.* The force needed to separate the bricks, is applied by pouring sand, at a uniform rate, into the bucket *e.* The weight of the sand and bucket, the mark on the beam where the weight was applied, and the weight of the *poise,* enable us to ascertain the force necessary to tear the bricks asunder. In the tables, the force required to separate the bricks is reduced to the proportional force required to tear up a surface of one square inch: so that if there were 16 square inches of actual contact, and the force used in separating the bricks was 1000 pounds, the table would represent the tenacity of the mortar by $62\frac{1}{2}$lbs.—equal to $\frac{1000}{16}$.

The hardness of the mortars was determined by ascertaining the weight, applied on a circular plane surface of 0.16 of an inch in diameter, (or .02008 of an inch area,) which the mortar would support. This mode of trial is represented in fig. 10, Pl. II. The circular surface at the extremity *a*, presses upon mortar still adhering to one of the bricks. The arms of the lever *b*, are of equal length, so that the upward force at *c* is equal to the pressure at *a*. The force is applied by means of a steelyard and sand, as in the preceding case.

The experiments were generally made with several pairs of bricks, and a mean was taken of the results; unless it had obviously been subjected to some accident or disturbance, being made to contribute to the mean. Very few results were rejected. There could be only as many trials of *tenacity*, in each particular experiment, as there were pairs of bricks. But for *hardness*, it was often possible to make a considerable number of distinct trials on the same surface of mortar: on the other hand, it would sometimes happen that the surface would be left too ragged and uneven for this trial: and in several instances this test seemed to be entirely inapplicable—the mortar beginning to yield with light weights, and continuing to yield more and more as the weight was increased, the whole effect being a gradual crumbling. In a great majority of cases, however, the effects were sufficiently decided to leave no doubt as to the moment when the power prevailed over the resistance—and sufficiently consistent to afford useful comparisons.

The method, just described, of trying the strength of mortars, was adopted in the Fort Adams experiments, on account of the facility of application. There was, in the first instance, no purpose of extending the experiments beyond what was deemed indispensable to a proper choice, and judicious application of materials. in the construction of a work of some magnitude, then being begun. One series of experiments, however, involved another and another, until the series became extended and the experiments too numerous and valuable, not to make it desirable that subsequent ones should be comparable with them, and, consequently, the same mode of test was continued.

It is probable that the method followed by Genl. Treussart, of making rectangular prisms of mortar, and subjecting them to fracture by weights suspended from the middle, is the best mode. It, at any rate, has the advantage of allowing mortars made in different places, and at distant times to be compared. This mode was adopted in some of the later trials at Fort Adams.

The following table exhibits the mean results of all the experiments made from 1825 to 1832; comprising seven series. The time of exposure of the 1st series was 5 months; of the 2nd. series, 10 months; of the 3rd, 10 months; of the 4th, 5 months; of the 5th, 10 months; of the 6th, 25 months; and of the 7th, 11months. In the 1st series, there were 2 pairs of bricks to each experiment; in the 2nd, 3 pairs; in the 3rd, 3 pairs; in the 4th, 1 pair; in the 5th, 4 pairs; in the 6th, 2 pairs; and in 7th, 3 pairs.

The first column prefixes a number to each kind of mortar, for convenient reference; the 2nd column expresses the nature, or composition of the mortar; the 3rd column, whether the bricks were *wet* or *dry* when joined together; the 4th, the number of series of which the results are a mean as to *tenacity*; the 5th, the *tenacity*, as expressed by the number of pounds required to tear open a joint of one inch square; the 6th, the number of series of which the results are a mean as to *hardness;* and the 7th, the number of pounds required to force into the mortar a circular plane surface of 0.16 of an inch in diameter.

Table No. LXV.

No.	Nature and Composition of the mortar.	Bricks wet or dry.	Tenacity.		Hardness.		Remarks.
			Number of series affording the mean.	Mean tenacity.	Number of series affording the mean.	Mean hardness.	
1	New York Hydraulic cement B, alone	W	1	32.6			
2	do. do. do. A, alone	W	5	56.2	4	1053	
3	Roman cement (Parker's English) alone	W	1	18.5	1	260	
4	do. (do.) alone	D	1	22.6	1	412	
5	Lime alone	W	1	10.5	1	98	
6	Hydraulic cement A in powder 1 / Sand No 3 .50	W	1	61.9	1	1055	
7	Cement A do. 1 / Sand the same 1	W	6	40.3	5	993	
8	Cement A do. 1 / Sand the same 1.50	W	5	33.1	4	918	
9	Cement A do. 1 / Sand the same 1.50	D	2	30.4	1	765	
10	Hydraulic cement A in powder 1 / Sand No. 3 2	W	3	17.5	3	670	
11	Cement A do 1 / Sand the same 3	W	3	19.8	2	367	
12	Cement A do. 1 / Lime slaked to powder .50 / Sand the same 1.50	W	2	29.6	3	573	
13	Cement A do. 1 / Lime the same .50 / Sand No. 2 2	W	4	20.1	3	509	
14	Cement A do. 1 / Lime the same 1 / Sand No. 2. 2	W	4	28.3	3	778	
15	Cement A do. 1 / Lime the same 2 / Sand No. 2 4	W	4	17.1	3	545	
16	Cement A do. 1 / Lime the same 2 / Sand No. 2 6	W	4	16.2	3	267	
17	Cement A do. 1 / Lime in paste, .50 / Sand No. 2 1.50	W	1	44.4	1	765	
18	Cement A 1 / Lime in paste .50 / Sand No. 2 1.50	D	1	54.7	1	915	
19	Cement B do. 1 / Sand No. 3 1	W	2	18.9			
20	Cement B do. 1 / Sand No.2 1.50	W	1	23.4			
21	Cement B do. 1 / Sand No. 2. 2	W	2	14.7			

Table No. LXV—Continued.

No.	Nature and Composition of the mortar.	Bricks wet or dry.	Tenacity. Number of series affording the mean.	Tenacity. Mean tenacity.	Hardness. Number of series affording the mean.	Hardness. Mean hardness.	Remarks.
22	Cement B do. 1 / Lime in powder slaked .50 / Sand No. 2 2	W	2	17.5			
23	Cement B do. 1 / Lime the same 1 / Sand No. 2 2	W	2	19.1			
24	Hydraulic cement B in powder 1 / Lime slaked in powder 2 / Sand No. 2 4	W	2	18.1			
25	Cement B 1 / Lime the same 2 / Sand No. 2 6	W	2	15.0			
26	Roman cement 1 / Sand No. 2 .50	W	1	19.2	1	397	
27	Roman cement 1 / Sand No. 2 1	W	1	16.8	1	309	
28	Roman cement 1 / Sand No. 2 1.50	W	1	13.5	1	286	
29	Roman cement 1 / Lime in paste 0.50 / Sand No. 2 1.50	W	1	26.7	1	471	
30	Roman cement 1 / Lime in paste 0.50 / Sand No. 2 1.50	D	1	29.1	1	787	
31	Lime in powder 1 / Sand No. 3 3.50	W	3	12.3	1	159	
32	Lime in powder 1 / Sand No. 3 6	W	1	5.6	1	107	
33	Lime in paste 1 / Sand No. 3 .50	W	1	14.3	1	208	
34	Lime in paste 1 / Sand No. 3 1.50	W	3	15.4	2	275	
35	Lime in paste 1 / Sand No. 3 3	W	4	12.8	2	146	Made with a hoe.
36	Lime in paste 1 / Sand No. 3 2.50 a 3	W	6	14.3	3	202	Made in mortar mill.
37	Lime in paste 1 / Sand No. 3 2.50 a 3	D	5	14.9	4	254	do. do.
38	Lime in paste 1 / Sand No. 1 2.50 a 3	W	1	13.7	1	217	do. do.
39	Lime in paste 1 / Sand No. 1 2.50 a 3	D	1	16.2	1	200	do. do.
40	Lime in paste 1 / Sand No. 1 2	W	1	33.8	1	242	Lime different.
41	Lime in paste 1 / Sand No. 1 2	D	1	26.6	1	231	

Observations on the Experiments of Table No. LXV.

1st. Generally, within the limits of the experiments, *a mortar made of lime and sand, or of hydraulic cement and sand, or of hydraulic cement, lime and sand—whether it was cement A, or cement B, or Roman cement, was the stronger, as the quantity of sand was the less.* In 24 comparisons, 3 exceptions.

In 13 comparisons of *tenacity*, 2 exceptions.

In 11 comparisons of *hardness*, 1 exception.

2nd. *It appears that with cement A, or cement B, any addition of sand weakens the mortar.* In all the cement experiments, except one, composed of Roman cement 1—sand ½ (No. 26,) the cement alone, was stronger than when mixed with sand in any proportion whatever. Cement A (No. 6,) would seem to be another exception, but it is not; the strength of cement A, alone, as given in No. 2, is the average of five results with different specimens of cement, some of which were of inferior quality; while the result given in No. 6 is of one trial only, and that of a cement proving to be the best used; the particular result of No. 2 which corresponds with No. 6— that is to say, which was afforded by the same specimen of cement, gave for *tenacity* 74.7 lbs. and for *hardness* 1063 lbs., while No. 6 shows a *tenacity* of 61.9 lbs. and a hardness of 1055 lbs.

3rd. *It appears that when cement mortars are not required to be the strongest that can be made—a little lime may be added, without great loss of tenacity, and, of course, with a saving of expense.*

4th. *Mortar made in the mortar-mill was superior to mortar made by being mixed, in the common mode, with the hoe.*

5th. *When the bricks were dry and the mortar more fluid than usual, the mortar was better, both as to* TENACITY *and* HARDNESS—*in five cases out of seven, than when the bricks, being wet, were put together with mortar of common consistence.*

In the next table there is a comparison of the three kinds of lime—of the three modes of slaking, of various proportions of sand—of the effect of wet and of dry bricks on the mortar, &c.

In most cases six pairs of bricks were put together at the same time, and of the same materials; of which three pairs were separated after about 6 months, and the remainder after the lapse of 4 years and 5 months.

Table No. LXVI.

Showing the tenacity and hardness of mortars variously composed after exposure in the air.

No.	Nature and composition of the mortar.	Bricks wet. Tenacity per square inch. After 6 months.	After 4 years and 5 months.	Hardness. After 6 months.	After 4 years and 5 months.	Bricks dry. Tenacity per square inch. After 6 months.	After 4 years and 5 months.	Hardness. After 6 months.	After 4 years and 5 months.	Remarks.
		lbs.	lbs.	lbs.	lt s.	lbs.	lbs.	lbs.	lbs.	
1	Paste of Smithfield lime slaked by DROWNING 1 / Sand No. 2 1	20.4	42.8	119	220					There are two kinds of Fort Adams lime in the table. The first, A, was imperfectly calcined: the second B, was thoroughly burned.
2	Lime the same 1 / Sand No. 2 2	15.2	18.8	130	297					
3	Lime the same 1 / Sand No. 2 3	12.6	16.6	182	232					
4	Lime the same 1 / Sand No. 2 4	13.2	16.4	85	203					
5	Paste of Thomastown lime slaked by DROWNING 1 / Sand No. 2 1	11.3	38.3	216	300		40.3		355	
6	Lime the same 1 / Sand No. 2 2	17.1	38.3	123	273		39.1		310	
7	Paste of Thomastown lime, slaked by DROWNING 1 / Sand No. 2 3	24.7	27.6	265	240		38.0		220	
8	Lime the same 1 / Sand No. 2 4	15.1	21.7	214	210		35.4		203	
9	Paste of Fort Adams lime A slaked by DROWNING 1 / Sand No. 2 1	13.4	21.9	105	273		34.0		186	
10	Lime the same 1 / Sand No. 2 2	9.9	18.8	68	175		22.5		110	
11	Lime the same 1 / Sand No. 2 3	12.6	22.7	75	93		22.8		187	
12	Lime the same 1 / Sand No. 2 4	9.6	11.5	92	93		21.4		102	
13	Paste of Thomastown lime, slaked by SPRINKLING 1 / Sand No. 2 1	26.8	49.1	259	798		40.6		787	
14	Lime the same 1 / Sand No. 2 2	26.4	35.6	225	666		57·3		370?	
15	Lime the same 1 / Sand No. 2 3	26.3	37.0	285	392		26.2		625	
16	Lime the same 1 / Sand No 2 4	25.2	31.0	289	313		38.0		347	
17	Paste of Fort Adams lime B slaked by SPRINKLING 1 / Sand No. 2 1	32.9	47.8	446	900		56.7		620	

No.	Nature and Composition of the mortar.	Bricks wet.				Bricks dry.				Remarks.
		Tenacity per square inch.		Hardness.		Tenacity per square inch.		Hardness.		
		After 6 months.	After 4 years and 5 months.	After 6 months.	After 4 years and 5 months.	After 6 months.	After 4 years and 5 months.	After 6 months.	After 5 years and 5 months.	
		lbs.	lbs.	lbs.	lbs.	lbs.	lbs.	lbs.	lbs.	
18	Lime the same 1 / Sand No. 2 2	33.1	54.5	228	600		52.4		507	
19	Lime the same 1 / Sand No. 2 3	28.9	43.1	221	327		51.8		266	
20	Lime the same 1 / Sand No. 2 4	23.5	30.4	254	258		52.6		233	
21	Paste of Smithfield lime AIR SLAKED 1 / Sand No. 2 1		22.4		126					
22	Lime the same 1 / Sand No. 2 2		9.9		85					
23	Paste of Thomastown lime AIR SLAKED 1 / Sand No. 2 1				37?					Sand 5.00
24	Lime the same 1 / Sand No. 2 2		6.0		20?					
25	Paste of Fort Adams lime B AIR SLAKED 1 / Sand No. 2 1		29.2		664					
26	Lime the same 1 / Sand No. 2 2		21.6		281					Cement 0.33 do. 50
27	Paste of Fort Adams lime B slaked by DROWNING 1 / Brick dust 0.40 / Sand No. 2 1.40	16.3		104						
28	Lime the same 1 / Dust of burnt clay .50 / Sand No. 2 .50	17.5		168						
29	Paste of Thomastown lime slaked by SPRINKLING 1 / Brick dust 2	35.0		360						*Equal, lime 1
30	Paste of Thomastown lime slaked by DROWNING, measured before slaking 1 / Sand No. 2 5	12.2	18.5	102	263		22.5		192	
31	Lime the same* 1 / Cement A .33 / Sand No. 2 5.50	15.4	23.1	165	192		42.6		230	
32	Paste of Fort Adams lime B slaked by DROWNING, measured before slaking 1 / Sand No. 2 5	25.7	48.8	130	650		17.8		652	Sand 5.50 Cement 0.33 Lime 1
33	Lime the same* 1 / Cement A .33 / Sand No. 2 5.50	22.7	46.7	194	849		46.2		303	
34	Cement A in powder 1 / Sand No. 2 1.50	63.3	72.4		1508	467	88.4		1659	

Observations on the experiments of Table No. LXVI.

1st. *Within the limits of the experiments, whatever was the mode of slaking, or the kind of lime, the mortar was the stronger as the quantity of sand was less.*

The lime being measured in paste, the proportions were 1 of lime to 1 of sand; 1 of lime to 2 of sand; 1 to 3, and 1 to 4 of sand.

In all the corresponding trials of the table,

1 lime in paste, to 1 sand, gave the strongest mortar in 35 cases of tenacity, and in 13 cases of hardness.

1 lime in paste, to 2 sand, gave the strongest mortar in 3 cases of tenacity, and in 1 case of hardness.

1 lime in paste, to 3 sand, gave the strongest mortar in 2 cases of tenacity, and in 2 cases of hardness.

1 lime in paste, to 4 sand, gave the strongest mortar in 0 cases of tenacity, and in 1 case of hardness.

2d. *Slaking by* DROWNING, *or using a large quantity of water in the process of slaking, affords weaker mortar than slaking by* SPRINKLING.

In 24 corresponding cases of the table—The quantity and quality of the materials being alike: and there being no other difference than in the modes of slaking the lime.* ,

Lime slaked by SPRINKLING, gave the best mortar in 22 cases of tenacity, and in 24 cases of hardness.

Lime slaked by DROWNING, gave the best mortar in 2 cases of tenacity, and in 0 case of hardness.

The average strength in all the 24 cases in which the lime was slaked by *drowning* was, as to tenacity, 23.79 lbs., and as to hardness, 187.00 lbs.

While the average strength in all the 24 cases in which the lime was slaked by *sprinkling* was, as to tenacity, 38.63 lbs., and as to hardness 417.33 lbs.

The relative tenacity then is as 1 to 1.62; and the relative hardness as 1 to 2.23.

3d. *The experiments with air* SLAKED LIME, *were too few to be decisive—but the results were unfavourable to that mode of slaking.*

Average strength of the mortar made of *air-slaked* lime as to tenacity 20.80 lbs., and as to hardness 202.18 lbs.

Average strength of the corresponding mortars made of lime slaked by *drowning*, as to tenacity 27.10 lbs., and as to hardness 207.50 lbs.

Average strength of the corresponding mortars made of lime slaked by *sprinkling*, as to tenacity 46.70 lbs., and as to hardness 533.83 lbs.

4th. *The mortars were very materially stronger at the end of 4 years and 5 months, than at the end of the first half year.*

Of the 26 mortars which enter into this comparison, the average strength at the end of 6 months was, as to tenacity, 22.54 lbs., and as to hardness 166.33 lbs., and at the end of 4 years and 5 months it was, as to tenacity, 35.45 lbs., and as to hardness 367.37 lbs.

The relative tenacities being as 1 to 1.57, and hardness as 1 to 1.97 lbs.

5th. *Brick dust, or the dust of burnt clay, improves the quality of mortars both as to tenacity and hardness.*

6th. *Hydraulic cement added, even in small quantities, to mortars, improves their quality sensibly.*

* Except in their being two different burnings of Fort Adams lime

7th. *The tenacity of mortars seems to have been increased by using dry bricks, and making the mortar a little more fluid than usual. But the hardness of the mortars was rather the greatest when* WET BRICKS *were used.*

In 21 corresponding instances, *wet bricks* and mortar of common consistency gave the best results, as to tenacity, in 5 instances; and, as to hardness, in 12 instances. *Dry brick* and mortar more fluid, gave the best results as to tenacity in 16 instances; and as to hardness, in 9 instances.

Table No. LXVII.

Trials in December, 1836, of mortars made in December, 1835. The results show the weights in pounds required to break prisms of mortar 2 inches square, 6 inches long and 4 inches in the clear between the supports.

No. of the comparison.	Sand No. 2.	Lime } slaked to powder with 1-3 of its bulk of water, measured in paste.	Cement A, cask No. 1, measured in paste.	Lime from the same barrel. Mortars made with the least possible quantity of water	Mortars made rather thin.	Mortars made with equal parts of water and bitter-water.	Mortars made with bitter-water alone.	Mortars made of cement A, cask No. 2, which required much more time to set under water than cask No. 1.	Mortar made of calcined clay instead of cement A, cask No. 1.	Mortar made of sand No. 4, instead of sand No. 2.	Stone Lime. } Lime slaked with water enough to make a thin paste—and made into mortar after 12 hours.	Shell Lime	Lime from the same barrel. Lime slaked with ¼ its bulk of water, after being kept sealed hermetically in a jar 3 months.	Lime slaked to cream at first, and kept in that state in a keg under ground for 3 months.	Lime allowed to slake spontaneously for 3 months.	Lime slaked to powder with 1-3 its bulk of water and kept dry in a tight keg for 3 months.
1	1		½	497	370	323										
2	1		¾	562	502											
3	1		1	655	525	703	206									
4	1		1¼	782	516											
5	1		1½	707	721	1125	483									
6	1		1¾	783	712											
7	1		2	844	694	984	452									
8	1	1	¼		117			103	115	197						
9	1	⅓	½		351		220									
10	1	1	½		155			164	178	211						
11	1	1	¾		337			173	155	412						
12	1	½	1		469		295									
13	1	1	1		426			178	206	328						
14	1	1	1¼		328			305	187	469						
15	1	1	1½		295		295	267	206	426						
16	1	1	1¾		337			305	206	351						
17	1	1	2					548		511						
18	1	1	3		417		454	455								
19	1	1	4		389		455	520		806						
20	1	1	5		492		548	530		633						
21	1	1	6		576		553	649		862						
22	1	1									206	141	401	286	253	286
23	2	1									155	129	412	225	244	
24	3	1									122	173	356	160	159	244
	4	1									131	89	286	169	150	220

Observations on Table No. LXVII.

It results from this table, and from the tables from which it has been abridged,

1st. *That in mortars of cement and sand (no lime) the strength is generally greater as the quantity of sand is less.* In 33 comparisons, 12 exceptions.

2nd. *That in mortars of sand, cement and lime—the lime remaining the same in quantity, the mortars were stronger as the quantity of sand was less in proportion to the cement.* In 57 comparisons, 10 exceptions.

3rd. *That in mortars of cement, sand and lime—the quantities of cement and sand being the same—the mortars were stronger as the quantities of lime were less.* In 52 comparisons, 15 exceptions.

4th. *That mortars made of cement and sand were materially stronger when the least possible quantity of water was used, than when the mortars were made thin.* In 14 cases, 1 exception.

5th. *That mortars made of cement and sand with the least possible quantity of water, were stronger when kept in a damp place, than when kept in a dry one.* In 7 comparisons, 1 exception. The experiments did not prove this to be true with reference to mortars made thin. These results were afforded by the experiments but are not included in the above table.

6th. *That in mixtures of lime and sand in various proportions, the mortar was generally stronger as the lime was slaked with less water.*

The average strength of several trials with 0.30 of water being represented by 80—with .40 of water, it was 98—with .60 of water, it was 72—with .80 of water, it was 60, and with 1.00 of water, it was 57. These results were afforded by the experiments, though not included in the table.

7th. *That mortars of lime and sand are materially improved by the addition of calcined clay, but not so much as by the addition of cement A.*

8th. *That sand freed from dust by washing and then pounded fine, gives much better mortars, than a sand composed of particles of every size from dust (no dirt) up to grains $\frac{1}{12}$ of an inch diameter.* In 21 comparisons, 2 exceptions.

9th. Many experiments were made to ascertain whether of two cements of the same manufactory, the difference being, probably, only difference of age, that cement which sets the quickest under water will give the strongest mortars in the air after a considerable lapse of time. The results leave the matter in doubt. The quick cement sometimes giving stronger mortars, and sometimes weaker.

10th. Of lime kept for three months after being slaked, before being made into mortar—the lime slaked into powder by sprinkling one-third of its bulk of water, gave the strongest mortar—represented by 250 lbs.; the lime slaked into cream gave the next strongest mortar—represented by 210 lbs., and the lime slake spontaneously during three months, the weakest mortar, represented by 202 lbs. All these mortars being much inferior to that made of the same lime which had been carefully preserved from slaking by being sealed hermetically in a jar—this last mortar being represented by 364 lbs. It must be remarked here that this result is very extraordinary for fat lime and sand; and it is probable this particular barrel of lime was somewhat hydraulic.

11th. Mortars of cement and sand in which bitter-water alone was mixed (Bitter-water being the mother water after the separation of muriate of soda from sea water,) were weaker than those in which water, or a mixture of equal parts of water and bitter-water, was used. But a mixture of equal parts of water and bitter-water gave much better mortar than water alone—the strongest composition we had, being cement $1\frac{1}{2}$, sand 1, and equal parts of water and bitter-water. In 8 comparisons, 2 exceptions.

The trials that afforded the two exceptions were with mortars containing a smaller proportion of cement than the six others. These facts seem to show that the addition of bitter-water, within certain limits, improves the cement, but that beyond these limits it is injurious; and that where the proportions of cement are great, an increased addition of bitter-water may be advantageous. These particular experiments were made in consequence of finding that the addition of a little bitter-water hastened the setting of cement A when immersed.

12th. *Mortars of cement and sand are injured by any addition of lime whatever, within the range of the experiments; that is to say from sand* 1, *lime* ½, *and cement* ½; *to sand* 1, *lime* 1, *and cement* 2. No exceptions in 67 comparisons.

13th. *Stone-lime, in the proportions tried, gives better mortar than shell-lime, as* 153 *to* 133: but some previous trials had afforded results slightly the best with shell-lime.

Table No. LXVIII.

Trials made in June, 1836, *of mortars made in September,* 1835.

The results show the weights, in pounds, required to separate each inch square of surface of bricks joined by mortars. The object is to compare grout with mortar.

No.	Sand No. 2.	Lime slaked to powder and measured in paste.	Cement A.		Mortar.	Grout.
1	2	1		Lime and cement the same.	30.12	17.19
2	2	1	⅛		33.33	17.84
3	2	1	¼		31.35	15.13
4	2	1	½		32.14	25.14
5	2	1	¾		41.06	21.42
6	2	1	1		39.64	34.68
7	2	1		Lime and cement the same.	22.94	23.08
8	2	1	⅛		28.38	14.22
9	2	1	¼		27.07	12.67
10	2	1	½		29.93	16.96
11	2	1	¾		33.79	22.71
12	2	1	1		36.69	19.75

Observations on Table No. LXVIII.

In order to compare the strength of grout with that of mortar, bricks were joined (as before described) with the mortar given in the table—there being four pairs to each kind of mortar. To obtain similar joints of grout, bricks were supported on their ends and edges, in a box large enough to contain all, in such a way as to admit the proper quantity of grout to flow in between each pair. The box was not disturbed until the grout had become quite stiff, when it was first laid on one side, and then taken to pieces. The excess of grout was carefully cleared away from the bricks, which were removed without injury to any of the pairs, and put away by the side of the bricks joined with mortar.

It will be seen that, in every case but one, the grout was much inferior to the mortar. The average strength of all the mortars in the table is 31.78, and the average strength of all the grouts is 20.06

Changes of bulk on slaking lime—making mortar, grout, &c.

A great many measurements were made of the changes of bulk in the operations of slaking lime, making mortars, &c., and the results, as might be expected, varied with the qualities of the lime. The following condensation of the results may be useful.

					trials.	varying from
1 lime and $\frac{1}{4}$ water made, as a mean, 2.25 of powder.					27	1.56 to 2.97
1 do. $\frac{1}{3}$ do.	do.	1.74	do.		4	1.55 to 1.83
1 do. $\frac{1}{2}$ do.	do.	1.81	do.		4	1.63 to 1.95
1 do. 1 do.	do.	2.06	do.		4	1.77 to 2.39
1 do. 2.54 do.	do.	2.68 of thin paste.			3	2.50 to 2.82

Slaked by drowning.

				trials.	varying from
1 do. 1.70 do.	do.	1.98 do.		6	1.73 to 2.36

Slaked by sprinkling.

Lime in powder.	Water.			trials.	varying from
1	0.40 made, as a mean, 0.66 thick paste.			2	0.65 to 0.67
1	0.50 do.	do. 0.76 thinner paste.		19	0.67 to 0.94

1 lime air-slaked gave, as a mean, 1.84 powder   3   1.37 to 2.41

1 of air slaked lime in powder and 0.50 water made, as a mean, 0.75 thin paste, 2 trials varying from .70 to .80.

1 of lime (quick) pounded to powder, made 0.90 of powder, 1 trial.

1 of lime slaked to powder, kept dry for 3 months, still measured 1.00, 1 trial.

Sand.	thin paste.	cement.		mortar.	trials.	varying from.
1	52	00 made, as a mean,		1.17	13	1.06 to 1.21
1	58	0.125	do.	1.25	23	1.70 to 1.50
1	55	0.25	do.	1.37	3	1.29 to 1.54
1	61	0.35	do.	1.43	3	1.38 to 1.57
1	72	0.50	do.	1.60	2	1.50 to 1.70
1	1.00	0.125	do.	1.78	1	
1	1.00	0.25	do.	1.85	1	
1	1.00	0.50	do.	2.18	1	
1	1.10	0.75	do.	2.14	1	
1	1.40	0.25	do.	2.20	1	
1	1.28	1.00	do.	2.36	1	
1	1.00		do.	1·71	1	
1	2.00		do.	2.14	1	

1	50	00	do.	0.32 water, made 1.27 grout.
1	50	0.062	do.	0.45 do. do. 1.50 do.
1	50	0.125	do.	46 do. do. 1.55 do.
1	50	.25	do.	51 do. do. 1.66 do.
1	50	.375	do.	52 do. do. 1.78 do.
1	50	.50	do.	61 do. do. 1.88 do.

202 of mortar with 87 of water made 290 of grout.
213 do. 87 do. do. 305 . do.
430 do. 180 do. do. 604 do,
467 do. 201 do. do. 660 do.
430 do. 180 do. do. 620 do.
495 do. 176 do. do. 664 do.
553 do. 180 do. do. 711 do.

CHAPTER XXIV.

Observations and experiments on Concrete, &c.

It was ascertained, by careful measurement, that the void spaces, in 1 bulk of sand No. 1, taken from the middle of the heap, amounted to 0.33: the cementing paste, whatever it may be, should not be less therefore, than one-third the bulk of this sand. Taking one bulk of cement A, measured in powder from the cask, and a little compacted by striking the sides of the vessel, water was added till the consistence was proper for mortar: 0.35 of water was required to do this, and the bulk of the stiff cement paste was 0.625. To obtain, at this rate, an amount of cement paste equal to the voids (0.33) in the sand, will require, therefore, 0.528 cement in powder, and 0.185 of water, or

Dry sand,　　　　　1.000
Cement in powder,　　.528　} making a bulk of 1.000 of mortar.
Water,　　　　　　　.185

It is by no means certain that a mortar composed on this principle will be the most tenacious that can be made—on the contrary our experiments indicate that the mortar would be stronger with a smaller proportion of sand; but possessing the minimum quantity of cementing constituent, which is by far the most expensive ingredient, it affords the cheapest admissible mortar, made of cement and sand; and as it was probable, that it would shrink very little on drying, it was tried as a *pointing* for exposed joints, and also as *stucco*, and it answered very well for both purposes—becoming very hard, and never showing the slightest crack. An excess of cement, and a very *slight excess of water*, above the stated proportions, should be allowed for imperfect manipulation, because the proportions suppose every void to be accurately filled.

Extending the application of this principle to concrete—experiment showed that one bulk of stone fragments (nearly uniform in size, and weighing about 4 oz. each) contains 0.482 of void space. To convert this bulk of stones into concrete, we, in strictness, need use no more mortar than will fill this void space; and to compose this mortar we need use no more cement than is necessary to occupy, in the state of paste, the voids in 0.482 of sand. This concrete would therefore be composed as follows:

Stone fragments about 4 oz. each,　　　1.000
Sand No. 1　　.　　　　　　　.　　.482　} making a bulk
Cement in powder,　　　.　　　　.255　} of 1.000 of
Water,　　　　.　　　　　　.　.089　} concrete.

Obtaining thus a cubic yard of concrete by the use of one-fourth of a cubic yard of cement in powder, (about one and a half bbls.)

But the above fragments were of nearly equal size, and of a form approaching the spherical: affording more void space than if they had been more angular, and had varied in size from about six oz. to less than one oz. such as would commonly be used. We have found that clean gravel, quite uniform in the size of the pebbles, which were about half an inch in average diameter, afforded voids to the amount of 0.39. And Mr. Mary, a French Engineer, used pebbles, probably mixed of coarse and fine, of which the voids were 0.37. The above allowance of 0.482 for void space is therefore quite large.

In all cases of the composition of concrete, the quantities expressed above, should be ascertained by actual measurement of the particular cement, sand and fragments, or pebbles, that are to be used. No better mode of measuring the void spaces, will be found, probably, than measuring the quantity of water that can be poured into a vessel already filled with stone fragments, pebbles, or sand, as the case may be.

Although the hydraulic property of cement will be the cause, in all cases of its use in concrete, it may happen that the cement at hand is more energetic than is actually necessary, and that the concrete would fully accomplish the object in view, even if it should be two or three weeks in becoming hard and impervious to water. Under such circumstances lime may take the place of part of the cement, with great economy. The lime may be added either in the state of powder that has been slaked some time, or in the state of paste: but in either case, the previous slaking must be complete.

The mortar is to be made first, and then the pebbles, or broken stones, may be mixed therewith by turning them over several times with the shovel.

When it is to be deposited under water, it is still a disputed point whether the concrete, prepared as above, should be used immediately, or be left in heaps to stiffen to such a degree as to require the use of pickaxes to break down the heaps: but, in works out of water, there can hardly be a case in which it will not be best to place it at once in its allotted space, where it should be compacted by ramming till none of the stone fragments project above the common surface. One or two trials will show how much mortar over and above the strict proportion is necessary in each case.

In circumstances where ramming cannot be applied, as when depositing concrete in deep water, the concrete should be more yielding and plastic —containing a larger proportion of mortar, and the mortar should be rammed before being deposited, in order thoroughly to imbed the larger constituents.

In many situations where concrete may be resorted to with great advantage, the economy need not stop at the above proportions. This substance may be rammed between, and upon, stones of considerable size—the only indispensable precaution being, to make sure that the stones are perfectly clean, are well imbeded in the concrete, and are far enough apart to permit the full action of the rammer between them.

The following case occurred at Fort Adams in October, 1836.

The proportions adopted were, *fragments of granite*, of

nearly uniform size, and about 5 oz. each,	1.000	Bulk of
Sand No. 1	0.500	concrete, a
Cement A, in powder,	0.280	little more
Water rather more than	0.100	than 1.000.

Experiment gave 16.683 as the number of cubic feet of concrete made by 1 barrel of cement—187 barrels were consumed which afforded 115.52 cubic yards of concrete. There were also used, 11.29 struck Winchester bushels of sand, and 22.58 struck Winchester bushels of granite fragments.

187 barrels of cement at $2.45			$ 458.15
1129 struck bushels of sand at $0.37			41.77
2258	do.	granite fragments at $0.04	90.32
		Carried over,	$ 590.24

Brought over, $ 590.24

There were 151 days labour, applied to making mortar—making concrete—depositing the concrete in its proper place, ramming it into a compact mass, and doing all other work required in the operation.

151 days at $ 0.92.	138.92
Supervision	10.00

Cost of 115.52 cubic yards, $ 739.16

Cost of one cubic yard $ 6.40

Springs of water flowed over this work continually; and were allowed to cover each day's work. The next morning the concrete was always found hard and perfectly set.

Had we dispensed with one half of the cement used, and used in lieu thereof, as much paste of lime, as the cement dispensed with would have furnished of paste of cement, the cost would have been materially reduced, and the work have been still very hydraulic, and very strong. In that case, the bulk would not have been altered, but would have been as before, 115.52 cubic yards. We should have used 93½ bbls. of cement less than we did: and, as cement, in passing to the state of paste, diminishes in bulk in the proportion of 1 to .625, we should have used $93.5 \times .625$ equal to 58.43 barrels of paste of lime. Saving, thereby, the difference between the cost of 93.5 barrels of cement and 58.43 barrels of paste of lime.

93.5 barrels of cement at $ 2.45	$ 229.07
58.43 do. of paste of lime at $ 0.60	36.06

Amount saved $193.01

$ 739.16, less $ 193.01, equal $ 546.15; the cost of 115.52 cub. yards. Cost of one cubic yard $ 4.73.

Another Instance.

Proportions—Clean gravel,	1.000	
Sand No. 1,	.530	Bulk of concrete about
Cement A, in powder,	.430	1.15
Water about,	.140	

This was rammed into a mould of the capacity of 13.786 cubic feet.

Cement A,	4.35 struck bushels at $ 0.59			cost $ 2.57
Sand No. 1, washed	5.44	do.	"	0.04	.22
Gravel	10.00	do.	"	0.04	.40
Cost of all the labour,					1.03

Total cost of 13.786 cubic feet, $ 4.22

Being $ 0.306 per cubic foot, or $ 8.26 per cubic yard.

This became very hard, and is a very good substitute for stone, in certain applications.

Another Instance.

Proportions—Clean gravel,	1.000	
Sand No. 1,	.625	
Cement A, in powder,	.333	
Water, about	.125	

This was rammed into a mould of the capacity of 7.812 cubic feet; and the whole cost was $ 2.15, being $ 0.276 per cubic foot, or $ 7.45 per cubic yard.

This became a hard mass, but the concrete was rather too incoherent to make the best factitious stone.

Another case.

In this instance, a box containing 7.812 cubic feet was filled, first, with pieces of a stone of slaty structure—laying the pieces on their beds; a grout was then poured in, until all the interstices were filled. The composition of grout was as follows.

Washed sand No. 1,	1.000
Cement A in powder,	1.000
Water,	.910

The whole cost was $2.40—being $0.31 per cubic foot—or $8.37 per cubic yard.

This mass became hard, but was not so strong as those made of mortar instead of grout.

Numerous objects have, at different times, been moulded at Fort Adams, with analogous compositions, and always with success. Sometimes concrete was used, the entire mass being rammed into the mould: at other times the mortar without the fragments was used *as mortar*; bricks, or fragments of stones, being laid therein, in successive strata, until the mould was filled. Shafts of columns—the Doric echinus, abacus, &c., thus formed many years ago, resist the climate well, although less perfect than we should now be able to produce.

All our experiments concur in showing that much sand weakens cement mortar essentially; at least when exposed to the air. The improvement to be applied to the foregoing proportions should consist therefore, if the expense be no objection, in increasing the quantity of cement—taking care to keep the quantity of water as low as possible, in order to retain the shrinkage of the indurated mass at a minimum. It is surprising how much water may be driven out of an incoherent and apparently half-dry heap of cement-mortar, by hard ramming: and it is still more surprising, after the exact quantity necessary to saturation has been supplied, how small a quantity of water will suffice to convert a dry and powdery heap, if well worked, into a thin paste. Cements vary in their capacity for water: hence the dose of water is a matter that must be established by experiment in each case. The true quantity for concrete, and moulded objects in air, is that which, with hard ramming, affords a stiff paste, with a *little* free water on the surface: a state to which it can be brought with difficulty under the trowel or under the shovel. More water than this is attended with the double disadvantage of lessening the density of the mortar when dry, and of causing cracks by the shrinkage. If the quantity of water be thus regulated, the quantity of cement may be increased at pleasure, but the expense will increase rapidly with every addition of cement. In the first concrete above, the bulk of the dry cement is about one half the bulk of the sand, and the expense per cubic yard is $6.40; make the dry cement to equal the sand in bulk, and the expense per cubic yard will be about $10.00, all other proportions remaining, as they ought, the same.

In the preceding proportions it has been supposed that the concrete was to be used in the air, and that nothing would prevent the free use of the rammer. But if the concrete is to be deposited under water beyond the reach of this instrument, there should be a change of the proportions; and the quantity of mortar should be so increased that the fragments will be certain to be severally imbedded therein from their own weight, the gentle operation of the rake and other leveling instruments, and the pressure of the superincumbent concrete. Attention must be paid to the constituents of the mortar, in reference to hydraulic energy, also, especially in running water: this mortar must not only be very hard after a time—it must become hard speedily; and to attain this end, the materials at command may demand proportions quite different from those required to fill the voids in the sand.

The following instances are derived from the practice of the French.

M. Mary, Engineer des Ponts et Chausseés, states that he ascertained the voids between the stones to be .37 of the whole bulk—that filling .90 parts of a box with stones, .10 parts$+(.37\times.90=.33)=.43$ parts of mortar would be required, in theory, to fill the box: but he found that the box was more than full, showing that some of the mortar designed to occupy the voids did not reach them, from imperfect manipulation. Instead of .90 parts, he then filled .87 parts of the box with stones, which required that the mortar should amount to .13$+(.37\times.87=.32)=.45$ parts of mortar; and this he found filled the box very exactly. He also found that the transportation of the concrete, in wheelbarrows, from the mortar bed to the place where it was to be deposited, produced agitation enough to settle all the stones to their places, and bring the excess of mortar to the top. M. Mary is not aware that so large a proportion of stones had been employed any where else than at Pont-de-Remy, at Abbeville, and at the upper dam of Saint Valery; but at these places, no disadvantage resulted from the quantity, and the concrete was impervious to water. The mortar mixed with these stones was composed of 0.22 parts of feebly hydraulic lime measured in paste—0.225 of sand—and 0.225 of brick, or tile, dust ("*cement.*") The proportions of this concrete were therefore, as follows:

Stones,	.87	
Sand,	.225	
Brick, or tile dust,	.225	Total bulk 1.000
Feebly hydraulic lime in paste	.22	
Water,		

Or—	Stones,	1.000	
	Sand,	.259	
	Brick or tile dust,	.259	1.15
	Feebly hydraulic lime in paste,	.253	
	Water,		

At the lock of Haningue the cube of concretes was composed as follows:

Pebbles,	.69	
Sand,	.40	Bulk 1.00
Hydraulic lime in paste,	.22	
Water,		

As to this case M. Mary observes that it is probable the pebbles were a mixture of coarse and fine gravel; because, with these quantities, in order to make up the cube of 1.00, the void spaces could amount to only about .09. This would be about 13 per cent. only of the measure of the pebbles, instead of 37, found by M. Mary, himself, in the case stated above. Expressing, as in the other cases, the proportions used at this lock, in parts of the measure of pebbles—it would stand thus,

Pebbles,	1.00	
Sand,	.58	Bulk 1.45
Hydraulic lime in paste,	.32	

To found the pier of the suspension bridge communicating between la Grève and l'ile de la Cité, at Paris, a concrete was used which was much more hydraulic than those just mentioned. It was thus composed:

Fragments of Buhrstone,	1.00	
Sand,	.50	
Factitious puzzolana of M. St. Leger,	.25	Resulting bulk 1.50
do. hydraulic lime do. (unslaked)	.25	
	2.00	

This concrete was placed in a bed eight feet thick, which, owing to a flood in the Seine, was about six weeks in being deposited. Masonry was begun upon it in eight days after its completion, and in six weeks it had the whole pier to support; and before the concrete was four months and a half old it sustained the weight of the pier of the bridge, and of the proof load, without the least appearance of subsidence.

At the Saint Martin canal, where great quantities of concrete were used, the proportions were:

Pebbles,	1.00	
Sand,	1.00	Bulk 1.63
Hydraulic lime	.33	

In another case, these proportions were used, viz:

Siliceous pebbles,	1.00	
Tile dust and brick dust,	.28	
Fat lime made from chalk used at the moment of slaking—measured as quicklime,	.56	Bulk 1.34
Water, more or less,	.53	

Another case.

Rounded gravel about the size of a hazle-nut,	1.000	Bulk 1.15
Mortar,	0.500	
The mortar being composed of brick-dust,	1.00	
Slaked lime, in powder,	1.00	
Sea-sand,	1.00	

After three months immersion in salt water, this concrete sustained a pressure on one end of the mass of 260,000 pounds per square foot of surface without impression. On being broken up, it showed that the gravel was well imbedded in mortar. The void space in the gravel was found to measure 0.35.

Another.

The aqueduct of Guétin, which conducts the Loire canal across the Allier, is composed of 18 arches of 53½ feet span, and of 17 piers of 9.84 feet in thickness. Immediately at one end of the aqueduct are three connected locks, whereof the mass forms the left buttress of the bridge.

The right buttress and its wing-walls, the 17 piers, and the three connected locks, are built on a general "radier" or platform, 1594 feet long, 57.42 feet wide, and 5.41 feet thick; on the upper and lower sides of the platform are two guard walls 6.56 feet thick, and 14.76 feet deep—these walls, like the rest of the platform, rising to within 1.64 feet of the level of the water in the river in its lowest state.

The whole of the guard walls, as well as the lower layer of the platform for a thickness of 3.28 feet, were formed of concrete deposited in the water. The concrete used amounted to near 22,000 cubic yards.

The operation of depositing the concrete was confined to the 4 or 5 months between the spring and autumn floods; and at the end of the second season it supported the superstructure above described.

The following is the composition of the concrete:

Stone fragments,   1.000 ⎱
Mortar,   1.000 ⎰

     The mortar was composed of sand,   1.50 ⎱
     Hydraulic lime measured in powder,   1.00 ⎰
     Artificial puzzolana of M. St. Leger,   0.50 ⎰

And the puzzolana was formed by calcining, at a heat not great, a mixture of four parts of earthy clay measured in paste, and one part of fat lime measured in the same way—the mixed pastes being formed into small prisms, dried in the sun, calcined and pulverised.

In order to obtain some evidence of the actual strength of concrete, and to compare several varieties of compositions, the experiments contained in the following table were made at Fort Adams: some prefatory remarks are necessary in relation to them.

The *cement* was obtained by taking several casks of hydraulic cement A, of nearly equal energy—emptying them into one heap on the floor, and after mixing the contents intimately, returning the cement into the casks, and heading them all tightly, until they were severally wanted. As the casks were opened, in succession, for use, the quality of the mixture was tried with the test wire, and was found to be very uniform—about half an hour being required for the setting. This cement had been on hand about four months.

The *lime* used was Fort Adams' unground lime. It was slaked to powder by the affusion of one-third its bulk of water, and allowed to stand several days. As it was about to be used, it was reduced to paste and passed through a hand paint-mill, by which it was made very fine. It should be borne in mind that this lime is slightly hydraulic.

The *sand* used was sand No. 1

The larger constituents of the concrete were of four kinds, viz: 1st. *granite fragments*, angular, average weight of each 4 oz.; 2d, *brick fragments*, angular, average weight 4 oz.; 3d. *stone-gravel*, made up of rounded pebbles from ¼ to ¾ of an inch in diameter; and, 4th. *brick gravel*, composed of angular fragments of bricks from ¼ to 1 inch in their greatest dimensions. All were perfectly free from dirt, and were drenched with water before mixing them with the mortar.

The measure of the void spaces in the granite and brick fragments was .48; and of the stone gravel and brick gravel, .39.

One set of experiments was made by using, in each case, a measure of mortar equal to the measure of void space—and another set, by using two such measures of mortar.

The mortar was made with as small a quantity of water as possible. On this account, the mixture of the constituents was probably somewhat imperfect; and to this may, in part, be attributed the irregularities observable in the results. The concrete, before ramming, was quite incoherent, especially when only one measure of mortar was used. It was, in every case, consolidated by ramming into boxes that afforded rectangular prisms of concrete 12 inches by 6 inches by 6 inches.

The prisms were made in December 1836, and being kept in a damp place, safe from frost and accident, were broken in June, July, and August following. In breaking the prisms the two edges of the supports were 9 inches apart, leaving $1\frac{1}{2}$ inch resting at each end: weights were applied, by adding about 60 lbs. at a time, to a scale-pan suspended from a knife edge which bore on the middle of the prism.

Table LXIX.

Trials made in June, July, and August, 1837, of the strength of concretes made in December 1836. The results show the weight in pounds required to break prisms of concrete 12 inches by 6 inches by 6 inches—the distance between the supports being 9 inches.

No.	Composition of the Concrete	Mortar No. 1. (Cement A. 1.00, Sand No. 1. 0, Lime 0)	Mortar No. 2. (Cement A. 1.00, Sand No. 1. .50, Lime 0)	Mortar No. 3. (Cement A. 1.00, Sand No. 1. .50, Lime .25)	Mortar No. 4. (Cement A. 1.00, Sand No. 1. 1.00, Lime 0)	Mortar No. 5. (Cement A. 1.00, Sand No. 1. 1.00, Lime .25)	Mortar No. 6. (Cement A. 1.00, Sand No. 1. 1.50, Lime 0)	Mortar No. 7. (Cement A. 1.00, Sand No. 1. 1.50, Lime .25)	Mortar No. 8. (Cement A. 1.00, Sand No. 1. 2.00, Lime 0)	Mortar No. 9. (Cement A. 1.00, Sand No. 1. 2.00, Lime .25)
1	Granite fragments, with 1 measure of mortar	4973	4142	2778	3989	2721	2045	2056	lost	1574
2	do. with 2 do.	4068	4983	5064	4088	5366	1547	3537	1643	1972
3	Brick fragments, with 1 measure of mortar	3242	2117		4127	3254	1788	2136	1567	3649
4	do. with 2 do.	2805	5047	2826	4232	1178	3655	3856	2320	4803
5	Stone gravel, with 1 measure of mortar	1097	1049	1240	1256	1066				
6	do. with 2 do.	2347	4247	2655	1295	3351				
7	Brick gravel with 1 measure of mortar	5437	6183	3088	lost	4726				
8	do. with 2 do.	6025	5712	5480	3142	2699				
9	Stone fragments, grouted,	3278	1846	2012	1158	1178				
10	Brick fragments, grouted,	1634	2305	2869	2726	2770				

Observations on the experiments given in the above table.

It is to be regretted that such discrepancies are to be noted in the table. They are ascribable, in the first place, as suggested above, to the difficulty of bringing the mixture always to the same condition as regards the dissemination of the ingredients, when worked in so dry a state; but, probably, chiefly to the difficulty of filling the moulds always with equal accuracy, and ramming every part with equal force, when using so incoherent a mortar, united with so large a proportion of very coarse ingredients.

Notwithstanding these discrepancies, however, several deductions may be fairly drawn from the table, which, if confirmed by future trials, will be useful.

1st. *When the mortar was made of cement, sand, and lime, or of cement and sand without lime, the concrete was the stronger as the sand was less in quantity* In 50 comparisons 19 exceptions. *But there may be 0.50 of sand and 0.25 of lime without sensible deterioration; and as much as 1.00 of sand and 0.25 of lime, without great loss of strength.*

2d. *A mortar of cement and sand does not seem to be improved by the addition of lime, while the bulk of sand is only equal to, or is less than, the bulk of cement; but as the quantity of sand is further increased, the mortar appears to be more and more benefitted by the addition of a small quantity of lime.*

3d. *Two measures of mortar, in concrete, are better than one measure; that is to say, a quantity of mortar equal to the bulk of the void space does not give as strong a concrete as twice that quantity of mortar.* In 30 comparisons, 7 exceptions. Nevertheless, the strongest example was with one measure of mortar, and it is not unlikely that the deficiency of strength in the other cases resulted from the difficulty of causing all the voids to be accurately filled, when the mortar was a minimum, and the space into which it was forced so small. It is not improbable that the voids may be perfectly occupied, even with one measure of mortar, when the mass of concrete is large enough to permit the full effect of the rammer.

4th. The results of the experiments recommend the several compositions of the table, in the following order, namely:

1. Brick gravel,   with 2 measures of mortar,   No. 8.
2.   do.   with 1   do.   7.
3. Brick fragments,   with 2   do.   4.
4. Granite fragments, with 2   do.   2.
5.   do.   with 1   do.   1.
6. Brick fragments,   with 1   do.   3.
7. Stone gravel,   with 2   do.   6.
8. Brick fragments, grouted   10.
9. Stone fragments, grouted   9.
10. Stone gravel,   with 1 measure of mortar   5.

5th. *It appears that the best material to mix with mortar to form concrete, is quite small, angular, fragments of bricks: and that the worst is small, rounded, stone-gravel.*

6th. *Grout, poured amongst stone, or brick fragments, gave concretes inferior to all, but one, of those obtained from mortars.*

A piece of sound and strong *red sand-stone*, 12 inches by 4 inches by 4 inches, required a weight of 3673 pounds to break it—there being 9 inches between the supports. According to the formula $P=R.\dfrac{ab^2}{c}$,* prisms of

* In this formula P is the weight causing fracture, c the distance between the supports, a the breadth, and b the depth of the prisms.

this stone of the size of our prisms of concrete, would require the weight of 12,396 lbs. to break them; whence it appears that the strongest prism under trial, was, after eight months exposure, half as strong as this sand stone.

CHAPTER XXV.

Some recent experiments with Mortars made of Lime and Sand.

There will be presented, in conclusion, some experiments, made very recently at Fort Adams, with lime mortars without cement; they were instituted in reference to the best proportions of lime and sand, and also to a comparison of coarse and fine sand, and salt and fresh water.

In making these, a cask of fresh Smithfield lime, of the best quality, was taken, and the lumps broken into pieces of about the size of a pigeon's egg. These being carefully screened, in order to get rid of all dust and fine lime, and carefully intermixed, in order to obtain uniformity of quality throughout, were slaked by the affusion of water to the amount of one third the bulk of lime. When cold, the slaked lime was returned to the barrel, which was carefully headed and put in a dry place; and on all occasions of withdrawing a portion of this lime for use, the cask was carefully re-headed.

The sands used were those described in page 4, as sand No. 1, sand No. 2, sand No. 3, and sand No. 4.

In making the mortars, just enough water was added to the slaked lime taken from the cask, to make a stiff paste. This paste being passed through a hand paint mill, which ground it very fine, was mixed, by careful manipulation, with the due proportions of sand. Much care was bestowed upon the operation of filling the prism-moulds with mortar; and each prism was submitted to a pressure of 600 lbs. for a few minutes, that is to say while the succeeding prism was being formed.

About one week was consumed in preparing the prisms—namely, from the 7th to the 15th of May, 1838. And they were broken on the 1st of July, 1838, making the average duration of the experiment, 50 days.

Three prisms were made of each composition. But, on the principle that there are several causes which tend to make a prism weaker than it should be, and few or none that tend to make it stronger, only the maximum result of each experiment is given in the following table.

It may, however, be well to state that precisely the same inferences are deduceable, if the mean of the results be taken instead of the maximum.

Table No. LXX.

Trials made on the 1st of July, 1838 of the strength of the mortars made between the 7th and 15th of May, 1838 (50 days.) The results show the weights, in pounds, required to break prisms of mortar 6 inches long, by 2 inches by 2 inches: the distance between the supports being 4 inches, and the power acting midway between the supports.

Composition of the mortars.	Sand No. 1.—Lime. Fresh water.	Sand No. 2.—Lime. Fresh water.	Sand No. 3.—Lime. Fresh water.	Sand No. 4.—Lime. Fresh water.	Sand No. 1.—Lime. Salt water.	Sand No. 3.—Lime. Salt water.
Lime in stiff paste 1—Sand 0	262½					
do. 1 do. ¼	224	220½	248½	353½	192½	234½
do. 1 do. ½	213½	234½	234¼	241½	210	199½
do. 1 do. 1	248½	220½	227½	234½	178½	178½
do. 1 do. 2	164½	199½	161	178½	140	178½
do. 1 do. 3	157½	189	185½	157½	119	119
do. 1 do. 4	126	227½?	157½	136½	101½	154

Observations on the experiments of table No. LXX.

1st. Within the limits of the experiments, the mortar was the stronger as the quantity of sand was the less—in 96 comparisons, 12 exceptions.

2nd. Although the above inference is derived from the whole range of the table, still, when the quantity of sand was less than the quantity of lime, the weakening effect of the sand on the mortar was not very sensible. And it would seem from table No. LXV. that from one-fourth to one-half of sand may be slightly beneficial.

3rd. It appears that coarse sand, or, rather, sand composed of coarse and fine particles, (sands No. 1 and 2,) is a little inferior to sand that is all fine (sands No. 3 and 4;) in 36 comparisons, 16 exceptions; and also that sand reduced by pounding to a fine powder (No. 4,) afforded some of the best results of the table. It is to be regretted that no experiments were instituted in order to compare sand all coarse, with sand all fine.

4th. It appears that the mortars made with salt water—that is to say, the water of the ocean, was decidedly weaker than those made with fresh water; 1 exception in 12 comparisons. The aggregate strength of all the prisms made of coarse sand and salt water was 2674 lbs.; while the aggregate strength of the corresponding prisms of coarse sand and fresh water was 3174 lbs. And the aggregate strength of all the prisms of fine sand and salt water was 2800lbs. while the aggregate strength of the corresponding prism of fine sand and fresh water was 3346 lbs.

DESCRIPTION OF THE PLATES.

PLATE I.

Fig. 1. *a, a,* Prism of mortar under trial.

b, b, Iron stirrups, supporting the prism.

c, c, Iron collar, embracing the prism.

d, d, Iron link, to which the ropes of the scale-pan are fastened.

e, e, check, against which the collar rests when on the middle of the prism.

f, f, Timber, to which the stirrups are attached.

g, Scale pan, in which the weights to break the prism are put.

Fig. 2. *h,* Interior of the furnace.

i, Door of the furnace.

k, k, Chimney.

l, Register.

m, m, Arches, under the hearth, in which the fuel is placed.

n, n, Conduits, to lead the flame and a current of air into the furnace.

Fig. 3. *o,* Plan of lime kiln.

p, p, Nut of the kiln.

q, q, Steps descending to the doors of the kiln.

r, Steps, up which the materials are carried to the top of the kiln.

s, s, Doors of the kiln.

t, t, Portions of spherical arches leading to the doors of the kiln.

PLATE II.

Figs. 4, 5, 6, 7 and 8, represent Mr. Petot's *"curves of energy"* of fat lime, hydraulic lime—plaster-cements—calcareous puzzolanas, and clay.

Fig. 9. *a, b,* Half staples, driven into the floor.

f, g, A pair of bricks united by mortar.

c, c, Iron piece, embracing the ends of the upper brick, and suspended from the steelyard.

d, Steelyard.

e, Bucket, into which sand flowed from the trough.

h, Trough.

i, Floor.

Fig. 10. *a, b, c,* Iron lever, with a steel point at *a* to impress the mortar *f,* on the brick *g.*

d, Steelyard, connected with the lever *a, b, c,* at *c.*

e, Iron rod, from which the steelyard is suspended.

h, h, Uprights, supporting the rod *e.*

i, Uprights of iron, supporting the fulcrum of the lever *a, b, c.*

FINIS.

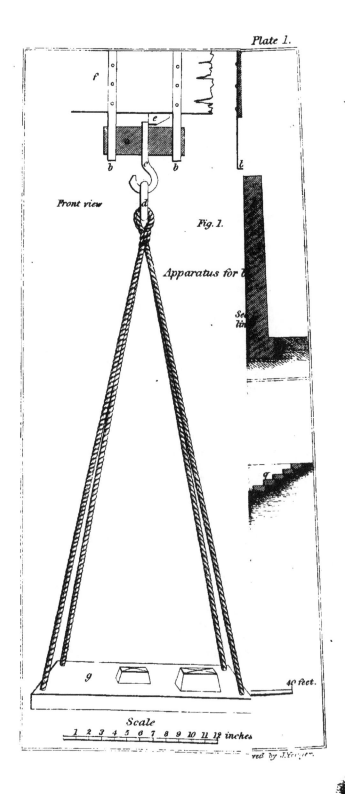

Plate 1.

Front view

Fig. 1.

Apparatus for [...]

Se[...]
lin[...]

40 feet.

Scale
1 2 3 4 5 6 7 8 9 10 11 12 inches

ved by J.Ye[...]

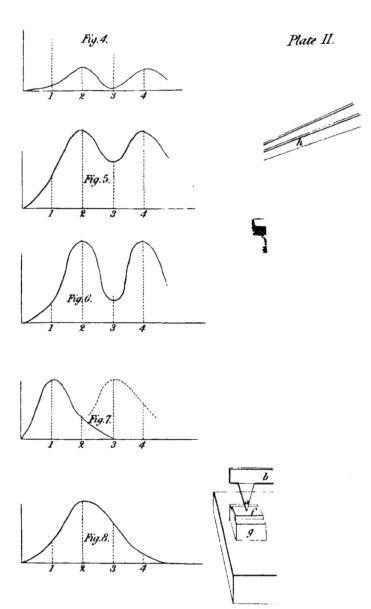

Fig. 4.

Plate II.

Fig. 5.

Fig. 6.

Fig. 7.

Fig. 8.

ERRATA.

PAGE.
160. Line 18 from bottom—for *pieces*, read *piers*.
" Line 17 " do do
161. Line 9 from bottom—for *least*, read *last*.
164. Line 12 from top—substitute for *or*, the words *such as*.
" Line 16 " substitute for *wrong*, the word *advantageous*.
168. Line 7 " for *amelioracion*, read *amelioration*.
" Line 7 " for *work*, read *works*,
177. Line 22 from bottom—for *trass*, read *copper*.
180. Table 48, last line—for *calcined*, read *melted*.
" Line 4 from bottom, and in every other case where the word occurs—for *plastic cements*, read *plaster-cements*.
184. Line 27 from bottom—insert the words *stone of the*, before the word *Pouilly*.
189. Table 51, 3d column—for 54, read 51. 4th column, for 51, read 54.
190. Line 5 from top—for *cases*, read *causes*.
" Table 52, 7 line from top—for *one-half of quartzose sand*, read *one of quartze sand*, and in the last column, for 12.31, read 13.31.
" Line 10 from bottom—for *Biard*, read *Brard*.
198. Line 16 from bottom—for 76.00, read 74.00.
211. Line 9 from top—for *that of 1-5 of clay*, read *as much as 1-5 of clay*.
213. Line 16 from top—for *Rine de Geir*, read *Rive-de-Gile*.
219. Table 57, column 3—for *clay from Bidoreau*, read *clay from Bedouan*.
222. " 60, column 4—for 0.159, read 0.059.
" " 5—for 0.019, read 0.059.
223. Table 61, column last—for 19, read 79.
225. Table 63, No. 17—for *minerals*, read *mineral*.
226. Table 64, No. 10—for 09.4, read 59.4.
" " No. 53—for 293.8, read 239.8.
227. Bottom line—for *three*, read *thin*.
229. Line 16 from bottom—for *instance*, read *instants*.
232. Line 10 from top—insert the words *each result*, before the word *unless*.
233. No. 19—for *Sand, No.* 3, read *Sand, No.* 2.
239. No. 9, 3d column—for ½, read ⅓,
242. Line 25 from bottom—for 1.70, read 1.10.
244. Line 8 from bottom—for 11.29, read 1129.
" " 7 " for 22.58, read 2258.
" " 4 " for $0.37, read $0.037.
247. Line 16 from bottom—for *Haningue* read *Huningue*.

[Philadelphia, February, 1839.

CAREY & HART'S

CATALOGUE

of a

VALUABLE COLLECTION OF BOOKS,

IN THE VARIOUS BRANCHES OF

ARCHITECTURE, ENGINEERING,

AND SCIENCE.

MOST OF WHICH HAVE BEEN

RECENTLY IMPORTED

AND ARE FOR SALE

AT THE CORNER OF FOURTH AND CHESNUT STREETS,

PHILADELPHIA.

ARCHITECTURE, CIVIL ENGINEERING, MECHANICS, &c.

ADCOCK'S
ENGINEER'S POCKET BOOK,
FOR THE YEAR 1839,

Containing ruled pages for daily cash accounts and memoranda; British weights and measures; tables of squares and cubes, and square and cube root; mensuration of surfaces and solids; tables of the areas and circumferences of circles, circular segments and zones; the mechanical powers; animal strength; wind and water mills; steam engines; the strength of railway bars; hydraulics; pneumatics; heat; artificial light; the strength and weight of materials, &c., &c., in pocket book form.

Analytical Essay on the Construction of Machines, translated from the French of Lanz and Betancourt, 4to.

Allason's Picturesque Views of the Antiquities of Pola, in Istria, 1 vol. folio.

Arcana of Science and Art; or an Annual Register of Popular Inventions and Improvements, for 1839, 12mo.

Adye's Pocket Gunner, with notes by Egerton.

BREES, S. C.
RAILWAY PRACTICE,
IN ONE HANDSOME QUARTO VOLUME,
With 80 or 90 Large Folding Plates,

Containing more practical details than are usually found in double the number of engravings *embellished with a brilliant Frontispiece* by Andrew Picken; from an original drawing by the editor, showing the excavation of the North Church Tunnel, in progress of execution, containing a series of Examples, selected from Railways, and other extensive works connected with the science. The whole forming a most useful volume, particularly at this moment, when real working plans, which these may answer for, are necessary in making correct estimates for projected railways, likewise it being a class of art not yet illustrated.

BY S. C. BREES, C. E., &c.

A collection of working plans and practical details of construction in the public works of the most celebrated Engineers, comprising tunnels and tunnel fronts; turnpike road bridges; occupation bridges in embankments and in cuttings; ornamental bridges, with various designs for iron rails and framing; viaducts of several descriptions; retaining walls; culverts; sidings; cuttings and embankments; permanent ways; chairs, blocks, &c.; cuttings in rock, and undersetting; aqueducts; turn-tables; cranes, and railway depots, with sheds, &c. on the several railways, canals, &c. throughout the kingdom.

The arrangement is clear and style familiar; the illustrations are upon a large scale, and in express imitation of the original drawings made for the purpose; the subjects are represented under every variety of local circumstance, and in contrasted modes of construction, accompanied by detailed specifications, accurate descriptions, and appropriate remarks.

A series of original designs for every description of railway works, in various styles of architecture, complete the volume. The whole of the information necessary for this treatise is derived from the only legitimate source—the direct communications of the Engineers to the several works, who have kindly sanctioned and promoted the undertaking.

Barlow, Peter. A Treatise on the Strength of Timber, Cast Iron, Malleable Iron, and other Materials, with rules for application in Architecture, construction of Suspension Bridges, Railways, &c.; with an Appendix on the powers of Locomotive Engines on horizontal planes; and Gradients, 8vo.

Barlow, Peter. Second Report on the London and Birmingham Railway, founded on an inspection of, and Experiments made on, the Liverpool and Manchester Railway. Wood cuts, 8vo.

Barlow, Peter. An Elementary Investigation of the Theory of Numbers, with its application to the Indeterminate and Diophantine Analysis, the Analytical and Geometrical Division of the Circle, and several other curious Algebraical and Arithmetical Problems, 8vo.

Beamish, R. A Treatise on Hydraulics, which will be found of considerable value to the Practical Civil Engineer. Translated from the French of Mon. T. F. D'Aubuisson de Voisins, Ingenieur en Chef au Corps Royal des Mines, &c., &c.

Contents of the Work.—On Running Waters in Canals, Rivers, Conduits, and Jets d'Eau, and which, in the original, occupies 230 pages. The Second Part to exhibit water as a motive power, and to show its applicability to various Machines, 313 pages. The whole compressed in an octavo volume with several plates. A new edition, with additions, by G. Rennie, Esq., C. E., F. R. S.

Buchanan, R. Practical Essays on Mill-work and other Machinery; on the Teeth of Wheels, the Shafts, Gudgeons, and Journals of Machines; the Couplings and Bearings of Shafts; disengaging and re-engaging machinery in Motion; equalising the motions of Mills; changing the velocity of Machines in Motion; the Framing of Mill-work, &c.; with various useful Tables. By Robert Buchanan, Engineer. Revised, with notes and additional articles, containing new Researches on various Mechanical Subjects. By Thomas Tredgold, Civil Engineer. Illustrated by plates and numerous figures. 2 vols. 8vo.

Britton, John. Dictionary of the Architecture and Archæology of the Middle Ages; Including the words used by Old and Modern Authors. By John Britton, F. S. A., &c. 1 large volume royal 8vo., illustrated by 41 Engravings, by J. Le Keux.

Banks, John. Treatise on Mills, 8vo.

Berthollet on the Art of Dyeing, with notes by Andrew Ure, 2 vols. 8vo.

Badnall, N. Treatise on Railway Improvements, explanatory of the chief difficulties and inconveniences which at present attend the general adoption of Railways, and the means by which these objections may be overcome, 8vo.

Bruff, Peter. Treatise on Engineering Field Work, containing Practical Land Surveying for Railways, &c. with the Theory, Principles, and Practice of Levelling, and their application to the purpose of Civil Engineering. Also, every information necessary to be known in the elementary parts of Civil Engineering, with plates, 8vo.

Britton and Pugin's Illustrations of the Public Buildings of London, in 2 vols. 4to, with upwards of 60 plates, beautifully engraved.

Benjamin, Asher. Practice of Architecture, containing the Five Orders, and an additional column and entablature, with all their elements and details explained and illustrated, 4to.

Brown, R. The Rudiments of Drawing Cabinet and Upholstery Furniture; containing ample Instructions for designing and delineating the different articles of those branches perspectively and geometrically. Illustrated with appropriate Diagrams, and Designs, on 25 plates, many of which are coloured; second edition, royal 4to.

Bloxam, M. H. The Principles of Gothic Ecclesiastical Architecture, 12mo.

Bigelow, J. Elements of Technology, 8vo.

British Cyclopedia of the Arts and Sciences, including Treatises on the various branches or Natural and Experimental Philosophy, the Useful and Fine Arts, Mathematics, &c. By C. F. Partington, 2 vols. 8vo. plates.

Bourdon's Algebra, by Professor Farar, 8vo.

Bonnycastle's Algebra, 2 vols. 8vo.

Beauchant's Naval Gunner.

Bridge's Treatise on Mechanics, 8vo.

———

CHAMBERS.
A TREATISE
ON THE
DECORATIVE PART OF CIVIL ARCHITRCTURE,
ILLUSTRATED BY SIXTY-TWO PLATES,
Engraved by Rooker, Grignion, Gladwin, &c.
By SIR WILLIAM CHAMBERS, K.P.S.
Late Surveyor-General of His Majesty's Works, &c.

FIFTH EDITION,

With nine Plates, Illustrative of Grecian Architecture,

To which are added copious Notes, and an ESSAY on the PRINCIPLES of DESIGN in ARCHITECTURE,

BY J. B. PAPWORTH, Architect.

Chevallier, Rev. T. The Study of Mathematics as Conducive to the Development of the Intellectual Powers, 8vo.

Creswell, Dr. Treatise on Geometry con-

taining the first Six Books of Euclid's Elements, methodically arranged, and concisely demonstrated, 8vo.

Curtis, John G. C. Tables for Correcting

Lunar Distances, with rules for finding the errors and rates of Chronometers, 8vo.

Cavelar, Wm. Select Specimens of Gothic Architecture, comprising the most approved examples in England, from the earliest to the latest dates; forming a complete Chronology of that admired style, including plans, sections, elevations and details, 4to.

Cumming, T. G. Description of the Iron Bridges of Suspension erected over the Strait of Menai, &c., &c., with three views. Also, some account of the different Bridges of Sus-

pension in England and Scotland, with calculations of the strength of malleable Iron, founded on experiments, 8vo.

Charnock's History of Marine Architecture, 3 vols. 4to., plates.

Cotman, I. S. Architectural Antiquities of Normandy. Descriptive notices by D. Turner, 2 vols. folio.

Coney, John. Engravings of Ancient Cathedrals, Hotels de Ville and other Public Buildings of celebrity in France, Holland, Germany and Italy, 1 vol. folio.

DIX'S
TREATISE ON LAND SURVEYING,
ILLUSTRATED WITH
NEARLY TWO HUNDRED DIAGRAMS;
SIXTH ED., CORRECTED AND IMPROVED;
By SAMUEL MAYNARD, 8vo.

Davy, Sir H., On the Safety Lamp, 8vo.

Decorations for Parks and Gardens—Designs for Gates, Garden Seats, Alcoves, Temples, Baths, Entrance Gates, Lodge Façades, &c., 55 plates, 8vo.

Dupin's Mathematics, with Additions by Birkbeck.

Douglass, Sir Howard, Treatise on Gunnery, 8vo.

Do. do. On Bridges, 8vo.

EMERSON'S
PRINCIPLES OF MECHANICS:
EXPLAINING AND DEMONSTRATING

The General Laws of Motion, the Laws of Gravity, Motion of Descending Bodies, Projectiles, Mechanic Powers, Pendulums, Centres of Gravity, &c.; Strength and Stress of Timber, Hydrostatics, and Construction of Machines.

BY WILLIAM EMERSON.

To which is now added an Appendix, containing Explanatory Notes, Illustrations, and Observations.

By G. A. SMEATON, CIVIL ENGINEER.

A New Edition, corrected; Illustrated by Eighty-three Copper-plates, and other Figures in wood. Octavo.

Eastman, S. Treatise on Topographical Drawing, 8vo.

Evans, Oliver. Millwright and Miller's Guide. By Oliver Evans. New Edition, with Additions and Corrections, by the Professor of Me-

chanics in the Franklin Institute of Pennsylvania; and a Description of an Improved Merchant Flour Mill. With Engravings. By C. & O. Evans, Engineers.

Euler's Algebra, by Farar, 8vo.

FAIRBAIRN'S TREATISE
ON THE
POLITICAL ECONOMY OF RAIL ROADS.
IN WHICH THE
NEW MODE OF LOCOMOTION

Is considered in its Influence upon the Affairs of the Nation. 1 vol. 8vo.

Francœur's Complete Course of Pure Mathematics, Translated from the last French Edition, by R. Blakelock.

Farar's Astronomy, 8vo.

Fisher's Elements of Natural Philosophy, 8vo.

GORDON'S TREATISE

ON

ELEMENTAL LOCOMOTION AND INTERIOR COMMUNICATION,

Wherein are Explained and Illustrated the History, Practice and Prospects of Steam Carriages, the Comparative Value of Turnpike Roads, Railways, and Canals, with Plates and Appendix, *Third Edition.*

CONTAINING A SUPPLEMENT,

Wherein are given Rules and Tables, and the Description of a Uniform Road—Surveying Instruments for determining the comparative value of different roads. 1 vol. 8vo.

Gregory, O. A Treatise on Mechanics, Theoretical, Practical and Descriptive. Containing the Theory of Statics, Dynamics, Hydrostatics, Hydrodynamics and Pneumatics; with Remarks on the Nature, Construction and Simplification of Machinery; on Friction, Rigidity of Cords, First Movers, &c.; and Descriptions of many curious and useful Machines. With numerous plates. In Three Volumes Octavo.

Gregory's, O., LL.D., Mathematics for Practical Men; being a common-place book of Principles, Theorems, Rules and Tables, in various departments of pure and mixed Mathematics, with their most useful Applications, especially to the pursuits of Surveyors, Architects, Mechanics, and Civil Engineers, 2d edition, 8vo. boards.

Gray on Rail Roads, 8vo.

Guest, R. Compendious History of the Cotton Manufacture; with a Disproval of the Claim of Sir Richard Arkwright to the Invention of its Ingenious Machinery. In Quarto, with Twelve Plates.

Galloway and Hebert's History and Progress of the Steam Engine; with a Practical Investigation of its Structure and Application, containing also minute descriptions of all the various improved boilers; the Constituent Parts of Steam Engines; the Machinery used in Steam Navigation; the New Plans for Steam Carriages, and a variety of Engines for the application of other Motive Powers; with an Experimental Dissertation on the Nature and Properties of Steam and other Elastic Vapours, &c., Illustrated by upwards of 300 Engravings, 1 vol. 8vo.

Garry, James. Treatise on Perspective; designed for the use of Schools; Illustrated by 15 plates, 8vo.

Gwilt, John. Sciography; or, Examples of Shadows, with Rules for the Projection intended for the use of Architectural Draughtsmen and other Artists, 8vo.

Gell's, Sir W., Topography of Rome and its Vicinity. 2 vols. 8vo. with several plates, and a very large Map of Rome and its Environs, (from a most careful trigonometrical Survey,) mounted on cloth, and folded in a case so as to form a separate volume. Uniformly bound in gilt cloth, in 3 vols. 8vo.

Glossary of Terms used in Grecian, Roman, Italian and Gothic Architecture, 2d Edition, with 400 wood cuts, 8vo.

Gwilt, John. Translation of the Architecture of Vitruvius, 4to., plates.

Gregory, G. New and Complete Dictionary of Arts and Sciences, 3 vols. 4to.

HEBERT'S

ENGINEERS' AND MECHANICS' ENCYCLOPÆDIA;

COMPREHENDING

PRACTICAL ILLUSTRATIONS

OF THE

MACHINERY AND PROCESSES

Employed in Every Description of Manufacture of the British Empire,

With nearly 2000 Engravings. By LUKE HEBERT. 2 vols. 8vo.

Hughes. The Practice of Making and Repairing Roads; Of Constructing Footpaths, Fencing, and Drains; Also, a Method of comparing Roads with reference to the Power of Draught required; with Practical Observations, intended to simplify the mode of estimating Earth-work in Cuttings and Embankments, 8vo.

Humfrey. An Essay on the Modern System of Fortification Adopted on the Rhine and Danube, and followed in all the works constructed since the Peace of 1815, in Germany. Illustrated by a copious Memoir on the Fortress of Coblentz, and accompanied by beautiful Plans and Sections of the works of that place. By Lieutenant-Colonel J. H. Humfrey, K.S.F., formerly of the Royal Artillery and Royal Staff Corps, and late Commanding Engineer to the

Corps of Cantabria, author of several Military Works, &c. Long resident in Germany, where he had opportunities of collecting information from the best sources.

Hart, John. A Practical Treatise on the Construction of Oblique Arches. 8vo., New Edition, with several Plates.

Hall, J. W. Crown Glass Cutter and Glaziers' Assistant, 8vo.

Hornby, Thomas. Treatise on the New Method of Land Surveying with an improved plan of keeping the Field Book, 8vo.

Hebert, Luke. Practical Treatise on Rail Roads and Locomotive Engines for the Use of Engineers, Mechanics and others, in which are the Mechanical Construction of Edge, Frame, Suspension and all other Railways, and the various Locomotive Carriages. Illustrated with 250 engravings, 8vo.

Harding, J. D. Elementary Art; or the Use of the Lead Pencil, adapted and explained, folio.

Hutton, Charles. Mathematics, new and greatly improved edition, by Professor Ramsay, 1 vol. 8vo.

Hutton, Charles. Mathematical Tables, containing the common hyperbolic and logistic Logarithms, &c., &c. 7th edition, enlarged and improved by Olinthus Gregory, 8vo.

Hutton, Charles. Tracts on Mathematical and Philosophical Subjects, comprising among the most important articles, the Theory of Bridges, 3 vols., 8vo.

History of the University of Cambridge, its Colleges, Halls and Public Buildings, 2 vols. 4to, splendidly illustrated.

History of the Colleges of Winchester, Eton and Westminster, with the Chapter House, &c. 4to, splendidly colored plates.

History of the Abbey Church of St. Peters, Westminster, its Antiquities and Monuments, 2 vols. 4to, colored plates.

JOPLING'S PRACTICE
OF
ISOMETRICAL PERSPECTIVE.
With Three Plates, and 170 *Figures, 8vo.*

Ibbetson, J. H. Specimens in Eccentric Circular Turning, with Practical Illustrations for Producing Corresponding Pieces of Art, 8vo.

Jonas, P. Theory and Practice of Gauging, a New Edition, by Tate, 8vo.

KATER AND LARDNER'S
TREATISE ON MECHANICS.
BY CAPT. KATER AND THE REV. DIONYSIUS LARDNER.
WITH NUMEROUS ENGRAVINGS. A NEW EDITION.

LOUDON'S ENCYCLOPÆDIA
OF
COTTAGE, FARM AND VILLA ARCHITECTURE.
New Edition, With upwards of Two Thousand Engravings.

Lugar. Plans and Views of Ornamental Domestic Buildings, Executed in the Castellated and Other Styles. By R. Lugar. On 32 Coloured Plates, with Descriptive Letter Press.

Lugar. Villa Architecture: a Collection of Views, with Plans of Buildings, executed by Robert Lugar, Architect. Engraved on 42 Folio Plates, and Elegantly Coloured.

Lugar. The Country Gentleman's Architect; containing a variety of Designs for Farm-Houses and Farm-Yards of different Magnitudes, arranged on the most Approved Principles for Arable, Grazing, Feeding, and Dairy Farms; with Plans and Sections, shewing at large the Construction of Cottages, Barns, Stables, Feeding Houses, Dairies, Brew-House, &c.; with Plans for Stables and Dog-Kennels, and some Designs for Labourers' Cottages and Small

Villas. The Whole adapted for the Use of Country Gentlemen about to build or to alter. Engraved on 22 Plates. By R. Lugar. 4to. A New Edition.

Lecount, Peter. Examination of Professor Barlow's Report on Iron Rails, 8vo.

Lefevre's Architecture, 4to.

Lardner. A Treatise on Hydrostatics and Pneumatics. By the Rev. Dionysius Lardner, LL.D., F. R. S., &c. A new American from the last London Edition, with Notes by Benjamin F. Joplin, M.D., Professor of Natural Philosophy in Union College.

Laing, David. Plans, Elevations and Sections of the Buildings, Public and Private, executed in the Various Parts of England, &c., including the New Custom House of London, 1 vol. folio, 59 plates.

McNEIL.
COMPLETE TREATISE ON BRIDGE BUILDING;
Being a Translation of such portions of Gauthey's, Perronet's, Wiebeking's and other celebrated Works as are deemed most essentially useful.
WITH AN APPENDIX OF VALUABLE MATTER,
AND
ADDITIONAL PLATES ELEGANTLY ENGRAVED ON COPPER,
TAKEN BY THE EXPRESS PERMISSION OF SEVERAL EMINENT
ENGINEERS AND ARCHITECTS FROM THEIR ORIGINAL DRAWINGS.
Edited by JOHN McNEIL, Esq., C.E., F.R.A.S., M.R.I.A., &c.

Embodying in its pages every thing worth knowing respecting this *most important* (particularly at this moment) branch of Science.

Moller's German Gothic Architecture, Translated. With notes and illustrations by W. H. Leeds, 8vo., cloth boards, and lettered.

Moses. A Collection of Antique Vases, Altars, Pateras, Tripods, Candelabra, Sarcophagi, &c.; from various Museums and Collections, engraved in Outline on 170 plates. By H. Moses. With Historical Essays, small 4to.

Matthews, Wm. Hydraulia; an Historical and Descriptive Account of the Water Works of London and the contrivance for supplying other Great Cities in different Ages and Countries, 1 vol. 8vo.

McKernan, H. Treatise on Printing and Dyeing Silks, Shawls, Garments, Bandanas and Piece Goods in the different colours, 8vo.

Mahan, D. H. Elementary Course of Civil Engineering, for the use of the Cadets of the United States Military Academy, 8vo, second edition.

Mifflin, C. W. Methods of Location or Modes of Describing and Adjusting Railway Curves and Tangents, as practised by the Engineers of Pennsylvania.

McAdam, John L. Remarks on the Present System of Road Making, 8vo.

Murphy, John Treatise on the Art of Weaving, illustrated by engravings, with Calculations and Tables for the use of Manufacturers, 8vo.

McNeil, John. On the Resistance of Water to the Passage of Boats upon Canals, and other Bodies of Water, 4to.

Maliphant, Geo. Designs for Sepulchral Monuments, Mural Tablets, &c. 4to.

Millington, John. Elements of Civil Engineering, Theoretical and Practical, in 1 large volume, 8vo., of upwards of 600 pages and 250 illustrative figures.

Microcosm of London, a splendid collection of illustrations of the Interiors of all Public Buildings of London, 3 vols. 4to., plates beautifully colored.

NICHOLSON'S
NEW PRACTICAL BUILDER,
AND
WORKMAN'S COMPANION;
Containing a full Display and Elucidation of the most recent and Skilful Methods pursued by
ARCHITECTS AND ARTIFICERS,
IN THE VARIOUS DEPARTMENTS OF
Carpentry, Joinery, Bricklaying, Masonry, Slating, Plumbing, Plainting, Glazing, Plastering, &c.
INCLUDING, ALSO,

New Treatises on Geometry, Theoretical and Practical, Trigonometry, Conic Sections, Perspective, Shadows, and Elevations; a Summary of the Art of Building; Copious Accounts of Building Materials, Strength of Timber, Cements, &c.; an extensive Glossary of the Technical Terms peculiar to each Department; and the Theory and Practice of the Five Orders, as employed in Decorative Architecture.

The Plates are engraved on Steel, in the neatest style, from the original Designs of the most eminent Architectural Artists. Numerous Schemes and Diagrams are introduced in the Letterpress, in order to illustrate, in the most perspicuous manner, those subjects which require it. The whole is fully completed, including "THE PRACTICAL BUILDER'S PERPETUAL PRICE-BOOK." 3 vols. 4to.

Nicholson, Peter. The Carpenter's New Guide, being a complete Book of Lines for Carpentry and Joinery, treating fully on Practical Geometry, Soffits, Brick and Plaster Groins, Niches of every description, Skylights, Lines for Roofs and Domes, with a great variety of Designs for Roofs, Trussed Girders, Floors, Domes, Bridges, &c., on 84 Copper-plates; including some Observations and Calculations on the Strength of Timber.

Nicholson, Peter. The Five Orders of Architecture; containing a Theoretical and Practical Treatise, with plain and simple Rules for Drawing and executing them in the purest style, with the opinions of Sir WILLIAM CHAMBERS, and other eminent Architects, both ancient and modern: exhibiting the most approved modes of applying each in Practice, with Directions for the Designs and Execution of various kinds of Buildings, both Useful and Ornamental, and suitable to the Climate of Great Britain, including a new and complete Historical Description of Gothic Architecture, showing its origin, and the development of the Byzantine, Saxon, and Norman styles, together with the first, second, and third periods of the Gothic style. Illustrated with specimens, selected from the most celebrated structures now existing, and numerous plans, elevations, sections, and details of various building, executed by Architects of great eminence; to which are added, in order to assist the student in drawing architectural objects with ease and accuracy, Treatises on Projection, Perspective, Fractions, Decimals, Arithmetic, &c., including a copious Index and Glossary of the Terms of Art, &c.

Nicholson, Peter. Practical Carpentry, Joinery and Cabinet-Making; being a new and complete System of Lines, for the Use of Workmen; founded on accurate Geometrical and Mechanical Principles, with 90 Plates, and numerous Diagrams.

Nicholson, Peter. Practical Masonry, Bricklaying, and Plastering, both Plain and Ornamental; containing a new and complete System of Lines for Stone-Cutting, for the use of Workmen; with the Formation of Mortars and Cements; including Practical Treatises on Slating, Plumbing, Painting, Glazing, and Materials used in these Arts, with 60 Plates, and numerous Illustrative Diagrams.

Nicholson, Peter. A Treatise on the Construction of Stair-Cases and Hand-Rails; shewing Plans and Elevations of the various forms of Stairs; methods of projecting the Twist and Scroll of the Hand-Rail; an expeditious method of Squaring the Rails, general methods of describing the Scroll, and forming it out of the solid. Useful also to Smiths in forming Iron Rails, Strops, &c. With a new method of applying the Face Mould to the Plank without bevilling the edge. Illustrated by 39 Engravings. By Peter Nicholson. 4to. bound.

Nicholson, Peter. Principles of Architecture; containing fundamental rules of Art in Geometry, Arithmetic and Mensuration; Geometrical rules for Shadows; also the Five Orders of Architecture, in 3 vols. 8vo.

Nicholson, Peter. Key to Nicholson's Popular Course of Pure and Mixed Mathematics, in which all the questions are worked at full length.

Nicholson, Wm. Introduction to Natural Philosophy, illustrated with plates, 2 vols. 8vo.

Newton, Isaac. Principia Mathematica, new edition, 2 vols. 8vo.

Nicholson, Peter. Architectural Dictionary, containing a correct nomenclature and derivation of the terms employed by Architects, Builders and Workmen; exhibiting, in a perspicuous point of view, the theory and practice of the various branches of Architecture, in Carpentry, Joinery, Masonry, Bricklaying, &c., the whole forming a complete guide to the Science of Architecture and the Art of Building, 2 vols. 4to.

OPTICS.
BY PROFESSOR FARAR.

PAMBOUR.
A PRACTICAL TREATISE
ON
LOCOMOTIVE ENGINES UPON RAILWAYS;

The construction, the mode of acting, and the effect of Engines in conveying heavy loads; the means of ascertaining, on a general inspection of the Machine, the velocity with which it will draw a given load, and the results it will produce under various circumstances and in different localities; the proportions which ought to be adopted in the construction of an Engine, to make it answer any intended purpose; the quantity of fuel and water required, &c.; with Practical Tables, showing at once the results of the Formulæ: *founded upon a great many new experiments* made on a large scale, in a daily practice on the Liverpool and Manchester, and other Railways, with different Engines and trains of Carriages. To which is added, an *Appendix,* showing the expense of conveying Goods by means of Locomotives on Railroads.

By the Chevalier F. M. G. DE PAMBOUR.

Pambour. A New Theory of Steam Engines; being the several papers read at the Institute of France. By Chevallier F. M. G. De Pambour, author of a Practical Treatise on Locomotive Engines, 8vo.

Pasley. A Complete Course of Practical Geometry and Plan Drawing; treated on a principle of peculiar Perspicuity. Adapted either for Classes, or for Self-Instruction. Originally published as the first volume of a Course of Military Instruction. By C. W. Pasley, C.B., Colonel Royal Engineers, F.R.S., &c., &c.

Pasley. Observations on Limes and Calcerous Cements, as applied to the Formation of Mortars, Stuccoes, and Concrete; together with Rules, deduced from numerous experiments, for making an Artificial Water Cement, similar in its properties, and equal in efficiency, to the best Natural English Cements, improperly styled Roman Cements. By Colonel Pasley, Royal Engineers, C.B., F.R.S., &c. &c. 8vo., with numerous wood-cuts.

Partington. A Manual of Natural and Experimental Philosophy; being the substance of a series of Lectures, delivered in the London, Russel, Surrey, and Metropolitan Institutions. By Charles F. Partington, author of an Historical and Descriptive Account of the Steam Engine, Gallery of Science, &c., &c. Illustrated by two hundred and fifty engravings, in 2 vols. 8vo.

Partington. Descriptive Account of the Steam Engine, and on Steam Navigation, third edition, corrected and improved, illustrated with 48 plates, 8vo.

Partington. Complete and Practical Guide to Carpenters, Joiners, Bricklayers, &c., 8vo.

Pugin. Specimens of Gothic Architecture, selected from various Ancient Edifices in England; Consisting of Plans, Elevations, Sections, and Parts at Large, calculated to exemplify the various Styles, and the Practical Construction of this Class of admired Architecture; accompanied by Historical and Descriptive Accounts. Also, a Glossary of Ancient Terms. The subjects selected, measured, and drawn by A.

Pugin, Architect. Illustrated by 114 plates, correctly engraved in outline, with the measurements figured to the parts. In 2 vols. medium Quarto.

This Work exhibits a Series of accurate Specimens of the early Architecture of England, from the Norman Dynasty to the Dissolution of the Monasteries; particularly adapted to aid the Architect and Decorator when employing this Style.

Pugin's Designs for Front Brass Work, 4to.

Parnell, Sir H. A Treatise on Roads; wherein the principles on which Roads should be made are explained and illustrated, by the Plans, Specifications and Contracts made use of by T. Telford, Esq., on the Holyhead Road. By the Rt. Hon. Sir Henry Parnell, Bart. Hon. Mem. Inst. Civ. Engin. &c. Second edition, much enlarged, with nine large plates, two of which are new; cloth.

A work that should not only be in the hands of every person in any way connected with the highways of the kingdom, but also on the shelves of every public library as a standard book.—*Civil Engineer.*

Pain, W. Practical House Carpenter; containing a great variety of useful designs in Carpentry and Architecture, 4to.

Playfair, John. Outlines of Natural Philosophy, 2 vols. 8vo.

Plaw. Rural Improvements; a series of Domestic and Ornamental Designs, suited to Parks, Plantations, Rides, Walks, Rivers, Farms, &c. 4to. numerous plates.

Prout, Samuel. Hints on Light and Shadow, Composition, &c., as applicable to Landscape Painting. Twenty plates, containing eighty-three examples, executed in the present improved method of Two Tincts, by Samuel Prout, Esq., F.S.A., Painter in Water Colours in ordinary to her Majesty. Imperial 4to. cloth lettered.

Peddie's Cotton Manufacturer's Guide, 18mo.

Peddie's Linen Draper and Woollen Manufacturer's Guide.

Powell's Treatise on Optics, 8vo.

ROSS.
A TREATISE ON NAVIGATION BY STEAM;

Comprising a HISTORY OF THE STEAM ENGINE and an ESSAY towards a SYSTEM of the NAVAL TACTICS PECULIAR TO STEAM NAVIGATION.

By SIR JOHN ROSS, R.N., K.S., &c. &c.

In 4to., with Plates.

Richardson. A Popular Treatise on the Warming and Ventilation of Buildings, showing the advantages of the Improved System of Heated Water Circulation, &c., &c., &c. By Charles James Richardson, Architect. In 8vo. illustrated with eighteen large folding plates.

Report on Steam Carriages, by a Select Committee of the House of Commons, 1 vol. 8vo.

Robson. A Treatise on Land Surveying, 8vo.

Renwick, Jas. Elements of Mechanics, 8vo.

Reid, Hugo. The Steam Engine; being a popular description of the Construction and Action of the Engine, with plates, 18mo.

Reports of the British Association for the Advancement of Science, 6 vols. 8vo.

Reid, Thos. Treatise on Clock and Watchmaking, practical and theoretical. By Thomas Reid, Edinburgh Honorary Member of the Worshipful Company of Clock Makers, London. Royal Octavo. Illustrated by numerous plates.

Robinson's Mechanical Philosophy, 4 vols. 8vo.

Riddle's Navigation and Nautical Astronomy, 8vo.

SIMMS.

PUBLIC WORKS OF GREAT BRITAIN;

CONSISTING OF

Railways, Rails, Chairs, Blocks, Cuttings, Embankments, Tunnels, Oblique Arches, Viaducts Bridges, Stations, Locomotive Engines, &c.; Cast-Iron Bridges, Iron and Gas Works, Canals, Lock-gates, Centering, Masonry and Brickwork for Canal Tunnels; Canal Boats, the London and Liverpool Docks, Plans and Dimensions, Dock-gates, Walls, Quays, and their Masonry; Mooring-chains, Plan of the Harbour and Port of London, and other important Engineering Works, with Descriptions and Specifications; the whole rendered of the utmost utility to the Civil Engineer and to the Nobility and Gentry, as monuments of the useful arts in this country and as examples to the Foreign Engineer.

EDITED BY F. W. SIMMS, C. E.

153 Plates, engraved in the best style of art, half-bound, very neat.

This work is on an imperial folio size, the Drawings and Engravings have been executed by eminent Artists, and no expense has been spared in rendering it highly essential to the Civil Engineer and Student; also, as an ornamental volume of Practical Representations of important Engineering Works in several parts of the kingdom. The work is bound in half-morocco.

Stevenson, D. Sketch of the Civil Engineering of North America; comprising Remarks on the Harbours, River and Lake Navigation, Light-houses, Steam-navigation, Water-works, Canals, Roads, Railways, Bridges, and other works in that country. By David Stevenson, Civil Engineer.

CONTENTS.

Chap. I. Harbours.
II. Lake Navigation.
III. River Navigation.
IV. Steam Navigation.
V. Fuel and Materials.
VI. Canals.
VII. Roads.
VIII. Bridges.
IX. Railways.
X. Water Works.
XI. Light Houses.
XII. House Moving, &c.
In one vol. 8vo.

Simms. A Practical Treatise on the Principles and Practice of the Art of Levelling, with Practical Elucidations and Illustrations, and Rules for Making Roads upon the principle of Telford; together with Mr. Macneill's Instrument for the Estimating of Roads, &c.—A work most essential to the Student. With plates, 8vo.

Sopwith. A Treatise on Isometrical Drawing, as applicable to Geological and Mining Plans, Picturesque Delineations of Ornamental Grounds, Perspective Views and Working Plans of Buildings and Machinery, and to the General Purposes of Civil Engineering; with Details of improved Methods of preserving Plans and Records of Subterranean Operations in Mining Districts. With 34 Copper-plate Engravings, By T. Sopwith, M. I. C. E. 8vo.

Smeaton. Reports, Estimates and Treatises on Canals, Rivers, Harbours, Piers, Bridges, Draining, Embanking, Light Houses, Machinery, Fire Engines, Mills, &c., with other Papers, drawn up in the course of his employment, with 74 Plates, engraved by Lowry. By J. Smeaton, Civil Engineer. In one vol. 4to.

Stalkartt. Naval Architecture; or the Rudiments and Rules of Ship Building, exemplified in a Series of Draughts and Plans; with Observations, tending to the further improvement of that important art. Dedicated, by permission, to his Majesty. By Marmaduke Stalkartt. 3d edition. Small Folio, with a large Atlas of Plates.

Stuart & Revett. Antiquities of Athens, and other Monuments of Greece, as Measured and Delineated, by James Stuart and N. Revett. 70 plates, beautifully engraved. Small 4to. Price $4 50.

Smeaton. The Builder's Pocket Manual; containing the Elements of Building, Surveying and Architecture; with practical rules and instructions in Carpentry, Bricklaying, Masonry, &c. Observations on the Properties of Materials, and a Variety of useful Tables and Receipts. With 12 plates. By A. C. Smeaton. Second edition.

Smeaton. The Painter's, Gilder's and Varnisher's Manual; containing Rules and Regulations in every thing relating to the Arts of Painting, Gilding and Varnishing; numerous useful and valuable Receipts; Tests for the detection of Adulterations in Oils, Colours, &c.; and a Statement of the Diseases and Accidents to which Painters, Gilders and Varnishers are peculiarly liable; with the simplest and best Methods of Prevention and Remedy. By A. C. Smeaton. A new edition, corrected, boards.

Simms, F. W. Rules for Making and Repairing Roads, as laid down by the late Thomas Telford, 8vo.

Stuart. R. Dictionary of Architecture; Historical, Descriptive, Topographical, Decorative, Theoretical and Mechanical, 3 vols., 8vo. illustrated by 1000 drawings of subjects referred to in the work.

Stuart's Descriptive History of the Steam Engine, a new edition, 8vo.

Smith, Jas. Panorama of Science and Art; embracing the principal Sciences and Arts, the methods of Working in Wood and Metal, and a miscellaneous selection of useful and interesting processes, 2 vols. 8vo. plates.

Sganzin. Elementary Course of Civil Engineering, translated from the French, 3d edition, 8vo.

Shaw, Edward. Operative Masonry; or, a Theoretical and Practical Treatise of Building, 8vo.

Smith, W. S. A Synopsis of the Origin and Practice of Architecture; to which is added a Dictionary of General Terms, 8vo.

Simpson's Conic Sections, 8vo.

Stuart, R. Historical and Descriptive, Anecdotes of Steam Engines, 2 vols. numerous plates.

Soane, John. The New Law Courts at Westminster, the Board of Trade, and the New Privy Council Office, 1 vol. folio, plates.

Smeaton, John. A Narrative of the Building, and a Description of the Construction, of the Eddystone Light House; to which is added an Appendix, giving an account of the Light House on Spurn Point built upon sand, 1 vol. folio.

TREDGOLD

ON THE

STEAM ENGINE AND ON STEAM NAVIGATION.

These very important and interesting volumes, comprising 125 very elaborate and beautifully engraved Plates, are in Sections, Elevations, Plans, Details, &c., of the highest utility to the Engineer and Student, to Manufacturers of Marine, Locomotive and Land Engines;—the science being elucidated and explained by the most eminent practical men of Britain; in 2 vols. 4to. entitled

The Steam Engine:

Comprising an account of its invention and progressive improvement, with an INVESTIGATION of its PRINCIPLES, and the PROPORTIONS of its PARTS for EFFICIENCY and STRENGTH; detailing also its application to NAVIGATION, MINING, IMPELLING MACHINES, &c., and the Result in numerous Tables for Practical Use, with Notes, Corrections and New Examples relating to Locomotive and other Engines.

Revised and Edited by W. S. B. WOOLHOUSE, Esq., F. R. A. S., &c.

The algebraic parts transformed into easy practical Rules, accompanied by Examples familiarly explained for the Working Engineer, with an ample

APPENDIX ON STEAM NAVIGATION,

Its present and progressive state, by illustrations of the various Examples of Engines constructed for Sea, War and Packet Vessels, and River Boats, by the most eminent Makers of England and Scotland, drawn out in Plans, Elevations, Sections and Details, with a Scientific Account of each, and on

STEAM NAVAL ARCHITECTURE,

Shewing, by existing and the latest examples, the Construction of War, Sea and Packet Vessels; their Naval Architecture, as applied to the Impelling Power of Steam for Sea and River purposes.

Tredgold. Elementary Principles of Carpentry, &c. A Treatise on the Pressure and Equilibrium of Beams and Timber Frames, the Resistance of Timbers, and the Construction of Floors, Roofs, Centres, Bridges, &c.; with Practical Rules and Examples. To which is added, an Essay on the Nature and Properties of Timber; including the Methods of Seasoning, and the Causes and Prevention of Decay; with Descriptions of the Kinds of Wood used in Building: also numerous Tables of Scantlings of Timber for different purposes, the Specific Gravities of Materials, &c. Illustrated by 22 Engravings. By Thomas Tredgold, Civil Engineer.

Tredgold. A Practical Essay on the Strength of Cast Iron and Other Metals; Intended for the Assistance of Engineers, Iron-Masters, Mill-wrights, Architects, Founders, Smiths, and others engaged in the Construction of Machines, Buildings, &c. Containing Practical Rules, Tables, and Examples, founded on a Series of new Experiments; with an extensive Table of the Properties of Materials. Illustrated by 8 plates and several wood-cuts. By Thomas Tredgold, Civil Engineer. Third edition, improved and enlarged. 8vo. boards.

Turnbull. A Treatise on the Strength and Dimensions of Cast Iron Beams. 8vo.

Tredgold. A Practical Treatise on Rail-roads and Carriages, showing the Principles of estimating their Strength, Proportions, Expense and Annual Produce, and the Conditions which render them Effective, Economical, and Durable; with the Theory, Effect, and Expense, of Steam Carriages, Stationary Engines, and Gas Machines. By T. Tredgold, Civil Engineer. With four plates, and numerous tables. 8vo.

Tredgold. Tracts on Hydraulics, edited by Thomas Tredgold, Civil Engineer; comprising Smeaton's Experimental Papers on the Powers of Water and Wind to Turn Mills, &c.; Venturi's Experiments on the Motion of Fluids; Dr. Young's Summary of Practical Hydraulics: with Notes by the Editor. Second edition, just published. Illustrated by seven plates. 8vo.

Tredgold. Principles of Warming and Ventilating Public Buildings, Dwelling-Houses, Manufactories, Hospitals, Hot-Houses, Conservatories, &c.; and of constructing Fire-places, Boilers, Steam Apparatus, Grates, and Drying-Rooms; with Illustrations, experimental scientific and practical; to which are added, Observations of the Nature of Heat, and various Tables useful in the Application of Heat. By Thomas Tredgold, Civil Engineer. Third edition. By T. Bramah, Civil Engineer.

Thomson's Retreats; A Series of Designs, consisting of Plans and Elevations for Cottages, Villas and Ornamental Buildings. By J. Thomson, Architect. In royal 4to., on 41 plates, coloured. The second edition just published.

Taylor's, Brook, Principles of Linear Perspective; or, the Art of Designing upon a plane the Representations of All Sorts of Objects as they would appear to the Eye from a given point. A new edition, with Additions, intended to facilitate the Study of this esteemed Work. By Joseph Jopling, Architect, Author of " *The Practice of Isometrical Perspective*," &c., &c. In 8vo. with plates and diagrams, boards.

Taylor, N. Scientific Memoirs, selected from the Transactions of Foreign Academies of Science and Learned Societies. 8vo.

Tingry, P. F. Varnisher's Guide, 12mo.

Treatise on the Manufactures in Metals, Iron, Steel, Brass, &c., 3 vols. 12mo.

Trigonometry, by Professor Farar, 8vo.

Topography, by Farar, 8vo.

Tingry, P. F. House Painter and Colourman's Guide.

URE'S

DICTIONARY OF

ARTS, MANUFACTURES AND MINES;

Containing a Clear Exposition of their Principles and Practice.

BY ANDREW URE, M.D.

F.R.S. M.G.S. M.A.S. LONDON;

M. ACAD. N.S. PHILADEL.; S. PH. SOC. NORTH. GERM.; HANOV.; MUHL. &c. &c.

Illustrated by upwards of One Thousand Engravings on Wood.

A book much wanted. It contains a mass of information, important to the generality of readers, divested of the difficulties of technicality, and the pedantry which generally confuses and deters the mere common-sense and common-capacity student.—*Times.*

Dr. Ure is so fully possessed of the minutest details of most of the processes which he describes, that there are, we should conceive, even few manufacturers who would not be able to gain some useful information from this well-planned dictionary.—*Courier.*

Ure, A. The Cotton Manufactures of Great Britain Investigated, illustrated by 150 figures, 2 vols. 12mo.

Ure, A. The Philosophy of Manufactures; or, An Exposition of the Scientific, Moral and Commercial Economy of the Factory System. Second edition. 1 vol. 12mo.

Vicat, L. J. A Practical and Scientific Treatise on the Choice and Preparation of the Materials for, and the the Manufacture and Application of, Calcareous Mortars and Cements, Artificial and Natural, supported by an Extensive Series of Original Experiments. By Mr. L. J. Vicat, Chief Engineer of Roads, &c. Translated from the French, with numerous and valuable Additions and Explanatory Notes, comprehending the most important known Facts in this Science, and with additional new Experiments and Remarks. By Captain J. T. Smith, Madras Engineers. In 8vo., with plates.

Vince's Complete System of Astronomy, 3 vols. 4to.

WOOD'S
PRACTICAL TREATISE ON RAIL ROADS,
AND
INTERIOR COMMUNICATION IN GENERAL.

Containing the Performances of Improved Locomotive Engines: with Tables of the Comparative Cost of Conveyance on Canals, Railways and Turnpike Roads.

By NICHOLAS WOOD, COLLIERY VIEWER.

Third Edition, much enlarged, with 13 plates, (several of which are new, and the rest have been re-drawn and re-engraved,) and several new woodcuts, in cloth.

An excellent manual and volume of general reference for Engineers.—*Monthly Chronicle.*

Waistell, Charles. Designs for Agricultural Buildings, including Labourers' Cottages, Farmhouses and Out-offices, conveniently arranged around Fold-yards, and adapted to farms of various sizes and descriptions. To which is prefixed an Essay on the Improvement of the Condition of Cottagers. 4to. with 12 plates.

Walker, Robert. Elements of the Theory of Mechanics, 8vo.

White's Century of Inventions, 4to.

YOUNG'S
SERIES OF DESIGNS,
IN THE PRESENT TASTE,
FOR
SHOP FRONTS, PORTICOES AND ENTRANCES TO BUILDINGS,
Public and Private,
BY J. YOUNG, ARCHITECT.

Engraved on 31 Quarto Plates. This Collection is in the style, and is adapted to advance the Improved Street Architecture of the present day.

Young's Algebra. An Elementary Treatise on Algebra, with Attempts to Simplify some of the more difficult parts of the Science, particularly the Demonstration of the Binomial Theorem in its most general form; the Summation of Infinite Series; the Solution of Equations of the higher order, &c., for the use of students. By J. R. Young, Professor of Mathematics in the Royal College, Belfast. A new American from the last London edition, revised and corrected by a Mathematician of Philadelphia. 1 volume, octavo.

BY THE SAME AUTHOR.

Elements of Geometry.
Elements of Analytical Geometry.
Elements of Mechanics.
Elements of the Integral Calculus.
Elements of the Differential Calculus.
Elements of Plane and Spherical Trigonometry.

2

ARNOT'S
ELEMENTS OF PHYSICS.
Two Volumes, 8vo.

Allan's Manual of Mineralogy, comprehending the most recent Discoveries in the Mineral Kingdom. 8vo.

BAKEWELL'S
INTRODUCTION TO GEOLOGY,

Intended to convey a Practical Knowledge, and comprising the most Important Recent Discoveries, with Explanations of the

FACTS AND PHENOMENA

Which serve to confirm or invalidate various Geological Theories. 8vo. New edition.

Bakewell, J. K. Introduction to the Study of Mineralogy, 12mo.

Brown, Thomas. Conchologist's Text Book, embracing the arrangements of Lamarck and Linnæus, with nineteen engravings, 18mo.

Brown, Thos. Taxidermist's Manual, plates, 18mo.

Brewster, Sir David. Treatise on Magnetism, 12mo.

Brewster, Sir David. Treatise on the Microscope, 12mo.

Brewster, Sir David. Elements of Optics. A new American edition, with Notes and Additions, by A. D. Bache, Professor of Natural Philosophy and Chemistry in the University of Pennsylvania. In one volume, 12mo.

Blumenbach's Natural History, translated by Gore, 8vo.

Boase's Treatise on Primary Geology, 8vo.

Burmeister's Manual of Entomology, translated by Shuckard, 8vo. plates.

Bridgewater Treatises. In seven volumes, octavo.

I.
The Adaptation of External Nature to the Moral and Intellectual Constitution of Man. By the Rev. Thomas Chalmers, Professor of Divinity in the University of Edinburgh.

II.
The Adaptation of External Nature to the Physical Condition of Man. By John Kidd, M. D., F. R. S. Regius Professor of Medicine in the University of Oxford.

III.
Astronomy and General Physics, considered with reference to Natural Theology. By the Rev. Wm. Whewell, M. A., F. R. S., Fellow of Trinity College, Cambridge.

IV.
The Hand; its Mechanism and Vital Endowments as Evincing Design. By Sir Charles Bell, K. H., F. R. S.

V.
Chemistry, Meteorology and the Function of Digestion. By Wm. Prout, M. D., F. R. S.

VI.
The History, Habits and Instincts of Animals. By the Rev. Wm. Kirby, M. A. F. R. S. Illustrated by numerous Engravings on Copper.

VII.
Animal and Vegetable Physiology, Considered with Reference to Natural Theology. By Peter Mark Roget, M. D. Illustrated with nearly Five Hundred Wood Cuts.

VIII.
Geology and Mineralogy, Considered with Reference to Natural Theology. By the Rev. Wm. Buckland, D. D., Canon of Christ Church, and Reader in Geology and Mineralogy in the University of Oxford; being the last of the Bridgewater Treatises on the Power, Wisdom and Goodness of God, as Manifested in the Creation; with Eighty-nine Copperplates and Maps. The whole bound in handsome embossed cloth, or neatly half bound with calf backs and corners —Any one of the Treatises can be had separately.

Barton, W. P. C. A Flora of North America, with 108 Coloured Plates, by W. P. C. Barton, M. D. In 3 volumes, Quarto.

Bonaparte, C. L. American Ornithology; or Natural History of Birds inhabiting the United States, by Charles Lucien Bonaparte. Designed as a Continuation of Wilson's Ornithology. 4 vols. large 4to. Coloured Plates.

Brande's Chemistry, 8vo.

Berzelius's Traité de Chimie, 8 vols. 8vo.

BUIST'S FLOWER GARDEN DIRECTORY, a new edition, entirely rewritten, greatly enlarged and improved, 8vo.

Bigelow's Medical Botany, 3 vols. 8vo.

Bigelow's Plants of Boston and its Vicinity, 8vo.

COMBE'S
PHRENOLOGY.

8vo., with Plates.

Combe, Geo. On the Constitution of Man, 12mo.

Do. Moral Rhilosophy.

Do. Philosophy of Digestion and Dietetics.

Do. Mental Derangement.

Complete Grazier, or Farmer and Cattle Breeders' and Dealers' Assistant, 8vo.

Comstock, J. L. Botany, being a Treatise on Vegetable Physiology, 12mo.

Do. Outlines of Physiology, Comparative and Human, 12mo.

Do. Mineralogy, 12mo.

Do. Chemistry, 12mo.

Conversation on Mineralogy, with plates, 2 vols. 12mo.

Combe, A. The Principles of Physiology applied to the Preservation of Health and to the Improvement of Physical and Mental Education, with 12 Illustrative Wood-cuts.

Catechism of Phrenology, 12mo.

Chaptal's Agricultural Chemistry.

Crouch's Introduction to Lamarck's Conchology, 4to. fine plates, coloured.

Do. do. do. do. 4to. fine plates, plain.

Cyclopædia of Practical Medicine, comprising Treatises on the Nature and Treatment of Diseases, Materia Medica and Therapeutics, Medical Jurisprudence, &c. Edited by

John Forbes, M.D.

Alexander Tweedie, M. D. and

John Connolly, M. D.

In 4 large Volumes, 8vo.

Cuvier's Animal Kingdom, Translated from the French by McMurtrie, 4 vols. 8vo. plates.

Cuvier's Revolutions on the Surface of the Globe, 12mo.

Conversations on Geology, 12mo.

Carus's Comparative Anatomy, 2 vols. 8vo. and a 4to. Atlas of Plates.

DAVY'S ELEMENTS
OF
AGRICULTURAL CHEMISTRY.

Sixth Edition, 8vo.

Davy, Sir. H. Elements of Chemical Philosophy, 8vo.

Drury's Illustrations of Foreign Entomology, wherein are exhibited upwards of 600 Exotic Insects, of the East and West Indies, China, New Holland, North and South America, Germany, &c., very few of which are figured in any other work. Engraved with the greatest accuracy by the celebrated Moses Harris, Author of the Aurelian, &c. All most correctly and beautifully coloured from the original specimens. New and much improved edition, with the following important additions—the Modern Names; Generic and Specific Characters; Synonymes of later Naturalists; Accounts of the Economy, Habitations and Food of many of the Insects; and Scientific and Alphabetic Indexes; by J. O. Westwood, Esq. F.L.S., 3 vols. 4to.

Dillwyn's Descriptive Catalogue of Shells, English and Foreign, arranged according to the Linnæan System, with the Synonymes of all preceding Authors, descriptive of the Size, Colours, Places where fonnd, &c., &c. 2 vols. 8vo.

Daniel's Meteorological Essays, 8vo.

Dandolo, Count. Art ot Rearing Silk Worms, 12mo.

Dana, J. W. System of Mineralogy, including an extended Treatise on Crystallography, with an Appendix, containing the application of Mathematics to Crystallographic Investigation, &c. 8vo.

Dubois. Epitome of Lamarck's Conchology, 12mo.

Dixon, R. W. Practical Agriculture; or, a Complete System of Modern Husbandry; with the best Methods of Planting and the Improved Management of Live Stock, illustrated with numerous Engravings, 2 vols. 4to.

De la Beche. A Geological Manual. By Henry T. de la Beche, Esq. F.R.S., F.G.S., Member of the Geological Society of France, &c. In One Volume, Octavo. With 104 Wood-cuts.

De la Beche. How to Observe—Geology. 1 vol. 12mo.

De Candolle, Aug. Pyr. Icones Selectæ Plantarum, Quas in Systemate Universali ex herbarii Parisiensibu, Præsertim ex Lessertiano.

ELECTRICITY AND MAGNETISM.

BY
PROFESSOR FARRAR.
OCTAVO.

Eaton, Amos. Manual of Botany for North America, containing generic and specific descriptions of the Indigenous Plants and common cultivated Exotics growing north of the Gulf of Mexico, 12mo. seventh edition.

FLEMING'S
MOLLUSCOUS ANIMALS;
INCLUDING SHELL FISH.

Containing an Exposition of the Structure, Systematical Arrangement, Physical Distribution, and Dietetical Uses, with a Reference to the Extinct Races. 12mo.

Flora Domestica, or the Portable Flower Garden, with directions for the Treatment of Plants, 8vo.

Forster's Pocket Encyclopædia, 12mo.
Fyfe's Manual of Chemistry, 12mo.
Farraday's Chemical Manipulations, 8vo.

GRAY'S
CHEMISTRY OF THE ARTS;
ON THE BASIS OF GRAY'S OPERATIVE CHEMIST.
Being an Exhibition of the Arts and Manufactures dependent on Chemical Principles.
With Numerous Engravings.

By Arthur L. Porter, M. D., late Professor of Chemistry, &c., in the University of Vermont.

Gray's Natural Arrangement of British Plants, 2 vols. 8vo.

Gall, F. J. On the Origin and Moral Qualities and Intellectual Faculties of Man, and the Conditions of their Manifestation, translated by Winslow Lewis, 6 volumes, 12mo.

Gardens and Menageries of the Zoological Society, delineated in 2 volumes, with numerous beautifully executed Wood-cuts.

KAPE'S
CLEOPTERIST'S MANUAL.
Containing the Lamellicon Insects of Linnæus and Fabricius. 8vo.

Dr. Hooker's Enlarged Edition of the Flora Londinensis, originally published by Curtis, revised and improved by George Graves, extended and continued by Dr. W. Jackson Hooker; comprising the History of Plants indigenous to Great Britain, their Uses, Economy, and various interesting Particulars, with Alphabetical Linnæan and other Indexes. The Drawings made by Sydenham, Edwards and Lindley. 5 vols. royal folio, containing 647 Plates. Exhibiting the full natural size of each Plant, with magnified Dissections of the parts of Fructification, &c. All beautifully coloured.

Huber, N. P. Natural History of Ants, 12mo.

Hayward on the Science of Agriculture, 8vo.

History and Description of Fossil Fuel, the Collieries and Coal Trade of Great Britain, 8vo.

Hoare, C. The Cultivation of the Grape Vine on Open Walls. By Clement Hoare. 8vo. new Edition, with Additions, cloth.

Herschel. Preliminary Discourse on the Objects, Advantages and Pleasures of the Study of Natural Philosophy. By J. T. W. Herschell, A. M., late Fellow of St. John's College, Cambridge.

Herschell. Treatise on Astronomy, with Plates. By Sir John F. W. Herschell, F. R. S., &c. In 1 vol. 12mo. with numerous Questions for Schools.

Haydon's Geological Essays, 8vo.
Humboldt's Essay on Rocks, 8vo.
Hare, Dr. R. Chemistry, 1 vol. 8vo.

JAMESON'S MINERALOGY;

ACCORDING TO THE NATURAL HISTORY SYSTEM; 12mo.

Jenyns, L. Manual of British Vertebrate Animals; containing Descriptions and Measurements of all the British Animals belonging to the Classes Mammalia, Aves, Reptilia, Amphibia and Pisces. By the Rev. Leonard Jenyns, M. A., F. L. S. &c. 8vo.

Jones, Silas. Practical Phrenology, 12mo.

KYAN

ON THE ELEMENTS OF
LIGHT AND THEIR IDENTITY.

With those of Matter radiant and fixed. 8vo.

Kirby and Spence. Introduction to Entomology; or, Elements of the Natural History of Insects. By W. Kirby, M. A., F. R. S., L. S., and William Spence, Esq., F. L. S. 5th edition, 4 thick volumes, 8vo. Plates and Portraits, boards.

LOUDON'S
ENCYCLOPÆDIA OF PLANTS;

Comprising the Description, Specific Character, Culture, History, Application in the Arts, and every other desirable Particular, respecting all the Plants Indigenous to, Cultivated in, or Introduced into Britain.

With nearly 10,000 Engravings on Wood. Second edition, corrected.

One large vol. 8vo. boards.

The most useful and popular botanical work that has ever appeared in the English language.—*Jameson's Philosophical Journal.*

Loudon, J. C. Hortus Britannicus; a Catalogue of all the Plants Indigenous to, Cultivated in, or Introduced into Britain. Part 1.—The Linnæan Arrangement, in which nearly 30,000 Species are enumerated, &c.; preceded by an Introduction to the Linnæan System. Part 2.—The Jussieuean Arrangement of nearly 4000 Genera; with an Introduction to the Natural History System, and a Description of each order. 8vo. cloth.

Loudon, J. C. An Encyclopædia of Gardening; comprising the Theory and Practice of Horticulture, Floriculture, Arboriculture, and Landscape Gardening; including all the latest Improvements; a General History of Gardening in all Countries; and a Statistical View of its Present State; with Suggestions for its Future Progress in the British Isles. New edition, greatly enlarged and improved; with nearly 1,000 Engravings on Wood. 1 vol. 8vo.

Loudon, J. C. Encyclopædia of Agriculture; comprising the Theory and Practice of the Valuation, Transfer, Laying out, Improvement, and Management of Landed Property; and the Cultivation and Economy of the Animal and Vegetable Productions of Agriculture; including the latest Improvements; a General History of Agriculture in all Countries; and a Statistical View of its Present State; with Suggestions for its future Progress in the British Isles. One large vol. 8vo. With nearly 1,300 Engravings on Wood. 3d edition.

Loudon, J. C. Arboretum et Fruticetum Britannicum; or, the Trees and Shrubs of Great Britain, Native and Foreign, Pictorially and Botanically delineated, and Scientifically and Popularly described; with their Propagation, Culture, Management and Uses in the Arts, in Useful and Ornamental Plantations, and in Landscape Gardening. Preceded by a Historical and Geographical Outline of the Trees and Shrubs of Temperate Climates throughout the World. 8 thick volumes, 8vo. (four of Letterpress and four of Plates,) consisting of above 3000 Pages of Letterpress, above 400 Octavo Plates of Trees, and upwards of 2500 Woodcuts of Trees and Shrubs.

It contains such a mass of information on the subject of trees as was never before collected together, and as must render it indispensable to every country gentleman and landed proprietor.—*Times.*

Loudon, J. C. Encyclopædia of Cottage, Farm and Villa Architecture and Furniture. By J. C. Loudon, F. L. S., &c. New edition, 1 large vol. 8vo. with above 1000 pages of Letterpress, and illustrated with upwards of 2000 Engravings.

Loudon, J. C. The Suburban Gardener and Villa Companion; adapted for Grounds from one perch to fifty acres and upwards in extent, and intended for the instruction of those who know little of gardening and rural affairs. By J. C. Loudon, F. L. S., H. S., &c. 1 vol. 8vo. cloth lettered.

The whole work contains so much sound good sense combined with the results of long experience, that it will be invaluable to every one who wishes to enjoy all the comforts of which a suburban residence is susceptible, with a due regard to economy, and it should be carefully perused by every person who resides in a house having a garden.—*Times.*

Lindley, J. Introduction to Botany, 2d edition, with Corrections and considerable Additions. One large vol. 8vo. with numerous Plates und Woodcuts, cloth.

The most valuable and perfect in any language we are acquainted with.—*Medical Gazette.*

Lindley, J. A Natural System of Botany; or, a Systematic View of the Organisation, Natural Affinities, and Geographical Distribution of the whole Vegetable Kingdom; together with the Uses of the most important Species in Medicine, the Arts, &c. 2d edition, with numerous Additions and Corrections, 1 vol. 8vo. cloth.

Lindley, J. Synopsis of the British Flora, Arranged according to the Natural Orders. 2d edition, with numerous Additions, Corrections and Improvements. 12mo. boards.

Lindley, J. Flora Medica; or, a Botanical Account of all the most remarkable Plants applied to Medical Practice in Great Britain and other Countries. 1 vol. 8vo. cloth, lettered.

Eminently useful.—*Medical Gazette.*

Low, David. Elements of Practical Agriculture; comprehending the Cultivation of Plants, the Husbandry of Domestic Animals, and the Economy of the Farm. 1 vol. 8vo. 2d edition, with Alterations and Additions, and above 200 Wood-cuts, cloth, lettered.

No work on agriculture has appeared in our time which will bear a comparison with this excellent, and, we would say, classical work, of Professor Low. It will become the manual of practical agriculture for the British Empire; and the judicious views and sound rules of our author will unquestionably prove beneficial to the agriculturists of other countries.—*Jameson's Edin. Philosophical Journal.*

Lithead's Electricity: its Nature, Operation and Importance in the Phenomena of the Universe. 18mo.

Leslie, Sir John. Natural and Chemical Philosophy. 2 small vols. 8vo.

Leithart on Mineral Veins: with the Application of several new Theoretical Principles of the Art of Mining. 8vo.

Lyell, Charles. Geology, 2 vols. 8vo.

La Place's System of the World, translated by Harte. 2 vols. 8vo.

Legendre's Geometry, by Farrar. 8vo.

MANTELL'S
WONDERS OF GEOLOGY. 2 vols. 12mo.

Mantell, Gideon. Fossils of the South Downs; or, Illustrations of the Geology of Sussex, in 4to. with 42 Illustrations.

Mammatt, E. Collection of Geological Facts and Practical Observations; intended to elucidate the Formation of the Ashby Coal Field; being the result of 40 years' experience and research. Illustrated by a Map and 102 Coloured Plates of Vegetable Fossils. 4to.

M'Intoch, Charles. The Practical Gardener and Modern Horticulturist, in which the most approved Methods are laid down for the Management of the Kitchen, Fruit and Flower Garden, the Greenhouse, Hothouse, Conservatory, &c., for every Month in the Year, including the New Method of Heating Forcing-houses with Hot Water, forming a complete System of Modern Practice in the various Branches of Horticultural Science. Coloured Plates of Fruits and Flowers, with Designs for Hot-houses, Green-houses, Conservatories, Hot-beds, &c. By Charles M'Intoch, C.M.C.H.S.

Mitscherlick, E. Practical and Experimental Chemistry, adapted to Arts and Manufactures, translated by Dr. Hamich. 8vo.

Macnish, Robert. Introduction to Phrenology. 12mo.

Maw. Descriptive Catalogue of Minerals. 8vo.

Murphy, P. Meteorology, considered in its Connection with Astronomy, Climate, and the Geographical Distribution of Animals and Plants, equally as with the Seasons and Changes of the Weather. 8vo.

Michaux, F. A. Sylva of North America; or, a Description of the Forest Trees of the United States, Canada and Nova Scotia, illustrated by 156 beautifully Coloured Plates. 2 vols. 8vo.

Mackenzie, Colin. One Thousand Experiments in Chemistry. 8vo.

Mitchell, Thos. D. Elements of Chemical Philosophy on the Basis of Reid, comprising the Rudiments of that Science, and the requisite Experimental Illustrations; with Plates and Diagrams. 8vo.

NEILL.

THE FRUIT, FLOWER, AND KITCHEN GARDEN.

12mo.

Nuttall, Thos. Introduction to Systematic and Physiological Botany. 12mo. 2d edit.

Nuttall, Thos. Ornithology. Land and Water Birds. 2 vols. 12mo.

Nichol, J. P. The Phenomena and Order of the Solar System, by J. P. Nichol, LL. D., F. R .S. E., Professor of Practical Astronomy in the University of Glasgow. Second edition, 8vo. with twenty-three Illustrative Plates, and many Cuts.

Nichol, J. P. Views of the Architecture of the Heavens. By Professor Nichol.

Naturalist's Library, conducted by Sir W. Jardine, with numerous coloured plates, descriptions, wood-cuts, and Lives of celebrated Naturalists, now publishing in monthly volumes, foolscap, 8vo. 20 volumes now ready, with numerous beautiful coloured plates.

PURSH.

FLORA AMERICÆ SEPTENTRIONALIS;

Or, a Systematic Arrangement of the Plants of North America.

2 volumes, 8vo.

Parkinson, James. Fossil Organic Remains, in 3 vols. 4to. with plates.

Parkinson, James. Introduction to the Study of Fossil Organic Remains, 1 vol. 8vo.

Philips, John. Treatise on Geology, 12mo.

Prince's Treatise on the Vine. 8vo.

Prince's Pomological Manual. 8vo.

Philips's Mineralogy, new edition, with numerous diagrams by Allen, 8vo.

Perry, Geo. Conchology, or the Natural History of Shells, containing a new arrangement of the genera and species, illustrated by 60 folio plates, coloured, each containing numerous specimens.

Pinkerton's Petralogy, a Treatise on Rocks. 2 vols. 8vo.

ROGET.

TWO TREATISES ON
PHYSIOLOGY AND PHRENOLOGY.

2 volumes, small 8vo.

Rydge, John. The Veterinary Surgeon's Manual, a complete guide to the cure of all diseases incident to horses, cattle, sheep and dogs.

SPURZHEIM'S
PHRENOLOGY.

2 volumes, 8vo. Plates.

Spurzheim's Phrenology, in connection with the Study of Physiognomy, with 35 plates. 8vo.

Spurzheim on Insanity. Plates. 8vo.

Spurzheim's Anatomy of the Brain, with a General View of the Nervous System. 8vo.

Spurzheim's View of the Elementary Principles of Education. 12mo.

Spurzheim's Answer to Gordon & Cheneire. 12mo.

Spurzheim's Natural Law of Man. 12mo.

Spurzheim's Outlines of Phrenology. 12mo.

Shepherd's Mineralogy. 12mo.

Strutt's Sylva Britannica. 8vo.

Silliman's Journal of Science and Art, complete, from commencement to present time.

Seale, R. F. Geognosy of the Island of St. Helena, illustrated in a series of Views, Plans, and Sections.

THOMSON'S

CHEMISTRY OF ORGANIC BODIES, VEGETABLES. 8vo.

Thomson's Chemistry of Inorganic Bodies. 2 vols. 8vo.

Thomson's Outline of Mineralogy, Geology, and Mineral Analysis. 2 vols. 8vo.

Thomson's Outlines of the Science of Heat and Electricity. 8vo.

Thenard's Essay on Chemical Analysis. 8vo.

URE'S DICTIONARY OF
CHEMISTRY AND MINERALOGY;
WITH THEIR APPLICATIONS.

Fourth Edition, with numerous Improvemets. 8vo. Plates.

———

WOOD'S CATALOGUE OF SHELLS;

Second Edition, with numerous Specimens Coloured after Nature. 8vo.

Woodward's Synoptical Table of British Organic Remains. 8vo,

Witham. H. T. M. Internal Structure of Fossil Vegetables found in the carboniferous and solitic deposits of Great Britain, described and illustrated. 4to.

Wyatt, Thos. Manual of Conchology, according to the system laid down by Lamarck, with the late improvements by Blainville. 8vo. with numerous colored plates.

Woodarch's Introduction to Conchology. 8vo.

———

YARRELL'S
HISTORY OF BRITISH FISHES;

Illustrated with nearly 400 beautifully executed Wood-cuts. 2 vols. 8vo.

———

JUST PUBLISHED,

IN ONE HANDSOME OCTAVO VOLUME,

The American Flower Garden Directory:

CONTAINING

PRACTICAL DIRECTIONS FOR THE CULTURE OF PLANTS

IN THE

FLOWER GARDEN, HOT HOUSE, GREEN HOUSE, AND ROOMS OR PARLOR WINDOWS:

With a description of the Plants most desirable in each, the soil, and situation best adapted to their growth, proper seasons for transplanting;

ALSO,

Full directions for the cultivation of the Grape Vine, with descriptions of the most Approved Vines, &c., &c.

Instructions for laying out a Flower Garden, for erecting a Hot House or Green House, &c.

The whole adapted to either large or small gardens, with lists of Annuals, Biennials, and Ornamental Shrubs, &c.

BY R. BUIST, *Nurseryman and Florist.*

VALUABLE WORKS

ON

THE ART OF DRAWING.

THE LITTLE SKETCH BOOK.

A SERIES OF VERY EASY STUDIES IN LANDSCAPE FIGURES, &C.

BY G. CHILDS.

Neatly Bound in 2 Volumes.

The Elementary Drawing-Book of Landscape,

BY G. CHILDS.

CHILD'S ADVANCED DRAWING-BOOK.

FOR THE USE OF THOSE WHO HAVE ACQUIRED SOME PROFICIENCY IN THE ART,

Containing Twenty-four Sketches of Hampstead and its vicinity, drawn from Nature, and on Stone, by G. CHILDS.

FAIRLAND'S JUVENILE ARTIST;

Or, Easy Studies for Beginners in Figures, Animals, Shipping, and Landscape. Neatly Bound in Cloth.

Tilt's New Progressive Drawing-Book

OF THE

HUMAN FIGURE,

IN A SERIES OF STUDIES BY THOMAS FAIRLAND.

NEW DRAWING-BOOK

OF

ANIMALS AND RUSTIC GROUPS,

A SERIES OF EARLY PROGRESSIVE STUDIES, DRAWN FROM NATURE,

BY T. S. COOPER.

ELEMENTARY ART;

OR, THE USE OF THE LEAD PENCIL ADVOCATED AND EXPLAINED.

This work is intended to teach the young student, and the amateur, by the practical use of the simplest, *but most valuable instrument in art*—THE LEAD PENCIL—how they may study Nature and acquire Art with the certainty of eventual success, and also to furnish them with assistance to which they may continually refer in the absence of their master. The work is illustrated by twenty-eight Lithographic Drawings by Mr. HARDING, and he has followed as nearly as possible the course which his experience in actual instruction has suggested to him.

HARDING'S EARLY DRAWING-BOOK,

Consisting entirely of Elementary Studies for Beginners. Bound in Cloth.

Harding's Drawing Book for 1837 and 1838.

Consisting of a series of Studies on a great variety of subjects. Printed in Mr. HARDING's new tinted style.

HARDING'S PORTFOLIO;

A Series of Twenty-four highly finished Sketches, tinted in exact imitation of the original drawings.

The improvements recently made in Lithography, particularly in the process of introducing the *whites*, enabling Mr. HARDING to give to his published Sketches all the appearance of Drawings. As the Sketches have been wholly drawn on Stone by Mr. Harding's own hand, they thus *possess all the value and interest of the originals.*

An Edition has also been prepared, beautifully coloured, under Mr. HARDING'S superintendence, so as exactly to imitate the original drawings.

Sketches at Home and Abroad.

This very beautiful Work consists of Sixty Views of the most interesting Scenes selected from a large collection of Foreign and Domestic Sketches made by Mr. HARDING, and executed by him in Lithography, in exact imitation of the original drawings, as they were made upon the spot, with Black Lead Pencil on tinted paper. The only addition to the original Sketches, which were made with scrupulous accuracy, being the introduction of appropriate objects, and figures in correct costume, thus improving the compositions of the subjects as well as adding national character to local interest.

VIVIAN'S SPANISH SCENERY;

OR, TWENTY-NINE SKETCHES FROM NATURE;

Executed in a similar style to Harding's "Sketches at Home and Abroad."

STANFIELD'S SKETCHES

ON

THE MOSELLE, THE RHINE, AND THE MEUSE.

PAINTING IN WATER COLOURS.

The Theory and Practice of Painting in Water Colours, as connected with the Study of Landscape, with hints on Perspective and Pencilling on Light and Shade, the Harmony of Colour, The Arrangement of Objects for Pictorial Effect: By G. F. PHILLIPS.

THE PRINCIPLES

OF

PRACTICAL PERSPECTIVE;

OR, SCENOGRAPHIC PROJECTION.

Containing universal rules for Delineating Architectural Designs on various surfaces, and taking Views from nature, Rules for Shadowing, and the Elements of Painting.

BY RICHARD BROWN.

In one Volume 4to., 50 Plates.

HINTS ON LIGHT AND SHADOW, COMPOSITION, &c.

AS APPLICABLE TO

LANDSCAPE PAINTING,

BY

SAMUEL PROUT, Esq. F.S.A.

20 Plates, containing 83 Examples, executed in the improved method of two tints.
"As maxims of experience, they deserve to be written in letters of gold."—*Spectator.*

ELEMENTS OF
DRAWING AND PAINTING IN WATER COLOURS.
BY JOHN CLARK.
With 24 Plates, mostly coloured, illustrative of Landscape Painting, Flower Painting, Portrait Painting, Historical Painting, and the Human Figure.

Colour as a Means of Art;
Being an adaptation of the Experience of Professors to the Practice of Amateurs; with eighteen coloured plates.
BY FRANK HOWARD, Esq.

THE SKETCHER'S MANUAL:
BY FRANK HOWARD.

BURNETT ON PAINTING.
Comprising hints on Light and Shade, Composition, on the Eye, &c.; accompanied by numerous Illustrations from the old masters. 1 vol. 4to.

THE YOUNG PAINTER'S MAULSTICK;
Being a Practical Treatise on Perspective; containing Rules and Principles for Delineation on Planes, founded on the clear Mechanical Process of VIGNOLA and SIRIGATTI, united with the Theoretic Principles of Dr. Brook Taylor.

BY JAMES MALTON, ARCHITECT.
With Twenty-three Plates, in Quarto.

SCIOGRAPHY,
OR
EXAMPLES OF SHADOWS,
With Rules for their Projection, intended for the use of Architects, Draughtsmen, and other Artists.
BY JOSEPH GWILT. 24 Plates.

TREATISE ON
TOPOGRAPHICAL PLAN DRAWING.
BY S. EASTMAN, U.S.A.

LESSONS IN FLOWER PAINTINGS;
IN A SERIES OF EASY AND PROGRESSIVE STUDIES.
BY JAMES ANDREWS.

Containing Twenty-four Sheets of Flowers, beautifully coloured. A duplicate of each is given in outline, printed on drawing paper, for the pupil to colour like the original.

Studies in Flower Painting.

Flora's Gems,
OR, THE TREASURES OF THE PARTERRE.
In twelve Bouquets, drawn and coloured by JAMES ANDREWS.

THE ROMANCE OF NATURE;
OR, THE FLOWER SEASONS ILLUSTRATED.
By L. A. TWAMLEY. Second Edition. 8vo., morocco, elegant.

Bryan's Dictionary of Painters and Engravers.
2 Vols. 4to.

Pilkington's Dictionary of Painters.
2 *Vols* 8vo.

BARRY'S WORKS COMPLETE
2 Vols. 4to.

NORTHCOTE'S LIFE OF TITIAN.

Sir Joshua Reynolds' Works.

TREATISES ON
PAINTING AND THE FINE ARTS.
By HAYDON and HAZLITT.

MAGAZINE OF FINE ARTS;
Containing a Variety of Papers, Lectures, &c. on Art. 4 Vols. Plates.

Lightning Source UK Ltd.
Milton Keynes UK
UKHW030703060521
383241UK00009B/764